Management
Decision-Making

Management Decision-Making:

Towards an Integrated Approach

MARK TEALE
VINCENZO DISPENZA
JOHN FLYNN
DAVID CURRIE

 Prentice Hall
FINANCIAL TIMES

An imprint of **Pearson Education**

Harlow, England • London • New York • Boston • San Francisco • Toronto • Sydney • Singapore • Hong Kong
Tokyo • Seoul • Taipei • New Delhi • Cape Town • Madrid • Mexico City • Amsterdam • Munich • Paris • Milan

Pearson Education Limited
Edinburgh Gate
Harlow
Essex CM20 2JE
England

and Associated Companies throughout the world

Visit us on the World Wide Web at:
www.pearsoned.co.uk

First published 2003

ISBN: 978-0-201-61922-5

British Library Cataloguing-in-Publication Data
A catalogue record for this book is available from the British Library

Library of Congress Cataloging-in-Publication Data
Management decision-making : towards an integrative approach / Mark Teale ... [et al.].
     p. cm
  Includes bibliographical references and index.
  ISBN 0-201-61922-9 (alk. paper)
    1. Decision-making. 2. Management. I. Teale, Mark.

  HD30.23 .M352 2003
  658.4'03--dc21   2002025811

10 9 8 7 6
08

Typeset in 9.5/12 pt Stone Serif by 30
Printed and bound in Great Britain by 4edge Ltd, Hockley. www.4edge.co.uk

The publisher's policy is to use paper manufactured from sustainable forests.

Contents

Acknowledgements

We would like to thank our colleagues David Lippiatt, Pat Mould, Joe Nason, Diane Reeve, Val Skerrow and Lorraine Warren for their advice, support and mentoring. Our thanks also go to Dave Powell, and to Angela McKiernon for her invaluable help in compiling Illustration 7.2 concerning forecasting service levels in the pertoleum industry. At Pearson Education we would like to thank Anna Herbert, Alison Kirk, Kevin Ancient, Carol Abbott, Rebekah Taylor and David Cox for their patience and support.

Publisher's acknowledgements

We are grateful to the following for permission to reproduce copyright material:

Table 3.2 from *Psychology: The Science of Mind and Behaviour*, 3rd Edn pp 12–13, reproduced by permission of Hodder/Arnold Ltd (Gross, R. 1996); Figure 5.1 from *Organisational Decision-making Study Guides*, p. 21 (Bell, S. and Reedy, P. 1999); Tables 5.1 and 5.2 from *Research Methods of Managers*, 2nd Edn, reprinted by permission of Sage Publishing Ltd 1991, (Gill, J. and Johnson, P. 1991); Table 6.1 from *Systems Thinking Systems Practise*, copyright 1993, © John Wiley & Sons Ltd, reproduced with permission (Checkland, P. B. 1993); Figure 6.4 from *Strategic Management and Organisational Dynamics*, p. 253, © 1996 Pitman Publishing (Stacey, R. 1996); Figure 7.2 from *Systems Thinking and Decision Making*, p. 102, Rea Publications (Daellenbach, H. G. 2001); Figure 8.5 from *Advanced Management Accounting*, 3rd Edn (Kaplan, R. S. and Atkinson, A. A. 1998) and Figure 14.2 from *The Financial Times Handbook of Management*, p. 1045 (Sadgrove, K. 1996) by permission of Pearson Education; Table 8.7 from *Accounting Financial Management for the Small Business* (Barrow, C. 1998); Figure 8.7, reprinted by permission of Harvard Business School Press, from *The Balanced Scorecard: Translating Strategy into Action* by R. S. Kaplan and D. P. Norton, Boston, MA 1996, p. 9, copyright © 1996 by the Harvard Business School Publishing Corporation, all rights reserved (Kaplan, R. S. and Norton, D. P. 1996); Figure page 22 from PROCESS CONSULTATION VOLUME 1 2nd EDN by Schein, © reprinted by permission of Pearson Education, Inc., Upper Saddle River, NJ (Schein, E. 1969).

In some instances we have been unable to trace the owners of copyright material, and we would appreciate any information that would enable us to do so.

Guardian Newspapers Limited for an extract from "Chelsea allsorts – not an Englishman in sight at the Bridge" published in *The Guardian* 28th December 1999 © The Guardian 1999; News International Newspapers Limited for an extract from "Problems at the top remain unresolved because board members tend to shy away from confrontation" by Margaret Coles published in *The Sunday Times* 23rd July 1995 © Margaret Coles / Times Newspapers Limited, London 1995; Pearson Education Inc. for an extract from *Organizational Psychology* by E. H. Schein; and The Yorkshire Post for an article on Yorkshire Water published in *Yorkshire Post* 8th July 1999.

About the authors

Mark Teale is a Senior Lecturer at the University of Lincoln. He is head of the Operations Management subject area and has taught this as well as Operations Research, Project Management and Logistics on a range of programmes in the UK and internationally for the past ten years. Prior to his academic career, he has had wide experience of management at all levels, including consultancy for British Coal's Operational Research Executive.

Vincenzo Dispenza is a Senior Lecturer at the University of Lincoln and has been teaching for over ten years, specialising in qualitative aspects of decision making. He is leader of the executive MBA programme at Lincoln.

John Flynn is a Senior Lecturer at the University of Lincoln with over 10 years experience in the application of statistical and mathematical techniques to industrial problems, including toxicology, agriculture and aerospace. He has developed training courses to support Project Management software. Along with overseas teaching, he has taught on professional Statistics courses for the Institute of Quality Assurance and the UK Accountancy professional bodies.

David Currie is currently Head of the Department of Human Resource Management at Lincoln Business School, University of Lincoln. He has over ten years experience teaching decision-making on the MBA at the University of Lincoln. Before entering teaching full time, he worked for nearly fourteen years in the Trading Standards departments of two large UK Local authorities.

Preface

As an academic subject, management decision-making consists of different theoretical approaches that reflect the individual interests, experiences, disciplines and biases of a wide range of authors. It embraces long-established concepts from psychology, sociology, mathematics and philosophy, and relatively new concepts from systems theory and chaos theory.

As a practical day-to-day activity, decision-making is a holistic phenomenon. As humans we do not consciously differentiate between psychological, sociological and philosophical dimensions to our actions; we simply act.

There is, therefore, a difference in the way we research and theorise about decision-making, and the way we actually make decisions. The study of management decision-making has tended to fragment into discrete and ever more specialised areas of analysis, whilst, arguably, managers continue to make decisions on gut feeling, intuition and the best available data. So, are the results of research into management decision-making in particular, and management and organisations in general, of any use to a manager? We think so, and that is probably the main reason we are writing this book.

The benefit of this text is that it attempts to combine and integrate usually distinct subject disciplines 'under one roof'. As authors we have faced many challenges in trying to adopt what we consider to be a genuinely interdisciplinary, rather than multidisciplinary, approach. The latter would have allowed us to present our ideas in a way that avoided integration by treating issues and themes from a series of perspectives, but without exploration of the interrelatedness of each. The former required us to actually talk to each other; to establish links between our different perspectives; to confront each other with challenging ideas; and sometimes to agree to disagree.

We have tried to develop a methodology for writing the book that challenges our own preconceptions of what integration means. It would have been easier to talk integration and espouse it; instead we chose to practise it. It has been a difficult but valuable process, and in turn it has informed our thinking and our practice. People often come together in organisations to address problems and issues, and in doing so create further problems and issues owing to a lack of understanding of each other's perspectives. We are no different.

There is a strong argument that knowledge grows paradigmatically, that is, debates happen between authors who, although they may disagree with the detail of the argument, share the same fundamental assumptions regarding the nature of reality, knowledge and human nature. We certainly did not all share the same basic assumptions and, therefore, faced a daunting problem in attempting to produce an integrative text. What we did share was an interest in decision-making. We also shared a willingness to engage in intellectual debate. These were some of our challenges. Now, what do we expect of you?

Challenges you may face when reading this book

Management texts too often attempt to oversimplify complex issues by adopting a prescriptive, 'this is how to do it' approach. We do not intend to do this. You may find this frustrating at times; you may even say we are abrogating responsibility. If you do get frustrated, that is good. If you find that you end up with more questions than answers, that is even better. If this is the case, we have gone some way to achieving our purpose. Integration, to some extent, implies disintegration of our existing perspective. We intend to put you off your balance. We have been taken out of our own comfort zones at times as authors, but this is all part of the learning and unlearning process. We say 'learning' because you will undoubtedly acquire new knowledge; we say 'unlearning' because your existing knowledge will sometimes be called into question. As you first glance at this text you may be drawn to particular chapters at the expense of others. Some of you may have a fear of psychology, whilst others may have a phobia of numbers. Any book that attempts to be truly integrative must address this kind of issue.

Although this book addresses management issues and problems, we want to challenge the misconception that only managers make decisions in organisations by avoiding a managerial authorial voice. Many management texts are written from a predominantly managerial perspective and are based on certain assumptions about managers. It is almost as though managers are a breed apart. We hope to redress some of the false assumptions made about managers as rational, neutral, organisational technicians who make decisions purely 'for the good of the organisation'.

Integrative themes

Although it could be argued that each decision is a unique occurrence, it is equally true that decision-making often follows patterns or phases. In this text, decision-making is characterised by four themes:

- uncertainty
- research
- choice
- implementation

Decisions usually affect, or are affected by, a change in the status quo. Either way, we may find ourselves in a period of *uncertainty* for all sorts of reasons, personal, interpersonal or organisational. To address some of these uncertainties we consciously or unconsciously attempt to make sense of the situation. In effect, we undertake some kind of *research*. The results of this sense-making process, or research, may present us with a *choice* from a number of alternative courses of action; action implies some kind of implementation process. There is, as ever, a feedback loop. Anyone who believes that implementation is ever complete is denying the inherent uncertainty and ambiguity of life. Hence, we must evaluate and re-evaluate our actions in order at least to attempt to ensure the effectiveness of our decision-making processes.

Having created this thematic structure, we issue a warning. It *appears* to be a rationally based approach, but not all decisions are primarily rationally driven, nor are they necessarily linear or sequential. What we have presented is the nice, neat version of events – the reality is always a bit messier. However, we set out with the aim of integration in mind and, in doing so, felt the need to develop an alternative to the usual topic-based framework, which tends to treat perspectives in a discrete way. As part of that process we were forced to share our ideas and come to a consensus (our shared rationality).

In order to facilitate integration, we swapped drafts of each chapter and commented on each other's work. Each chapter is the product of dialogue between at least two of the authors. We believe we have addressed issues in sufficient depth to provide you with a critical view of decision-making. We hope that the thematic structure we have created encourages you to embrace perspectives you may otherwise have found inaccessible.

Remember, the boring bits are the bits you probably need to read the most.

PART ONE

Uncertainty

Preface to Part One

In the first part of the book we explore the complex environment within which decisions are taken. Notions of uncertainty are discussed from three points of view in the three subsequent chapters. Chapter 1 attempts to locate the subject of management decision-making within a broader theoretical framework. Within Chapter 2 we begin by examining uncertainty from primarily a management science perspective, by exploring notions of risk and rationality. How we can measure and manage risk is outlined. Chapter 3 locates decision theory within the environment of the individual. That is how an individual's psyche affects the process of decision formulation and implementation. In Chapter 4 the uncertainty theme is expanded to encompass chaos theory. Chaos theory, in its many branches, encourages managers to consider wider environmental issues as well as the internal dynamics of the firm.

The primary concern of Part One is that decisions are taken within contexts that are changeable and difficult to describe. Hence information needs to be collected, people need to be involved and decisions need to be taken with due regard to their complexity and importance.

Management decision-making in context

On completing this chapter you should be able to:

- Locate approaches to decision-making within a broader theoretical context.
- Recognise and evaluate normative models of decision-making.
- Identify and evaluate descriptive models of decision-making.
- Distinguish between programmed and non-programmed decisions.
- Distinguish between structured and unstructured decisions.
- Reflect upon your own decision-making behaviour and actions.

1.1 Introduction

In Samuel Beckett's play *Waiting for Godot*, the character Vladimir states 'It's the start that's difficult', to which his companion Estragon replies, 'You can start from anything.' Vladimir retorts, 'Yes, but first you have to decide' (Beckett, 1981: 63). Their words point to some of the difficulties faced by decision-makers. They allude to the risks involved in having to act when faced with uncertain outcomes, yet recognise the potential to experiment with new behaviours and experiences through the power to decide. Indeed, one can start from anywhere, at least in theory. In reality, the starting point for decisions is often determined by many factors, be they internal (to the individual) or external. Our starting point, for reasons that will become apparent, happens to be a rather apocalyptic tale (Illustration 1.1).

Illustration 1.1 On the road to Jaffa

It was a rainy day in Israel. Two university lecturers had just conducted a staff development workshop with some Israeli colleagues and were returning to their hotel. The session had overrun slightly, to the frustration of the driver who had been waiting to take them back to their hotel further up the coast. They had settled into the rear seat and had begun to debrief the session. They were not wearing seatbelts. They were, as they later confirmed to each other, both aware of the agitation the driver was expressing through his rather erratic and aggressive driving. The taxi was weaving in and out of surrounding traffic as the windscreen wipers struggled to clear the volume of water and dirt. In spite of the apparent dangers, neither acted individually to put on their seatbelts; nor did they share their concerns with each other; nor, perhaps most significantly of all, did they take any steps to influence the driver to modify his behaviour.

To be continued ...

Activity 1.1 Have you ever been in a situation where, against your better judgement, you have taken no steps to avoid what, with hindsight, may have been a fairly predictable outcome?

We return to this example later, but for now we want to address the issue of integration.

1.2 Problems of integration

In the preface we stated that the initial philosophy for the book was founded on the desire to attempt to integrate opposing philosophical views. How this can be achieved in practice is not an easy issue. One approach might be to deconstruct decision scenarios and treat each decision as a unique event. We could attempt to evaluate cases from different perspectives. In the event we have reverted to a 'structured' approach that pigeonholes decision theory into major subject areas. On reflection, this style takes the easy way out. It may be easier for the reader to consider issues under labels such as 'culture' or 'modelling'. It is certainly easier for the authors, because we can centre our research on established texts that match our own preconceived notions of what a text on decision-making should include. The grand idea of philosophical integration is extremely problematical as it implies that we can aggregate and synthesise fundamentally different points of view.

Easton (Easton and Schelling, 1991) addresses this very issue of integration by using the example of the Humpty Dumpty story as a metaphor for the way in which knowledge, at least in western civilisations, has become fragmented and reductionist through disciplinary divisions. In everyday life we are confronted with whole problems, not fragmented parts of problems. According to Easton (Easton and Schelling, 1991: 12–13):

To understand the world it has seemed necessary to analyze it by breaking it into many pieces – the disciplines and their own divisions – in much the way that Humpty Dumpty, now the egg of knowledge, fragmented when he fell off the wall. But to act in the world, to try to address the issues for which the understanding of highly specialized knowledge was presumably sought, we need somehow to reassemble all the pieces. Here is the rub. Try as we may, we have been no more able than all of the king's horses and all of the king's men to put our knowledge together again for coping with the whole real problems of the world.

Easton (Easton and Schelling, 1991) identifies the problem of integration in business management education in particular. He argues that business schools are mini universities that mirror the wider university structures of which they are a part. They are structured along the lines of traditional disciplines and any integration that takes place is, usually, left to the individual student to accomplish. It is implicit that this is unsatisfactory, but explicit that, to date, no obvious solution exists.

Reluctantly, our initial attempts at integration have fallen off the same wall as Humpty Dumpty. The book taken as a whole may offer up an integrated account of management decision-making, but there is no grand theory or any isolated solutions to the multifaceted nature of decision-making. However, that is not to say that we should not attempt an integrative approach. Our own efforts have shown us that it can be an invaluable, if frustrating, experience. It leads to a more reflective and reflexive approach to thinking about one's own behaviour, and challenges the assumptions on which our very concept of what constitutes an appropriate underpinning theory is based.

The book is structured around themes and topics. The four themes are uncertainty, research, choice and implementation. Each theme contains a number of discrete topics. However, within each theme and topic there are commonalities, contradictions and confluences. As these surface we refer to the relevant section.

Whilst it may be tempting to the reader to 'dip into' the book and selectively engage with separate chapters, we would urge you to engage with chapters that you may not be so predisposed to read. To put it another way, if you are a 'numbers person', force yourself to read the more qualitatively-underpinned chapters and vice versa. We return to this issue later in the chapter under the heading of 'Qualitative and quantitative dimensions' (section 1.10).

This chapter continues with a broad introduction to the area of decision-making and its various dimensions. Decisions are often parts of sequences that we may have had no control over or, at least, perceived ourselves to have had no control over; reactions to the actions and decisions of others. Or they may be products of our own and others' a priori assumptions. In short, there are many types of decision and there are many types of decision-maker. In this first chapter we begin by examining the following questions:

1 What types of decision are made?

2 Who makes decisions?

3 Where are decisions made?

4 Why are decisions made?

5 How are decisions made?

Illustration 1.1 (continued)

Meanwhile, back on the road to Jaffa, the traffic came to a sudden halt as a large vehicle carrier neared a low bridge about 200 metres ahead. The taxi braked suddenly but the road conditions meant that it did not stop in time to avoid the vehicle in front. Crunch. Unfortunately, this was also the case for the vehicle behind. Consequently, the two lecturers found themselves in a motorway pile-up just outside the city of Jaffa.

Why did the two lecturers fail to act – either individually or collectively? It hardly seems rational that they should identify their lives were literally at risk yet take no action whatever to minimise the impact of the impending outcome. Better still, why not avoid the outcome altogether by requesting the driver to slow down?

If only it were always so obvious. Who can honestly say that they have not been on the road to Jaffa, figuratively speaking? How did you answer the question at the end of the first part of the story, for example? Our experience of decision-making as a process suggests that emotional and cultural factors, to name but two, can affect our behaviour in decision-making situations. Perhaps the lecturers had been socialised into not criticising the actions of another person, even where they were paying for a service. Perhaps as visitors in an alien culture, they felt unable to act owing to uncertainty about what would be an acceptable way of confronting the driver. Perhaps such was the emotion of the situation that they did not even think about putting their seatbelts on. Perhaps, perhaps, perhaps. In fact, the only thing we can be certain about in this scenario is that the post-crash reflections, over a couple of very large brandies back in the safety of the hotel bar, led to the initial motivation for writing this book.

We explore some of the issues that these questions raise for decisions, for decision-makers and for decision-making. As a point of departure it may be useful to provide some definitions of decision-making, though some would argue that definitions may be counterproductive if they are regarded as justifications for not exploring a subject in further depth. We urge you to view these definitions as a point of departure for further exploration of a complex but fascinating subject.

1.3 Definitions of decision-making

Acts of choice between alternative courses of action designed to produce a specified result, and one made on a review of relevant information guided by explicit criteria.
(Rose, quoted by Weeks in Salaman and Thompson, 1980: 187)

A conscious and human process, involving both individual and social phenomena, based upon factual and value premises, which includes a choice of one behavioural activity from one or more alternatives with the intention of moving towards some desired state of affairs.
(Shull *et al.* in Harrison, 1999: 4)

A moment, in an ongoing process of evaluating alternatives for meeting an objective, at which expectations about a particular course of action impel the decision-maker to select that course of action most likely to result in attaining the objective.
(Harrison, 1999: 5)

A *commitment* to action.
(Mintzberg, 1983: 188)

Activity 1.2 Referring to the definitions of decision-making given above, identify the words that you consider to be key to defining management decision-making. When you have identified them, place them in a sequential order, according to how you believe decisions are made. We return to this list when considering normative models of decision-making later in the chapter.

One of the difficulties with defining a phenomenon such as decision-making lies in the fact that it is a concept which, when operationalised, takes many forms. In other words, decision-making can be varied and multifaceted and, whilst we may identify elements of a decision that may be common to other decisions, it does not necessarily follow that all decisions are similar in nature. Words such as 'choice', 'evaluation' and 'commitment' can be used to describe elements of a decision, but in practice the nature of a decision will be more readily analysed with regard to its immediate context and to the participants involved in the decision scenario. The definitions presented, for example, do not convey a sense of the emotions that can be stirred in an individual when faced with certain choices. However, this should not deter us from trying to learn more about the processes involved in making decisions. Generalising and hypothesising can allow us to raise our vision beyond our immediate concerns and, in turn, allow us to evaluate our existing beliefs and actions in a new light. Of course, it could be that as a result the way in which we make decisions is changed, and not necessarily for the better. It all depends on the criteria by which we judge success. For instance, are promptness of action and 'decisiveness' the main criteria by which a decision is judged? Or is the main criterion a successful decision outcome? What *is* a decision? The definitions you have just read all purport to define decisions, yet they focus on different elements of a decision. It might be a useful start to think about decisions in terms of decision *processes* and decision *outcomes*. This book aims to increase your awareness of decision-making processes in order to increase your chances of achieving favourable outcomes. In reality the two form part of a continuum. Achieving an objective requires action leading to a desired outcome. In theory, *how* one proceeds should inevitably affect *what* one achieves, and in turn this should affect future actions. Ultimately, it should be remembered that no amount of knowledge, experience, skill or awareness guarantees success.

1.4 The structure of decisions

This section addresses the question: what types of decision are made? There is a generally accepted typology concerning the structure of decisions. This includes: structured, unstructured, programmed, non-programmed, strategic and operational. We return to these later; in the meantime we offer the following brief explanations of each. *Structured decisions* are decisions that are considered to be clear, unambiguous and easily definable. As you would expect, *unstructured decisions* are unclear, ambiguous and difficult to define. *Programmed decisions* are decisions that rely on some form of predetermined organisational apparatus or routine, for example an administrative procedure which is invoked when a particular problem, say an industrial dispute, occurs. *Non-programmed decisions* are those for which no such procedural guidelines exist. *Strategic decisions* are those that involve a fundamental change in the ideology and/or authority, and therefore, the direction of an organisation. *Operational decisions* concern the day-to-day running of the organisation.

Illustration 1.2 Hillsborough tragedy

On 15 April 1989, Liverpool football fans arriving late for the FA cup semi-final game with Nottingham Forest, were allowed into the Leppings Lane standing enclosure of the Hillsborough stadium in Sheffield. As they surged onto the top of the terraces, a wave of pressure was caused to pass down towards the front, in turn causing the fans at the front to be crushed against the retaining wall and fences. In order to escape this pressure the fans attempted to climb over the structures that were designed as crowd control barriers. As some fans managed to make their way onto the pitch the police officers in attendance started to respond to what they perceived to be a pitch invasion. They had been trained to prevent further ingress onto the pitch in such situations and, therefore, defined the situation as aggressive behaviour rather than a desperate act of survival. The act of attempting to return fans to the terraces no doubt contributed to the scale of the disaster. Ninety-six people died as a result of the events of that day.

The Taylor Report, following the official inquiry into the disaster, identified one of the contributory factors as the police's programmed, structured response to what was, in essence, a non-programmed, chaotic and unforeseen event. This led, *inter alia*, to a fundamental re-evaluation of police training, ultimately resulting in a change of philosophy from one of programmed, structured responses to set situations, to a more reflective, analytical approach in which officers are encouraged to think situations through as they unfold.

The principal decision-making issue here may be the extent to which we ever know what we are actually dealing with in any given situation.

There are variations in the use of language to identify the different types of decision. For example, Harrison (1999: 21) distinguishes between category I and category II decisions. He uses the term 'category I' to describe decisions that are 'routine, recurring, and certain', as opposed to 'category II' decisions which are 'nonroutine, nonrecurring, and uncertain'. In essence, Harrison is differentiating between what are more usually described as structured and unstructured decisions, or operational and strategic decisions. However, it is worth noting that not all strategic decisions are unstructured. Likewise, it does not necessarily follow that all operational decisions are structured.

1.5 The decision body

Who makes decisions? Depending on your view, everyone or no one. When does behaviour become action? When does action become decisive action? We could simply state, 'managers make decisions'; but managers are not the only people who make decisions, even in profit-driven organisations. Everyone has the potential to make decisions, albeit decision-making in organisations is presented as the legitimate right of managers. That is not to say that people without the title of manager do not engage in some form of decision-making. Doctors, lawyers, teachers, architects, shop assistants, and so on, all make decisions of some kind. It is an activity, however, that has increasingly come to be regarded as the specific domain of managers. One of the reasons for this could be that a very narrow definition of organisational decision-making has been adopted, in which decisions have been regarded as involving the control, coordination and allocation of (human and material) resources.

Perhaps the question 'who makes decisions?' should generate the answer 'everyone'. In the context of this book we refer primarily to managers and to the people they manage. It would be naive to address management decision-making without also addressing organisational decision-making. The 'who' of decision-making is therefore context-specific. Cooke and Slack (1991) define the 'who makes decisions?' issue as 'the decision body' and suggest that decisions are made by individuals and groups. They argue that the way in which decisions are made is easier to understand when the decisions are made by individuals than when they are made in conjunction with others. We explore the merits and disadvantages of both in later chapters.

1.6   The decision context

Where are decisions made? Having stated that our concern is organisational decision-making in particular, you might assume that the answer to this question is relatively straightforward: in organisations. However, organisations do not exist in a vacuum; they are part of wider societies. This holds political, cultural and ethical implications for organisational decision-making. It would, therefore, be myopic to address organisational decision-making in isolation from wider socio-cultural factors.

Activity 1.3	Close your eyes and imagine a manager making a decision. When you have done so, address the questions below.

1 In what kind of surroundings did you locate your imaginary manager?

2 Was the manager you described a woman or a man?

3 What was the manager doing?

The traditional notion of a manager (usually male) in a suit, making decisions in open meetings or in his office is one that is continually reinforced by media images. However, many decisions are made in less formal settings of corridors, car parks, in restaurants over a long lunch break and so on.

1.7 The purpose of decisions

Why are decisions made? Management decisions are made for a host of reasons. The commonest assumption is that they are made because decision-making is a fundamental aspect of the management functions (of coordinating, controlling etc.) and management decision-making is therefore a key management role. This classical view detracts attention from the more psychological and political reasons why managers might make decisions. There has been growing acceptance that managers are people and, as such, have their own personal needs, drives and motives.

In *The Foundation of Management* (1986), Peter Anthony distinguishes between what he calls the official theory of management and the real theory of management. It is worthwhile mentioning Anthony's work in order to encourage critical reflection about management decision-making theory and its relationship to the ways in which managers make decisions in practice. Anthony (1986: 175–6) describes official theory as the predominant account of management as a 'rational, purposive activity directed at the achievement of goals usually determined in economic terms'. In terms of official theory, management is a rational process. Emphasis is placed on objectivity rather than subjectivity. It is portrayed as a purposive activity, and managers are seen as organisational stakeholders who provide direction for others. Managers' actions are primarily directed at making profit, and the focus is on getting things done in the name of the organisation.

Alternatively, he describes real theory as behaviour that is social and political in nature. He arrives at this position by arguing that real theory focuses on what he and others (he refers to Dalton) suggest happens in real life (empirically):

> The inability of superordinates to learn from their subordinates about what was going on, the self protective feigning of ignorance, the side-stepping of official procedures to gain personal advantage, the deliberate use of change and confusion ... the construction and maintenance of ambiguous rules, and the claims and obligations of friendship.
>
> (Anthony, 1986: 178)

In terms of real theory, management is far from a rational activity. The emphasis is on politics and self-interest. It is, indeed, purposive, but only to the extent that managers pursue their own personal goals. Management, in real theory terms, is primarily directed at maintaining personal power, which is not necessarily the same as maximising profits.

Anthony (1986: 178) states:

> What official theory seems to provide, then, is some basis for persuading others that managers know what they are about, and some comfort for the managers in maintaining the illusion with the necessary confidence. In either case, official theory does not seem very real. More and more evidence has accumulated ever since the Hawthorn [sic] experiments that a great deal of the behaviour of the subordinates in organizations cannot be understood by attempting to enclose it in a theory of rational, goal-directed activity subsumed under the organization's grand design and purpose.

It therefore follows that our expectations of decision-making, and of the behaviour of decision-makers, may be influenced by our implicit assumptions concerning the very nature of management. If we hold a primarily official-theory-centred view of management, then our expectations of the purpose of decisions will focus more on the well-being of the organisation as a whole, the pursuit of organisational profit and so on. Likewise, we may implicitly assume that individuals make decisions on criteria based more on their organisational roles and objectives than on personal agendas.

If we hold a primarily real-theory-centred view of management, we may assume that managers are driven mainly by personal needs and goals, and seek to pursue these goals under the guise of legitimate organisational business.

It is also worth noting that our implicit assumptions, be they official or real, will affect our orientation to questions concerning the structure, body, context and methodology of decision-making.

1.8 The methodology of decision-making

How are decisions made? This is the area in which most research into management decision-making has taken place. This is hardly surprising because managers are practitioners and, as such, want information that will enable them to get better results. However, we argue that practice can become more effective not only as a result of tackling the 'how' questions, but also by addressing all of the preceding (who, where, what, and particularly, why) questions. The type of research undertaken in addressing this question includes research into: rationality; irrationality; risk-seeking and risk-averting behaviour; optimising and satisficing behaviour. We examine these later in the context of qualitative and quantitative approaches to management decision-making.

1.9 Objectivity and subjectivity

In everyday usage, the words 'objective' and 'subjective' hold certain connotations. To be objective is regarded as a virtue and a sign of considered judgement and impartiality. To be subjective is to see a problem from one view alone, that is, your own, and to disregard the views and opinions of others. Subjectivity, therefore, is regarded pejoratively. In the context of exploring decision-making, these value-laden connotations are unhelpful. In order to facilitate understanding of some of the ideas presented in this book we need to define what we mean by both words.

At its simplest level, the objective world is the world outside our heads. Objectivity is the notion that the world can be made sense of in terms of structures that exist outside of any individual's consciousness. So, we can say that a 'manager' is an objective phenomenon because we all recognise that managers exist 'out there' in the real world. People experience managers as existing;

managers transcend individual consciousness; management is a shared social phenomenon. If an individual manager ceases to exist, the objective phenomenon of management will live on. Again, to put it simply, the subjective world is the view that each one of us has from our own unique standpoint. In Activity 1.2 , for example, you were asked to imagine a manager. Was the manager you described an imaginary manager or an actual one? Was it a composite of all the managers you have known? Was it a vague media-perpetuated stereotype? Was it your own manager? Was it another manager you know? Was it you? In recognising our request to imagine such a person we must have shared at least some vague, objective notion of what constitutes a manager. Ultimately, however, the image of the manager will have been subjectively experienced by you.

Subjectivity is the notion that the world can be made sense of in terms of how each of us views it through our individual consciousness. Emphasis is placed on the reality inside one's head. So, taking our example of a manager, a subjective view might emphasise the way in which an individual makes sense of either being a manager, being managed, or experiencing management in some other way. In essence, subjectivity is the way in which we make sense of our individual experience, and use that knowledge to interpret the phenomena that surround us.

Illustration 1.3 Subjectivity masked as objectivity

In an essay on the use of statistics as a basis for public policy published in 1954, British economist Ely Devons drew parallels between decision-making processes in formal organizations and magic and divination in tribal societies. He noted that while organizational decision-makers would not normally think of examining the entrails of a chicken or of consulting an oracle about the futures of their organization or the state of the economy, many of the uses of statistics have much in common with the use of primitive magic. In primitive society magic decides whether hunting should proceed in one direction or another, whether the tribe should go to war, or who should marry whom, giving clearcut decisions in situations that might otherwise be open to endless wrangling. In formal organizations techniques of quantitative analysis seem to perform a similar role. They are used to forecast the future and analyze the consequences of different courses of action in a way that lends decision-making a semblance of rationality and substance. The use of such techniques does not, of course, reduce risks. The uncertainties surrounding a situation still exist, hidden in the assumptions underlying the technical analysis. Hence Devons's point that the function of such analysis is to increase the credibility of action in situations that would otherwise have to be managed through guesswork and hunch. Like the magician who consults entrails, many organizational decision-makers insist that the facts and figures be examined before a policy decision is made, even though the statistics provide unreliable guides to what is likely to happen in the future.

Source: Morgan, 1986: 134

Since the advent of the human relations school of management, which drew attention to the importance of understanding the effects of human agency in organisations, more objective and predictive notions of organisational process have been called into question. The recognition that we are thinking, feeling, active beings who influence our environment and are not machines, as might have been implicitly assumed in earlier notions of organisation, has led to greater emphasis on more qualitative approaches to the study of organisations. Nonetheless, Devons' comments are based on a rather dated view of the role of quantitative analysis in making sense of organisational processes. Management science has evolved significantly in the areas of understanding systems and describing them both mathematically and figuratively, as later chapters demonstrate. Perhaps most significantly is the idea that models are interpretive, in both their construction and their use. That is not to say that 'magicians' do not exist in contemporary organisations. Consider, for instance, the role that many management consultants serve in contemporary organisations.

1.10 Qualitative and quantitative dimensions

In this book we describe and examine some theories about management decision-making in particular, and decision-making, organisations and management in general. We explore what we have described as quantitative and qualitative dimensions of decision-making. First we need to suggest what we mean by both terms. The qualitative dimension of decision-making relates to the elements of a decision-making process that are primarily viewed as subjective. The quantitative dimension of decision-making relates to the elements of a decision that are defined as objective and which utilise numerical values.

The qualitative–quantitative classification is a common way of describing and distinguishing the different approaches to decision-making. Why is it so common? One reason may be that the academic subject of decision-making has emerged from different disciplines, all of which – economists, operational researchers, psychologists, sociologists, social psychologists, mathematicians and so on – claim a stake in it. It could be said that decision-making does not really exist as a subject, rather it is a broad concept that is interpreted differently depending on the context. Decision-making will hold quite different meanings for a statistician and a psychologist. There is a danger of overstating what we earlier identified as the problem of fragmentation of knowledge in decision-making. Whilst statisticians may place greater emphasis on the use and value of numbers in understanding and solving management problems, it does not necessarily follow that this undermines qualitative approaches. Similarly, if social psychologists choose to emphasise more qualitative critical factors that may lead to successful management, this does not in itself undermine quantitative approaches.

In western civilisations, for example, we are encouraged to make sense of the world around us in terms of bipolar opposites which, when held up to scrutiny, are far from bipolar. We speak of black and white; male and female; top and bottom; good and evil, and so on. So why do we choose to make sense of reality (or at least talk about it) in terms of either/or?

Pirsig (1974) suggests that a process of discrimination ensues as we start to divide what we have selected. This process is what he refers to as the knife, which divides the conscious universe into parts. The process is never ending as we continue to divide and classify. You may perceive similarities between Pirsig's knife metaphor and our earlier exploration of the fragmented egg of knowledge.

Illustration 1.4 Phaedrus's knife

Pirsig (1974: 75) uses the concept of Phaedrus's knife to describe the process of analytical thought:

> The application of this knife, the division of the world into parts and the building of this
> structure, is something everybody does. All the time we are aware of millions of things
> around us – these changing shapes, these burning hills, the sound of the engine, the
> feel of the throttle, each rock and weed and fence post and pieces of debris beside the
> road – aware of these things but not really conscious of them unless there is something
> unusual or unless they reflect something we are predisposed to see. We could not pos-
> sibly be conscious of these things and remember all of them because our mind would
> be so full of useless details we would be unable to think. From all this awareness we
> must select, and what we select and call consciousness is never the same as the aware-
> ness because the process of selection mutates it. We take a handful of sand from the
> endless landscape of awareness around us and call that handful of sand the world.

Pirsig distinguishes between two ways of seeing the world: classical and romantic. Classical approaches, he argues continuing the sand metaphor, are
'concerned with the piles and the basis for sorting and interrelating them'.
Romantic approaches are concerned with 'the handful of sand before the sorting
begins'. He goes on to state that both are valid, yet irreconcilable, ways of looking at the world. From a personal point of view, you may find that you are more
comfortable dealing with one set of approaches to decision-making than
another. As we mentioned earlier in the chapter, you may find it easier, for
instance, to deal with statistical techniques than to analyse the psychology of
decision-making, or vice versa. You may be drawn to certain chapters. If so, why
is this? It could be that the way in which you see the world has a lot to do with
assumptions you hold regarding reality, knowledge and human nature. Some
theories may seem more valid to you because they are based on basic assumptions that confirm your view of the world.

In this book we proceed on the premise that knowledge is far from neutral.
Indeed, Easton (Easton and Schelling, 1991) emphasises the highly politicised
nature of the process of knowledge fragmentation and the vested interests inherent in each of the (competing) disciplines. We, therefore, adopt a critical
approach, which encourages us to recognise the means by which knowledge
itself is constituted. An understanding of underlying assumptions regarding the
study of social sciences can help us to evaluate how knowledge can be political
and may be used to promote certain world views at the expense of others. Thus,
for example, the use of statistical techniques in decision-making may promote a
view that it is predominantly a scientific practice. But is it really?

The most difficult phenomena to address are those that we take for granted.
You may have heard the saying 'nobody knows who discovered water, but it's
unlikely to have been a fish'. In other words, if we are surrounded by a seemingly natural phenomenon, then we are less likely to see it as a subject for study;
we simply *live* it. However, there are also social phenomena that we take for
granted and call 'natural' when that is far from the case. For example, in group
decision-making situations, is it 'natural' that a leader will emerge? Or have we
have been socialised into expecting this, thereby creating a self-fulfilling
prophecy? In labelling social processes as 'natural' we ignore the potential for

---

Illustration 1.5 Management decision-making: art, science or ...?

Wittgenstein thought that if you want to understand a type of discourse, such as religious discourse or any other type of discourse, look at the role that it actually plays in people's lives. For him [Wittgenstein], the characteristic mistake of twentieth-century intellectual life was to try to treat all intellectual endeavours as if they were attempting to be like a science. He thought that science had its place like anything else, but that it was a mistake to treat subjects which were plainly not forms of science and technology as if they were second-rate attempts to achieve science and technology.

Source: Searle, quoted in Magee, 1987: 335

---

learning and change. If we say 'that's just the way it is', then we are closing the door on further analysis. We rarely turn our attention to subjects such as reality or knowledge; we simply *experience* the world and we *use* knowledge to study and classify phenomena rather than see the world as a valid subject for study in itself. In doing so we run the risk of believing that everything can be measured, classified or quantified in some way.

The theories presented in this textbook are the product of human thought and action. As such, they are the product of individuals or groups of people that hold a particular set of assumptions about reality, knowledge and human nature. It is worth remembering this, as well as the fact that you too carry a set of assumptions which underpin your 'normality'. This is discussed in more detail in Chapter 5 when we introduce a discussion about ontological and epistemological issues.

Illustration 1.6 The paradoxical platypus ... an illusory search for certainty?

The inability of conventional subject–object metaphysics to clarify values is an example of what Phaedrus called 'platypus'. Early zoologists classified as mammals those that suckle their young and as reptiles those that lay eggs. Then a duck-billed platypus was discovered in Australia laying eggs like a perfect reptile and then, when they hatched, suckling the infant platypi like a perfect mammal.

The discovery created quite a sensation. What an enigma! It was exclaimed. What a mystery! What a marvel of nature! When the first stuffed specimens reached England from Australia around the end of the eighteenth century they were thought to be fakes made by sticking together bits of different animals. Even today you still see occasional articles in nature magazines asking, 'Why does this paradox of nature exist?'

The answer is: it doesn't. The platypus isn't doing anything paradoxical at all. It isn't having any problems. Platypi have been laying eggs and suckling their young for millions of years before there were any zoologists to come along and declare it illegal. The real mystery, the real enigma, is how mature, objective, trained scientific observers can blame their own goof on a poor innocent platypus.

Zoologists, to cover up their problem, had to invent a patch. They created a new order, monotremata, that includes the platypus, the spiny anteater, and that's it. This is like a nation consisting of two people.

Source: Pirsig, 1991: 104–5.

Activity 1.4

Have you considered that your behaviour as a decision-maker may have been learned in your formative years? The following activity is designed to encourage you to think about the links between self and decision-making, and to explore your own assumptions concerning reality, knowledge, and human nature.

Think of at least five proverbs, sayings or nursery rhymes that you learned as a child. Write them down. Now ask someone else to write down what they believe may be any hidden messages that each proverb could be conveying. For example, the saying 'a bird in the hand is worth two in the bush' may convey a sense of caution and prudence. You may come to make links between the underlying message here and the notion of satisficing, or 'making do', described later.

There are a number of different approaches to management decision-making, each dependent upon underlying assumptions concerning the judgement capability of the decision-maker and the level of certainty surrounding the decision-making situation.

1.11 Normative models

Normative approaches are prescriptive and attempt to provide advice for how decisions *should* or *ought* to be made. Their basis is, therefore, an idealistic one rather than a descriptive one.

In essence, simple normative models (as exemplified in Figure 1.1) tend to assume that decision-makers:

- have an extremely sound basis of knowledge available to them, so they can know a great range of alternative options available to them, and successfully predict an extensive variety of possible outcomes;
- have excellent judgement, so they can rank all possible outcomes in terms of value;
- are logical, rational and objective in the way they make decisions.

Referring back to Activity 1.1, your list of key words could have included: individual phenomenon; social phenomenon; conscious; choice; courses of action; relevant information; evaluating; alternatives; ongoing; meeting objectives; desired state of affairs; commitment; action. If we were to take all the words and present them in some linear, sequential format, according to how decisions are made *in general* we would most likely end up with a typical normative model of decision-making. In essence, this is what the normative approach reflects – a general, context-free theory of decision-making. It is general in that it is often used to identify abstract stages in a process that purports to represent the way decisions are made. It is context-free because, being general and abstract, it need not concern itself with the vagaries and problems of actual decisions made by specific individuals in particular organisations.

Many authors who adopt or describe normative models acknowledge their limitations. For example, Cooke and Slack (1991: 10) depict the decision process

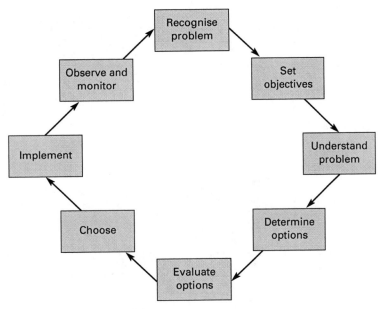

Figure 1.1 A typical normative model

as a cycle with a continual feedback loop. The authors acknowledge that management decision-making is rarely so clearly defined and sequential in practice. Nonetheless, their model of decision-making is normative in the sense that it is reductionist, that is it attempts to identify and describe elements of a decision that can be generalised.

1.12   Descriptive models

Max Bazerman (1998) distinguishes prescriptive and descriptive models of decision-making. Prescriptive models, as the label suggests, are models that prescribe methods to obtain optimal solutions and are synonymous with normative models. Descriptive approaches are more concerned with the 'bounded' manner in which decision-makers operate. Figure 1.2 provides a light-hearted example of a 'model' that many managers may be able to relate to. Whilst it concentrates on the problem-solving element of decision-making, it can be used to illustrate the principle of bounded rationality in several ways. Our rationality is bounded not just by psychological factors (for instance as can be seen in Chapter 3), but also by sociological factors (for instance as will be seen in Chapter 12). The 'real-life' model presented in Figure 1.2 is particularly popular with practising managers as it identifies key factors of decision-making such as self-preservation and avoidance of responsibility. It also alludes to the importance of political manoeuvring and the notion of risk avoidance.

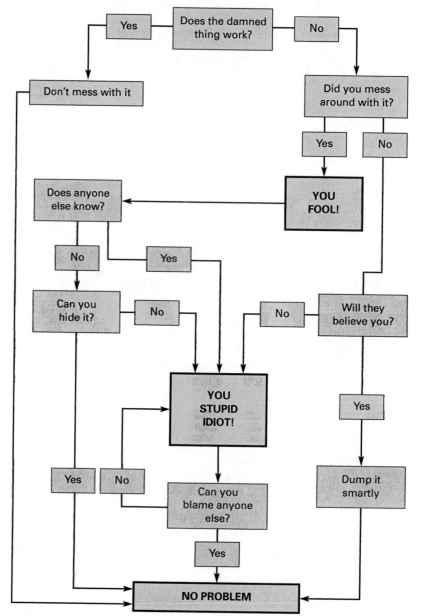

Figure 1.2 A descriptive 'real life' model?

1.12.1 **Bounded rationality**

Simon (1982) uses the term 'bounded rationality' to express the idea that, as humans, our capacity to process large amounts of data is limited in different ways. It is sometimes described as 'limited rationality' or 'subjective rationality'. We examine some of the factors that might constitute our rationality in Chapter 3.

1.12.2 Incrementalism

Lindblom (1954) coined the phrase 'muddling through' to describe how managers make decisions with the implicit criterion of remaining close to current practices and existing courses of action. In other words, it is a process-driven rather than a goal-oriented way of making decisions. The primary drive for the decision-maker is not to achieve a predetermined goal but to look for logical, alternative ways of progressing current courses of action, hence to muddle through. The advantages to this method include the fact that it builds on existing tried-and-tested experience and actions; it therefore allows the decision-maker to avoid significant risk. The corollary of this is that the future is not always certain and current courses of action will not necessarily be appropriate in future situations. As a result, significant dangers may be unforeseen; as may significant opportunities.

Another danger lies in the assumption that the status quo is appropriate. There is less likelihood of current ways of operating being called into question in an incremental process. We may develop excellent organisational mechanisms for making decisions; however, we may be making the wrong decisions. In essence, we end up making the wrong decisions in the right way.

An incremental approach lends itself to programmed and structured decisions in which the element of uncertainty is lower. However, there is evidence to suggest that managers are more likely to make decisions incrementally at times of greater uncertainty. Psychologically, as individuals we may try to create an illusion of certainty and predictability when we feel most threatened. When goals become more ambiguous owing to external pressures, such as the loss of a major contract, or internal pressures, such as changes in senior management, decision-makers are more likely to fall back on the psychological crutch of the past, which at least is more certain.

 Summary

As you have probably noted from reading this chapter, we have been critical of normative approaches to decision-making as we have attempted to explore the complexity of the decision-making process. You have been encouraged to focus on *what actually happens* rather than what *should* happen. In order to help you to continue this reflective approach, we suggest that you start a diary to log your own decision-making behaviour. Having said this, we should not be too critical of normative approaches. Many of the techniques you will encounter in this book have been developed as a result of trying to improve decision-making. If we were to adopt a purely descriptive approach to what goes on in practice, then there would be a danger of that practice becoming anachronistic, and of practitioners becoming dogmatic. Paradoxically, although normative approaches are intrinsically dogmatic in attempting to prescribe methods, they can also act as a mechanism for counteracting potentially dogmatic practices. That is, they may show the practising manager how it *could* be done another way, as well as how it should be done another way.

? Decision diary

You will already have noticed that we are encouraging you to interact with the text by including activities. This is based on the precept that participative learning is more effective, particularly in developing skills of reflection and analysis. As you read through this book you will be asked to keep a decision diary. The diary will serve two main purposes. First, it acts as a longitudinal, continuous summary of key learning points from each chapter. Second, it acts as a reminder that this book aims to encourage you to put your learning into practice. So, you are encouraged to make your own entries on decision-making issues as you encounter them and to 'track' them through the diary as you progress in the book. You will also find that we tend to pose questions to help stimulate reflection and analysis on the theories and concepts broached chapter by chapter.

As a first diary entry you are asked to reflect on a recent, current or ongoing decision. As a starting point to get you to think about your particular decision, we recommend you complete the following general statements as fully as you can.

1 The best decision I ever made was .... because ....
2 The worst decision I ever made was .... because ....
3 I think a good decision is one that ....
4 I think a bad decision is one that ....
5 In order to improve my decision-making I need to ....

Now describe the decision you have chosen to address in the diary. We suggest you write it as a mini case study, or mini 'soap opera' ... feel free to embellish the tale as best you can. Write it from your own perspective (first person) or in reported (third person) style.

Once you have written your account, address the following questions, bearing in mind what you have read in Chapter 1.

■ Have you chosen to describe a one-off decision or an ongoing decision?
■ Think about the decision in terms of process:
  – Was the process easy or difficult?
  – What words might you use to describe it?
  – What factors do you think contributed to its being so?
■ Think about your own role in the decision-making process. How might you have done things differently?
■ Identify other people that you think played a significant part in the scenario. Think about what influence they may have had on you.
■ Would you describe the decision as structured or unstructured? Programmed or unprogrammed?
■ Think about the outcomes of the decision:
  – How easy were they to identify?
  – Were they positive or negative?
  – What other words might you use to describe them, for example 'ambiguous'?
  – Who determined whether they were positive, negative, etc?

References

Anthony, P.D. (1986) *The Foundation of Management*. London: Tavistock.

Bazerman, M.H. (1998) *Judgment in Managerial Decision-making*, 4th edition. New York: Wiley.

Beckett, S. (1981) *Waiting for Godot*. London: Faber.

Berger, P. and Luckmann, T. (1966) *The Social Construction of Reality*. Harmondsworth: Penguin.

Cooke, S. and Slack, S. (1991) *Making Management Decisions*, 2nd edition. Hemel Hempstead: Prentice Hall International.

Easton, D. and Schelling, C.S. (1991) *Divided Knowledge, Across Disciplines, Across Cultures*. Newbury Park, CA: Sage.

Harrison, E.F. (1999) *The Managerial Decision-making Process*, 5th edition. Boston, MA: Houghton Mifflin.

Lindblom, C. (1954) 'The science of "muddling through"', *Public Administration Review*, 29: 79–88

Magee, B. (1987) *The Great Philosophers*. London: BBC Books.

Mintzberg, H. (1983) *Power in and Around Organizations*. Englewood Cliffs, NJ: Prentice Hall.

Morgan, G. (1986) *Images of Organization*. London: Sage

Pascale, R.T. and Athos, A.G. (1982) *The Art of Japanese Management*. Harmondsworth: Penguin.

Pirsig, R. (1974) *Zen and the Art of Motorcycle Maintenance. An Inquiry into Values*. New York: Corgi.

Pirsig, R. (1991) *Lila. An Inquiry into Morals*. London: Bantam Press.

Salaman, G. and Thompson, K. (1980) *Control and Ideology in Organizations*. Milton Keynes: Open University Press.

Simon, H.A. (ed.) (1982) *Models of Bounded Rationality: Behavioral Economics and Business Organization*, Volume 2. Cambridge, MA: MIT Press.

Glossary

Bounded rationality:	a concept used to describe the ways in which people's capacity to process large amounts of data is limited. Sometimes called 'limited rationality' or 'subjective rationality'.
Incrementalism:	this emphasises the way in which decision-makers base their decisions on existing situations and practices, rather than on projected goals. Sometimes referred to as 'muddling through' or 'logical incrementalism'.
Non-programmed decision:	a decision for which there is no established procedural mechanism. Sometimes called 'unroutinised' decisions.
Normative:	an approach which gives advice on how, or how not, to proceed.
Objectivity:	this emphasises the notion that the world exists independently of human consciousness.

Operational decisions: decisions concerning the day-to-day running of the organisation. They concern matters of more immediate relevance in terms of time and scope, that is, they deal with short- to medium-term matters and concern part or parts of the organisation rather than the organisation as a whole. In reality, operational and strategic decisions may not be so easily differentiated. Operational decisions may have strategic implications both in time and scope, and strategic decisions invariably affect operations.

Programmed decision: this relies on a predetermined procedural mechanism. Sometimes called 'routinised' decisions

Strategic decisions: decisions directly concerned with the overall direction of the organisation and usually made by senior managers. They may also be decisions that are not to do with direction but with scope, that is, they have implications for the organisation as a *whole*.

Structured decision: one that involves a seemingly clear, unambiguous and well-defined context.

Subjectivity: this emphasises the notion that individual human consciousness determines how we perceive the world.

Unstructured decision: one that involves a seemingly unclear, ambiguous and ill-defined context.

2 Risk, uncertainty and rationality

Learning outcomes

On completing this chapter you should be able to:

- Define the nature of risk and uncertainty.
- Formulate and solve a simple decision tree under terms of uncertainty.
- Use expected values to explore the contribution of probability-based data to the decision-making process.
- Assess the impact of risk on your personal approach to decisions.
- Define the nature of rationality.
- Debate the assumptions and limitations of risk models, the contributions of subjective and objective information, and the implications of analysis.

2.1 Introduction

This chapter explores the important complementary themes of risk and uncertainty and discusses some of the techniques to evaluate decision unknowns. But, straight away you ask, 'How can you know the unknown? and 'Is that a myth?' Perhaps, then, it is all really about finding the most practicable solution to a problem. Being a contentious area for discussion, risk analysis brings into focus the real tension between quantitative and qualitative approaches to decisions and assessment of the outcomes.

The notion of risk infiltrates all our decision-making processes, whether we are considering decisions about forecasts and simulations (Chapter 7), financial issues (Chapter 8), or addressing the ethics of a decision (Chapter 14). A requirement of our risk assessment might be that it is consistent, personally relevant and rational in approach. Uncertainties and risks in the decision-making process can be due to language used. This may extend beyond 'communication problems' and take us into philosophical debates about meaning.

In attempting to measure risk, we have to consider the probability of the occurrence of the risk and the consequences of the risk itself. These two contributions are treated separately according to the theory we utilise. Using complementary examples, we proceed to consider the dilemmas faced by personnel who are risk-seekers, risk-neutrals or risk-avoiders. The strategy for risk avoidance, then, seems to be one that is tied in with a personal reference point.

When we are trying to balance the philosophy of decision-making, the skills and needs of the decision-maker and the role of the decision within an organisation, the importance of the risk analysis will depend on the objectives of the decision – but this assumes that the objectives are certain and consistent. A wise approach to decision-making might seek contributions from different angles, some strongly quantitative, others qualitative and subjective, perhaps mechanistic or merely intuitive. The importance placed on data analysis, management skills, organisational awareness, and custom and practice in the assessment of risk would be vital. Critical thinking about assumptions and limitations of models, the role of subjective and objective information, an understanding of the implications of analysis, and the construction of a solution to a problem would be further requirements. Ultimately, from a personal perspective, it is important to have confidence in analytical techniques with proven practical applicability although we may find it difficult to 'measure' risk and anticipate its consequences.

2.2 The nature of risk and uncertainty

Decision-makers are used to assessing risk because decision-making is usually associated with some degree of risk taking, but not all outcomes are easily assessed. Some unknown outcomes may not previously have been seen or experienced and so they are 'uncertain'. In theory, the outcome may have a low probability of occurrence but be quite troublesome if encountered in practice.

Take as an example the Millennium Dome. The Dome was built in London as a tourist attraction to celebrate the arrival of the year 2000. Obviously, the owner of an attraction aims to provide a happy 'tourist experience', but the tourist may be willing to accept a flaw in the portfolio of exhibits because of the possibility of merely being at the attraction. Any uncertain outcome or event ought to be 'interesting' to the owner and tourists alike. This might be a simple 'error', e.g. an exhibit fails to function, or an exhibit is controversially attacked by a critic in the media. In the case of the Dome, neither party might have anticipated that one day in November 2000 a bungled jewel raid on the building might bring danger, excitement and fame to increase the Dome's attraction. This third-party intervention had a low probability of occurrence but the consequences were huge from the security angle in terms of the loss of confidence by the party that was lending the jewels to the Dome for exhibition.

Attendance figures at the Dome provide an interesting risk scenario. The owner had to contend with falling attendance figures month by month and bad publicity and, hence, needed to review the economics of the pricing policy. Tourists might then imagine that the Dome was less crowded and thus more attractive to visit. Such opinions (a form of risk assessment) can make or break any business relationship. For the owner, fresh performance data may identify an adjustment to the Dome's business processes to encourage the visitors but, of course, that still leaves other decisions to be addressed concerning the uncertainties of the politics, strategy, finance and logistics before the business relationship could be deemed perfect.

A further cause of difficulty in decision-making is *ambiguity*. Uncertainty and doubt will always interfere with managerial decision-making unless clarified through improved communication and risk assessment. This is addressed further in Chapter 4.

Illustration 2.1 Do all crises have to become disasters? Risk and risk mitigation

Risks may become a crisis if left unattended. The manager who is often charged with recovering the supporting services may have to adopt a range of strategies to recover. The worst disaster is where the main income generating activities are seriously affected. Eighty per cent of firms who suffer a computer disaster go bankrupt within 18 months, because they do not have contingency plans.

Facility managers are encouraged to start disaster planning with hazard analysis, an assessment of risk. Is it possible to minimise risk and limit disasters? Natural disasters (typhoons, floods, falling trees etc.) and man-made ones (bombs, computer failure etc.) are one-off events beyond anyone's control to influence. What are the identifiers of potential accident situations in the making?

- Toleration of gaps in important information
- Failure to reveal information to members who do not understand the significance
- Rigid hierarchies that inhibit the flow of relevant information
- Blinkered outlooks
- Operation of outdated regulations
- Complacent attitudes
- Pressured or preoccupied managers
- Ignoring alarm signals

These all indicate poor management at the organisational level. These errors can become compounded or cumulative. The failure of the Chernobyl nuclear reactor was, ironically, caused by testing of the fail-safe mechanisms that led to an unstoppable chain reaction.

Source: adapted from Davies and Walters, 1999: 5–9

Risk mitigation involves the adoption of a safety culture and a number of organisational strategies which can affect and limit risk. It could be argued that optimum decision-making is where decisions are pushed to the lowest level commensurate with skills available. The poorest style of mitigation is, usually, centralised and with little or no input from the outside environment. A practical solution is to make every person responsible for every problem by educating and training in safety culture.

Activity 2.1 **Doctors – making decisions on a knife edge.** Spare a thought for doctors – faced with complex situations, they have to make decisions which could later hit the headlines.

Patients denied details on failing doctors. The government's new openness proposals will shed light on rationing decisions, but information on poorly performing doctors is likely to still be out of bounds.

Using the two BBC News headlines above from 1999, consider the decision-making perspective. Comment on what are the likely risks that ensue for a patient and a doctor, and the degrees of ambiguity and risk that exist for both parties.

At any level, risk 'awareness' usually influences our decision-making process, perhaps through our education or a type of gambling instinct. It is sometimes said that many projects are brilliant ideas – until they are 80 per cent or more of the way down the road ... to ruin. Risks and uncertainties fill any project where the management of change across a timescale is taken on (Chapter 10), but sometimes these risks are gladly welcomed – the thrill is conquering them.

2.3 Definition of the nature of risk

Within a managerial decision-making context, a risk might be viewed as 'the chance of a negative *outcome* for a decision which has a possible uncertainty element, usually on the downside'. For example, in discussing a winning marketing/management model to create competitive advantage in project business, Cova and Holstius (1993: 117) say: 'Risk management can be operationalised as the number of different kinds of project risks that are analysed, and the readiness to evaluate risk probability and to choose the appropriate strategies. This applies especially to the financial risks linked with price, escalation formula, terms of payment and warranties.' Further, Cova and Holstius place risk management within the key success factor of the entrepreneurial culture, meaning that it contributes highly in the analysis of the competitive situation and its relevant risks.

For comparison, Duckworth's (1998: 10) qualitative definition of risk states: 'The potential for exposure to uncertain events, the occurrence of which would have undesirable consequences.' Other definitions of risk combine the probability (chance or likelihood) of the undesirable event with the magnitude of the consequence. It then follows that the anticipated value of the loss of taking the risk is assessed by multiplying together two components of the risk: its likelihood and its consequence:

Impact of the risk = Likelihood of the risk × Consequence of the risk

This eclectic definition requires a value for the likelihood and its associated consequence, a potent combination as we explore aspects of rational decision-making. This could be applied to decision-making in any context, at any level, whether social, technical or cultural.

2.3.1 **Likelihood, probability and chance**

Likelihood, probability and chance represent the same concept but their measurement cannot always be precise. It may be impossible to do more than estimate that the likelihood of a risk is low, medium or high. In health studies, values such as 1 in 10,000 might be used to identify low-level risk. In education, failure in university exams might be acceptable at around the 10 per cent rate.

There are two constraints in the theory of probability:

1 The probability of an event is expressed as a value between the limits of 0 and 1. A probability of 0 indicates that the event cannot happen, and a probability of 1 shows that the event is certain to occur. It could be argued that anything else is uncertain and would be placed somewhere on the scale between the limits.

2 The sum of all the probabilities of all outcomes *accumulates* to exactly 1.00 (100%) by the addition rule of probability (Thomas, 1997: 57–9). This implies that something *will* happen.

The second constraint is more difficult to accomplish than the first, but it stimulates decision-makers to check that their subjective assessments of probability accurately represent all outcomes. It is worth noting here that risk is not a measurable quantity and should not be used synonymously with probability (Duckworth, 1998: 10). Probabilities are generally defined as 'frequencies in the long run' and the magnitude of the risk is measured in terms of its frequency.

Some people will admit that the consequence of the risk is given higher emphasis than the probability component, e.g. a millionaire's view of financial loss, or the consequences of risks in air travel (death, severe injury, etc.) which outweigh the actual probabilities of a crash. A crash on a bicycle at 25 kilometres per hour is rarely fatal, though it occurs more frequently.

The increased number of accidents of a particular type will influence the layperson's estimate of the risk. Commercial decisions might not be in this category because they are often well planned and well executed. A 'pure' project will rarely be influenced by accident rates but the estimate of its chance of failure and its margin of error remain highly desirable, at least for heuristic purposes. Every estimate has an estimable margin of error which changes in value depending on the sample size from which the data are drawn.

It may be worth reversing the approach to the problem by suggesting a magnitude of risk and then asking what kind of evidence is required to support, claim or deny the existence of the risk. The conditions for risk, e.g. greater speed in a car, or anticipated faster change to banking practice, or improvements to genetically modified food, may all constitute risk.

2.4 Probability/impact matrix

For each risk, it is appropriate to examine its position on some sort of consistent scale so as to help the decision-maker identify relevance, strength or weakness of all risks being discussed. The matrix in Figure 2.1 classifies the impact of the risk (from low to high) and its associated probability (from low to high). Recall that

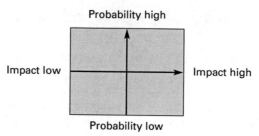

Probability high

Impact low ←———————→ Impact high

Probability low

Figure 2.1 Matrix to show the impact of risk

the best estimate of the probability may be limited to a high, low or medium non-numerical classification.

Activity 2.2 Place on the matrix in Figure 2.1 the following four risks:

1 Change in cost of raw materials in a volatile economy

2 Act of terrorism when travelling on an aeroplane

3 Technical design error for a new product

4 Cultural change in managers after participation in information technology awareness programme.

Students usually see the four risks listed in Activity 2.2 as fitting into four separate quadrants. 'Change in cost of raw materials in a volatile economy' is seen as high probability with high impact, an 'act of terrorism when travelling on an aeroplane' is judged to be low probability but high impact. A 'technical design error for a new product' is usually high probability and low impact because it can be reworked and solved, and 'cultural change in managers after participation in information technology awareness programme' is seen as low probability and low impact. However, you might disagree with these assessments.

What if the three probabilities calculated by John in Illustration 2.2 were to change – would that augur well for the church membership or suggest that one of the outcomes should be chased as being preferable? It is worth 'updating' the probabilities or recalculating the pay-offs which have been measured in terms of growth or decline in people. For example, if the probability of recruiting within six months suddenly increased to 0.5 and the other two outcomes were predicted to have equal probabilities of 0.25 then the impact values would change to 5, –6.25 and 0 respectively, yet the best outcome would remain at appointing within six months.

John's view could be criticised for not being inclusive of all the data, within the context of the criticism he received at the meeting.

Statisticians might aspire to measuring risk with one number but hard-pressed managers usually believe they are measuring risk appropriately without a number. Have they foreseen all the outcomes, do all associated probabilities add up to one (second constraint)? In risk management, frequently used measurements are themselves providers of risks in the equation because they are estimates. Happily, risks are normally capable of being insured against by

Illustration 2.2 Church minister recruitment

A small church needs to recruit a new minister to replace the current minister who is seriously ill. The church leaders asked John, a member of the congregation, to help them in making their decision as he was an expert on quantitative methods and was known to be writing a book about decision-making. John soon identified the following outcomes: the minister will be recruited within six months, or from six months to two years, or the church will utilise its members to run the church in a form of democracy.

John attended a special meeting of the church leaders and made the following presentation.

"I have identified three outcomes in our search for a new minister. All three outcomes have a forecast 'pay-off' in terms of anticipated change in church membership, with an estimated chance of its occurrence:

Outcome	Change in membership	Estimated chance of outcome's occurrence
Recruit within 6 months	Increase by 10 people	0.2
Recruit within 6 months to 2 years	Decrease by 25 people	0.7
Run as a democracy	No change	0.1

The impact of the risk of recruiting within 6 months is $0.2 \times 10 = 2$
The impact of the risk of recruiting within 6 months to 2 years is $0.7 \times -25 = -17.5$
The impact of the risk of running as a democracy is $0.1 \times 0 = 0$

What we now do is neatly rank the three outcomes (let us call them the 'decisions'), on the basis of the impact values (sometimes known as expected value). The best outcome is to recruit within six months, if possible, because of the highest, favourable impact value of 2. The worst outcome is to take longer than six months to recruit, with the lowest impact value of –17.5. Perhaps this would be a convenient point to pause and take any initial questions."

The chairperson of the committee thanked John for his diligence and clear presentation of the options and stated: 'It is obvious that there is only one viable option and John has proved it scientifically beyond dispute. So, without further delay I propose that we implement the first option and ensure that we recruit the new man within six months. I take it we all agree?'

'Well, actually, it might not be a man,' came a response from Dave, one of the committee members.

'Oh, let's not get hung up on that one again. It's just a turn of phrase. Of course it might be a woman,' responded the chairperson.

'Well, actually, that isn't really the point I want to make. What I'm much more interested in is for John to tell us just how he was able to produce such a definite set of options for us?'

'Er, well, let me see. Ah yes, I based the range of options, the likely probability of occurrence and the nature of the outcome on my past experience of similar situations,' came John's reply.

'In other words, you made them up,' came Dave's retort.

'Mmm, you could say that,' John rather timidly replied, 'but they are my best estimates. Do you have anything better?'

insurance companies who use knowledge of risks and potential loss to evaluate the premium to be paid.

2.4.1 Exploring your understanding of uncertainty

Moore and Thomas (1988: 127–8) discuss the language of uncertainty and explore expressions which convey meaning but not an exact, quantitative standard of value. The authors refer to an experiment in which 250 executives were shown to be inconsistent in ranking the 'value' of the following ten words, which can all be said to represent uncertainty:

- Probable
- Quite certain
- Unlikely
- Hoped
- Not certain
- Possible
- Not unreasonable that
- Expected
- Doubtful
- Likely

In the business of a courtroom, important judgements are reached and, ideally, decisions are made correctly on the basis of evidence and debate. There is a need for consistency of meaning in the language used. In Figure 2.2, the circle runs from 0 per cent to 100 per cent (two extremes of the probability scale) in inter-

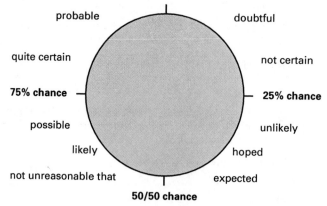

Figure 2.2 The language of uncertainty and the values communicated by words

vals of 25 per cent in a clockwise direction. The ten words around the circle have been inserted, subjectively, onto the scale where they might be suitable.

For example, if I prefer to rank 'likely' as being lower in value than 'possible', I might give 'likely' a value of 0.6 but 'possible' a value of 0.7. If we can communicate the exact value of these words then our feelings about the effects of uncertainty would be communicated explicitly into the decision process. However, this is rarely the case.

At the bottom of the circle, the 50/50 chance place, the equal chance of two outcomes occurring might be a useful place of agreement. This is the same as asking 'how do penguins make a decision?' to which the answer, jokingly, is 'they flipper coin': the 50/50 decision mechanism.

Activity 2.4	Using Figure 2.2, estimate a numerical probability value for all the words around the circle. Get a friend to attempt likewise. Compare notes on where you have agreed and disagreed.

Moore and Thomas (1988: 128) argue that if executives are inconsistent in their use of words, the treatment of uncertainty is downgraded in importance from the consideration of other items, such as costs, that are thought capable of being measured and communicated in a precise manner. The inconsistency among practising managers with this exercise indicates an obviously weak contribution to the decision-making process. You also might begin to realise that your words can be open to interpretation about their exact meaning. As other words are introduced into the decision process, what values would you give to 'virtually certain', 'reasonable cause to suspect' or 'substantial evidence'?

Words are so incapable of accurately representing the truth, and you might concur that numerical sophistication has been replaced by semantic sophistication. Now question yourself as to whether you proceed with your day-to-day decisions at the 'virtually certain' level of risk or at the 'certain' level, and whether it makes any difference.

The marrying of quantitative techniques to available, timely data will help to drive the decision-making so that unexpected outcomes may be thoroughly explored, analysed and debated. Such techniques are helpful in processing and converting accurate, reliable data into management information. Even a risk like a last-minute change to your perfect plan, perhaps an objection from a third party, can be considered and prepared for. Some practitioners argue that it is all about asking the right question at the right time to discern the risk, or compiling a risk register based on experience.

In Illustration 2.3, the theatres in which many 'risky' managerial decisions are made include takeovers, customer care, human resources, franchising arrangements, economic development, etc. Cash flow has been identified as a risk, but supportive accountants suggest all future expansions will be handled satisfactorily.

Illustration 2.3 Cleaning and disposable

CPD is in the cleaning and paper disposibles market, with a current annual turnover of £4 million, but a longer-term objective to grow to £10 million or better, and to be placed in the top 5 per cent of companies operating nationally in its type of business. A major risk will be any approach for a takeover, or a weak cash flow to fuel the desired growth. Accountants and solicitors have throughout the 11 years of trading been very supportive, indicative of good relationships.

However, in turning down very good offers for the business, the managing director shows he wishes to retain executive control. One bonus has been that he was able quite recently to buy all the shares of an equity partner who had been with him since the beginning. The benefit for the latter is the significant return on the initial investment he made. Other problems over the years have been the shedding, retaining and recruitment of staff.

Major objectives are quite clear for future expansion plans – to expand within the existing customer base, or acquisitions to move into different market sectors. The latter are sometimes unhappy affairs because acquisitions are known to bring down the acquirer.

Activity 2.5

Identify the aspects of risk and uncertainty in CPD's case. Try to rank these risks in order of importance. Do you think the organisation has handled the uncertainty and the risks well in getting its business to a healthy level?

2.5 Decision trees

A useful way of graphically presenting decisions made under risk is by a *decision tree*. An important element of these diagrams is the concept of *expected monetary value* (EMV). The EMV for a decision is simply the sum of the possible pay-offs of the alternative outcomes, each weighted by the probability of that pay-off occurring. This is an extension to our earlier definition of the impact of a risk, illustrated in Illustration 2.2. EMVs are particularly useful to financial decision-makers, enabling them to develop the comparative analysis of several projects, often expressed in terms of the *present value* of the cash surplus or deficit (Arnold and Turley, 1996: 59–68). This is discussed further in Chapter 8.

EMV = (Pay-off of first outcome) × (Probability of first outcome) +
(Pay-off of second outcome) × (Probability of second outcome) + ... +
(Pay-off of final outcome) × (Probability of final outcome)

The EMV for each decision is calculated and the largest value is noted. This EMV corresponds to the decision most likely to anticipate the best return.

Structurally, all decision trees are similar in that they have decision points and 'states of nature' points, represented by symbols:

□ – A decision node from which several alternative decisions may be chosen.

○ – A 'state of nature' node out of which one of the states of nature (outcomes) will occur.

A decision tree needs three pieces of numerical data:

1 An estimate for all the outcomes (perhaps in terms of volume of sales, profits or losses) and their chance of occurrence (the distribution of probabilities). Sometimes these have to be qualitative in terms of high/medium/low ratings.

2 A list of the alternative decisions available to meet the decision's objectives.

3 The cost or revenue for each of the alternative decisions.

Example 2.1	A materials manager, Fred, works for a firm assembling roller-bearings for earth-moving equipment. Fred is analysing three alternative decisions concerning the fabrication of a certain part, a steel ball-bearing. It can be purchased from a supplier for £8.00 each or produced in-house using either a low-speed or a high-speed polishing machine.

1 The firm can make the part for £5 each, but will need to invest £8,000 in a new high-speed polishing machine.

2 Another alternative, using a low-speed polishing machine would produce the ball-bearings at a cost of £6 each, with a fixed cost of only £4,000.

Fred has also estimated that annual demand will be 7,000, 8,000 or 9,000 units, with a probability distribution for these three 'states of nature' of:

Bearings demanded (states of nature)	Probability
7000	0.15
8000	0.45
9000	0.40

Which alternative should Fred select?

Solution
The decision tree will show three alternative decisions, each with three anticipated outcomes.

The costs associated with the states of nature can be calculated from the sum of the variable and fixed costs for each possible outcome, hence giving the pay-offs (Figure 2.3). For example:

To purchase 7,000 units will cost $7,000 \times £8.00 = £56,000$

To make in-house 9,000 units with the high-speed polisher will cost $9,000 \times £5.00 + £8,000 = £53,000$

The EMV can be then estimated for all the decisions. As described earlier, to do this we sum all of the possible outcomes for each state of nature taking into account the probability values:

EMV of 'Purchase' $= (56,000 \times 0.15) + (64,000 \times 0.45) + (72,000 \times 0.4)$
$= £66,000$

▶

Example 2.1

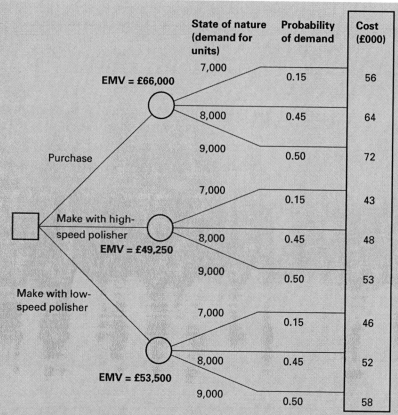

Figure 2.3 Decision tree diagram for Example 2.1, showing costs, chances of outcomes of EMV's of each decision

EMV of 'Make with high-speed polisher'
$$= (43{,}000 \times 0.15) + (48{,}000 \times 0.45) + (53{,}000 \times 0.40)$$
$$= £49{,}250$$

EMV of 'Make with low-speed polisher'
$$= (46{,}000 \times 0.15) + (52{,}000 \times 0.45) + (58{,}000 \times 0.40)$$
$$= £53{,}500$$

These are positioned inside (or near to) the circles representing the state of nature nodes (Figure 2.3).

The three EMVs of £66,000, £49,250 and £53,500 suggest that to minimise the costs it is likely to be more appropriate to select the high-speed machine option.

A decision tree approach presents all such information as that derived in Example 2.1 in one diagram in an effective manner, summarising managerial data and promoting discussion on the decisions. The problem with decisions of this type is that using EMV does not always lead to the 'best' decision. Let us think about the criteria for best decision. In this case, if we go for the high-speed option and make the bearings in-house we will take on the burden of managing the process. The *utility value* of having someone else do the buying-in has not been taken into account.

Arnold and Turley (1996: 59–68) state that, from a management accounting angle, the EMV ignores the level of risk hanging over the decision and the level of funding available to support the decision. Further, whether we are risk-avoiders or risk-takers is not clear. In fact, giving each decision an equal criterion by which to judge it, the decision-maker is assumed to be neutral in terms of risk analysis. These ideas are discussed later in the chapter.

2.6 Decision-making, outcomes and pay-offs

The general structure within which decision-making occurs can be summarised as a matrix (Figure 2.4). We can partition some decisions into a type of voluntary direct management control, others into involuntary management control, where there is little that can be done to influence the decision. Some outcomes of the decisions are not always certain to occur, so they can be categorised as predictable or unpredictable. A third-party intervention in a project could be regarded as unpredictable. There is a pay-off for each combination of decision and outcome, being a price, cost, profit or loss to be minimised or maximised according to the decision objectives.

Conceptually, discrimination between any dominant risks or trivial outcomes, those not worthy of attention or those which must be monitored most carefully, will help the decision-maker. In theory, sector A will tend to produce decisions with least risk and least impact (voluntary management control and predictable outcomes). Conversely, sector D will tend to produce decisions with highest risk and worst impact (involuntary management control and unpredictable outcomes). A valuable principle is that voluntary decision control for a predictable outcome leads to effective decision-making.

2.7 Judgement, values and factual data

Some of the issues in decision analysis clearly involve judgement, experience and teamwork, but factual data can be used to develop estimates of the chance of success or failure. Furthermore, studying the underlying assumptions in the

	Predictable outcomes	Unpredictable outcomes
Decisions under voluntary management control	A	B
Decisions under involuntary management control	C	D

Figure 2.4 Matrix of decisions and outcomes

decision process might validate the phase of comparison and evaluation of any proposed models. We would propose the following ground rules:

1 Decision-making is associated with a combination of factual evidence and human values.

2 The interpretation of factual, or 'hard', data is a core element in decision-making.

3 Values can be thought of as a filter that will affect our individual perception of factual data when we are engaged in making judgements or decisions. There is not likely to be one set of universal human values.

4 Acknowledge some of the inconsistency, human bias or personal agendas within complex problem situations.

Good decision-makers minimise some of the risk of being wrong using personal skill, trusted approaches and tactical awareness of issues. An outcome may be personal to oneself, perhaps with social, cultural or financial implications. Our values will be influential in assessment of the problem and choice of decision. Naturally, the more exposures to the risky outcome, the larger the expected losses due to the risky outcome.

It seems logical to propose that all activities be assessed for risk, either by imagining all the possible things that could go wrong, or by using historical 'database' values of some sort to quantify their frequency of occurrence. Critically, our ability to imagine and extrapolate is limited in all sorts of ways, and historical data may give a false sense of certainty in the estimates of chance of success and failure.

2.8 Simple risk scale

In our ground rules we proposed that 'decision-making is associated with a combination of factual evidence and human values'. Now we will explore some of the personal issues that are evaluated when analysing risk. For example, how would you compare the risks of 'rock climbing for the first time' with 'driving above the speed limit whilst tired', 'flying a glider', 'taking an employee to court for stealing', or 'smoking 20 cigarettes a day'? Think about the implications for yourself as you weigh up the risks. Some of these risks have consequences for sports enthusiasts that could be immediate death, premature death or tremendous exhilaration. Other risks might involve accidents to property or destruction of a livelihood. Managers and sports enthusiasts thrive on uncertainty and, in order to perpetuate their role and purpose, they create projects as well as solve them, taking on and accepting hazards and risks as part and parcel of life. But what level of consistency in attitude to risk is adopted?

Duckworth's (1998: 10–12) simple risk scale for the public allows new risks to be calibrated against familiar risks. This neat scale is intended for use by any individual who may voluntarily (or involuntarily) be exposed to the potential hazard. The mathematical theory of this work is outlined further in Appendix 1 to this chapter. Duckworth gives some examples of the quantification of risk by a risk number **R**. The range of the values is from the safest value, near 0, to the most risky, near 8:

R = 0.3 for 100 mile train journey (very safe)

R = 1.9 for 100 mile car journey (sober, middle-aged driver)

R = 4.2 for rock climbing (one session)

R = 5.5 for an accidental fall (new-born male)

R = 6.4 for deep-sea fishing (40 year career)

R = 7.2 for Russian roulette (one game)

R = 8.0 for suicide

Note that these risk numbers have been calculated for the UK only and for life-time exposures, with a discount rate of 2 per cent per annum.

You can probably think of all sorts of questions. Does travelling by car to the rock-climbing event make you twice as risky? Can some risks be swapped with others or traded off? Can managerial risks be neatly ranked within this list? Which risks do we welcome and which do we avoid? A single figure can be mis-leading as an estimate of intangible risk because the value usually depends on so many factors, assumptions and our personal agenda. This is a particular criticism of the expected monetary value approach (above) because it takes little account of the ability to cope with a large loss of money, or the funding necessary to finance an option, or the complexity of decisions which can confuse the partici-pants in their attitude to risk.

2.8.1 Risk-averse, risk-neutral and risk-seeking

Work in the area of behavioural decision-making has emphasized the role of ref-erence, or target, levels in the analysis of risky choices. The measurement of *utility* (Moore and Thomas, 1988: 166–88) is a method of quantifying and meas-uring a decision-maker's preference pattern for the alternative outcomes arising from the different courses of action available (Cooke and Slack, 1991: 197–207).

Moore and Thomas state that:

> A majority of individuals exhibit a mixture of risk-seeking and risk-averse behav-iour, with the range of returns, where these two risk preferences are the predominant modes of behaviour, being intimately connected with the notion of a "target return". For returns below the target, a large majority of individuals appear to be risk-seeking. For returns above target, a large majority appear to be risk-averse.

Utility is a measure of the total worth of an outcome in a decision as seen by the decision-maker. Reflecting again on the ground rules given earlier, the value we put on the factors such as the profit, the loss and the consequences will influ-ence how far a person will go towards accepting a decision as being best.

Somebody who is *risk-neutral* would accept the EMV ('average value') for gain or loss as being helpful to the choice of decision, exhibited by a linear utility function. People who are *risk-averse* (conservative) reject the chance to win large amounts of money because they could lose an amount of money that is beyond the threshold that they consider safe. A *risk-seeker* (optimist) would have a utility profile that represented an attitude to losing a large amount of money that was welcoming, or positive, in comparison with the opportunity to gain a large amount of money. Utilities can be compared graphically (Figure 2.5). The

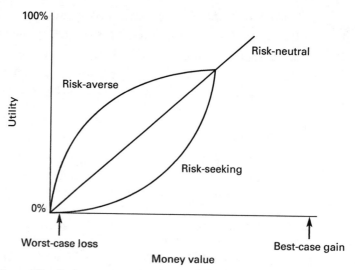

Figure 2.5 Three utility functions, comparing attitudes to risk

horizontal scale represents the level of money being considered (the usual variable of interest in such analysis) and the vertical scale the value of the utility to the person (here scaled to be from 0 to 100%).

Example 2.2

Suppose, in a gambling game, you and I toss a coin for which the two sides (head and tail) are equally likely to appear with a 50/50 chance (0.5). You will win from me £1.00 if the coin is a head, but you will lose to me 10 pence if it is a tail. A decision tree of the outcomes and their chances is represented in Figure 2.6.

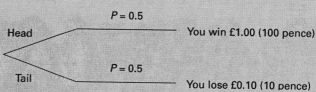

Figure 2.6 Outcomes in a simple gambling game

In pence, your 'expected' winnings are:

$0.5 \times 100 + 0.5 \times (-10) = 50 - 5$
$= 45$ (you can 'expect' to win 45 pence in one game)

Expectation is about estimating over a number of similar games what you could, on average, win. For example, over ten separate games, you can 'expect' to win 450 pence, the long-run expected value. You might be puzzled because the stakes are 100 pence and 10 pence and we are not playing for 45 pence at all. When questioned about your decision to play this game, you might perhaps state that you prefer to win 100 pence rather than lose 10 pence, that you enter into this gamble quite happily. Thus, we then summarise that the utility to you, personally, of winning 100 pence is greater than the utility to you of losing 10 pence, i.e.

$U(100 \text{ pence}) > U(-10 \text{ pence})$

Activity 2.6 In the above example (Figure 2.6), reduce the value of the probability of winning to 0.3 and determine the new expected value. Under those conditions what will that do to the value of your utility function?

You might find in Activity 2.6 that the new expected value of 0.3 × £1.00 + 0.7 × –£0.10 = £0.30 – £0.07 = £0.23 impacts upon you in some way. Perhaps, as the expected value reduces from £0.45 and gets closer to zero, you feel the game is not worth playing at all. If you are unhappy about playing then your utility assessment might be:

$$U(100 \text{ pence}) < U(-10 \text{ pence})$$

which clearly has changed since we first looked at the example.

Activity 2.7 Again, in Example 2.2, suppose we now raise the stakes when winning from £1.00 (3 small bars of chocolate) to £1,000 (a good quality PC and printer), and the stakes when losing from £0.10 to £100 (two seats at the FA Cup Final). The odds remain at 50/50 for the coin's outcomes (Figure 2.7). Discuss your attitude to the risks involved, and calculate your utility (preferences).

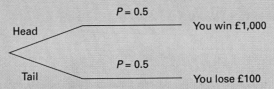

Figure 2.7 Gambling game with increased stakes

In Activity 2.7 the stakes have changed to winning £1,000 and losing £100 but, on average, you can 'expect' to win £450 in each game of tossing the coin. Your utility might change because of the high amount you could lose. Indeed, suppose you were to refuse to play – we can then summarise:

$$U(£1000) < U(-£100)$$

This does not represent a risk-neutral policy. It is somewhat risk-averse because you prefer not to lose £100 rather than to take the chance of winning £1,000.

Some would argue the other way, that you should seize the opportunity to play because you face the same odds of winning and losing as before, i.e. 50/50, but others would agree that the same chance of losing £100 is more important than winning £1,000, given that £100 is a large amount of money. A millionaire would have a further perspective, being prepared to accommodate losses and take risks, being self-insured.

Illustration 2.4 Shifting utilities

A further illustration of the above type of decision-making occurred in 2001 on *Who Wants to be a Millionaire?*, a popular British TV quiz show which involves a contestant answering a sequence of questions for money prizes that build up to a final jackpot of £1 million.

A contestant had already won £8,000 in the quiz, which is normally full of suspense and tension, and could leave the quiz with that amount if she so wished, but would win another £8,000 if she answered the next question correctly. The next question for the contestant was: 'On an oven, what is Gas Mark 6?' After some time of deliberation over the four possible answers, the rules allow the four answers to be reduced to two, one of which is incorrect (180 degrees centigrade or 350 degrees Fahrenheit) and the other correct (200 degrees centigrade or 400 degrees Fahrenheit). If she gave an incorrect answer she would lose £7,000 of her £8,000 winnings, thus leaving the show with £1,000 only.

The contestant admitted she would have to guess the answer (200 degrees centigrade). She chose to take her 'safe' £8,000 by not answering the question. For her, the utility function of her risk-averse policy can be represented as:

$$U(£8,000) > U(£16,000)$$

although her expected winnings by 50:50 guesswork alone on this question were:

$$0.5 \times £16,000 + 0.5 \times -£7,000 \quad = £8,000 - £3,500$$
$$= £4,500$$

Clearly, at that moment she had moved away from risk-neutral into risk-averse mode. Perhaps she may not have been so risk averse if the gains and losses were only £80 and £70, with a base cushion of £10. A subjective assessment guided her decision-making, but also the obvious strain and emotion of losing £7,000 tended to force the issue.

2.8.2 Value system inconsistencies

Up to now we have spent time covering personal decision-making, without much regard for the strategic perspective of the decision. An interesting example of an investment decision that went wrong was when Nick Leeson's trading strategy brought down Barings Bank in the mid-1990s. Much of his dealing was being made in a 'virtual dimension' based on numbers alone. Usually, investment advisers state that past performance is no guide to future performance due to the complexity of the outcomes involved. Speculation takes place and decisions are made by people who have no vested interest in the tangible commodity. For example, if a crop fails and people starve, does the investor really feel that loss?

We now consider managerial risk where the manager has strong reasons of accountability for 'getting it right'. Cooke and Slack (1991: 48–54) summarise the contributions of our values and value systems to managerial decision-making. Their findings suggest that our values operate at the unconscious and non-conscious level, they affect the choice among alternatives. Our personal values are 'normal' to us but our value systems are not always consistent and this inconsistency prevents the operation of perfect judgement in the evaluation of alternative courses of action.

2.9   Effective risk management

An ancient dictum suggests, 'You cannot manage what you don't measure'. Some firms try to develop a proactive risk assessment by anticipating the risk, its possible outcome and how to manage its danger.

Unilever's approach in Illustration 2.5 appears realistically pragmatic, suggesting the influence of quantitative techniques as well as a very organised and subjective, consultative approach, being very specific in identifying options for risk solution.

Illustration 2.5   Unilever

Unilever is a worldwide company specialising in products of a chemical, pharmaceutical and household nature. Hundreds of projects are in hand at any one time, but the overall risk is spread according to the company's financial portfolio. An account of good practice goes like this:

> How do we get the issues out in the open? We use decision trees and acknowledge that costs determine the crucial items to get right. Open-ended, non-threatening interviews allow each team member to declare what has to go right for the project to succeed. This leads to a risk management plan, rehearsed and with contingency for everything. The philosophy is that you will get a better decision if you have thought about it. Active listening by the interviewer will pick up conditions and assumptions likely to affect the outcome. The risk register will prioritise any pre-launch activities, probing each area thoroughly.
>
> Economic losses are a 'disaster', being the contribution of the intersection of several events, probably simultaneously. A risk audit assesses the occurrence of probabilities and their consequences. There will often be a difference between the actual and perceived probability. Rare events also have to be 'modelled'. We might summarise at this point by saying that we can avoid, reduce or retain a risk (whether it is unintentional or passive), we can pool risks or transfer risk in an economic sense. This might be called risk portfolio management. The modelling of these rare and common events are through the application of three commonly occurring probability distributions. A probability distribution is the accumulation of data about the occurrences of many events with their estimated chances. The Normal, Binomial and Poisson distributions are among the best-known distributions (Thomas, 1997: 55–91).

(adapted from Whittall, 1999)

Compare this approach to the risky shift ideas of Dunford (Chapter 11).

2.9.1 The role of the risk analyst

Actuaries are a good example of risk analysts who address insurance and medical risks. Other business analysts might be working on a wide variety of issues that include the development of statistical models to understand risk, or reporting and interpreting historical experience so that appropriate actions can be taken. This would enable new products to be developed whilst enabling business opportunities to be examined systematically and profitable options identified.

A risk analyst will have excellent training and a career path, possessing good analytical, problem-solving skills. For example, a major banking organisation would attract risk analysts at a variety of levels for various divisions of its retail credit risk department. These analysts would have an interest in finance and good information technology experience.

2.9.2 Service sector risk management

Where risk is associated with the health of the public, for example, then very clear protocols exist for minimising such risks. The negative effects of bad publicity can destroy a public utility's reputation. For example, the toxicity of drinking water is a high priority for Yorkshire Water, a British company which had a lot of negative publicity in the mid-1990s concerning the quantity of water available in a drought for a region of several million customers. Illustration 2.6 focuses on the discolouration of the same company's water.

Now, all four authors of this book are customers of Yorkshire Water, a monopoly company with no competitors apart from bottled water suppliers. The report sounds very good; a failure rate of 0.19 per cent (19 in every 10,000 samples) might be seen as acceptable for this type of service provision and it has been publicly quoted. But, this depends on whether failing a test where levels of tri-halomethanes are too high is a serious threat to human life. However, the water

---

Illustration 2.6 Yorkshire's water

Water quality in the Yorkshire and Humber region is said to be improving but concern remains over the number of cases of discoloured water last year. The Drinking Water Inspectorate (9th annual report) praised Yorkshire Water for supplying high-quality water and reducing the number of samples failing the standard for manganese.

11 out of 15 water quality incidents in 1998 involved discolouration where levels of tri-halomethanes failed to meet tough standards. In the region, 99.81% of the 268,100 tests by Yorkshire Water reached the required levels. (Tri-halomethanes (chloroform, bromoform, bromodichloromethane, and chlorodibromomethane) are common contaminants of chlorinated drinking water. Although animal data indicate that these compounds may be reproductive toxicants, little information exists on their relation to spontaneous abortion in humans.)

The region's principal Drinking Water Inspectorate, Chris Jackson, said 'Yorkshire Water continues to provide drinking water of a high quality'.

Source: Yorkshire Post, 8 July 1999

company will be aware that sales of bottled water are rising, which is a sign of loss of confidence by the public.

A level of failure of 0.19 per cent can be favourably compared with other service sector examples. Evans and Lindsay (1999: 607) estimate that the USA encounters the following numbers of 'failures' in public services when a failure rate of 0.27 per cent is achieved:

- At least 20,000 wrong drug prescriptions per annum
- More than 15,000 babies dropped each year by nurses and obstetricians
- No electricity, water or heating for about 9 hours per annum
- 500 incorrect surgical operations each week
- 2000 lost pieces of mail each hour

As a consumer, would you be satisfied with such quality? These failure rates are indicative of some 'real' risks which seem terrible when extrapolated into a national population. The failure rates are typical for such services despite massive initiatives to furnish a total quality management (TQM) philosophy and reduce the failure rates towards zero so as to inspire consumer confidence.

In local government, risk management is a relatively new phenomenon encompassing insurance, auditing, financial control, planning and, above all, health and safety. The tools to monitor and control risk are situated within a limited resource base, with time constraints always evident. The decision support for managers involves operational definitions of risk, perhaps encompassing statistical models. The outcome of a large organisation's decisions will determine the performance of that organisation, again within the idea of a portfolio of shares or resource bidding. Risk is taken when any capital is staked under conditions of uncertainty which could be technical or organisational in its context.

2.10   Rationality

Some people avoid walking under a ladder placed against a wall. Others jump onto a stool when a large spider scurries across the kitchen floor in the late hours of the night. These people are clearly 'risk averse'. A manager could not, rationally, make big decisions when risk averse to such an extent.

Chambers Concise 20th Century Dictionary defines something to be rational when it is: 'sane, intelligent, commensurable with natural numbers, a rational being or quantity'. Further, when we rationalise we are 'free from irrational quantities'.

In one sense, being 'free from irrational quantities' implies that reason is employed. Take three extreme sports, such as bungee jumping, white-water rafting and abseiling. What rational behaviour do we encounter in these three sports from young and old participants alike in a world that is, normally, trying to minimise risk?

The risk of success or failure is very relevant to our personal, business and social lives. The publishers of this book have taken a risk with funding us to write it; the exact future purchasers have not been identified as yet, the quality of our book will depend on our approach, research, writing abilities and other vital inputs to a 'risky' venture. Yet, in a rational fashion, both we and the publisher have taken on the project because we know we can make it work.

A car travelling at 40 km/h is dangerous if a tyre bursts but the consequences are probably less than if it were travelling at 120 km/h. The type of injury could be quite different, possibly fatal, and to some extent the consequences are better at the lower speed. We rationalise away the risks by claiming that 'they will happen to somebody else', but few of us dare venture out from our home environment without insurance against illness, death, robbery, and so on.

Social and biological sciences require masses of facts to determine general behaviour and risk because of wide variation in individuals. In the physical sciences, precisely controlled laboratory experiments can be used to predict response. These give background data, essential for understanding a risk-associated issue. For example, in quantifying individual risks from air pollution, adverse health outcomes are important areas of concern. A time series analysis usefully models the daily count of some health outcome, e.g. deaths or hospital admissions, with data on various air pollutants and climatic variables in conjunction with other confounding variables. There is a general tendency for these studies to report a weak positive association between health outcomes and pollutants, but the risk relationships vary in their nature and strength.

Sjoberg (1999: 6) points out that the risk from smoking is very much greater than the risk of living close to a nuclear power plant. Hence, why does the public not accept nuclear power because it has clearly accepted smoking? This illustrates the personal preference for a risk that is voluntary over a risk that is imposed. Clearly, a human life has 'infinite' value, creating an ethical tension. The latter has created turmoil in many countries, which Sjoberg calls the 'psychometric paradigm'. For example, the Swedish parliament wished in the late 1990s to eliminate all road-related deaths, with no extra resource, from a base point of 400 deaths per year. Is that really possible? The implications for road speeds, redesign of car features, road management and, hence, the costs, are serious. Sweden hosted a high-level meeting with other EU countries in 2001 on new technology for safe and environmentally sound road transport as part of its Vision Zero policy of 1997, which declared that no one needed be killed or injured by road traffic.

As for nuclear safety, the experts' risks are qualitatively similar to those of the public, but often at a significantly different level of risk. Of course, the higher the risk the more the public wants it reduced, and it falls to management to reduce the chance of occurrence and not only the seriousness of the consequences.

Teigen *et al.* (1999: 124) address the question of lay respondents' views on risk. Here,

> the consequence component is given more weight than the probabilities, and risk judgements are influenced by other factors than probability for a specified outcome (deaths, injuries), like voluntariness of exposure, the possibility of exerting control, the novelty of the hazard, and less measurable qualities of the outcome, like its 'catastrophic' character. Factors of this kind are often held responsible for lack of correspondence between lay and expert estimates of the relative riskiness of various hazards.

2.10.1 Evidence-based societies

We can pose the question: who is imposing risks on whom? Likewise, who pays the costs? Who receives the benefits of taking a risk? How do we measure and monitor relevant utilities? It is likely to be true that, as regards current population health policy, the future generations stand to gain more than the current generation in benefits.

The decision-maker is identified and confronted with a set of possible outcomes, or flow of consequences, each with an outcome of some uncertainty. The expected utility is the preferred action, or the person and people to whom the risk is applicable might debate the preferred action and then choose. For example, a patient might be advised in a hospital that only 10 per cent of patients with a certain type of lung tumour live longer than five years. The patient's personal approach will assess age, reason to live, financial cost, etc. The utility assessment may focus on survival or preferred treatment (chemotherapy, surgery or a combination of the two).

In another medical example, the debate might be over the utility of a clinical trial and what is being done to patients compared with the quality of information to be gained from the trial. Who allows whom to be the decision-maker? Who is managing the risk?

A conceptual model, formal or otherwise using database and analysis techniques, gives useful output. Is the source of the data known? The parameters within the structure could also be uncertain, so a *stochastic* probability-based analysis is advocated that builds uncertainty and variation into the parameter estimates.

With all modelling of decisions, there is need for an audit on the scientific sensitivity analysis and the probabilities calculated so as to inspire 'public' confidence. The decision-maker has to find compatibility with the data and support from experts. Theoretically, all models are flawed – but many are useful because

---

Example 2.3

A firm specialises in making lamps and mirrors. Its delivery schedule from 30 suppliers shows the percentage of parts delivered within the last three months. The amounts delivered on time have been recorded as a percentage and, for simplicity, are presented in ascending order:

0, 0, 0, 46, 53,	55, 56, 59, 72, 76,	78, 80, 81, 85, 87
88, 89, 90, 91, 96,	97, 97, 98, 99, 99,	100, 100, 100, 100, 100

For example, supplier 15 in the list delivered on time 87 per cent of its scheduled parts.

The mean average supply rate is only 75.6 per cent, although we note that the median average supply rate is higher, at 87.5 per cent (the latter would be regarded as more representative of the average rate because of the skewed data distribution). This implies that there is a 50 per cent chance that the supply rate will be 87.5 per cent or better because the median divides the data into two equal portions, 50 per cent above and 50 per cent below the average.

A decision is required to improve the delivery schedule. The evidence suggests that, by eliminating the worst five suppliers in terms of their supply record, the average amounts supplied would improve and, hence, the overall risk of poor delivery service would be reduced. This rational decision is free from any form of bias.

risk issues are real and complex and a model encourages debate about the issues. However, statisticians agree that the quantitative formalism should not be pushed beyond the limits of public defensibility.

Samples give historical data that are valuable in market research, cost control, quality control, and research and development problems. Probability-based data are merely the relative frequency of occurrence. Using the lamps and mirrors data in Example 2.3, the probability-based forecast that any supplier will provide nothing in the next three-month period is 3/30, i.e. 10 per cent, using the observation that 3 suppliers out of the 30 supplied nothing at all on time.

The risk is not so much in the data, more in the importance of the decision depending on the data.

2.10.2 Subjective views

What is the probability of another world war? Your personal belief is not necessarily like personal faith (being sure of what you hope for and certain of what you do not see), because you just do not know. We would expect a group of rational people to put forward similar estimates for the probability of an event such as a war, or we can expect a similar consensus of opinion although different amounts of knowledge and experience may lead to numerically different values. For example, in 1997 the Bank of England moved to a situation where 27 experts are now tasked with forecasting the inflation figures for the next period. This is an example of the *Delphi method* to forecast by a group consensus technique that provides a relatively narrow spread of opinions within which the majority of experts concur.

Risk is more easily defined when its associated outcome has occurred before, and it may happen again, with predictable relative frequency, a probability-based argument. Also, many decisions are based on factors that are not really expressed in financial terms. The pay-offs, or negative consequences, are not known in uncertainty analysis and when there are so few data to predict the outcome we begin to realise that we cannot tell the difference between risk and uncertainty.

2.11 The equivalence of frequencies and probabilities

Psychological studies by Teigen *et al.* (1999: 123) have shown that people are skilful at processing frequency information but are not always consistent in forming estimates of risks and probabilities. It is safe to say that people reason differently when faced with frequencies rather than probabilities. Statistical data are evidence of some sort, but a probabilistic data value might include or exclude the frequency data. A subjective estimate may be absolutely accurate in estimating the future, but frequency data may be less than helpful in their accuracy. Here, we are mainly concerned with the magnitude of the risk and it is suggested that when problems are represented in a frequentistic rather than probabilistic way the bias described elsewhere may be eliminated.

Fischhoff and De Bruin's (1999: 149–51) research shows that bias is often obvious in the personal assessment of common risks. The overestimation or underestimation of the risk often becomes clearer when 'official' data are checked to validate the size of the 'claim'. This can be a cause of worry and anxiety for many people, which is unnecessary. For example, a police force might claim that the crime rate for burglaries and assaults has declined in recent years. However, the public often overestimates the probability of the risk of being a victim of burglary in the next year, and yet all of us probably know someone who has been 'recently' burgled. For example, you might estimate that your risk of being burgled in the next year is 20 per cent, but a retrospective assessment might show that only 5 per cent of people in your district actually encounter a burglary in any one year. Thus, frequencies are dependent on the risk and probabilities, rather than vice versa.

The translation of subjective feelings into quantitative estimates is long established. It is generally acknowledged that drawing a person's attention to a quantitative value, however irrelevant to the task, can pull that person in the direction of the value if you ask them to provide an estimate of the risk. What is termed a 'high anchor' can influence the probability judgement of an individual.

2.11.1 The 50/50 probability value

Sometimes, when faced with uncertainty, we look for a probability value to summarise our feeling. When we 'don't know', then often we settle for 50/50, a sign of 'ignorance' or epistemic uncertainty rather than an exact assessment of the risk's value. This leads to overestimation when the real probability is somewhat smaller than 50 per cent. Fischhoff and De Bruin (1999: 150–1) advise that when we have no idea of the probability of an outcome, it is unwise to allocate a value of 50/50 as this artificially biases the value upwards. If a subjective override were preferred for the quantitative risk value, this again shows the danger of providing a number for the risk analysis.

The authors argue that it is better to 'present a probability scale so as to reduce epistemic uncertainty or the ability to express it'. Epistemic uncertainty occurs when we do not know what probabilities to use when expressing our uncertainty. The production of a probability scale halves a respondent's use of the 'absolutely no idea' option. Better to have imperfect information than perfect 'misinformation' because a fateful event with severe consequences is one in which we may be particularly reluctant to commit ourselves to a value. When we need to produce a numerical estimate of the probability it can be helpful to have a probability scale from 0 to 100 per cent, or perhaps Duckworth's riskometer, on which to place the value.

◆ Summary

As you have probably noted from reading this chapter, we have taken a very practical view of the context of risk, uncertainty and rational decision-making. The simplicity of decision-making may at this stage seem less obvious now as we explore the complexity of the process and engage in our preliminary assessment of the risks, their level and seriousness.

Attitude to risk may be personal to oneself, or form part of a nation's cultural policy. In all aspects the consequences of the risk and its probability-based assessment of occurrence are important inputs to the decision-making. Although normative approaches have been previously introduced as intrinsically dogmatic in attempting to prescribe methods, the reality is that quantitative and qualitative theory have to marry so that analysis can begin to provide estimates of the risks involved in decisions.

The practising manager might be a seasoned subjective decision-maker, but one who fails to plan an examination of the context of the risk analysis does so at risk to self.

? Decision diary

Develop a day-by-day list of risks that you take. Question yourself as to whether you proceed with your day-to-day decisions at the 'virtually certain' level, or at the 'certain' level. Refer back to Figure 2.2, the language of uncertainty, and evaluate any quantitative data that show whether the risk is changing over time or whether, subjectively, there is little change.

References

Arnold, J. and Turley, S. (1996) *Accounting for Management Decisions*, 3rd edition. Hemel Hempstead: Prentice Hall International.

Cooke, S. and Slack, N (1991) *Making Management Decisions*, 2nd edition. Hemel Hempstead: Prentice Hall International.

Cova, B. and Holstius, K. (1993) 'How to create competitive advantage in project business', *Journal of Marketing Management*, 9: 105–21.

Davies, H. and Walters, M. (1999) 'Do all crises have to become disasters? Risk and risk mitigation', *Property Management*, 16(1).

Doll, R., Peto, R., Wheatley, K., Gray, R. and Sutherland, I. (1994) 'Mortality in relation to smoking: 40 years' observations on male British doctors', *British Medical Journal*, 309: 901–11.

Duckworth, F. (1998) 'The quantification of risk', *Royal Statistical Society News*, 26(2).

Evans, J. and Lindsay, W. (1999) *The Management and Control of Quality*, 4th edition. Cincinnati, OH: South-Western College Publishing.

Fischhoff, B. and De Bruin, W. (1999) 'Fifty-fifty = 50%?', *Journal of Behavioral Decision Making*, 12: 149–63.

Moore, P. and Thomas H. (1988) *The Anatomy of Decisions*, 2nd edition. Harmondsworth: Penguin.

Sjoberg, L. (1999) 'Factors in risk perception', *Royal Statistical Society Conference Abstracts, Warwick, England, July*.

Teigen, K. Brun, W. and Frydenlund, R. (1999) 'Judgments of risk and probability: the role of frequentistic information', *Journal of Behavioral Decision Making*, 12: 123–39.

Thomas, R. (1997) *Quantitative Methods for Business Studies*. London: Prentice Hall.
Whittall, P. (1999) 'If you can keep your head ... (some tips on risk management)', *Royal Statistical Society Conference Abstracts, Warwick, England, July.*

Websites of interest

See www.geog.ucl.ac.uk/safety for a Health and Safety approach to risk assessment, hazards and control of types of risk.

Go to www.bancdirections.co.uk then the operational risk areas.

See www.hse.gov.uk for the Health and Safety Executive's reports.

See www.riskworld.com for more issues of a topical nature.

Go to www.acq.osd.mil/io/se then follow the risk management option.

Go to www.pertmaster.com then follow the risk analysis/high power option and eventually look at the brainteaser.

Go to www.google.com then search for risk assessment software.

Go to www.4pm.com then follow the lead to risk management.

See www.learnrisk.com/downloads.checklstpdf.pdf for a simple risk assessment sheet which looks at risk factors, categorises them according to weighting factors and eventually uses a scoring method to provide a total score for each risk factor.

Go to http://www.uk.cgey.com/services/or/ and follow the link to risk analysis with a case study on the telecoms industry.

Glossary

Ambiguity:	the quality or state of being uncertain due to being understood in several ways.
Decision trees:	these show the sequential nature of the decision-making process by combining data about decisions, outcomes and associated probabilities.
Delphi methods:	these provide forecasts using questionnaire techniques by a group consensus process that provides a relatively narrow spread of opinions within which the majority of experts concur.
Expected monetary value (EMV):	the financial result of a decision taking account of all known outcomes and probabilities.
Outcomes ('states of nature'):	the possible chance events that occur and which affect the pay-offs associated with a decision.
Present value:	the value of an amount of money at the present time when a discounting process is applied to the known future value of the money.

Probability distributions:	these summarise the accumulation of data about the occurrences of many events with their estimated chances. The Normal, Binomial and Poisson distributions are among the best-known distributions and are used widely in several industries where the assessment is routinely dependent on quantitative techniques.
Quantitative approaches:	these analyse the quantitative facts and data associated with the problem. Mathematical expressions will describe the objectives and constraints of the problem.
Qualitative approaches:	these are likely to be used by managers, increasing with experience. These approaches are especially useful when the problem is simple or has been experienced previously.
Risk averse:	people who are risk averse tend to decide to avoid the risk of losing an amount of money that is above the threshold that they consider safe. In so doing, they normally miss the chance to win larger amounts of money.
Risk-seeking:	risk-seeking people tend to decide to accept the risk of losing an amount of money that is above the threshold that they consider safe. In so doing, they normally accept the chance to gain larger amounts of money.
Stochastic models:	models that contain at least one uncontrollable input which is uncertain and subject to variation.
Utility value:	the measure of worth of a particular outcome, reflecting the decision-maker's attitude based on a group of factors such as quality, profit, loss etc.

Appendix 1 Example risk numbers, R (Duckworth, 1998: 12)

The following are some calculated values of **R**. For smoking, data are from Doll *et al.*; for other risks they are from the Health and Safety Executive. A discount rate of 2 per cent is used throughout. All figures refer to the UK and are for lifetime exposures except where a specific exposure is given.

100 mile journey	0.3
Destructive asteroid impact (newborn male)	1.6
1,000 mile flight	1.7
100 mile car journey (sober middle-aged driver)	1.9
Rock climbing (one session)	4.2
Homicide (newborn male)	4.6
Lifetime car travel (newborn male)	5.5
Accidental falls (newborn male)	5.5
Rock climbing over 20 years	6.3
Deep-sea fishing (40 year career)	6.4
Continuing smoking cigarettes	
male aged 35, 10/day	6.7
male aged 35, 20/day	6.9
male aged 35, 40/day	7.1
Russian roulette (one game)	7.2
Suicide	8.0

3 A psychological dimension

Learning outcomes

On completing this chapter you should be able to:

- Understand how theories from the discipline of psychology can enhance your appreciation of decision-making.
- Appreciate the different philosophical bases of the theories considered.
- Recognise factors that may affect decision-makers' rationality.
- Begin to explore your own decision-making behaviour using theories from psychology.

3.1 Introduction

In this chapter you will encounter a number of theories from competing perspectives in the field of psychology. Some of the theories (for instance, cognitive psychology) focus on the perceptual processes of the individual, and therefore primarily concern themselves with the internal workings of the mind. Other theories (for example, social psychology) address the ways in which individuals come to make sense of themselves and their surroundings as social beings. We describe and examine a number of cognitive and social psychology theories and their implications for management decision-making. As you can imagine, a number of cognitive and social psychologists have applied their skills and knowledge specifically to evaluate decision-making. We address some of their findings in this chapter. Ultimately, no amount of study into psychology will guarantee successful outcomes. However, an increased awareness of the psychological dimension can increase our chances of being more vigilant decision-makers, and consequently improve our chances of success.

3.2 Nomothetic and ideographic approaches

Different theories in psychology are often broadly categorised in terms of whether the theory is nomothetic or ideographic. Each represents a particular set of underlying assumptions about what constitutes a valid methodology for studying people. Nomothetic means 'law giving', so we would expect such theories to be concerned with making predictions about people in general. Ideographic (sometimes spelt 'idiographic') approaches to psychology are concerned with the uniqueness of individuals. Quantitative approaches to decision-making are often presented as essentially nomothetic; qualitative approaches as essentially ideographic. You will discover that many theories in psychology try to establish general rules and classifications when studying personality and are in essence nomothetic. Others are more ideographic, relying on studying the individuals in depth and not attempting to extrapolate findings. However, there are theorists who use ideographic methodologies by focusing on detailed studies of a few individuals, and subsequently attempt to extrapolate their findings by making generalised statements about larger populations – this is a common source of criticism of Freud's work.

Buchanan and Huczynski's (1997: 63) summary of the differences between the two approaches is presented in Table 3.1.

Table 3.1 Nomothetic and ideographic approaches

Nomothetic approach	Ideographic approach
Has a positivist bias	Has a phenomenological bias
Is generalising; emphasises the discovery of laws of human behaviour	Is individualising; emphasises the richness and complexity of the unique individual
Uses objective questionnaires	Uses projective tests and other written and spoken materials
Describes personality in terms of the individual's possession of trait clusters or personality types	Describes personality in terms of the individual's own understanding and interpretation of his or her identity
Views personality as composed of discrete and identifiable elements	Believes that personality has to be understood and studied as an indivisible, intelligible whole
Believes that personality is primarily determined by heredity, biology, genetics	Believes that personality is primarily determined by social and cultural processes
Believes that personality is given at birth and cannot be altered	Believes that personality is adaptable, open to change through experience.

Source: based on Buchanan and Huczynski, 1997: 163. For an explanation of positivism and phenomenology see Chapter 5.

Before we discuss the various theories related to psychological decision-making, can you identify any decisions that you would take instinctively and those that you would stop and think about?

In Activity 3.1, you may have included as your instinctive decisions, diving into a river to rescue a child and swerving to miss a person crossing the road. Your 'stop and think' decisions may have been whether to buy a car or some other item. However, both decisions could involve an element of reflection, for example 'what would my friends think if they knew I did not try to save the child?' or 'If I buy the car, will I regret it later?'

3.3   Schools of thought

Table 3.2 may be helpful in categorising the different approaches in psychology.

Table 3.2 Five major approaches in psychology

	Psychoanalytic or psychodynamic (e.g. Freud)	Behaviourist or stimulus–response (e.g. Skinner)	Humanistic– existential (e.g. Rogers)	Neurobiological or biogenic	Cognitive
Nature of human beings	Individual is in conflict due to opposing demands made by different parts of the personality – id, ego, superego. Behaviour is largely determined by unconscious forces	Human behaviour is shaped by environmental forces (reinforcement) and is a collection of learned responses to stimuli. The key learning process is conditioning (classical and operant)	The individual is unique, free, rational and self-determining. Freewill and self-actualisation make human beings distinct from animals. Present experience is as important as past experience	Behaviour is determined by genetic, physiological and neurobiological factors and processes. The influence of the central nervous system (especially the brain) is crucial	The human mind is compared to a computer. People are information processors, selecting information, coding it, storing it and retrieving it when needed. Memory, perception and language are central
Nature of psychological normality	Adequate balance between id, ego, superego. But conflict is always present to some degree	Possession of an adequately large repertoire of adaptive responses.	Ability to accept oneself, to realise one's potential, to achieve intimacy with others, to find meaning in life	Properly functioning nervous system	Proper functioning of cognitive processes and the ability to use them to monitor and control behaviour

Source: Gross, R. (1996) *Psychology: The Science of Mind and Behaviour*, 3rd edn. Reproduced by permission of Hodder/Arnold Limited.

Table 3.2 Five major approaches in psychology *continued*

	Psychoanalytic or psychodynamic (e.g. Freud)	Behaviourist or stimulus–response (e.g. Skinner)	Humanistic–existential (e.g. Rogers)	Neurobiological or biogenic	Cognitive
Nature of psychological development	Psychosexual stages: oral (0–1) anal (1–3) phallic (3–5/6) latency (5/6–puberty) genital (puberty – maturity) Sequence determined by maturation. The individual is shaped by early childhood experiences	None as such. No stages of development. Different behaviour is selectively reinforced at different ages, but the differences between a child and an adult are merely quantitative	Development of self-concept, in particular self-regard (self-esteem). Satisfaction of low-level needs as prerequisite for higher-level (growth) needs (in Maslow's hierarchy of needs)	Stages of behavioural/ psychological development based on changes in brain growth which are genetically determined (i.e. maturation)	Stages of cognitive development (e.g. Piaget): sensorimotor 0–2) preoperational (2–7) concrete operational (7–11) formal operational (11–15) Information processing approach – development of memory, perception, language, attention, etc.
Preferred method(s) of study	Case study (clinical method)	Experiment (animals and humans, but mainly non-human animals)	Case study Q–sort (Rogers)	Experiment (mainly non-human animals)	Experiment (mainly humans) Artificial intelligence/ computer simulation
Major cause(s) of abnormal behaviour	Emotional disturbance or neurosis caused by unresolved conflicts stemming from childhood. Abnormal behaviour is symptomatic of such conflicts. Main feature is anxiety	The learning of maladaptive responses or the failure to learn adaptive ones in the first place No distinction between symptoms and behaviour disorder	Inability to accept and express one's true nature, or take responsibility for one's own actions and to make authentic choices. Anxiety stems from denying part of the self	Genetic disorders, organic (bodily) disorders (e.g. brain disease or injury), chemical imbalance, food allergies. Mental illness gives rise to behavioural and cognitive symptoms (e.g. thought disorder and schozophrenia)	Unrealistic or irrational ideas and beliefs about self and others. Inability to monitor or control behaviour through appropriate cognitive processes
Preferred method(s) of treatment	Insight-oriented psychotherapy (e.g. psychoanalysis). The unconscious is revealed through dream interpretation, free association, transference	Behaviour therapy or modification, e.g. systematic desensitisation aversion therapy, flooding, behaviour shaping, token economy	Client-centred therapy; insights come from the client, as present experiences are explored with the therapist	Physical (somatic) treatments, e.g. chemotherapy (drugs), electro-convulsive therapy (ECT), psychosurgery	E.g. cognitive behaviour therapy, rational–emotive therapy, Zen mediation and behavioural self-control

Table 3.2 Five major approaches in psychology *continued*

	Psychoanalytic or psychodynamic (e.g. Freud)	Behaviourist or stimulus–response (e.g. Skinner)	Humanistic– existential (e.g. Rogers)	Neurobiological or biogenic	Cognitive
Goal(s) of treatment	To uncover and work through unconscious conflicts to make them conscious. To achieve reasonable balance between id, ego and superego	To eliminate maladaptive responses and to acquire adaptive ones	To rediscover the whole self, which can then proceed towards self-actualisation	To alleviate symptoms and/or actually reverse the underlying causes(s) of the illness	To correct unrealistic/ irrational ideas and beliefs so that thinking becomes an effective means of controlling behaviour

Source: Gross, 1996: 12–13

We now address some implications of each school of thought, and assess how they can be used to inform our knowledge of decision-making.

3.4 A psychodynamic approach

3.4.1 Transactional analysis

Transactional analysis (TA) was developed by Eric Berne (1968) who suggested that the human psyche consisted of three 'ego states', namely Parent, Adult and Child, and that at any given time an individual will be in one of these states. It is generally considered that Berne derived inspiration for his ideas from the earlier work of Sigmund Freud, and that his identification of three ego states is, in many ways, closely related to Freud's notion of the id (child), ego (adult) and superego (parent). Whilst Freud used Greek words to describe the different elements of our personality, Berne made use of more accessible language to describe, what is in essence, the same basic notion.

The three ego states in TA are generally depicted in the following model:

Parent ego state

The parent ego state may be likened to a tape recording of our parents' (or guardians') sayings and attitudes made when we are in the first few years of our lives. How often do you find yourself saying something just like your parents? In our parent ego state we either admonish/punish others – referred to by Berne as the 'punishing parent' – or nurture them – referred to as the 'nurturing parent'. So the language associated with this state is generally typified by commands, admonishments and inquiries about another's well-being.

Adult ego state

It is in our adult ego state that we analyse issues and achieve whatever level of objectivity it is possible to attain. In the adult ego state we are able thus to evaluate and critique. We are able to be calculating and unemotional. We would be seen to be serious-minded when in this ego state.

Child ego state

The child ego state, like the adult ego state, is formed in the first few years of life. It is in our child ego state that we have fun and are mischievous. We are also at our most creative. In the child ego state we are at our least rational. When we are impulsive, giving no consideration to the consequences of our actions, this is referred to by Berne as the 'natural child'. When we change our behaviour in response to 'parental' admonishments, this is referred to as the 'adapted child'.

Given what was said about the dominance of rational models of decision-making in Chapter 1, there seems to be an implicit assumption that decision-makers should predominantly make decisions in an adult ego state. This, however, denies our capacity to be creative, impulsive individuals who often behave in a far from rational manner. It could be that we often make decisions in a child ego state and, subsequently, try to justify the decisions to others in an adult state. An example of this is the senior manager who was describing his decision to go on a training programme in the Far East. As he described his decision in an MBA seminar he adopted a rational model to talk through the criteria he had employed to make his decision. On further questioning by his classmates he became more animated and admitted that his 'real' reason was that he had not been there before and, more importantly, neither had any of the other senior managers in the organisation, so he would be a pioneer.

It is important to note that it is not suggested that we progress through life from one ego state to the next in a developmental process. Rather, even in very old age our child ego state will still be functioning. Importantly, Berne argues that a psychologically sound human being needs to have all three ego states in good working order. The model therefore develops into:

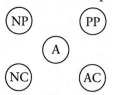

If you wish to read about TA in more depth, we recommend Stewart and Joines (1987). TA has been a very controversial concept since Berne introduced it in 1968. Others have developed and refined Berne's original concepts. As Stewart and Joines point out, many writers have been selective in their interpretation of Berne's ideas and have tended to present them in an oversimplified way.

There is far more to TA than what is generally called the PAC model and its use to analyse communication transactions (a process sometimes called TA proper). The psychodynamic model, which was developed to generate personal insights into behaviour (see Illustration 3.1), has also been used to train people to manipulate and exploit others. The ethical issues this raises have been addressed by some authors. TA is a good example of a theory that is often taught

---

Illustration 3.1 Transactional analysis

A purchasing decision: the problem

A few years ago David noticed that Saturday afternoon shopping trips with his wife were becoming quite problematical. The main source of conflict stemmed from his persistent (and indiscriminate) demands to buy items on display and his wife's equally persistent denial of his requests. It was getting to the stage that she didn't want him to accompany her to the shops. Something had to be done. Although his initial inclination was to blame his wife for this problem – if she agreed to the purchase of whatever item he demanded that would be the end of the matter – he was forced to admit to himself that most of the items were non-essential and the core of the problem lay with his indiscriminate demands to make the purchases. But what was causing him to behave in this way?

As implied above, David was quickly able to establish that he didn't have any real need for the vast majority of the items, so the matter couldn't be resolved in simple terms of *stimulus* (he needed something) – *response* (if he bought the item it would satisfy his need). He had to look beyond the items and consider the overall need to purchase (unnecessary) items. He wasn't depressed, so he couldn't rationalise his need to buy in terms of trying to cheer himself up. There was something else driving this behaviour. But what was it?

A purchasing decision: analysis

David remembered having read the book *Staying Okay* by Thomas and Amy Harris, in which the authors refer to a process called 'trackdown'. Trackdown is based on the theory known as transactional analysis (TA) developed by the humanist psychologist Eric Berne. The process of trackdown involves thinking about a particular situation and trying to identify the feelings associated with it. The next stage is to try to identify the ego state associated with those feelings. Finally you have to try to identify when you first experienced the particular collection of feelings. In the case of David wanting to buy things, the main feelings he had were frustration, powerlessness and deprivation. He then tried to track down these feelings. To his astonishment he remembered an event from his childhood. He was surprised how readily he recalled, what was in essence, a forgotten event from some 25 years beforehand. He came from a working-class background in Glasgow, Scotland. He had an older brother. There was never much money to spare and they only really received what could be described as luxury items on their birthdays and at Christmas. His brother, however, had a couple of part-time jobs and even from an early age appeared to be blessed with the Scottish stereotypical virtue of not spending money. What money he did spend, was always done after a long and tortuous process of trying to fully evaluate whether he really needed the item and whether the proposed place of purchase was offering the item at the lowest price. David, on the other hand, was never able to save money. As soon as he had any money, he went out and spent it. If they went on a day trip together, his brother would come back having spent only his bus fare; David would come back owing someone the money for his bus fare. In TA terminology, it might be suggested that David's brother had a very dominant adult ego state, whereas David tended predominantly to be in the (natural) child ego state.

The particular situation David recalled concerned the purchase of a reel-to-reel tape recorder. This was in about 1965/66 when he was 8 or 9 years old. His brother, five years his senior, had decided to buy a model made by Grundig. As it happened, the domestic appliance store near to their house sold the desired machine and the asking price was £20. Now, had it been David making this purchase, he would have been straight into the shop across the road and bought it – no messing about. Not his brother though. He wanted to make sure that the tape recorder couldn't be purchased any cheaper. So he started to shop around. Their house was about five miles from the city centre in Glasgow and it became his brother's Saturday mission for several weeks to walk into town to check out the price in the various shops that stocked the recorder. David dutifully accompanied his older brother on his numerous route marches into town to conduct this pre-purchase research. This was no straightforward matter. In those days, not many shops bothered to price items in their window displays; what prices were shown couldn't always be relied on as up until 1968 it was not illegal to indicate a false price. Where the Grundig recorder was displayed but no price was given, his brother refused to go into the shop to ask the price. It became David's task to go into the shops and ask the price. The price was always around £20; never less and certainly never more than a few pence more.

Would his brother go in and buy the machine? No he wouldn't. One Saturday, David made it fairly obvious to his mother that he did not want to go into town with his brother. Her immediate thought was that they must have been fighting. But no. David explained to her his growing frustration over his brother's refusal to buy the tape recorder in spite of having verified the price and being fully satisfied that it was indeed the tape recorder of his dreams. His mother said that he need not go to town with his brother if he didn't want to. But there was a slight problem. David felt certain that his brother would eventually buy the machine and he wanted to be there when he did. He could not afford the machine himself, so watching his brother buy it would be the next best thing. His brother did eventually buy that Grundig reel-to-reel tape recorder – for £20 in the shop across the road from their house.

And so, as he remembered this event, David seemed to have successfully tracked down the source of his present feelings from his Saturday trips with his wife. The feelings of frustration, deprivation and powerlessness experienced on those Saturdays with his brother were resurfacing in his present trips. Armed with this insight he was able to try to do something about his present behaviour on the outings with his wife. When he started to find himself wanting to buy something, he was able to engage in a rational process by staying in his adult ego state: he tried to be rational – did he really need this item or did he just want it? As a result, their Saturday shopping trips became a much more pleasant event.

Limitations of the analysis

David couldn't *prove* that the source of his desire to buy items lay in his Saturday trips with his brother. There could be other factors and he remains open to the possibility of alternative analyses. It might, for example, just be a reaction to there not having been much money to spare in his family when he was young. We could alternatively conclude, for instance, that his identification of the source of the problem and subsequent reaction to that new knowledge, could be seen as one of Kelly's (1961) personal constructs, to name but one alternative. Whatever the case might be, the important issue in this example is that the process of trackdown led him to an insight that enabled him to change his behaviour.

to managers in training courses. Whilst there is no doubting that an individual may use the concepts in a personally positive manner, there is evidence to suggest that TA has been used in a highly manipulative way. This is particularly common in many sales techniques that draw heavily on the capacity of sales staff to get potential customers into their child ego state. We are at our least analytical in this state – so we are less likely to critically evaluate the actual need for the purchase. Often the reality of the situations encountered in organisations is such that there are advantages and ethical dilemmas involved in the use of any theoretical instrument.

Activity 3.2	**Management or manipulation?**

Many managers will use whatever means at their disposal to help them to manage more effectively. So, if they think that applying some psychological technique or other will assist their purposes they will do so. A manager uses TA to help analyse a problem and, therefore, to manage subsequent interactions with her staff.

1 Does manage = manipulate in this context?

2 Do you think that it is ethical of her to use the psychological insights gained in an instrumental way?

3 If the outcomes turn out to be mutually beneficial, does the end justify the means?

(You might like to refer to the chapter on ethics in order to develop your argument.)

Berne suggested that in the early years of a child's life (the first seven years approximately), through the process of being nurtured and socialised by its parents or guardians, the child takes on 'positions'. In spite of these positions being adopted at an age when the child cannot possibly understand the implications of so doing, nonetheless they will carry these through the remainder of their lives in the form of 'life scripts' unless something occurs to bring about a change in position. It may well be the case that we find ourselves, or our scripts, being challenged in the face of a difficult decision. It may also be that we seek to reinforce our scripts through decision-making.

Scripts are used as an analytical concept by theorists in psychology and sociology. Whilst a detailed examination of such theories is beyond the scope of this present chapter, it may be helpful to say something in brief. Erving Goffman (1959) suggests that the theatre provides a useful metaphor for social interaction. Just as the actor thoroughly learns her script, puts on a suitable mask, wears an appropriate costume, has the right props and ensures that the stage has been set in a way that assists a polished performance of her part; so too does the teacher, the bus driver, plumber, husband and so on to ensure effective performance of whatever role is being enacted. We tend not to let people go backstage and it is generally understood that the actor on stage is only reading from a script. There is no suggestion that the actor is the same off-stage as on. The significance for decision-making is that we may come to see group situations, committee meetings and so on in a slightly different light. People may be more concerned about maintaining the appearance of competence in their role, than with the outcomes of the decision-making process.

It is important to note that Goffmann approaches the idea of scripts from a sociological perspective, whereas Berne's approach is psychological. Both perspectives offer insights into how our 'reality' is structured. In sociology the focus is on the dynamics of interaction and the attainment and maintenance of social order. In psychology the focus is on the way in which the individual consciously or subconsciously structures time and meaning. In general terms, the analysis of self in sociology invariably involves consideration of 'other'. In psychology, except for social psychology, the focus is generally restricted to self. Considering both sociological and psychological perspectives generates a more holistic understanding, underlining the value in attempting to take an interdisciplinary approach.

3.5 A behaviourist approach

The behaviourist approach stresses that the individual can be shaped by experience and learning into acting in a particular way. Learning is one of the fundamental processes underlying behaviour. Learning is the process by which a relatively enduring change in behaviour takes place, as a result of practice. So, in Illustration 3.2, had the redundancy experience shaped the person's current behaviour?

From a behaviourist perspective, two types of learning that are important to decision-making are classical conditioning and operant conditioning. Classical conditioning theory was developed by a Russian physiologist, Pavlov (1927). Pavlov noted that beings (in this case, dogs) could be conditioned to respond in prescribed ways. He first noted that presentation of food, an unconditioned stimulus, led to salivation by the dog, an unconditioned response. By training a dog to receive food at the same time as hearing a bell ring, he found that the dog salivated at the mere sound of the bell. Thus, he had produced a circumstance in which a conditioned stimulus led to a conditioned response.

In classical conditioning the sequence of events is independent of the subject's behaviour. In operant conditioning behaviour can be controlled by altering the consequences by using reinforcers and punishments, known as operants. In the workplace, many behaviours could be considered as operant, for example reading reports, attending meetings, operating a machine and so on. Illustration 3.3 represents an example of operant conditioning.

There are links here with the notion of sociological scripts, mentioned earlier. Scripts could be seen in terms of a series of stimulus–response interactions that combine to form a routinised situation. As can be seen in Illustration 3.3, the handing back of an assignment could become scripted behaviour. For example, stimulus 3 might be instigated by the student blaming their poor performance on the tutor's poor teaching methods. We leave you to imagine the likely response from the tutor.

The nature and effects of reinforcement have obviously been considered as important by management writers. Reinforcement can come in a number of pos-

---

Illustration 3.2

Some years ago a new member of staff joined an organisation. She seemed to be fitting in well and generally performing her duties to a good standard. A routine discussion with her mentor revealed that she felt insecure in her new role and was actually certain that she was performing so badly that it could only be a matter of time before she was dismissed. Her mentor tried to reassure her that this was not the case but to no avail. The mentor started to explore with her what the source of insecurity might be. She quickly related to her last job where she had been made redundant. Her mentor asked if she had been made redundant because of her incompetence? But she explained that her whole section had been made redundant at the same time. Her mentor asked if all her colleagues were incompetent. Far from it, she replied, they were highly skilled and highly regarded in the organisation. It then emerged that the reason for the redundancy was due to a restructuring in the company. It was only after systematically revisiting the redundancy situation with her that she was able to locate the reasons at the 'correct' level of analysis. Up to that point she had been focusing inappropriately at the level of self whereas the cause was due to financial problems within the company arising from the wider economic situation which prevailed in the company at the time.

It may be salutary at this stage in the book to offer this cautionary tale that we can examine situations in terms of

- self;
- self and others;
- wider organisational/ societal factors.

It may not always be immediately obvious which level is appropriate. There will also be situations where there is more than one possibility and we then have to manage the resultant ambiguity.

---

itive or negative forms. In the armed forces, for example, recruits were traditionally taught to slip comfortably into conditioned responses in a combat situation. These responses were 'drilled' into all ranks in the early days of training and then continually reinforced through practice for the rest of their careers. It is worth reflecting on Illustration 1.2 about the Hillsborough tragedy in Chapter 1. Clearly, the old police training methods were predicated on the principles of operant conditioning. It has become apparent in the UK that the armed forces have also moved away from an operant conditioning approach.

Illustration 3.3 An example of operant conditioning

Stimulus 1	**Response 1**	**Stimulus 2**	**Response 2**
A memo from your tutor to submit your assignment – conditioned stimulus	Preparing your assignment – conditioned operant response	Receiving valued praise from your tutor – reinforcing stimulus	A sense of satisfaction

3.6   A humanistic approach

Gross (1996: 763) suggests ' "Humanistic" is an umbrella term referring to a group of theories which all share the belief that scientific attempts to study human beings are misplaced and inappropriate, because "...to see man at second hand through his behaviour as against his experience is ultimately to see ourselves at second hand and never be ourselves" (Evans, 1975)'. Gross (1996: 763) goes on to say that humanistic theories could be considered as philosophical rather than psychological in that they emphasise characteristics that are uniquely human, because of the focus on 'experience, uniqueness, meaning, freedom and choice; we have first hand experience of ourselves as persons'. Humanistic theories are characterised by an emphasis on growth and self-actualisation of the individual. They emphasise an holistic approach to understanding the individual. Carl Rogers (1967) has been particularly influential in the field of humanist psychology.

Referring back to Chapter 1, you may recall the image of the shattered 'egg of knowledge'. Psychology has become a fragmented subject area, though the primary focus has remained on attempting to find out what 'makes people tick'. In fragmenting in such a way, each area has come to focus on distinct elements of human thought and behaviour. What humanist psychology attempts to do is to regard the individual as a whole person who acts in the world. Rogers' notion of client-centred therapy exemplifies this emphasis on the whole person.

Some of the best explorations of the humanist, or existentialist, perspective can be found, not in psychology or management textbooks, but rather in the novels of writers such as Italo Calvino, Umberto Eco, Milan Kundera , Franz Kafka, Albert Camus and Julian Barnes, to name a few. The 'real-life' situations into which they plunge their characters are usually more graphic and, paradoxically, given their supposed status as works of fiction, more realistic (true to life), than the case study approach much loved of traditional textbooks.

What tends to emanate from fiction is the complexity of 'experience, uniqueness, meaning, freedom and choice' as presented by the authors, perhaps mirroring their own lives and experiences. This may be why we are able to relate to their works, as the characters they describe are composites of the people we have come to know in our own lives. Moreover, the situations they describe are presented as rich pictures that provide us with common, recognisable reference points to relate to from our own experience. This can be contrasted with generalised and abstracted models of behaviour such as normative models of decision-making. Abstracted models provide us with heuristic devices that allow us to develop insights into our own behaviour, if we recognise the limitations of their usage. However, personal accounts and biographies, be they fictional or otherwise, provide us with the opportunity to transcend speculation and to explore the actual implications of actions.

Protherough (in Golding and Currie, 2000: 78) states:

> the study of literature could empower students and lecturers to question the nature of what is often called the 'mainstream' management curriculum, a pedagogy that sees the teacher as expert with 'answers', the downgrading of the personal and emotional, and the separation from lived experience. It could prompt greater awareness of the way in which managers are made (or made up) and of the political and cultural dimension within which management knowledge is socially situated and constructed (Clegg and Palmer 1996).

3.7   A neurobiological approach

With its emphasis on behaviour as determined by genetic, physiological and neurobiological factors, a neurobiological approach to decision-making has, at first sight, fewer implications for decision-making. It has certainly received less attention in the decision-making literature. This may be because it has, until recently, become less fashionable to regard behaviour as genetically determined. It may also be that science has not so readily provided us with 'answers' concerning the chemical processes that constitute our brain. More recently, however, research into genetic engineering has enlivened the traditional nature/nurture debate, that is, are our personality and behaviour determined by genetics or by socialisation?

Experimentation with the cloning of animals has led to speculation about the cloning of human beings. Whilst it may have been expected that this kind of research into genetic engineering would confirm the predominance of hereditary factors in the formation of personality, more recent research into genome theory (the gene pool) suggests that we have a smaller number of genes than was previously thought. It has, therefore, been suggested that our interacting in the social world mainly influences our behaviour.

3.8   A cognitive approach

Cognitions are the things that we know about ourselves, our behaviour and our environment. One theory which has major implications for understanding decision-making is that of **cognitive dissonance**. Festinger (1962) used the term to describe the state of disequilibrium that we find ourselves in when we simultaneously hold two contradictory beliefs. For example, we may believe that subordination is degrading, yet we may find ourselves working in an extremely hierarchical organisation in order to earn a living. In order to achieve consonance, that is a state of psychological comfort, we may attempt to change our attitudes towards one of the dissonant factors. In this case, we may convince ourselves that subordination is 'a fact of life' and we may associate with other people who have similar experiences in order to confirm this. When making a difficult choice between equally attractive alternatives, we may attempt to rationalise away the rejected alternative by attaching negative values to it. We do so in an attempt to reduce dissonance.

The work of Jean Piaget is of importance. He was interested in the way that cognition is developed in children. His work also introduces a moral dimension into our evaluation of intentions and outcomes. Gross (1996: 694) suggests that Piaget identified that parents tended to be more consistent in punishing what was perceived as naughty behaviour than in rewarding good behaviour. A discussion in one MBA group which initially focused on rewarding staff, and especially letting them know when they had done a good job of work, soon shifted to that of 'blame'. From their direct experience both as managers and of being managed, the managers in the group could relate to blame much more than they could to being thanked or rewarded. This points to possible organisational implications arising from Piaget's work. Could this be how 'blame cultures' develop in organisations? You may remember the 'real-life model of decision-making' illustrated in Chapter 1 (Figure 1.2). This may have been an attempt at humour, but it is surprising how much it resonates with the experience of practising managers.

Up to this point we have considered general psychological approaches and have attempted to provide some exemplary links to decision-making. We now consider some theories that have evolved as a result of research specifically concerning decision-making.

3.9　A psychology of the decision-maker

You may recall that in Chapter 1 we introduced a normative approach to management decision-making. In doing so, we stated that normative approaches have been widely criticised on the grounds of their underlying assumptions about the knowledge available to decision-makers; the capacity of decision-makers to judge situations correctly; and their capacity to act rationally and logically. Psychologists have grappled with issues concerning judgement, rationality and commitment in decision-making for decades. Much of the early research set out to understand and improve the decision-making processes of politicians, high-ranking military officials, public policy administrators and other key decision-makers in society. Janis and Mann (1977) examined one-off decisions (such as the Kennedy administration's decision to invade Cuba on April 17, 1961) and other high-profile ongoing decisions (such as the continuing commitment to US military intervention in Vietnam in the 1960s). They suggested that their findings concerning the flawed nature of decision-making could be generalised and applied to more common consequential decisions that managers would be more likely to face in organisations. They acknowledged the need to make a conceptual leap; nonetheless they believed that certain characteristics are common to decision-making in different contexts, although the stakes may be different. Much of the authors' argument centres on identifying, either through their own or others' research, the human psychological factors that limit rationality and therefore make people less vigilant in stressful situations. So how do decision-makers make decisions?

In Chapter 1 we briefly introduced the notion of bounded rationality in the context of descriptive theories that set out to explain how we make decisions, rather than how we ought to make decisions (normative theories). Herbert Simon (1976) set out to identify how people actually make decisions and, in doing so, described a process by which people decide as a result of not having the 'wits to maximise'. Rarely do we act on the basis of having perfect information at our fingertips; what is more, we may ignore the information that we do have, or use information that is irrelevant to the decision. We are bounded by our own subjective rationality, which is limited in all sorts of ways. In essence, we do the best we can with what we have available to us. In addition to being thinking decision-makers, we are emotional ones. Emotions have a bearing on how we think and act. This is what Janis and Mann (1977: 45), using Abelson's term, call 'hot cognitions'.

All this raises a number of questions:

- What processes are involved in the way we decide?
- How do we act when faced with a choice?
- How do we make sense of our actions?

In order to address these questions we will explore the following:

- Perceptual processes
- Internal conflict
- Ego defence mechanisms

3.9.1 Perceptual processes

The research into perceptual processes has been the domain of cognitive psychologists. It is commonly recognised that, as individuals, we see the world differently. This is hardly surprising when there is so much to see. The word 'see' has to be elaborated in this context. We see as a result of our physiological capability, that is we use our senses to see, hear, touch, feel and taste. However, the way in which we interpret the information provided by the senses is a perceptual process; we therefore perceive rather than see. We may see the same objective phenomenon but perceive it in very different, or subtly different, ways. This has obvious implications for normative models of decision-making that attempt to provide general, abstracted accounts of how decisions are, or should be, made. For example, many normative models require us to identify a problem. What problem? The problem as I see it, or as you see it? What if I do not think there is a problem? The definition of a problem may be extremely subjective. When we add to this the notion of contrasting and competing stakeholder agendas in organisations, the difficulties are compounded. Who defines a phenomenon, situation or person as problematical? Often, what constitutes a problem for one person, may constitute an opportunity for another. Moreover, if we accept a working consensus that a problem exists, then we face the same kinds of issues in setting objectives, and coming to a shared understanding of the problem, and determining what might constitute an option available to us, and so on.

A number of theorists have pointed to the existence of perceptual processes that may lead us to distort objective phenomena to suit our own particular needs. One generally accepted concept is 'selective attention'. This refers to the fact that we focus on particular aspects of the sensory data that we are confronted with. This may often be an unconscious process. We could not possibly give our undivided attention to all the sensory stimuli around us at any given time; we simply do not have the mental capacity to take in so much sensory data. We therefore have to filter the data in order to turn them into meaningful patterns by categorising or classifying them in some way. We do this through a process involving internal and external factors. Internal factors might include our motivation, or learning and experience based on the way we have been socialised into perceiving certain stimuli. Janis and Mann (1977: 61) give the example of a guardsman who, during a race riot in Detroit in 1967, was called by a nightwatchman whose premises were being looted. On hearing gunshots, the guardsman feared he was being fired upon and, seeing a black man holding a firearm, decided to shoot to kill. The black man turned out to be the nightwatchman. Although the authors use this as an example of flawed decision-making due to 'hypervigilance' (a state of extreme panic) under stressful circumstances, it can also be used to exemplify how our perceptual organisation can lead to grave misinterpretation with possibly grave circumstances. Although an extreme example, the fact that the guardsman came to the equation 'black + gun = criminal' illustrates what we all do to some extent, that is we classify, categorise and organise stimuli in order to come up with a meaningful pattern to explain events. The danger lies in that pattern being flawed, as it will invariably be to a lesser or greater extent.

External factors might include the way we give attention to particular stimuli at the expense of others, for example, what would you do if you were a camouflaged soldier in the field of combat at night and an enemy flare lit up the area around you? Your instinct might be to throw yourself to the ground. However, you would be trained to stand perfectly still; the premise being that the enemy would more likely to spot you as a result of your movement than any other factor. We are more likely to perceive stimuli that stand out from the surrounding context in some way, either through movement, colour, shape, size, sound and so on.

The guardsman in the example could be seen to have held a *stereotype* of a black person in a riot situation. We all stereotype to a degree. The process is a way of filling in the gaps in stimuli. Humans are interpretative beings with a capacity to make sense of situations, even when faced with a dearth of information. In fact, it is both a strength and a weakness that we have a capacity to attempt to make sense of situations with inadequate data. It allows us to think, learn and act in creative and intuitive ways. It may also lead to problems as we attempt to create certainty in whatever way we can, or in ways in which we have been taught to. We may work on the unconscious process of 'any interpretation of people, events or data, even if it is flawed, is better than no interpretation at all'. In order to make the task of making sense easier for ourselves, we employ a number of conscious and unconscious devices.

3.9.2 Internal conflict

As humans we are often reluctant decision-makers who will avoid having to make a choice between alternatives if the stakes are high. As managers, we cannot always avoid making decisions, as it is an expectation of the role. In the words of Goffman (1959: 37):

> When an actor takes on an established social role, usually he finds that a particular front has already been established for it. Whether his acquisition of the role was primarily motivated by a desire to perform the given task or by a desire to maintain the corresponding front, the actor will find he must do both.

Decision-making is widely regarded as a key management function. As such, managers have to act *decisively*. It becomes apparent that managers may, therefore, be motivated as much by the desire to be seen to be acting, as by the desire to solve a problem or deal with a pressing issue. The 'do nothing' option may sometimes be the most difficult one to take as others may interpret it as decision-making avoidance.

Janis and Mann (1977: 49) suggest that internal conflict is at its highest when we are faced with a choice, more specifically, 'the intensity of physiological and psychological symptoms of stress appears to depend upon the *perceived magnitude* of the losses the decision-maker anticipates from whatever choice he makes'.

If we are faced with a number of conflicting decisions, such as taking a new job, or buying a new car, then we are likely to suffer the effects of stress. Stress is an important behavioural effect and has been widely researched. Cox (1978), quoted in Gibson *et al.* (1982), has listed a number of consequences of stress on the individual:

- *Subjective effects* – anxiety, aggression, apathy, boredom, depression, fatigue, frustration, loss of temper, low self-esteem, nervousness, feeling alone.

- *Behavioural effects* – accident-proneness, drug abuse, emotional outbursts, excessive eating drinking or smoking, impulsive behaviour, nervous laughter.

- *Cognitive effects* – inability to make sound decisions, poor concentration, short attention span, hypersensitivity to criticism, and mental blocks.

- *Physiological effects* – increased blood sugar, increased heart rate and blood pressure, dry mouth, sweating, dilation of the pupils, hot and cold flushes.

- *Organisational effects* – absenteeism, lower productivity, alienation of co-workers, job dissatisfaction, reduced organisational commitment and loyalty.

3.9.3 Ego defence mechanisms

With the sorts of effect listed above being experienced from stressful events, it is not surprising that we try if possible to avoid decision-making in some instances. Decisions may carry emotional connotations and may engender feelings of fear, rage, pleasure, sadness, aggression, jealously, hatred, panic and anger. To lessen the impact of unpleasant feelings we unconsciously employ a variety of ego defence mechanisms. One such process that is relevant to decision-making is 'anticipatory regret'. When faced with a number of choices we are often drawn towards the choice that will offer the least potential for embarrassment. Janis and Mann (1977: 223) identify five factors that stimulate this phenomenon:

1 The preferred choice is not necessarily superior to any alternative.

2 The negative consequences that might ensue from the decision could start to materialise almost immediately after the decision is made.

3 Significant persons in the decision-maker's social network view the decision as important and will expect him or her to adhere to it.

4 New information concerning potential gains and losses can be obtained.

5 Significant persons in the decision-maker's social network who are interested in this particular decision are *not* impatient about his or her current state of indecision and expect him/her to delay action until he/she has evaluated the alternatives carefully.

Other defence mechanisms that are particularly relevant to the process of decision-making include procrastination, shifting responsibility, bolstering, projection, withdrawal and rationalisation.

3.10   Involvement and commitment

You may, by now, have gained the impression that humans are reluctant decision-makers. There is certainly plenty of evidence to suggest that we try to avoid making decisions, or even making choices from a range of alternatives. In researching consumer buying behaviour, Laurent and Kapferer (1985) identified four factors that affect involvement in a decision:

1 *Self-image.* Involvement is likely to be high when the decision potentially affects one's self-image. For example, empowerment initiatives may generate greater commitment from the workforce if accompanied with a perceived increase in status.

2 *Perceived risk.* If there is a risk that a decision could adversely affect the group, then the group will be keen to be involved in the decision-making process. For example, if the company is considering relocating, then the workforce will be keen to involve themselves in that process.

3 *Social factors.* When social acceptance is dependent upon making a correct choice, then involvement is likely to be high. The choice of a new yacht will influence one's standing in the sailing club.

4 *Hedonistic influences.* If the decision is capable of providing a high degree of pleasure, then involvement is usually high.

Decision-makers who are highly committed to decisions are less likely to change their course of action should new information become available, or if circumstances change.

One negative consequence of commitment relates to crime-related decisions. *Slippage* involves a series of reprehensible acts that tend to escalate to avoid the negative consequences of the first decision (see Illustration 3.4).

Illustration 3.4 An example of slippage

One Monday morning, slightly late for work, a motorcyclist sets off down the M1 motorway. Not far from home and travelling at about 100 miles per hour, he notices a police car in his mirror. He accelerates and leaves the police car standing. At the next exit he leaves the motorway, goes home and dumps the bike in a local park. He then contacts the police and reports the bike stolen. After a three-hour interview at the station he is released without charge.

Illustration 3.4 is a good example of what Bazerman (1998) calls a non-rational escalation of commitment. The motorcyclist compounds his initial negative choice (accelerating to get away) in a state of hypervigilance. His conscience may be telling him that his initial action is unwise, and may inevitably lead to unwelcome outcomes. However, having made a commitment to this action, he finds himself caught up in a sequence of events that he would not normally have considered appropriate.

We now address the implications that theories from psychology can have for wider organisational decision-making.

3.11 A psychoanalysis of organisations

Hitherto, we have dealt with the way in which psychological factors can affect individual decision-makers. It has also been argued that organisations can experience collective psychological difficulties.

Morgan (1986) describes the 'allegory of the cave' from Plato's *Republic*. Plato described a community of cave dwellers. They lived a rather strange life as they were all chained to the back wall of the cave. As such, they were unable to see out of the mouth of the cave to the outside world. Had they been able to see out, they would have observed that at the mouth of the cave there was a fire that burned brightly and caused the shadows of the cave dwellers to be cast on the wall. These shadows were the reality of the dwellers' existence. They knew of no other world. Plato suggested that if one of the dwellers were to escape from the cave, he would discover a vast world outside, and realise that the shadowy reality of the dwellers was but a pale reflection of the wonderful world beyond the cave. Plato further postulated that if after a time in the outside world the escapee were to return to the cave, far from welcoming the vision of an exciting world outside, he would be met with hostile resistance from the rest of the cave dwellers. Indeed, this attack on their understanding of reality would cause the cave dwellers to cling even more fervently to the belief in their world of shadows. The escapee would realise that he could no longer be a part of the community as the world of shadows could never be enough for him again and so he would become an exile.

Karen Legge's (1984: 6) statement seems particularly apt.

> The evidence we have of the circumstances in which evaluation findings are most likely to be used by decision-makers is hardly reassuring: findings tend to be listened to when they confirm what decision-makers already believe or disclose what they are predisposed to accept (Weiss, 1975, p.23); when they lend support to facts already known, or confirm suspicions already entertained (Patton, 1978, pp. 29–30). What rarely seems to happen is decision-makers acting upon findings that disconfirm their existing beliefs or suggest a radical and politically or ideologically unpalatable change in direction.

Developing the allegory of the cave, Morgan (1986) suggests that organisations may fall into the trap of favoured ways of thinking. He points to three ways in which this might manifest itself. We deal with two of them here: success and organisational slack. The third, groupthink, is addressed in Chapter 11.

3.11.1 Trapped by success

Organisations can become prisoners of earlier success. Morgan (1986) cites the US motor industry as an example, but affirms that other industries have suffered similar consequences owing to their smugness.

The US motor industry was so convinced about its technical superiority that it failed to recognise the threat of the small car during the OPEC oil crisis of the early 1970s. The industry took justifiable pride in its ability to produce high quality cars at a competitive price, but ignored the fact that the cars they produced contained large, fuel-guzzling engines. Hence, they failed to recognise the very real threat from the Japanese manufacturers, who were about to enter the US and other markets by capitalising on the general appeal of more economical vehicles. This makes an interesting comparison with Janis and Mann's account of the events leading up to the Japanese invasion to Pearl Harbour. Admiral Kimmel and other senior officers in the US Navy repeatedly ignored warnings of the possibility, and growing probability, of attack. The authors use the events to illustrate how, through defensive avoidance mechanisms, a series of warning signs (including an official war warning from the chief of naval operations in Washington) were ignored.

'Kimmel and his advisers shared the unwarranted belief that Japan would never risk attacking their "invulnerable" fortress at Pearl Harbor, and assumed that the messages from Washington must refer only to the necessity to be prepared for possible acts of sabotage' (Janis and Mann, 1977: 125–6).

Kimmel eventually paid the price for his lack of vigilance by being court martialed and demoted. The government investigation committee concluded that there had been an 'unwarranted feeling of immunity from attack' (Janis and Mann, 1977: 126).

3.11.2 Trapped by organisational slack

Just as individuals bolster themselves at times of perceived threat, so do organisations. One of the ways in which companies have traditionally dealt with uncertainty is by 'building in slack'. In other words, companies hold additional production capacity available in case it is ever needed, and build up buffer stock in case there is a shortage in the future. Whilst the slack generated may indeed come in useful at a future date, it is also a very costly tactic. Buffer stocks, for example, not only mean using employees and raw material to produce items not yet needed, they also tie up storage space and need to be kept secure. The slack can also encourage sloppiness in procedures ('it won't be a disaster if I make a mistake cutting out this piece of sheet metal, there's plenty more in the stockroom'). By changing their ways of thinking, many companies have revolutionised the workplace and made impressive financial savings. Concepts such as zero defects and just-in-time are important challenges to the old ways of creating costly organisational slack. As Morgan (1986: 202) comments: 'Interestingly, the ideas of zero inventory and zero defects were never really considered as practicable possibilities until the Japanese showed that it was feasible to organise in this way: the need for inventory and buffered forms of organization were treated as a given'.

Thinking back to the rational model, we can see that we may think that we are considering lots of different options and being both vigilant and creative, but the reality may be that we are acting within very narrow conceptions of what we think possible.

Are the implications of Morgan's analysis that we will inevitably fall into these traps never to escape? The likelihood is that unless some event happens which causes us to question the underlying assumptions we are operating from, we are indeed likely to continue to act as we always have. In the case of the US motor industry, the event was the severe economic loss due to the business that the Japanese manufacturers prised from US manufacturers.

You can probably think of circumstances in which you as an individual have been obliged to re-evaluate your own assumptions because of changes that have been forced upon you. In his book *The Teachings of Don Juan*, Carlos Castaneda tells of his encounters with a Mexican Indian, Don Juan. Through these encounters, Castaneda realises that Don Juan has been introducing him to a completely different way of seeing the world. It takes Castaneda many years to gain an understanding of Don Juan's perspective because he constantly attempts to make sense of his teachings from an American, western civilisation world view. From this perspective much of what Don Juan has to say seems nonsensical to Castaneda. It is only when he is able to set aside his usual way of seeing that Castaneda ultimately comes to understand the coherence of Don Juan's philosophy. Don Juan refers to this process as 'stopping the world'. This may be a difficult, but necessary, process if we are to improve our decision-making.

Returning to Plato's allegory, Morgan (1986) points to collective and individual actions in organisations, which defy rational explanation. He further suggests that many organisational actions may be grounded in the psychodynamics of the founders or senior managers of the organisation. He gives as an example the work of Frederick Winslow Taylor, the founder of scientific management, which is closely associated with time and motion studies and the strict control by management over how tasks are to be completed. The production line, although developed by Ford, owes much to the ideas of Taylor. Similarly, the McDonald's burger chain is generally held up as a prime example of a company that draws heavily on scientific management principles, specifying the details of even apparently insignificant tasks in operating manuals.

Morgan proposes that Taylor's theories resulted from his own personal need for absolute control over every aspect of his life; a need Morgan attributes to Taylor's extremely anal-retentive personality, based on Freudian theory of human development that postulates that our personality is formed in the first six years or so of our life. Morgan recounts stories of how, as a young boy, Taylor would insist on measuring out the exact circumference of the baseball pitch before starting a game; or how, as a youth, he would generate a system that would allow him to dance with the optimum amount of girls at the Prom. In effect, Morgan is drawing our attention to the fact that seemingly objective, and apparently rational organisational phenomena may be the result of highly subjective, individual, psychological processes.

Morgan goes on to say that, just as babies and children have their favourite toys, so do executives in organisations. In speculating about her former boss's seemingly irrational behaviour, a colleague once vividly described him as 'a little boy with a toy gun; only he doesn't realise he's firing real bullets'. Many apparent peculiarities can be made sense of in relation to a psychoanalytical analysis of the organisation. The important point to remember is that not all action in organisations can be traced back to a rational source. Morgan rightly draws our attention to the possible limitations of a psychoanalytical approach. As he suggests, the use of psychoanalysis, as seen in our exploration of Plato's allegory of the cave, can encourage 'utopian speculation and critique'. Psychology is a vast discipline and we may delude ourselves into thinking that we are more knowledgeable than we actually are and may read much more into a given situation than is actually there. Nonetheless, speculation can often be the main strategy available to us in trying to make sense of ambiguous and uncertain situations.

◆ Summary

Far from being a rational, logical process, involving much deliberation, much of our decision-making behaviour may actually involve little or no thought. If that is indeed the case, then it would seem that it may be more important for decision-makers to discover the extent to which they act in such an unthinking way. The ideas presented in this chapter may indicate that the apparent level of rationality in the behaviour of people in organisations is probably vastly over-stated. However, we should not necessarily define this as negative. Perhaps the actions that seem least rational of all are the actions that most clearly demon-strate that we are human. In this we agree with Janis and Mann (1977: 45): 'a world dominated by Dr Strangelove and like-minded cost accountants might soon become devoid of acts of affection, conscience, and humanity, as well as passion'. The arrogance of people may come from their belief that a rational explanation exists for everything. On the other hand, an overemphasis on self-analysis, reflection or impulsive behaviour, may lead, respectively, to defensive avoidance, paralysis or rash decisions that are later regretted. There is perhaps a case for both self-awareness and structured evaluation.

❓ Decision diary

Think of a recent decision in which you were directly or indirectly involved. Identify, if you can, an occurrence in which you felt comfortable or uncomfort-able in some way. Reflect on the experience and try to make sense of the situation using one or more theories from this chapter.

References

Bazerman, M.H. (1998) *Judgement in Managerial Decision Making*, 4th edition. Chichester: Wiley.

Berne, E. (1968) *Games People Play*. Harmondsworth: Penguin.

Buchanan, D. and Huczynski, A. (1997) *Organizational Behaviour: An Introductory Text*, 3rd edition. Hemel Hempstead: Prentice Hall International.

Castaneda, C. (1990) *The Teachings of Don Juan: a Yaqui way of knowledge*. London Arkana.

Festinger, L.A. (1962) *A theory of cognitive dissonance*. Stanford University Press.

Gibson, J.L. Ivancevich, J.M. and Donelly, J.H. (1982) *Organizations: Behavior, Structure, Processes*. Plano, TX: Business Publications.

Goffman, E. (1959) *The Presentation of Self in Everyday Life*. Harmondsworth: Penguin.

Gross, R. (1996) *Psychology: The Science of Mind and Behaviour*, 3rd edition. Hodder & Stoughton.

Janis, I.L. and Mann, L. (1977) *Decision-making: A Psychological Analysis of Conflict, Choice, and Commitment.* New York: Free Press.

Kelly, G. (1961) *The Abstraction of Human Processes. Proceedings of the 14th International Cognitive Psychological Conference, Copenhagen,* pp. 220–9.

Laurent, G. and Kapferer, J.N. (1985) 'Measuring Consumer Involvement Profiles', *Journal of Marketing Research,* February 12, pp. 41–53.

Legge, K. (1984) *Evaluating Planned Organizational Change.* London: Academic Press.

Mangham, I.L. (1988) *Effecting Organisational Change.* Oxford: Basil Blackwell.

Morgan, G. (1986) *Images of Organization.* London: Sage.

Pavlov, I. (1927) *Conditioned Reflexes.* Oxford University Press.

Protherough, R. 'Reconstructing the study of management' in Golding, D. and Currie, D. (2000) *Thinking About Management.* London: Routledge.

Rogers, C.R. (1967) *On becoming a person.* London: Constable.

Simon, H.A. (1976) *Administrative Behavior: A Study of Decision-making Processes in Administrative Organization,* 3rd edition. New York: Free Press.

Stewart, I. and Joines, V. (1987) *TA Today: A New Introduction to Transactional Analysis.* Kingston-on-Soar: Lifespace.

Further reading

Kets de Vries and Manfred, F.R. (1984) *The neurotic organisation.* London: Jossey-Bass.

Glossary

Ideographic: approaches to psychology that are concerned with the uniqueness of individuals, therefore emphasising more in-depth research with a smaller sample size. Unlike nomothetic theories, they make no claim to generalisable findings.

Nomothetic: means 'law-giving', so nomothetic approaches to the social sciences are concerned with making general predictions about human behaviour from their research findings.

Optimising: an approach that promotes the idea of decision-making as finding a best or optimal solution or pay-off.

Satisficing: an approach that presents decision-makers as people who 'make do' by finding 'good enough' solutions.

CHAPTER 4

The Armageddon factor

4.1 Introduction

There is a grandeur in this view of life, with its several powers, having been originally breathed by the creator into a few forms or into one; and that, whilst this planet has gone cycling on according to the fixed law of gravity, from so simple a beginning endless forms most beautiful and most wonderful have been and are being evolved.

– Charles Darwin (1979)

In the book *Jurassic Park*, the mathematician Malcolm endeavours, in vain, to explain the potential effects of chaos on the dinosaur theme park. Unfortunately for the characters, what he predicts comes true (a very unlikely phenomenon in chaos theory). The theme park goes horribly wrong and illustrates that you cannot take anything for granted.

We finish this first part of the book on uncertainty with an exploration of aspects of chaos theory, which can emerge as an influence at all stages of decision-making. It crosses the boundaries of quantitative and qualitative analysis. It can be described as quantitative, because the underlying mathematics (for some elements) is attempting to explain those irrational elements of a business that defeat the most elaborate analysis. It can be described as qualitative because the nature and source of irrationality are, by definition, intangible (we are not even aware of them). We felt it appropriate to use chaos theory as a convenient bridge to Part Two, where we look at issues of research and model building and begin to look at those elements of an organisation that form perhaps the most chaotic influence: people. If nothing else, the chapter will test your powers of imagination and philosophical thought.

When we make a decision we implicitly make assumptions and speculate about how the decision will affect or be affected by future events. Most people are aware that the future is rather unpredictable. Decisions are often based on limited and inaccurate information to which inappropriate techniques are then applied in order to manipulate the data into a form that is perhaps very misrepresentative of the situation. Some applications of chaos theory attempt to rationalise irrationalities (for example, see Sanders, 1998) and once again provide logical answers for issues that ultimately might be described as truly obscure. However, within this world of mathematics and systems analysis (see Chapter 6), some important new concepts have been generated; how we can apply these successfully remains to be seen.

4.2 The nature of chaos

You believe in a God who plays dice, and I in complete law and order, in a world which objectively exists, and which I, in a wildly speculative way, am trying to capture. I firmly believe, but hope that someone will discover a more realistic way, or rather a more tangible basis than it has been my lot to do. Even the great initial success of the quantum theory does not make me believe in the fundamental dice game, although I am well aware that your younger colleagues interpret this as a consequence of senility.

– Albert Einstein, letter to Max Bonn

A mathematics student was struggling with the concept of addition. To verify a particular theory, she conducted a survey. She asked her tutor what 1+1 was. 'It's 2, silly,' responded the tutor. She asked her statistics tutor: 'It's in the region of 2,' came the reply. She asked a tutor in engineering 'It's 2, but we'll say 9 for safety.' What the statistician and engineer had done was appreciate that we cannot rely on events always meeting some established rules, they build into their calculations what we shall term 'the Armageddon factor'. Put simply, any mathematical model that attempts to describe an outcome could be written:

$$Y = X + \alpha$$

where: X = any mathematical or qualitative description of a problem area

α = the Armageddon factor

Y = the outcome, dependent on X and α

This whole chapter is related to the Armageddon factor, which is impervious to traditional, rational and reductionist attempts to predict its behaviour, its size, its timing and its magnitude.

Einstein's letter to Bonn can be found in Ian Stewart's prologue to his book *Does God Play Dice?* (1989), which has helped popularise the theory of chaos. The accusers of Einstein's senility were perhaps premature. Rational people are still searching for objective and quantifiable explanations of phenomena and Stewart's question is transformed in the book to, 'how does God play dice?'

Chaos theory, and we use the term loosely, is a largely a product of western civilisation. We have distinct notions of good and evil, right or wrong. We tend to see a clockwork universe and have convinced ourselves that determinism can predict behaviour towards a predetermined end. Management is based on meliorism, we tend to attempt to control and dominate nature and business. Chaos theory to some extent perpetuates this philosophy.

The Eastern mind tends to have a different philosophical outlook. The Hindus, for example, recognise an underlying unity of order and disorder. In Hindu mythology the cosmos passes through three major phases: creation, maintenance and destruction – mirroring birth, life and death. Brahma is the god of creation, Vishnu the god of maintenance (order), and Shiva the god of destruction (disorder). Shiva represents creativity and non-conformity, the individual, the rebel, the untamed, the hermit who withdraws from human society. The distinction between the order of Vishnu and the disorder of Shiva is not that between good and evil. It represents instead two different ways in which divinity makes itself manifest: kindness and anger; harmony and discord. The Chinese Yin (darkness) and Yang (light) are interdependent and one follows the other to enable further creation (a simple parallel would be as man and woman). In the heart of Hong Kong, high-tech skyscrapers mingle with bamboo scaffolding erected for maintenance and construction purposes.

As the discussion of chaos develops, consider the pervading and sometimes stifling effect of the Vishnu factor or the necessary oscillations of the Yang and Yin.

Chaos theory is concerned with the ambiguous parts of life by trying to explain or eliminate ambiguity or uncertainty. One might describe *ambiguity* as a situation where there is no clear interpretation of phenomena or events; the evidence that is available supports more than one interpretation. On the other hand, *uncertainty* may be lessened through the collection of more facts or data.

Chaos theory moves on from this distinction to the notion that everything is in essence ambiguous, but the way a situation develops will follow certain laws of nature. Uncertainty does not exist, as more data cannot make the system less ambiguous. In a sense, things are both ambiguous and certain at the same time. So if we 'know' the underlying factors affecting a situation we can predict an outcome, however many aspects of chaos point to the fact that we do not know the underlying factors.

Under the banner of chaos theory are a number of distinct approaches linked by a central theme of uncertainty and predictability. This chapter outlines the fundamentals of the philosophy.

4.2.1 **The butterfly effect**

Attempts by Lorenz to predict weather led to awareness that some systems are extremely sensitive to initial starting conditions. Lorenz had developed an *algorithm* to predict some aspect of weather. One day in 1961, he wanted to see a particular sequence again. To test the results of this forecast Lorenz repeated the experiment. To save time, he started in the middle of the sequence, instead of the beginning. He entered the numbers from his printout and re-ran the calculations. When he examined the results an hour later, the sequence had evolved differently. Instead of the same pattern as before, it diverged from the pattern, giving a wildly different forecast compared with the original (see Figure 4.1). Eventually he figured out what had happened. The computer stored the numbers to six decimal places in its memory. However, he had it print out only to three decimal places. In the original sequence, the number was 0.506127, and he had only used the first three digits, 0.506.

On comparison, the two forecasts, although similar over the short term, displayed marked differences further from the starting point. Lorenz proved that this small difference in input (one part in a million) has a major effect on the outcome. This gave rise to what has become known as the butterfly effect, that is small errors in data collection will affect any resulting analysis. For example, if we do not take into account the flapping wings of a butterfly in Japan we will not be able to forecast the hurricane in America. Laplace's proposal of knowing all past and future from determining the present state of the universe and then using Newton's mechanics to predict future conditions is impossible, since the present state of classical systems cannot be known with infinite precision. The inability to determine the present state of a system will eventually lead to a divergence of system behaviour from that predicted. The scale of the divergence is dependent on the system's *sensitivity* to initial conditions and the *period*.

These general observations have led to the development of *deterministic chaos*. Deterministic chaos is defined as 'the aperiodic bounded dynamics in a deterministic system with sensitive dependence on initial conditions' (Kaplan and Glass, 1995: 27). *Aperiodic* means system states occur irregularly, i.e. one cannot predict the time interval between similar states. *Bounded* means that the system is constrained within certain parameters, i.e. it cannot explode. For example, it will not snow in the Sahara in June, neither will there be a tropical monsoon at Antarctica in July. *Deterministic* means that the spatial interactions and temporal dynamics are regulated by definitive rules. *Sensitive dependence on initial conditions* means that although systems may have 'similar' starting conditions they will evolve differently. Non-linear systems may exhibit *low-dimensional* or *high-dimensional* chaos, which determines the predictability over time of the system. The weather

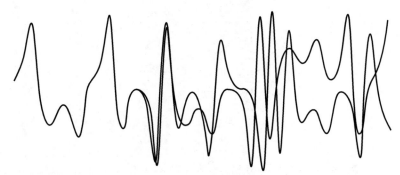

Figure 4.1 Lorenz's Experiment – the difference between the starting curves is 0.000127

Source: Stewart, 1989:141

exhibits high-dimensional chaos; temperatures of land and sea, cosmic effects and so forth, all independently affect weather conditions. Low-dimensional chaos has few variables affecting the performance of the system. For example, ambient temperatures and qualities of fuel and oil affect car engines. In business, large projects would exhibit high-dimensional chaos, the bottle-filling line of a cosmetics company low-dimensional chaos.

4.2.2 Fractal geometry

Clouds are not spheres,
mountains are not cones,
coastlines are not circles,
and bark is not smooth,
nor does lightning travel in straight lines.

– Benoit Mandelbrot (1982)

Mandelbrot's work on fractals (measurements in fractional dimensions) resulted in the development of the *Mandelbrot set*, a colourful, intricate, never ending pattern of random symmetry (Figure 4.2). Every picture is different depending on the starting conditions, but can be duplicated if these conditions are known. In the development of this set we observe some order emerging out of the apparent chaos. Stable pockets are joined by elaborate patterns. If we examine, or magnify, each part of the set we find a similar pattern.

If you use the picture as a visual metaphor, you can interpret the picture in many ways. It could be a large stable core of an organisation, with turbulent sparks of interaction with the environment, where small pockets of stability are created, in the form of new markets or new processes. Creativity and innovation only occur at the edge of the set or, for the organisation, where people and processes are not constrained by the straitjacket of the organisation.

Similarity and scales of measurement

Physical and some subjective phenomena usually take place on some characteristic scale of measurement. The distance within the universe, for example, is

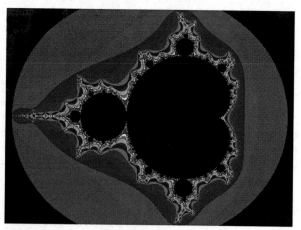

Figure 4.2 The Mandelbrot set

described in scales of millions of light years. Cell measurement involves scales closer to a micrometre. Some feelings may follow terms of disgust, indifference and delight (if one could measure them). Stewart (1989: 216) suggests that such scales are 'an artefact of the limitations of the human mind, rather than a genuine truth about nature. Our minds just cannot grasp something as big as the universe on a level of fine detail. So we dissect it up into large-scaled structures, like galactic super-clusters, and dissect those into galaxies, and galaxies into individual stars, and so on. Nature, in contrast, operates on all scales simultaneously (emphasis added).'

The small but discernible circle (the third from the right in Figure 4.2) is magnified in Figure 4.3. This illustrates the concept of self-similarity, where similar elements recur throughout the picture.

Orthodox shapes of geometry – triangles, circles, spheres, cylinders – lose their structure when magnified. A circle becomes a featureless straight line when viewed on a large scale. The distance around the coastline of any country, or indeed lake or puddle, varies with the method and instrumentation of measurement (Mandelbrot, 1967). Try to estimate the perimeter of a puddle using a hard ruler then a piece of string, then cotton. People who think the Earth is flat do so because that is the way it looks to a tiny human being. Mandelbrot invented the term *fractal* (a measurement in a fractional dimension, that is, similar over a range of scales) to describe a very different type of geometric object: one that continues to exhibit detailed structure over a large range of scales. Indeed, an ideal mathematical fractal has structure on an infinite range of scales.

Self-similar objects, by definition, do not have a characteristic length scale: they look much the same on many different scales of measurement. Does the same hold for social systems? Will decisions be made in a pattern that is common at all levels of the organisation, and will this in turn reflect patterns in the country as a whole? Is this the essence of what we term 'culture' (see Chapter 13)?

Fractals and the mathematical underpinning of the Mandelbrot set demonstrated how apparently random systems show elements of repetitive order. Parallels can be drawn with social systems. As individuals we are all very similar: a nurse, lawyer, pilot and criminal only fill these roles for a small fraction of their

Figure 4.3 Similarity in a Mandelbrot set

lives, we eat, breath, sleep and so on almost identically. In business, similarity occurs within many operations. For example, meetings at which employees from all levels of the organisation are present usually demonstrate a similar format across many industries. The highest-ranking person usually sits in a central or top position. Lower-ranking staff usually show respect and deference, which is not openly reciprocated. Managers appear in many guises in their changing roles, or as Shakespeare would have it, life is a stage and we are all actors.

Activity 4.1	Reflect on your various roles. In them, are people around you acting in similar ways, or ways that 'fit' with the situation? Try to alter this behaviour; for example, pretend you are doing your favourite pastime whilst you are at work (don't get the sack though!). Or ask to work in another department at another hierarchical level if possible. If you can do this you will get a completely different view of the world.

Dripping taps and exploding populations

One of the earliest experiments in chaos involved dripping taps (Yorke and Tein-Yien Li, 1975). The steady drip of a tap can be maddeningly constant. As the volume of water increases there comes a point at which the drops merge and mix and display erratic behaviour. Organisations are characterised and controlled by feedback. Formally in the deliberate development of procedural controls and informally through communications, which themselves can be directed, as in the Chancellor of the Exchequer's annual 'state of the nation' talk, or random as in rumour. The way in which these random feedbacks occur, including their frequency, is one of the factors that *period doubling* is attempting to explain.

Period doubling attempts to explain how a system might move from apparent stability to instability and back to stability through small changes in the environment. If we can spot when this change is going to occur, we can prepare ourselves for it. A simple analogy would be a whistle. If we blow into a whistle, increasing the volume of air, then the whistle will alternate between notes increasing in pitch and brief periods of instability, where no sound or distortion is heard. Likewise, an organisation may exhibit periods of stability and disorganisation as it changes in response to the environment. Griener (1972: 421) describes how these instabilities may be exhibited in business. As firms grow, various points of instability occur. For example, the small entrepreneurial firm reaches a crisis of leadership when initial creative skills give way to more needed direction. As the firm grows, more tasks are delegated and a crisis of control is reached, and so forth.

Starting with very small changes, the number and magnitude of changes can escalate and a system can move from relative stability to one of chaos. Mathematicians and scientists working on non-linear equations and ecological modelling have concluded that chaotic systems could form repetitive patterns and that life itself utilised some sort of non-linear formulations to generate patterns.

In the prediction of biological populations within the field of ecology, the equation would be simple if population continues to just rise indefinitely. However, the effect of predators and a limited food supply make simple linear relationships incorrect. The simplest equation that attempts to model this is:

Next year's population = $R \times$ This year's population $\times$ (1 – This year's population)

where 'population' is a number between 0 and 1, where 1 represents the maximum possible population and 0 represents extinction. R is the growth rate as a percentage. How does growth rate affect the equation? First thoughts might suggest that a high growth rate would result in a high population, whilst a low growth rate might result in a low population. For some growth rates this holds, but not for all cases.

One biologist, Robert May, decided to see what would happen to the equation as the growth rate value changed. At low values of the growth rate, the population would settle down to a single number. For instance, if the growth rate value is 2.7, the population will settle down to 0.6292. As the growth rate increased, the final population would increase as well. Then, something weird happened.

As soon as the growth rate passed 3, the line broke into two distinct sections (see Figure 4.4). Instead of settling down to a single population, it would jump between two different populations. It would be one value for one year, go to another value the next year, and then repeat the cycle. Raising the growth rate a little more caused it to jump between four different values. As the parameter rose further, the line bifurcated again. The bifurcations came faster and faster until suddenly, apparent chaos appeared. Past a certain growth rate, it becomes impossible to predict the behaviour of the equation. However, upon closer inspection, it is possible to see white strips. Looking closer at these strips reveals little windows of order, where the equation goes through the bifurcations again before returning to chaos.

In business, economists are trying to determine underlying patterns in economic and financial data. Like the search for the holy grail they are looking for the 'magic number' that will enable them to take the randomness out of the apparent random nature of the stock market.

Black holes and stagnation

The term *attractors* is given to the obvious influences of the organisation, often we can assume that they conform to physical, psychological and mathematical rules or are otherwise predictable. The Earth revolving around the Sun, an electron revolving around the nucleus of an atom. For the business, the attractors are the rules, the procedures, the products, the culture, the control systems and the personalities.

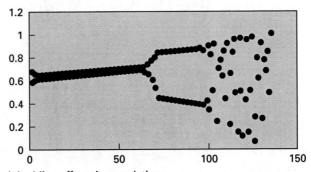

Figure 4.4 Period doubling effects in populations

Strange attractors are the forces pulling the firm into new directions: for example globalisation, innovation and technology. The effects of change are stabilised by attractors. Strange attractors are one way to explain the apparent irrationality within the system. Imagine a black moon, which by virtue of its properties does not reflect light and allows light through it. It is invisible but still has mass. Now explain tides.

In Figure 4.5 a single line representing a state of weather alternates between two basic positions. Lorenz used this to illustrate that whilst we may never be able to predict a weather condition, we can associate it with a range of possible conditions. Attractors are one way of identifying the boundaries of the system.

Activity 4.2	List any markets, organisations, or systems that appear to be changing rapidly in response to pressures. In contrast to that, are there any systems that appear not to be changing? Focus on items described in news bulletins or by public bodies.

The *Guardian* newspaper offers two recent examples of systems that appear to be changing:

> On a personal level, Daniel Lee the head of Salomon brothers' German operations love of music, eventually precipitated his move from bond analysis to begin a country music career in the year 2000.
>
> (*The Guardian*, 28 December 1999)

> Spain is being pulled in two directions. Traditionally the Spaniards have enjoyed a three-hour siesta within the middle of an extended working day. Shifts in commuter patterns and increased European competition are threatening this way of life. To compensate for the missed nap, new relaxation parlours are emerging that provide a 30 minute fast food approach to the siesta.
>
> (*The Guardian*, 28 December 1999)

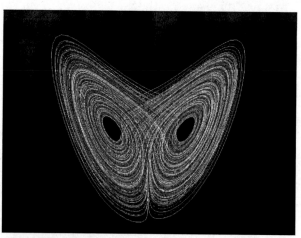

Figure 4.5 Lorenz attractors

There are many industries and systems that are changing rapidly in response to the environment. Industries such as banks have responded to technological change by introducing new methods of banking, they have responded to consumer pressure by becoming more customer-aware. Systems that are not responding, or respond in the 'wrong' way tend to go out of business. Attractors counterbalance the need for change in some cases; strange attractors are one way to explain the extraordinary.

However, when a system is in chaos these attractors break down. Strange attractors begin to take over the system, things that cannot be predicted or quantified. If a company could identify the nature of a strange attractor for a business then it would gain a significant advantage over its competitors, by being able to predict more accurately future events or influences.

Activity 4.3	Having read the introduction to chaos theory, how do you feel about what you have been learning up to this point?

4.3 Chaos becomes complexity

One response to Activity 4.3 is: 'what a waste of time'. If things are chaotic, why bother trying to understand what happens? Section 4.2 implies that it is futile to make plans and decisions because chaos theory tells us that, whatever we think, the future will more than likely show us to be wrong. In time, small errors in initial data collection, or factors being overlooked will lead to a fundamental shift away from the position where we thought we would be in the future, to one that we could not possibly have forecast. Or, for reasons of similarity, any course of action is likely to be channelled along a certain predetermined path.

Chaos theory is a relatively new concept in the world of business decision-making. Chaos itself is not a new phenomenon, it has been with us for some time and has been described using less vibrant words such as turbulence, confusion, instability, flux and, perhaps more relevant, irrationality. Reasons why we should be seriously considering the concepts of chaos when it comes to studying the social sciences include:

- *Increasing rates of change.* For example, in relation to planning, Cartwright (1991: 45) observes that even if local 'rules' are completely known, it may be impossible to predict global results and 'planning based on prediction is not merely impractical in some cases; it is logically impossible'.

- *Increasing emphasis on process research.* Although chaos is concerned with the dynamic evolution of complex non-linear systems (as evidenced in physical and natural sciences), similar processes can be observed in social systems, and hence the complexity sciences may contribute to an understanding of these processes.

- *Similarity of existing models of social behaviour.* Incorporation of non-linearity into existing models of social behaviour would allow exploration of the more significant implications of the complexity sciences.

■ *Disappointing results and lack of relevance.* Whilst there have been significant advances in understanding how organisations work, many of the individual studies lack transferability. It is difficult to compare findings unless we have some classification system on which to base the original research.

Apart from organisational classification, many studies suffer from poor analytical results, low correlation, low statistical significance and problems with replicability. These problems are due to using linear methods to evaluate the data, when systems with similar starting points and environments end up having different outcomes. Social and organisational researchers customarily conclude that either (a) significant, explanatory variables have been omitted from the study, (b) the measurement instrument is too imprecise and unsophisticated, or (c) the random or *stochastic* part of the problem has overwhelmed the patterned part (Gregerson and Sailor, 1993).

In the past we have tended to shrug off the effects of chaos with proverbs such as 'all good plans are lain to waste' or, as Illustration 4.1 demonstrates, a set of Sod's laws.

Having read the list of metaphysical 'laws', I'm sure that you can relate to a number of them. You could in fact add more laws, 'the toast', for example. Physical laws can in fact explain the reason why the toast falls buttered side down, i.e. objects will tend to fall with the heavier side down or the butter creates an aerodynamic surface. Although it is an annoying trait, it cannot be included in the above list, because there is a rational explanation.

Activity 4.4	Identify incidents at work, or within your environment, that appear irrational and, for each of them, try to identify the possible causes of that irrationality.

Some things you just cannot explain: the fact that a weather condition that is identical to one two years earlier suddenly turns into a raging tempest, instead of the idyllic summer day as was predicted. However, the weather is a poor simile for a business. The evolutionary forces at work in the weather system are very random, and alter rapidly in response to small fluctuations. This evolutionary factor is an important difference.

> So it is that the great Tree of Life fills with its dead and broken branches the crust of the earth, and covers the surface with its ever-branching and beautiful ramifications.
> (Darwin, 1979)

Darwin was perhaps the first indirect contributor to chaos theory. The quotation at the start of the chapter, taken from the conclusion to his classic book *The Origin of Species*, first published in 1860, was written with political intent. He was challenging the fundamental belief that the world was created in six days. He suggested that there was evidence that things had changed over a long time in response to the environment. Darwin used palaeontological and Earth sciences to reinforce his revolutionary theories. The time span is important: Darwin's arguments revolved around these changes, apparently random in themselves but established through natural selection taking place over thousands of years.

Illustration 4.1 Sod's laws of the universe

Why do things sometimes go wrong? These humorous (but not necessarily untrue) 'laws' of the universe suggest why rational methods of problem solving and decision-making do not always bring success to a business.

1 If anything can go wrong, it will.

2 Nothing is ever as simple as it seems.

3 Everything takes longer than you expect.

4 If there is a possibility of several things going wrong, the one that will go wrong first will be the one that will do the most damage.

5 Left to themselves, all things go from bad to worse.

6 If you play with something long enough, you will surely break it.

7 If everything seems to be going well, you have obviously overlooked something.

8 If you see that there are four possible ways in which a procedure can go wrong, and circumvent these, then a fifth way, unprepared for, will promptly develop.

9 Nature always sides with the hidden flaw.

10 It is impossible to make anything foolproof, because fools are ingenious.

11 If a great deal of time has been expended seeking the answer to a problem with the only result being failure, the answer will be immediately obvious to the first unqualified person.

12 Persons disagreeing with your facts are always emotional and employ faulty reasoning.

13 Enough research will tend to confirm your conclusions.

14 The more urgent the need for a decision, the less apparent becomes the identity of the decision-maker.

15 The more complex the idea or technology, the more simple-minded is its opposition,

16 Each profession talks to itself in its own unique language, apparently there is no Rosetta Stone.

Source: Eunson, 1988

Society and business are strange beasts. They consist of a number of interacting systems and each of these systems is undergoing an evolutionary process. This evolutionary process is probably chaotic in its nature, but is also subject to the forces of natural selection and all are taking place within different timeframes. Given the truly complex, multidimensional nature of any social system, it is perhaps strange that we are not in a continual process of flux and dramatic change, as chaos might imply.

Activity 4.5   Identify a system (for example, the local school, the hospital, a hotel). Try to say how quickly the systems are evolving or changing.

The difficult part is trying to guess how the system will evolve in the future or to determine the factors that have created the current climate. We also need to identify the classifications for the changes, so, for example, we might correlate time with teaching technology and curriculum issues in the university system, as shown in Table 4.1.

Table 4.1 Change in university technologies

Year	Event	Technology / curriculum
3500 BC	Neolithic	Sabre-tooth-tiger-scaring-with-fire – Specific (life enhancing)
350 BC	Aristotle and Greek philosophers / Hellenistic and Neoplatonism	Development of liberal arts / traditional / cultural
AD 1	Romans	Professional / law
400	Capella *De arte grammatica, De arte dialectica, De arte rhetorica, De geometrica, De arithmetica, De astrologia* and *De harmonia*	Liberal arts / Christian emphasis
1167	Oxford	Trivium, quadrivium / Christian
1440	Eton	Eton founded
1474	Thomas Caxton	Printing press / greater availability of books
1500	Desiderious Erasmus	Critical of theological issues / Reformation / mixed curricula
1570	Roger Ascham	English as the language to teach in / Reformist
1605	Francis Bacon *Advancement of Learning*	First important English book on learning
1640	Comenius *Pampaedia* (*Universal Education*)	Educator, proposing universal education in four streams, and a fifth College of Light.
1762	Jean-Jacques Rousseau	*Emile* / greater awareness of social issues / natural movement / child centred
1776	Adam Smith	Relevance to society / professionalism / national curriculum
1810	Humboldt	Examinations
1840	Rowland Hull	Postal service reform / wider access to education / distance learning
1852	John Henry Newman	Conformist / general / liberal art
1870	Elementary Education Act	Wider access to education
1900	Édouard Claparède	Child development / scientific realist
1920s	John Dewey	Experiential learning / progressive / naturalist
1950s	Psychologists (Freud 1920)	Educational psychology
1960s	Lord Robbins	Television / Open University / flexible learning / expansion to 10–30% of the population in the following 30 years
1980s	Bill Gates	Computers / distance learning
1990s	Ron Dearing	Communication technology / structural transformation
2000+	Who knows?	Centralised universities supported by distance learning technology and home-based tutors (perhaps)

In a similar way to the dinosaurs of old, firms may, by copying and cooperating, be following a redundant evolutionary branch; a discontinuity, unlike the small, fast mammal. A dynamic new firm may be waiting just around the corner, unencumbered by procedure and protocol, ready to pounce with the revolutionary product, which will replace one of your major products. Business is littered with such examples. The Dyson vacuum cleaner has revolutionised and revi-

> **Illustration 4.2 The real thing**
>
> Stacey (1996) describes an interesting example of how a small change can affect a business. In April 1985, the soft drinks giant Coca-Cola announced that the formula for the drink was to be changed. The change had come about after years of research and market testing. In the tests, most people preferred the new taste. The new product was estimated to generate an extra $200 million in sales. Early responses were good. However, a group of consumers were upset by the change and complained that a national symbol had been damaged. The complaints gathered momentum, with 5,000 calls per day and 40,000 letters arriving during the spring and summer. The test surveys were turned on their heads, with only 30 per cent liking the new drink as opposed to 53 per cent before the product launch. The new product was taken off the shelf and the company reverted to the old formula in July 1985.
>
> No cause and effect for this response has ever been found, although we can speculate that Coca-Cola has an iconic significance in North America. Tampering with it may therefore be seen as an un-American activity. What it demonstrates is how a small change in a business can create a major effect through the operation of positive feedback taking the form of herd instinct or bandwagon effects.

talised its industry; Amstrad Computers threatened IBM's complacency in the 1980s and so forth.

Given that we live in a blinkered world where unknowns are influencing change, how can we begin to control the destiny of the firm in which we work? We need some way in which to make sense of the irrational, or more importantly, an alternative way to understand the calm of a stagnant system.

4.4 Managing chaos

If we accept that in the longer term there is inevitably some uncertainty of outcomes to decisions, then we need a new framework within which we make our decisions. We need to accept that we cannot look into the future with any great accuracy. The theoretical maximum for an accurate weather forecast is two weeks; the best we can do at the moment (in the UK) is two or three days. We need to understand more about the irrationalities of the systems with which we are working. We need to develop contingency plans that deal with the uncertainty of the future and help with any unforeseen occurrences. We need to encourage visionary and innovative approaches to decision-making, management and internal entrepreneurship and creativity. Perhaps the most important element is that we need to create flexible organisations, that are in a position to respond rapidly when the goalposts move, the market shifts, or the founder of the company hands in the keys to the executive washroom.

Whilst chaos theory attempts to understand unpredictability, *self-organisation* is the balancing effect. Self-organisation is concerned with the issue that potentially complex dynamic systems can be constrained and generate organised and patterned temporal behaviours. However, as with the Yin and Yang, it is difficult to be both ordered and disordered at the same time. Chaos implies disorder; self-organisation implies stasis and inertia. Stewart (1993: 3) defines a successful system as being:

> At the transition between order and chaos: a central tenet of complexity theory is that selection or learning drives systems towards this edge of chaos. Systems that are too simple do not survive in a competitive environment, because more sophisticated systems can outwit them by exploiting their regularities. But, systems that are too random do not survive either. It pays in survival terms to be as complicated as possible, without becoming totally structureless.

Stacey (1996: 349), summarises this view of the complex organisation, as shown in Illustration 4.3. The theory has been annotated with our italics.

Illustration 4.3 A complexity theory of organisation

A complexity theory of an organisation is built on the following propositions:

1 All organisations are webs of non-linear feedback loops connected to other people and organisations by webs of non-linear feedback loops.

2 Such non-linear feedback systems are capable of operating in states of stable and non-stable equilibrium, or in the borders between these states, that is far from equilibrium, in bounded instability at the edge of chaos.

3 All organisations are paradoxes. They are powerfully pulled towards stability by the forces of integration, maintenance controls, human desires for security and certainty, and adaptation to the environment on one hand [*attractors*]. They are also powerfully pulled to the opposite extreme of unstable equilibrium by the forces of division and decentralisation, human desires for excitement and innovation, and isolation from the environment [*strange attractors*].

4 If the organisation gives in to the pull of stability, it becomes ossified and cannot change easily [*entropy*]. If it gives in to the pull of instability it disintegrates. Success lies in sustaining an organisation in the borders between stability and instability. This is a state of chaos, a difficult to maintain dissipative structure.

5 The dynamics of the successful organisation are therefore those of irregular cycles and discontinuous trends, falling within qualitative patterns, fuzzy but recognisable categories taking the form of archetypes and templates.

6 Because of its own internal dynamic, a successful organisation faces completely unknowable specific futures.

7 Agents within the system cannot be in control of its long-term future, nor can they install specific frameworks to make it successful, nor can they apply step-by step analytical reasoning or planning, or ideological controls to long-term development. Agents within the system can only do these things in relation to the short term.

8 Long-term development is a spontaneously self-organising process from which new strategic directions may emerge. Spontaneous self-organisation is political interaction and learning in groups. Mangers have to use reasoning by analogy.

9 In this way managers create their environment and the long-term futures of their organisations

Source: Stacey, 1996: 349

4.4.1 Managing the irrationalities

A number of authors have attempted to describe the irrational factors of a business. Samson (1991) describes how we should manage the interfaces of the business with surrounding systems. Peters (1989) explains why his excellent companies of a few years earlier are no longer excellent: because it is a chaotic world. Below is a suggested list of those factors that a company needs to manage, or at least be aware of, in order to try to retain some form of control:

- Company size
- Vertical integration and mergers
- Globalisation
- Technology
- Suppliers and contractors
- Customers
- People and the labour market
- Government and the environment:
    - safety
    - pollution
    - employment, wages and conditions
    - trade practice

Activity 4.6	Given that we need a new framework for making decisions that needs to take into account chaotic and irrational factors, draw up a list of what these factors might be.

Organisations need to continually strive to match what they are hoping to do with what the environment expects. They need to review what they are doing and the methods that they are employing to do it (whatever 'it' is). Some organisations reorganise themselves into new units but in essence keep to the same basic parameters. This is due in part to a lack of imagination on the part of the decision-makers. Their world view is limited and influenced by the jargon of the gurus or by the latest fad. They listen selectively to customers, employees and stakeholders and initiate a response only when the suggestion matches their own expectations and goals.

Table 4.2 illustrates how these factors might affect a firm's operations.

Chaos implies that planning becomes difficult when it is based on forecasts of future events. The distance into the future will depend to some extent upon the nature of the forces at work in the system. Does this mean then that companies who produce aggregate plans of 18 months are wasting their time? If it takes two years to build a new facility, and we think we need one (we have gone through all of the rational decision-making processes to this end), we need to take a chance and build, there is no other solution, unless it is one of stagnation. If we produce a strategic plan that states: 'In two hundred years we will be here', nothing has been lost, and shows some commitment to the long-term success of the

Table 4.2 Irrational factors and company responses

Factor	Comment	Business Response
Company size	Size used to be seen as the way forward, extending operations to gain advantages in economies of scale, but brings with it a lack of energy. Innovation is swamped in the bureaucratic complexity of the firm	Focus the business. Down-scope to simple structures that are effective and efficient in delivering customer requirements. Clear identification of market needs. Strategic business units set up to manage programmes. Integration of SBUs through common accounting and administrative procedures. Use collaborative task groups to manage project areas
Vertical integration	This again increases the complexity of the firm and potentially dilutes expertise. Directions become set and the firm is slow to respond to the environment	Think very carefully of the benefits of this. Many acquisitions of the 1980s have been thorns in the side of the acquiring company (e.g. British Leyland). Develop clearly defined quality control and accounting procedures. Improve technological integration to facilitate communication and teamwork initiatives
Globalisation	We are now a global market. Cross-fertilisation of products, technology and cultures are all adding a new dimension to virtually all business	Firms need to respond to global threats and opportunities. This can be done by continually monitoring competitors and new entrants through techniques such as benchmarking. Develop leading-edge market strategies that differentiate the product and identify customer requirements. Create product development teams that can rapidly meet these requirements
Technology	The rapid change in technology is leaving many companies behind. Manufacturing, service and logistics technologies enable companies to get better products quickly and at less cost to customers around the world	Technological forecasting, through informal research such as scanning, and directed research to respond to weaknesses needs to become a regular function of the R&D department. Research done through think-tanks that can collect, assimilate, and disseminate research to all members of the organisation
Customers	Customers are easily offended, are quick to shoot and slow to convince	Create differentiated markets that offer top quality, quickly and at low cost. Listen to customers and create a service ethos. Become student focused. Create relationships with the community. Become a firm without walls. Create research opportunities without always looking for a short-term financial payback
Suppliers and contractors	With downsizing comes reliance on third parties. Our suppliers, through strategic relationships, become an important element of our success; if they go down we may well follow. They themselves need to manage chaos in an effective manner	Relationships need to be carefully controlled through established and agreed procedures. These should include the need for the supplier to, for example, conduct technological forecasting

Table 4.2 Irrational factors and company responses *continued*

Factor	Comment	Business Response
People and the labour market	People could be the most irrational part of a business. Whether they are rational, or not, companies need to develop the most appropriate conditions to stimulate effective employee contributions. Europe is now open to interchange of skills across borders. If one country has a shortage of specific skills, it will import them. Demographic and political influences will determine the quality and quantity of the labour force. Companies need to address the training requirements of their workforce	The firm should review its human requirements in line with other audits to ensure that a flexible workforce is created. Innovation and creativity are important issues. Removal of fear, and enhancement of communication
Government and the environment	One of the more irrational elements and one that many companies have little control of. Government and environment influence business in a variety of ways by altering laws and taxes in such areas as: safety, pollution, employment, wages and conditions, and trade practice	The company needs to communicate with all the stakeholders as appropriate. New laws take time do react quickly to issues that they disagree with

---

Activity 4.7   For a company of your choice, how might that company begin to cope with managing the irrationalities? Use Table 4.2 as a framework for your thoughts.

---

company. Where the principles of chaos theory are really useful is in forcing companies to pay attention to details: in the short term, to ensure that the firm responds rapidly to changes in market conditions, technology and the environment; in the longer term, by having systems that ensure continual monitoring of the environment in which they are a part.

4.4.2 Risk management

A special case of irrational, or chaotic, events which is of importance to business is the management of risk. Disasters that affect human life, or the environment in which we live, have in recent years brought the issue of risk management in business organisations to the forefront in the press. Every year within the building industry, employees are killed, or events occur that could lead to loss of life. It can be estimated that the death in service of an employee, due to an accident on site, would cost the organisation at least £2 million. When an oil tanker runs aground it will potentially cost many millions in lost cargo, damage to the environment, and lost income from industries affected by the incident.

Activity 4.8 An important part of managing chaos is contingency planning. Most local government authorities will have contingency plans. For example, years ago these plans would have catered for the outbreak of a nuclear war. If you were the new chief executive for a large council (local government authority), what sorts of incident would you require contingency plans for, and what would be in those plans?

One way to approach Activity 4.8 is to ask, 'What would be bad for the local population?' This is the central question that would determine the need for a contingency plan and the contents of it, for example a strike of the workforce, a major epidemic, a major accident. Table 4.3 shows a possible response.

Table 4.3 Contingency plans

Incident	Contingency plan content
School burnt down	List of mobile temporary accommodation providers Alternative sites
Strike of park and garden staff	List of garden contractors Barriers to prevent entry into parks
Major air crash	Emergency incident plan to include procedures, telephone contact lists and alternative hospitals

In almost every case of disaster, the subsequent inquiry has identified poor management decision-making processes that have overlooked factors that may have been inconsequential at the time but which have either escalated into major factors or combined to create the ultimate disaster scenario. Illustration 4.4 identifies the major contributing factors leading to the Zeebrugge car ferry disaster.

Illustration 4.4 The Zeebrugge car ferry disaster

In September 1990 the trial for manslaughter of P&O Ferries and seven of its employees and managers started at the Old Bailey. The trial arose from the deaths of 189 passengers and crew on board the P&O ferry *Herald of Free Enterprise* that sank on 6 March 1987 outside the Belgian port of Zeebrugge. The ferry had sailed with its bow doors open, and the sea had flooded in when the ship built up speed. Only luck prevented the loss of all 539 on board. The death toll was the worst for a British vessel in peacetime since the sinking of the *Titanic* in 1912. How did such a lamentable disaster occur?

At first sight, the sinking was caused by neglect by three employees on the ship. The assistant bosun, who was supposed to shut the doors, overslept, and thus failed to shut them. The first officer, who had been involved with loading vehicles, waited until he thought he saw the assistant bosun approaching the door controls on the car deck, and then left to go to his assigned station on the bridge. The captain, who should have overall responsibility for ensuring the ship set sail in a safe condition, did not check to see that the doors had been closed.

At the court of investigation into the sinking it became apparent that the cause of the disaster went far beyond the neglect of three employees on one particular evening.

There were many factors which contributed to the sinking, among them:

■ Unstable working relationships, through poor shift patterns and a high turnover of officers.

■ Ambiguous work tasks and poor job descriptions.

■ Commercial pressures to sail early.

■ Negative reporting systems (reports filed only if things are wrong).

■ Five prior occurrences of the doors being left open and ignoring recommendations of previous inquiries.

■ Engineering requests for warning lights and pumps being cynically dismissed.

■ Inherent ship design faults.

■ No meetings between shore and ship management for two and a half years.

■ Passenger overloading.

■ Irresponsible management in P&O ferries.

The report of the investigation into the disaster castigates the management of the ferry company. It states that:

> A full investigation into the circumstances of the disaster leads inexorably to the conclusion that the underlying or cardinal faults lay higher up in the Company. The Board of Directors did not appreciate their responsibility for the safe management of their ships. The directors did not have any proper comprehension of what their duties were. All concerned in management, from the members of the Board of Directors down to the junior superintendents, were guilty of fault in that all must be regarded as sharing responsibility for the failure of management. From top to bottom the body corporate was infected with the disease of sloppiness ...

With regard for responsibility for safety, the report said that 'the Board of Directors must accept a heavy responsibility for their lamentable lack of directions. Individually and collectively they lacked a sense of responsibility. This left a vacuum at the centre.'

Although the report condemned the company and its management, the judge at the Old Bailey trial did not consider that there was sufficient evidence to justify the charge of manslaughter against P&O Ferries and seven of its employees and managers. After 27 days of a trial expected to last five months, he instructed the jury to find the defendants not guilty.

Source: based on Boyd in Ansell and Wharton, 1992: 194–7

| Activity 4.9 | You are the chief executive of P&O and have just left the court. What would be your immediate list of priorities to help prevent a similar experience? |

◆ Summary

The advocates of chaos theory offer some salutary thoughts on management decision-making for all aspects of businesses. The paradox of chaos is that aspects of the theory are based on assumptions of determinism and predictability within a context of randomness, ignorance and inaccuracy. Chaos theory implies that it is futile to make long-term plans and decisions, because whatever we think (based on perception, analytical models, forecasting, past events), the future will more than likely be wrong. Small errors or omissions in initial data collection will, in time, lead to a fundamental shift away from the position where we thought we would be in the future, to one that we could not possibly have forecast. On the other hand, chaos also shows that apparently all systems, although appearing to be chaotic or disordered, are in fact the very essence of order. Underpinning this are the assumptions that systems are non-linear and dynamic. Non-linear implies recursion and resonance, dynamic implies non-periodic and changing. Physical and biological sciences use non-linear methods to help model relatively simple systems. There are many reasons to suppose that social systems are more complex than these systems and contain significant elements of non-linearity. So the challenge for the decision-maker theorist is to determine the set of 'magic numbers' that might allow us to mimic this apparently random behaviour.

Chaos theory would imply, at first, that much of the past research on complex systems, such as social research, may be irrelevant now, because of changes in the system dynamics since the original research was undertaken. Past research is frozen in time, irrespective of any discussion of dynamics within the research. However, in common with all theories, chaos theory helps to frame the way in which we think and, in the case of past research, an awareness of it is likely to make this research useful again, within a chaotic context.

Chaos theory techniques have been used to model complex biological systems, such as population growth, epidemics and arrhythmic heart palpitations. Chaotic explanations of the apparent random fluctuations within stock market prices are more acceptable than simple deterministic attempts. More importantly for social systems and, in some ways more correctly, the term 'complexity' is used to replace chaos to reflect that, whilst unpredictable, many situations are not completely random. De Greene (1996: 292) suggests that if the new approaches

> act as perturbations and fluctuations, driving a restructuring of social science, and if they help generate new paradigm thinking, then the future can indeed be promising. If, however, the new theories function just as new tools (like a new form of regression analysis), then the social sciences may find that the exciting and challenging aspects of social reality have been usurped by the more dynamic, the more imaginative, and the more adventuresome, and that traditional economics, sociology, political science, and so on have become increasingly irrelevant.

? Decision diary

Try to identify those forces that guide your decision-making process. For these forces (e.g. maximisation of enjoyment, wealth, prestige, compassion) how universally held are they (are the same forces influencing your every decision)? How do they affect others in your world? Can you identify the rule-breakers? If so, what rules are they breaking? Can you identify any repeating patterns to decision-making? What happens if the pattern changes? How often do things change? Do things really change? Can you identify any attractors?

References

Ansell, J. and Wharton, F. (1992) *Risk Analysis, Assessment and Management.* Chichester: Wiley.

Darwin, C. (1979) *The Illustrated Origin of Species.* London: BCA

Eunson, B. (1988) *Managing Yourself and Others.* London: McGraw-Hill.

Gregerson, H. and Sailor, L. (1993) 'Chaos theory and its implications for social science research', *Human Relations*, 46(7).

Griener, L. (1972) 'Evolution and revolution as organisations grow', in De-Wit, B. and Meyer, R. (1994), *Strategy: Process, Content, Context.* St Paul, MN: West Publishing.

Kaplan, D. and Glass, L. (1995) *Understanding Non-linear Dynamics.* Berlin: Springer-Verlag.

Mandelbrot, B. (1982) *The Fractal Geometry of Nature.* New York: W. H. Freeman.

Peters, T. (1989) *Thriving on Chaos.* London: Pan Books.

Samson, D. (1991) *Manufacturing and Operations Strategy.* London: Prentice Hall.

Sanders, T.I. (1998) *Strategic Thinking and the New Science: Planning in the Midst of Chaos, Complexity and Change.* New York: Free Press.

Stacey, R. (1996) *Strategic Management and Organisational Dynamics*, 2nd edition. Harlow: Pitman Publishing.

Stewart, I. (1989) *Does God Play Dice? The Mathematics of Chaos.* Oxford: Blackwell.

Stewart, I. (1993) 'A new order (complexity theory)', *New Scientist*, 137(1859): 2,3.

Yorke, J. and Tein-Yien Li (1975) 'Period three implies chaos?' *American Mathematical Monthly*, 82.

Further reading

Bak, P., Tang, C. and Wiesenfeld, K. (1988) 'Self-organised criticality', *Physical Review A*, 38(1).

Bottery, M. (1994) *Lessons for Schools.* Cassell: London.

Brown, C. (1995) *Chaos and Catastrophe Theories*. Thousand Oaks, CA: Sage.

Cartwright, T.J. (1991) 'Planning and chaos theory', *APA Journal*, 57(1).

De Greene, K.B. (1996) 'Field-theoretic framework for the interpretation of the evolution, instability, structural change and management of complex systems', in Kiel, L.D. and Elliot, E. (eds), *Chaos Theory in the Social Sciences*. Ann Arbor: University of Michigan Press.

De-Wit, B. and Meyer, R. (1994), *Strategy: Process, Content, Context*. St Paul, MN: West Publishing.

Freldman, M. (1991) in Frost *et al*. *Reframing Organizational Culture*. Thousand Oaks, CA: Sage.

Keil, L.D. and Elliot, E (eds)(1996) *Chaos Theory in the Social Sciences: Foundations and Applications*. Ann Arbor: University of Michigan Press.

Krogh, G. and Roos, J. (1995) *Organisational Epistemology*. London: Macmillan.

Jantsch, E. (1980) *The Self-organising Universe*. New York: George Braziller.

Mandelbrot, B. (1967) 'How long is the coast of Britain? Statistical self-similarity and fractional dimension', *Science*, 156.

Ray, T.S. (1992) 'An approach to the synthesis of life', in Langton, G.C., Taylor, C., Doyne Farmer, J. and Rasmussen, S. (eds), *Artificial Life II*, Santa Fe Institute Studies in the Sciences of Complexity Volume 10. Reading, MA: Addison-Wesley.

Shaw, R. (1984) *The Dripping Faucet as a Model Chaotic System*. Santa Cruz: Aerial.

Stacey, R. (2000) *Strategic Management and Organisational Dynamics: The Challenge of Complexity*, 3rd edition. Harlow: Pearson Education .

Varela, F.J. (1984) 'Two principles of self-organisation', in Ulrich, H. and Probst, G.J.B. (eds), *Self-organisation and Management of Social System*. New York: Springer-Verlag.

Zelany, M. and Hufford, K.D (1992) 'The application of autopoiesis in systems analysis: are autopoeitic systems also social systems?' *International Journal of General Systems*, 21.

Website of interest

Dyson Inventions at http://www.dyson.com/

Glossary

Algorithm:	a set of rules or formulae used for problem solving especially connected with a computer.
Aperiodic:	of irregular occurrence.
Attractors/strange attractors:	parts of the system that are known and stabilise conditions or are unknown and have the potential to destabilise conditions.
Butterfly effect:	the notion that small or undetected variations in independent variables can lead to unforeseen future events.

Catastrophe theory:	is similar to dissipative structures but takes a modelling approach and attempts to evaluate revolutionary change in system behaviour.
Deterministic:	occurrences in nature, or social or psychological phenomena are causally determined by preceding events or natural laws
Dissipative structures:	are epitomised by instabilities, which alternate between periods of transitions and bifurcations. At these different states, the system is both quantitatively and qualitatively different from the previous one.
Fractals:	are distinct from the simple figures of classical geometry – the line, square, circle, sphere and so forth. They can describe the many irregularly shaped objects or spatially heterogeneous phenomena in nature that are beyond Euclidean geometric explanations. Examples of fractal phenomena can be readily seen in such objects as petals, snowflakes and tree barks.
Mandlebrot set:	a computer-generated picture, based upon non-linear algorithms.
Period doubling:	models system movements between stability and instability over small changes that result in a doubling or duplication effect (*see* Dissipative structures).
Self-organisation:	is concerned with the issue that potentially complex dynamic systems can be constrained and generate organised and patterned temporal behaviours.
Stochastic:	a phenomenon governed by the laws of probability, or characterised by a sequence of random variables.

PART TWO

Research

Preface to Part Two

In the second part of the book, information gathering is the major theme. Decisions are not taken out of context: there are always factors that influence a course of action. Our understanding of the situation influences the factors we include as part of the decision process. Our understanding of these factors, and importance accorded to them, comes from knowledge about the situation gained from research.

In Chapter 5 we examine the nature of knowledge and introduce the ideas of research methodology. We research in order to gain more information on which to justify and base our decision. In Chapter 6 we introduce a range of research methods that have been developed specifically for organisational analysis. In Chapter 7 we introduce the concept of model building and simulation to gain information on the effects of decisions before they are taken.

5 Research methodology

On completing this chapter you should be able to:

- Define key terms in research methodology.
- Explore the epistemological underpinnings of quantitative and qualitative approaches to decision-making.
- Recognise and distinguish positivist and phenomenological approaches to decision-making.
- Identify research methods that may help managers make more informed decisions.

5.1 Introduction

Why have we chosen to devote a chapter to research methodology in a book about management decision-making? Many management decision textbooks, this one included, present theories that have been formulated from research findings. These studies are often laboratory-type studies in which volunteers have been asked to contribute, and from which generalisations are made and passed on to managers. Alternatively, case studies are presented, complete with diagnostic work already supplied by the author. In reality, however, the problems faced by managers involve uncertainty and doubt. Whilst prescriptions and off-the-shelf solutions may help managers to broaden their knowledge base, ultimately the true test of decision-making rests in the evaluation of practical outcomes. Decision-making requires action. In this chapter the primary focus is on methodology rather than on method. The latter can be described as a set of tools and techniques for finding something out, or for reducing levels of uncertainty. The former addresses the philosophy of method in addressing such questions as 'is this the most appropriate technique?', 'how valid are my findings?', 'can the findings be extrapolated to other situations?' and so on. We openly try to persuade the reader of the value of questioning underlying assumptions about action. We argue that, wittingly or unwittingly, managers are all researchers, but how often do they question the basis of their research practice?

5.2 Research and decision-making

There are many parallels between decision-making and the research process. Gill and Johnson (1997: 3) note that:

> Managers need to be competent in investigative approaches to decision-making and problem-solving ... The research process, while being the means of advancing knowledge, also serves as a disciplined and systematic procedure of help in solving managerial problems.

Bell and Reedy (1999) take the research sequence, which Gill and Johnson (1997) borrow from Howard and Sharp (1983), and compare it to the decision-making part of a broader problem-solving cycle as defined by Cooke and Slack (1991: 5) – see Figure 5.1.

Figure 5.1 shows obvious parallels in the seemingly sequential nature of the process. Cooke and Slack actually present the process as a continuum in which there is a continual feedback loop, or what they call 'a recycling route' (Cooke and Slack, 1991: 10) based on observation and monitoring of the process. The authors acknowledge that the stages they identify are rarely so obviously defined

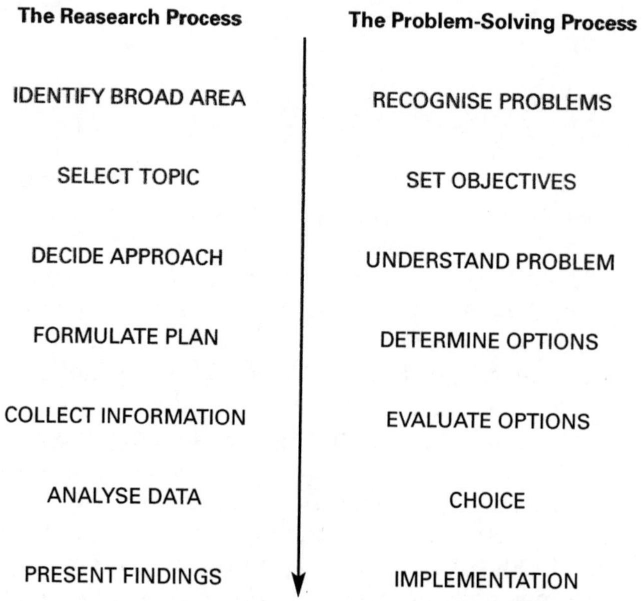

The Reasearch Process	The Problem-Solving Process
IDENTIFY BROAD AREA	RECOGNISE PROBLEMS
SELECT TOPIC	SET OBJECTIVES
DECIDE APPROACH	UNDERSTAND PROBLEM
FORMULATE PLAN	DETERMINE OPTIONS
COLLECT INFORMATION	EVALUATE OPTIONS
ANALYSE DATA	CHOICE
PRESENT FINDINGS	IMPLEMENTATION

Figure 5.1 The research process and problem-solving process compared
Source: adapted from Bell and Reedy, 1999: 21

in practice, nor are they recognised as a staged process by managers. What the model might be said to represent, then, is an idealised version of the process, as we noted in Chapter 1.

Many managers are probably involved in research without identifying it as such. The traditional tasks of management are usually defined in terms of planning, coordinating, controlling and so on. Research is rarely mentioned in the same breath as management unless it is in the context of management education, for example when part of a programme of MBA study. This is partly owing to the narrow conceptualisation of research as a specialised set of activities undertaken by presumed experts. In reality we are all researchers in some shape or form as we hypothesise, reflect, test our assumptions and generalise. However the process may not be as rigorous as it could be owing to a lack of theoretical underpinning for our thoughts, observations and actions.

5.3 Episteme and doxa

When asked to look back at empirical data in order to make future predictions (for example, time series analysis, Chapter 7), managers rarely question the value of this process. Yet, when asked to look back at the ideas of, say, writers on the human condition, in order to contextualise contemporary approaches to management, managers are more likely to question the value of such a process. Why might this be? One convenient way of explaining this might be to draw upon the ideas of the ancient Greek thinkers Plato and Aristotle, who distinguished knowledge in terms of episteme and doxa.

The terms can most easily be explained if we use the phrase 'immediately perceptible use value to the learner'. If you acquire new knowledge that you perceive as immediately applicable to a situation that you find yourself in or that you have come across in the past, then this could be described as doxa. You might, for example, come across some useful techniques as you read through this book. You may identify an immediate relevance for you in your work. You could, for instance, see the relevance of applying a network analysis to some problem you are facing, or of using a decision tree to help you clarify the feasibility of the options available to you in a decision scenario.

However, in this book you will also find yourself confronted by concepts that you may not see as *immediately* relevant, and such concepts could be described as episteme. This is not to say that they may not be of use to you in some way. You might, for example, find yourself questioning the value of some of the ideas put before you when we deal with issues of philosophical underpinning, as in this chapter. Hopefully, the relevance will become apparent over time.

Pascale and Athos (1982: 105) suggest that

> The inherent preferences of organizations are clarity, certainty and perfection. The inherent nature of human relationships involves ambiguity, uncertainty, and imperfection. How one honours, balances, and integrates the needs of both is the real trick of management.

As one of the aims of this book is to encourage readers to look beyond their existing world view, as suggested in Chapter 1, then this 'trick of management' surely requires the decision-maker to increase his or her 'uncertainty threshold' and embrace ambiguity. From an early age we are taught to recognise and value stability and order; in later life this is reinforced and compounded by having to compete and succeed in organised societies. Little wonder, then, that when we are confronted with ambiguity we try to ignore it or make sense of it in ways that reflect our own perception of the situation rather than the situation itself. We are 'given' a set of skills and a bank of knowledge in order to 'fit in', be it into an organisation, society or group. We thus perpetuate the order around us by means of our active involvement. As Berger and Luckmann (1966: 70) suggest, 'Social order is not biologically given ... Social order exists only as a product of human activity'. We 'become' artists, teachers, doctors, managers and so on, and in doing so, enact and develop the roles that have predated us and will outlive us. Through our primary and secondary socialisation, that is the way we are taught to see the world and our position in it as infants and subsequently as adults. Significantly, we are taught that most things can be explained through science. Those things that cannot be explained are less worthy of study. Hence, the study of the natural sciences takes precedence over the study of psychic phenomena, for instance. At least, this is the situation in 'advanced' societies in the western hemisphere.

Think back to the example of the paradox of the duck-billed platypus in Chapter 1 (Illustration 1.6). Rather than engaging with ambiguity, scientists attempt to create what are often arbitrary classifications to close down issues. Our stance here is that there may be more benefit to be derived, at least occasionally, from trying to be more tolerant of such ambiguity in order to generate new opportunities for learning.

Knowledge as doxa is more readily accepted in principle by learners who, seeing its immediate potential for applicability, may choose to match it with their needs and either accept or reject the new knowledge. The validity of knowledge as episteme is more likely to be queried and rejected outright. For example, when managers are presented with the principles and practice of, say, decision trees, they may easily see their applicability to current situations and may choose to use them or not. Whether they choose to use them or not, managers are still likely to regard decision trees as a legitimately useful device which could be drawn upon if necessary. However, when managers are introduced to concepts rather than techniques, the need to reflect on the new knowledge may be viewed as superfluous if they regard themselves as practically oriented 'doers' rather than as 'thinkers'. Currie (Golding and Currie, 2000: 135) tells the story of an MBA student who asserted, 'Look, I'm too busy trying to manage the core and periphery workers in my company to bother about all these theories.' The tutor pointed out to the student that the notion of core and periphery workers was indeed just such a theory. 'It was "invented" by Charles Handy and others in the 1980s when they were speculating on the future nature of work.'

In everyday life, thinking and doing are often presented as opposites rather than as a continuum. The phrase 'stop and think' identifies and reinforces a polarity rather than a continuum. But is this really the case? Theories of learning, for example, Kolb's (1985) experiential learning cycle, tend to emphasise the cyclical nature of learning by placing emphasis on action and reflection.

5.4 Positivism and phenomenology

Approaches to studying the social sciences are usually differentiated in terms of being either positivistic or phenomenological. Positivist approaches work on assumptions borrowed from the study of natural sciences. They therefore attempt to establish general rules and principles by using systematic techniques based on scientific methods. Much of the research undertaken in decision-making has its roots in positivism. Cognitive psychology, in particular, has attempted to establish general theories for understanding human behaviour. The well-established theories of organisational behaviour are often based on laboratory experimentation, control groups and so forth. As such, they have positivistic orientations.

More recently, there has been a growing amount of research that studies management by looking at managers in their 'natural' context. Researchers are adopting naturalistic modes of inquiry, such as participant observation, in order to understand situations. The underlying assumption here is that people cannot be studied in a similar way to objects. People are not inanimate objects who act on laws of cause and effect. In order to come up with worthwhile findings, we need to find motives as well as actions. Approaches that do this can be described as phenomenological. For example, Pirsig (1991: 55) argues that:

> Objects of scientific study are supposed to hold still. They're supposed to follow the laws of cause and effect in such a way that a given cause will always have a given effect over and over again. Man doesn't do this.

Similarly, Laing (in Gill and Johnson, 1997: 34–5) suggests, 'Persons are distinguished from things in that persons experience the world, whereas things behave in the world'.

The differences between positivism and phenomenology are summarised in Table 5.1.

Table 5.1 A summary of positivism and phenomenology with regard to basic beliefs and methods

	Positivism	Phenomenology
Underlying beliefs:	The world is external and objective Observer is independent Science is value-free	The world is socially constructed and subjective The observer cannot detach him/herself from what is observed Science is driven by human interests
Researcher should:	Focus on facts Look for causality and fundamental laws Reduce phenomena to simplest elements Formulate hypotheses and then test them	Focus on meanings Try to understand what is happening Look at the totality of each situation Develop ideas through induction from data
Preferred methods include:	Operationalising concepts so that they can be measured Taking large samples	Using multiple methods to establish different views of phenomena Small samples investigated in depth or over time

Source: adapted from Easterby-Smith *et al* (1991: 27)

5.5 Assumptions about reality

The next time you use the words 'natural' and 'normal', consider what you really mean in terms of the discussion that follows. The discussion sets out a broader theoretical context of approaches to the social sciences. The study of reality, sometimes called ontology, deals with issues concerning the nature of reality itself. When we say something is 'real', what do we mean? For instance, 'this is a real problem'. Real according to what criteria? What are the alternatives? What would the problem be if it were not real? Unreal? Imagined? Usually when we talk about 'reality' in this way, we are implicitly addressing philosophical questions such as, 'is reality external to the individual or is it the product of an individual's consciousness?' So, 'this is a real problem' may be interpreted as 'the problem is not just in my head; others obviously think there's a problem too'. The difficulty is that the use of the word 'real' in the context of everyday speech is not as rigorously delimited as it is within the context we are discussing it now, so the example could be dismissed as a semantic triviality. Nonetheless, that should not stop us from examining underlying reasons why we might behave and act in particular ways; after all, those ways might not always be appropriate and we might wish to change them.

Ontological issues deal with 'assumptions which concern the very essence of the phenomena under investigation' (Burrell and Morgan, 1979: 1). You should remember that these are theoretical positions, and it is likely that most people would believe that the answer to the question 'is reality a product of our mind or of the world outside it?' lies somewhere in the middle, that reality is the product both of our own consciousness and of our interaction with the external world.

It is fair to say that in western cultures the natural sciences are often advocated as the most valid way of researching social phenomena. This has tended to deflect attention from the idea of human agency. To paraphrase Berger and Luckmann (1966), as humans we are capable of producing a world that we then experience as something other than a human product; or as Morgan (1993) warns us: 'human beings have a knack of getting trapped in webs of their own creation'.

We can start to explore issues concerning reality by identifying different theoretical positions, for example, nominalism and realism. In studying social phenomena, a person with an inherently nominalist view of reality would emphasise the importance of the way in which the mind makes sense of the phenomena (a subjectivist approach). Reality is therefore more likely to be regarded as being socially constructed, that is, as humans we create and sustain structures as a result of our acting in the world. According to Burrell and Morgan (1979), the nominalist queries the notion that there is any 'real' structure to the world; structures are seen as being the creation of human interaction.

Realism, on the other hand, is grounded in an objectivist approach to the study of social sciences, and therefore regards reality as a product of the world external to our mind. For realists, therefore, social structures are hard and unchangeable. There is no doubt that they exist independently of the individual's consciousness. They might argue, for instance, that we are born into a world that predates us, and when we die, structures continue to exist. Burrell and Morgan (1979: 4) conclude that the realist sees the social world in terms of 'an existence which is as hard and concrete as the natural world'. We now turn to the 'problem' of knowledge.

5.6   Assumptions about knowledge

If ontology concerns itself with assumptions about reality, then epistemology deals with issues concerning knowledge, and encourages us to ask such questions as, 'what constitutes truth?', 'what are valid data?', 'what are "hard" data? and 'what are "soft" data?' Have you ever felt the need to produce hard facts to support a course of action you have taken? What does this mean? Does it mean, for example, that you needed to support your statement with some kind of evidence? What kind of evidence? The views of others? Statistics? If you have ever asked such questions, then you have grappled with epistemological issues.

Illustration 5.1   '0.49 capacity' or 'about half full'?

An external management consultant was asked to tackle an organisational problem in an expanding business. His task was to introduce a new computerised management information system to help managers acquire up-to-date information on which to base their decisions. In order to make his task easier he decided to examine the current system of collating stock control information. He chose an employee at random and asked her to explain a particular figure that appeared on her computer screen. The figure read 'Item A....0.49'. The employee explained that the stock item A, a bulk liquid, was currently being held at 50 per cent of its full capacity. When he asked her where she got the figure, he was given the name of an operative on one of the main operating lines, so he decided to walk across to see the relevant person on the line. After a brief introductory chat, the consultant asked, 'So, can you tell me how you come about this 0.49 figure?' The operative led the consultant to a large metal bulk liquid container and, tapping loudly on the sides, claimed, 'It's about half full.'

Activity 5.1

1   What issues does the story in Illustration 5.1 raise with regard to subjectivity, objectivity and the validity of data?

2   Do you think that information can be presented in such a way as to make it seem more convincing? Can you think of some examples?

3   Can the way in which data are presented actually misrepresent the 'real' situation? Can you think of examples?

4   Why might you choose to represent situations in ways which are more certain and precise than you really believe?

The different range of views on epistemology are sometimes presented as a spectrum (Burrell and Morgan, 1979) ranging from phenomenology to positivism. Phenomenological approaches to studying social phenomena are inherently subjectivist.

Phenomenologists argue that people or situations can be understood only from an 'internal frame of reference'. For an individual, that might include a detailed study of the person's biography, experiences and social context. For a group, it might include the detailed study of individuals' relationships and patterns of communicating. The emphasis is on the 'detailed' nature of inquiry, as phenomenology concerns itself with exploring the subjective nature of the social world and, therefore, focuses on the particular rather than the general. Humans are interpretive beings who make sense of themselves and their environment in unique, unpredictable and creative ways. The phenomenologist tries to examine this uniqueness.

Positivist approaches, on the other hand, are grounded in an objectivist view of the social sciences and set out to explain and predict by attempting to establish consistency and causality. For the positivist, generalisation is a virtue rather than a weakness. We might suggest, somewhat mischievously, that for positivists, human beings are obstacles to be overcome in the quest for absolute knowledge.

5.7   Assumptions about human nature

The final set of assumptions deals with issues regarding the relationship between humans and their environment. The answers to questions such as, 'are we conditioned by our environment?', 'can we actually change things around us?', 'are we social puppets or social actors?', might reveal our assumptions about human nature. If we believe that our environment conditions us, then we could be classed as deterministic. Alternatively, if we believe that we change society through our actions, we might be classed as voluntaristic. Determinists therefore regard humans as puppets rather than as actors. Social structures are seen as difficult, if not impossible, to alter, and human behaviour is seen as being determined by the environment. Voluntarists (or proponents of the 'freewill' argument), regard humans as social actors who have the potential and the ability to influence and change their environment. For instance, the phrase 'locus of control' is used to describe the extent to which individuals believe they have a measure of control over what happens to them. Those with an internal locus of control believe that they have a high degree of control over circumstances; those with an external locus believe that what comes to pass is beyond their influence. Locus of control may be determined by psychological and sociological factors. It often manifests itself at a cultural level through, for example, language. The English phrase 'I dropped it' cannot be literally translated into Spanish; it becomes 'it fell from me'. The latter expresses an external locus of control, and the former an internal locus. This is not just a semantic issue; language can express important cultural values, which may have their roots in history, religion and so on.

In summary, an awareness of methodology can help the decision-maker to:

- question underlying assumptions concerning reality and knowledge, in order to
- recognise and question the validity of other data, and
- appreciate the existence of other perspectives and methodologies, so as to
- make judgements based on more informed research, in order to
- take action based on examination of self as well as situation, hopefully leading to
- increased vigilance and thus
- favourable outcomes.

5.8   Induction and deduction

If we attempt to look at particular issues or problems with a view to coming up with findings that can be generalised, we are reasoning and acting inductively. If, for instance, we note from our observations that the female managers we know show good judgement in their decision-making, we might generalise that women generally make good decision-makers. We begin from specific observations and end with a general conclusion. Inductive approaches to research, therefore, are those that move from the particular towards the general. When we come across a female manager who shows poor judgement, we may start to modify our theory.

Deductive approaches begin with the general and work towards the particular. If we begin with a general rule, law, principle or hypothesis, and try to apply or test it in specific contexts, we are reasoning and acting deductively. Taking the example above, if we start from a general view that female managers make good decision-makers, and attempt to test this out in some systematic way, we are acting deductively. We may attempt to set up a hypothesis and test it by applying it to particular situations. This process is illustrated in Figure 5.2.

You may see similarities between the process of induction–deduction and the learning cycle described by Kolb (1985) referred to earlier in this chapter. This is not surprising if we consider that research is a learning process, and learning involves research of some description.

In summary, inductive methodologies are based on:

- analysing subjective accounts of individuals;
- 'getting inside' situations and becoming involved in everyday events;
- grounded theory (theory generated from observation);
- attempting to establish interpretational systems.

Deductive methodologies are based on:

- systematic protocol and methods borrowed from approaches employed in the natural sciences;
- attempting to test hypotheses;

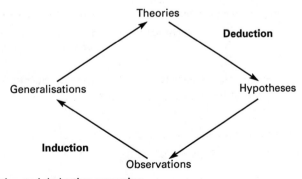

Figure 5.2 Inductive and deductive reasoning

- standards of 'scientific' rigour and standardised research instruments;
- trying to establish explanations and general laws of behaviour;
- quantifying concepts in an attempt to operationalise them.

Bechhofer (in Gill and Johnson, 1997: 2) provides an insight into why it might be difficult to adopt a systematic and sequential approach to research: 'The research process is not a clear-cut sequence of procedures following a neat pattern but a messy interaction between the conceptual and empirical world, deduction and induction occurring at the same time'.

5.9 Nomothetic and ideographic

The way in which we choose to research the social world depends on our assumptions regarding reality, knowledge and human nature and, depending on our assumptions, we may pursue either nomothetic or ideographic ways of researching the world (Table 5.2).

Nomothetic approaches stress the importance of rigorous, systematic protocol and scientific techniques. They have their roots in the natural sciences. The setting and testing of hypotheses are more likely to be regarded as valid, and greater emphasis is placed on quantifiable data than on subjective accounts.

Ideographic approaches to social science assume that you can understand social phenomena only by acquiring first-hand knowledge of the subject you are studying. A great deal of emphasis is placed on getting close to the subject, for example through examination of a person's biographical data. It becomes important to 'get inside' a situation and become involved in it in order to come up with a detailed account of events.

Table 5.2 A comparison of nomothetic and ideographic methods

Nomothetic methods emphasise	Ideographic methods emphasise
1. Deduction	Induction
2. Explanation via analysis of causal relationships and explanation by covering-laws (etic)	Explanation of subjective meaning systems and explanation by understanding (emic)
3. Generation and use of quantitative data	Generation and use of qualitative data
4. Use of various controls, physical or statistical, to allow the testing of hypotheses	Commitment to research in everyday settings, to allow access to, and minimise reactivity among the subjects of research
5. Highly structured research methodology to ensure replicability of 1, 2, 3 and 4	Minimum structure to ensure 2, 3 and 4 (and as a result of 1)

◄───►

| Laboratory experiments | Quasi-experiments | Surveys | Action research | Ethnography |

Source: adapted from Gill and Johnson, 1997: 37

5.10 Methods

Although we stated at the outset of this chapter that we would be focusing on methodology rather than on individual methods, we feel that it would be appropriate at this juncture to say something about some methods used in phenomenological research. We do so for two reasons. First, such is the pervasiveness of positivistic methods in common usage, that we may safely assume that most readers will have some understanding of the nature of those methods. Second, and more importantly, the methods which follow are particularly appropriate for decision-makers to have at their disposal, given the potential for such methods to help get 'inside' situations and to encourage the reader to become a reflective practitioner. What follows is far from a comprehensive exposition of the chosen methods. Our intention is to encourage further reading (see the list at the end of chapter) by illustrating the relevance of particular methods for practising managers.

5.10.1 Managers as action researchers

Management is often regarded as synonymous with action. Managers spend the majority of their time making or implementing decisions through the use of verbal interventions. It seems particularly relevant, therefore, that managers can be seen as action researchers in their own organisations. Action research is a form of organisational development that involves a process of systematic data collection, reflection and action planning. In essence, action research entails some form of planned intervention in a situation by an organisational agent, for example a manager or an external consultant. The effects of this intervention are subsequently monitored in some way and critically evaluated to see if the chosen course of action has produced the expected outcomes. The difference between action research and just managing is one of awareness and rigorous application of method. The argument is that managers can make more effective interventions by knowing more about the research options available to them, as well as about the theoretical assumptions on which they are based.

Theory has an important function in this process. It may be useful to differentiate its uses in two ways: in terms of our being theory-dependent and theory-laden. As decision-makers, we are:

- *theory-dependent*, because we create, apply and evaluate theories all the time. We act on speculation and explanations of phenomena, often in unconscious ways;

- *theory-laden*, because our observations are influenced by our prior theories and values. These values, together with our knowledge of theories, influence what we see and the value we attach to what we see.

5.10.2 Managers as ethnographers

As well as action researchers, managers may also be regarded as organisational ethnographers. Fetterman (1989: 11) describes ethnography as 'the art and science of describing a group or culture'. He goes on to compare the task of an ethnographer to that of an investigative reporter who interviews people, records events, and makes some kind of judgement about the events that have been reported. The difference is that ethnographers concern themselves with routines of everyday life rather than the unusual. Ethnography is in essence anthropology, and involves using techniques such as participant observation in a mainly inductive and naturalistic way. The concepts and practices of ethnography are particularly relevant if we accept the view of managers as a subculture, that is 'a social collectivity whose members share a set of implicit and explicit meanings acquired through innumerable communicative exchanges' (Gowler and Legge, in Earle, 1985: 198).

Ethnographers argue that the notion of a neutral, detached observer is a myth and, therefore, they should explicitly acknowledge their own role in the research rather than deny it. As a result of acknowledging bias, what was initially a fundamental problem – i.e. researcher bias – is turned into an opportunity to exploit active participation in situations as a means of generating a rich stream of data. As stated earlier, the main advantage of ethnography is that it takes place in natural settings, that is, ethnographers are part of the everyday settings in which they are researching. This has the advantage of reducing the researcher's possible impact on those being researched.

According to Sapir (Hawkes, 1977: 125), 'every cultural pattern and every single act of social behaviour involves communication in either an explicit or implicit sense'. An ethnographer attempts to explore this implicit sense by examining the use of signs, myth and language, and any possible contradictions between the implicit and explicit messages which are conveyed to organisational members via the 'vehicles' of signs, myth and language. Edgren (in Turner, 1990: 174) suggests that we let what he calls 'dead things', such as buildings, colours, interiors etc., send their messages to us. The ethnographer examines these 'dead things' as symbols that often take on a powerful role as *signifiers* of meaning to the extent that they acquire agency. That is, they may well be inanimate objects but they may influence people's actions. The meanings we attach to these signifiers are referred to as the *signified*. So, for example, an office chair can be regarded at a practical level as a piece of furniture that allows its occupant to undertake his or her work in comfort. However, it may also be a conveyer of alternative meanings, for example a symbol of its occupant's status relative to others, depending on its quality, comfort and appearance.

Another aim of the ethnographer may be to explore the ways in which we are controlled or impelled to act as a result of the myths that surround us. You may think of the word 'myth' as odd in this context, believing it to be more appropriate to studies of ancient Greece and Rome. Barthes (Hawkes, 1988: 131) considered myth to be 'the complex system of images and beliefs which a society constructs in order to sustain and authenticate its sense of its own being: i.e. the very fabric of its system of meaning'. When considered in light of Barthes' interpretation, it becomes apparent that myths are a common, everyday phenomenon.

We also internalise reality as an objective phenomenon through the medium of language that, according to Berger and Luckmann (1967: 153), 'constitutes the most important content and the most important instrument of socialisation'.

Reality is created through language. Language, whilst often regarded as neutral, can actually be regarded as a potent political device. In this sense, political refers to the degree to which we are influenced, through linguistic expression, to accept particular perspectives on a person, issue or event.

If we have no wider theoretical or experiential reference points by which to analyse everyday situations, then we are more likely to accept them as common sense and beyond question. If, however, we begin to address such concepts as power and symbolism, gender and power relationships, or we have external knowledge from other cultures that offers us other examples of social organisation, then we begin to locate our perceptions and experiences in a wider framework. Knowledge offers us the capability to widen our perspectives on life and sometimes we may begin to question what we have previously regarded as normal.

Ethnography emphasises the idea of the researcher as theory-builder, not just theory-consumer. We are all theory-builders, but theory has come to be defined in such narrow terms that we come to see ourselves as practical people who have little time for theory.

Summary

Theory often carries pejorative connotations for many managers. Our actions are theory dependent; we are all theory-builders whether we recognise it or not. And we are all theory-laden; we carry with us a set of assumptions about life, and we make sense of situations in certain ways. Our actions may be determined by theories we may not even realise we hold. We have argued that our way of seeing the world may be determined by our assumptions regarding the nature of reality, knowledge and human nature. All of these can determine our methodology when making sense of ourselves, our role, and our interactions with others, our organisation, and the wider environment.

Research is a fundamentally important, yet understated, element of the management decision-making process. We have tried to show that in order to improve decision-making skills, managers cannot afford to regard research as the exclusive domain of students or academics.

Decision diary

Think about a recent decision you have made. What sort of data did you rely on? Where did the data come from? How were the data generated? Did you think about the nature/quality of the data at the time or did you simply accept them and act upon them? On reflection, how suitable/reliable was the data? Does this analysis make you feel any differently about the decision made?

References

Barthes, R. (1973) *Mythologies*. St Albans: Paladin.

Bell, S. and Reedy, P. (1999) *Organisational Decision-making Study Guides*. Hull: University of Lincolnshire and Humberside.

Berger, P.L. and Luckmann, T. (1966) *The Social Construction of Reality*. Harmondsworth: Penguin.

Burrell, G. and Morgan, G. (1979) *Sociological Paradigms and Organisational Analysis*. London: Heinemann.

Cooke, S. and Slack, N. (1991) *Making Management Decisions*, 2nd edition. Hemel Hempstead: Prentice Hall International.

Denzin, N.K. (1989) *Interpretive Interactionism*. London: Sage.

Earle, M.J. (ed.) (1985) *Perspectives on Management*. Oxford: Oxford University Press.

Easterby-Smith, M., Thorpe, R. and Lowe, A. (1991) *Management Research: An Introduction*. London: Sage.

Fetterman, D.M. (1989) *Ethnography*. London: Sage.

Gill, J. and Johnson, P. (1997) *Research Methods for Managers*, 2nd edition. London: Paul Chapman Publishing.

Golding, D. and Currie, D. (2000) *Thinking About Management*. London: Routledge.

Handy, C.B. (1985) *Understanding Organisations*. Harmondsworth: Penguin.

Hawkes, T. (1988) *Structuralism and Semiotics*. London: Routledge.

Howard, K. and Sharp, J.A. (1983) *The Management of a Student Research Project*. Aldershot: Gower,

Kolb, D.A. (1985) *Experiential Learning: Experience as the Source of Learning and Development*. Englewood Cliffs. NJ: Prentice Hall.

Morgan, G. (1993) *Imaginization*. Newbury Park, CA: Sage.

Pascale, R.T. and Athos, A.G. (1982) *The Art of Japanese Management*. Harmondsworth: Penguin.

Pirsig, R. (1991) *Lila. An Inquiry into Morals*. London: Bantam.

Turner, B.A. (ed.) (1990) *Organizational Symbolism*. Berlin: De Gruyter.

Further reading

Argyris, C. and Schön, D.A. (1978) *Organizational Learning: A Theory of Action Perspective*. Reading, MA: Addison Wesley.

Blumer, H. (1969) *Symbolic Interactionism*. Englewood Cliffs , NJ: Prentice Hall.

Bryman, A. (ed.) (1988) *Doing Research in Organisations*. London: Routledge.

Gagliardi, P. (1991) *Symbols and Artefacts: Views of the Corporate Landscape*. Berlin: De Gruyter.

Morgan, G. (ed.) (1983) *Beyond Method*. London: Sage.

There are a growing number of up-to-date textbooks that concentrate on specific methods. Sage Publications, in particular, has a series of research methods texts that provide detailed accounts of different, practical modes of inquiry.

Alvesson, M. (1999) *Reflexive Methodology: New Vistas for Qualitative Research.* London: Sage.

Black, T. (1998) *Doing Quantitative Research in the Social Sciences.* London: Sage.

Du Gay, P. (1996) *Doing Cultural Studies: The Story of the Sony Walkman.* London: Sage.

Fink, A. (1995) *The Survey Kit.* London: Sage.

Firlej, M. and Heltens, D. (1991) *Knowledge Elicitation. A Practical Handbook.* Englewood Cliffs, NJ: Prentice Hall.

Georgakopoulu, A. (1997) *Discourse Analysis: An Introduction.* London: Sage.

Hall, S., Janes, L., MacKay, H. and Negus, K. (1997) *Doing Cultural Studies: The Story of the Sony Walkman.* London: Sage.

Have, P. (1998) *Doing Conversation Analysis: A Practical Guide.* London: Sage.

Hine, C. (2000) *Virtual Ethnography.* London: Sage.

Kendall, G. and Wickham, G. (1998) *Using Foucault's Methods.* London: Sage.

Morgan, D. (1998) *Focus Group Kit.* London: Sage.

Reissman, C. (1993) *Narrative Analysis.* London: Sage.

Silverman, D. (1999) *Doing Qualitative Research: A Practical Handbook.* London: Sage.

Stringer, E. (1996) *Action Research: A Handbook for Practitioners.* London: Sage.

Glossary

Doxa: knowledge that may be viewed as easily applicable in practice and of immediate use value. For example, instructions on how to boil water using a kettle may be regarded as a doxa.

Episteme: knowledge that may not be seen to have immediate, practical applicable use value. May be regarded as 'theoretical'.

Epistemology: the exploration and examination of issues concerning the nature of knowledge.

Nominalism: the view of reality as the product of individual consciousness.

Ontology: the exploration and examination of issues concerning the nature of reality.

Phenomenology: a social science perspective which regards the study of social phenomena as subjective.

Positivism: a social science perspective which regards the study of social phenomena as objective.

Realism: the view of reality as the product of the social world outside individual consciousness.

CHAPTER 6 Systems analysis

6.1 Introduction

Where lies the land to which the ship would go?
Far, far ahead, is all her seamen know.
And where is the land she travels from. Away,
Far, far behind, is all that they can say.

– A.H. Clough (1862)

As the poem implies, some on board the vessel do not know where they are. Hopefully, the captain knows to some extent the purpose of the voyage and the ultimate destination. It is only a recent phenomenon that an ocean going vessel, out of sight of land, knows exactly (to within 30 metres) where it is in relation to the rest of the world. Until the development of satellite navigational systems, navigators had to rely on a number of tools, such as charts, tide tables and compasses to measure direction, logs to measure speed, and sextants to record longitude and latitude, in order to calculate where they were. Once they knew where they were they could then set a course for home, the decision, in this case, of the direction to take. It is a repeated, short-lived decision, hence justifies automation. A similar process will be undertaken on a regular basis until the ship enters port.

Many decisions have potential longer-term consequences, in areas not immediately obvious. For example, a car manufacturer could decide to introduce a low pollution electric car, and as an unintentional result encourage greater awareness of environmental issues. This could lead to an increase in the use of public transport and bicycles. The sale of all cars might reduce and the car firm might then be forced to make something else or go out of business. Thus the effects of decisions may stray beyond the initially defined boundaries. In the example, a number of systems interact to produce the final event.

People are drawn towards rational approaches to decisions. Rational in this case means thinking that you are able to understand the decision context and thinking you can justify the measures taken to resolve it. Managers faced with a problem may be attracted by a 'how to fix' solution, the rationale being that if it has worked in the past it should work now. As such, when they have felt it necessary, managers have traditionally sought advice from business analysts brought in to implement technologies. Traditionally this implementation has always involved some elements of evaluation analysis and modelling that predict, optimise or simulate the effects of alternative decision scenarios. Historically this has meant that the 'management scientist' has observed processes, recorded quantitative and qualitative data, built and tested models and then used the analysis to advise the manager. The methods of analysis have grown in sophistication in response to problems of validity and applicability. Recently it has been appreciated that this analysis, although useful, needs to reflect to some extent the whole system within which the model has been created.

Systems Theory has evolved from an evaluation of various philosophical views of the world in order to attempt to create a way in which we can describe problem situations, with the ultimate object of improving things.

This chapter examines the nature of systems and how system analysis helps with decision-making.

6.2 Systems concepts

The *Oxford English Dictionary* defines a system as:

> a complex whole, a set of connected things or parts, an organised body of material or immaterial things.

It also gives a physiological definition as:

> a set of organs in the body with a common structure or function, e.g. the digestive system.

Common usage of the term 'system' normally has such a contextual element. We may talk of the telephone system, political system, digestive system or solar system. The phrase implicitly relates to the component parts; so when we talk of the telephone system, we may mean the wires, handsets, the communications software, the exchange, the delays or bad connections, the geographical presence and so on. The component parts we are aware of relate to our understanding of the system being described. Hence, when we use the term 'system' it has two very distinct elements: (i) the actual system and (ii) the part of the system we are aware of (and hence, for the individual, 'the system').

Systems can be simple or complex, closed or more typically and relevantly for our purposes, open. If people are involved in a decision-making process the system is going to be complex, although the problems to resolve might be fairly trivial.

Closed systems are characterised by being generally unaffected by the environment they operate within, for example, an engine or, under normal circumstances, the set of organs in a body (these can only be considered closed for short periods, i.e. both will fail if they are not maintained). They do not receive anything from, or give anything to, the environment beyond that within which they are operating. The engine, given an energy source, will operate in a predetermined fashion, determined by the configuration of the mechanical and electrical components, until the energy source runs out. As the energy source decreases, the system tends towards *entropy*, and unless the energy source is renewed the system will tend to operate erratically until it ceases to function and its organisation breaks down. For example, a music box will happily roll out a tune, until the spring winds down. In its final moments, notes become jerky until it finally stops. In reality, there are no truly closed systems; it is a theoretical concept. Although it can be argued that many organisations (or groups) are autopoietic, that is they create their own formative environment. Aspects of autopoiesis exist in organisations which show little signs of learning – 'we do things this way here'. This statement becomes closer to the truth with short time periods, i.e. organisations take time to assimilate changes in the environment. Changes, and responses to the environment, are restricted by a variety of mechanisms within a firm.

Open systems are subject to linear and non-linear feedback mechanisms. In the game of golf, the linear effect can be expressed in Newtonian mechanics. When the club strikes the ball the resulting motion will be a function sum of the respective momentums. Non-linear components reflect the variations in friction of the air and grass that will affect the final position of the ball. In an organisation wishing to improve quality, linear effects would be observed when implementing more quality checks to reduce the number of defects reaching the customer; non-linear effects would occur when deciding on a training programme to educate staff in total quality management.

In an organisation, energy is all of the inputs needed for the organisation to survive. The simplest of rational systems models, the *input–transformation–output* model (shown in Figure 6.1) illustrates these inputs. This model is extremely useful as a first stage in operational analysis as a simple mechanism for identifying the main parameters within an operational decision scenario.

Systems can be *discrete* or *continuous*. A computer is an example of a discrete system, it is on or off, processing discrete bits of digital information or not. The need for repairing a building is based on a continuous system, the effect of wind, sun, rain and frost having a continuous effect. Although a computer has discrete elements, on/off, document empty/completed, it approximates to a continuous system if we measure activities at specific periods. Every 15 minutes will see a page added to the document, every 15 seconds three words. Similarly, a continuous process could approximate to a discrete process. When describing the process of deterioration, we would measure the process at discrete points in time. If we record the deterioration of a road every year, we will see big changes in its state. If we record the same information every day, we get closer to the continuous deterioration that takes place.

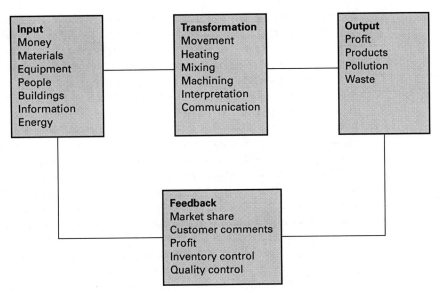

Figure 6.1 Input–Transformation–Output model

Most problem situations have a number of points in common. Often they deal with a decision, such as a need to achieve a set of goals or improve current levels of achievement. The answers to a problem are not always obvious, the information required to make the decision not available and all of the consequences of the decision may not be known.

Illustration 6.1 Severn Bearings

Severn Bearings manufactures roller bearings for large industrial and construction plant and fairground rides. Located in Sheffield, it has recently been acquired by an American company, to increase European capacity. The managing director, who is French, has responsibility for the Sheffield firm and his parent company located near Paris. The acquisition came about after Severn ran into cash flow problems, which were caused by poor productivity and high variable costs. The overall market for bearings is increasing (more fairground rides and world construction equipment), but Severn is failing to meet customer quality requirements and productivity improvements, hence its market share is in danger of decreasing.

The bearings are produced through a number of processes that include shaping steel discs, heat treatment and assembly of ball bearings and housings. Each machine is manned by skilled staff and powered by electricity and compressed air. Materials are moved by overhead cranes and forklift trucks and are stored in raw materials and finished goods storage sheds, before being shipped to the customer.

Activity 6.1

1. Describe Severn Bearings (Illustration 6.1) in terms of the input–transformation–output model.

2. Suggest ways in which Severn Bearings might adjust the system it is operating within.

The system is the environment within which these decisions are made. Relatively simple systems are those within the human body. Such systems are well researched and information is available on, for example, the short- and long-term effects of alcohol consumption at certain levels on the human body.

In order to have a successful (or continuing) operation, the value of the outputs must be greater than, or at least equal to, the value of the inputs. In the case of a for-profit firm, there must be sufficient profit to reinvest for continued operation. In the case of a public or voluntary organisation, there must be sufficient wealth creation to justify political or public subsidy. A manager needs to understand the relationships between the inputs and outputs, for example, to be confident that revenue exceeds costs. If the company can increase the number of sales, it may increase the amount of profit. In this case, we need to identify the market requirements then ensure the production system can meet these at a cost that warrants production. This would mean analysing the production system to determine where inefficiencies exist and act to resolve them. Inefficiencies take the form of quantifiably measured aspects such as machine breakdown, or qualitative factors such as employee motivation and morale.

Organisational and social systems are complex, with many subsystems, and interactions with other systems. A hospital is an open system interacting with its environment. It continues to exist by maintaining a cycle of input–transformation–output (Figure 6.2).

Feedback may be applied in a number of ways, including:

- Evaluation – setting objectives and evaluating the achievement of them, resulting in corrective action, or the resetting of objectives if the original ones are no longer valid.
- Negative and positive feedback.
- Research to identify the required outputs and social expectations.

A possible source of confusion is the range of systems-based methodologies that can be applied to describe and evaluate problems. We can express the issues as they relate to the degree of openness (how many parameters affect the decision) and discreteness (how easy are the parameters to measure) of the system compared with the approach in terms of soft and hard analysis, as shown in Figure 6.3 and explored later in the chapter.

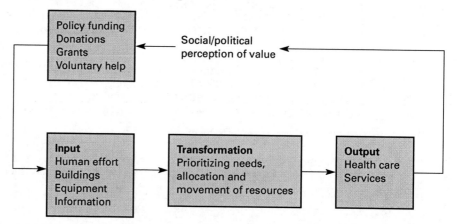

Figure 6.2 A hospital as a system

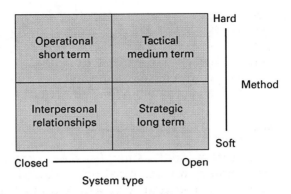

Figure 6.3 System characteristics

Boulding (1956) in his seminal paper provides a 'skeleton' upon which the 'flesh and blood' of all systems can be fitted. In this paper, systems are classed according to their complexity. This is set out in Table 6.1.

Table 6.1 A hierarchy of real-world complexity

Level	Characteristics	Examples (concrete or abstract)	Relevant disciplines
1. Structures and frameworks	Static	A rock, a house	Description, verbal or visual in all disciplines
2. Clock-works	Predetermined motion	Clocks, machines, the galaxy	Physics, classical natural science
3. Control mechanisms	Closed-loop control	Thermostats, homeostasis mechanisms in organisms	Control theory, cybernetics
4. Open systems	Structurally self-maintaining	Flames, biological cells	Theory of metabolism
5. Lower organisms	Organised whole with functional parts, 'predetermined' growth, reproduction	Plants	Botany
6. Animals	A brain to guide total behaviour	Birds and beasts	Zoology
7. Man	Self-consciousness, knowledge of knowledge, symbolic language	Human beings	Biology, psychology
8. Socio-cultural systems	Roles, communication, culture	Families, clubs, nations	History, sociology, anthropology, behavioural science
9. Transcendental systems	Inescapable unknowables	The idea of god	?

Notes
Properties emerge at each level.
Complexity increases the higher the level. It is more difficult to predict behaviour. There is an increasing dependence on unprogrammed decisions.
Lower-level systems are found in higher-level systems; properties emerge at each new level (holism).

Source: after Boulding (1956) and Checkland (1993)

6.3 Systems theory

Systems theory has evolved from the philosophy underpinning scientific research. At the core of the methodology are two sets of ideas: emergence and hierarchy, and communication and control.

6.3.1 Emergence and hierarchy

We can study any situation, from an atomic study of cellular DNA, through to the workings of a multinational organisation. At all levels, properties will emerge. As we increase the complexity of the study these properties will alter or be affected by the hierarchy within which they exist. For example, we can describe the molecules that constitute a chain of DNA, which gains the added property of being a code when all the molecules are together. Jacob (1974) illustrates this from a biological perspective:

> Every object that biology studies is a system of systems. Being part of a high-order system itself, it sometimes obeys rules that cannot be deduced simply by analysing it. This means that each level of organization must be considered with reference to adjacent levels.

6.3.2 Communication and control

It is only comparatively recently that control has been the subject of scientific investigation. Cybernetics (from the Greek kubernetes meaning steersman) deals with the way in which elements within a system interrelate and react to communications. Many factors are connected with the information exchanges. The basic ones are that a *message* is coded to produce a *signal* which is transmitted along a *channel*, which induces some *noise*, to arrive eventually at a *decoder*, which regenerates the original *message*. Our concern in decision-making is largely centred around the efficiency of this process.

Activity 6.2	Write down as many systems that you as a person, or your organisation, is involved in or interacts with.

Did you get as far as the education system, the political system or even the solar system in your answer to Activity 6.2? Daellenbach (1994: 27) describes the concept of a system as:

> The crucial ingredients of a system are its *components*, the *relationships* between the components, the *behaviour*, or the *activities* of the *transformation process* of the system, its *environment*, the *inputs* from the environment, the *outputs* to the environment, and the *special interest of the observer*.

As Activity 6.2 suggests, systems analysis would become difficult and meaningless, unless we define a boundary to the system.

The components, or entities, are the things within the systems, the people (customers, employees, suppliers), the machines, the paper, the electronic information and everything else that has some effect on the system. The relationships, how these entities affect each other, are vital for understanding a system, but often difficult to recognise or quantify. Activities describe what the entities do: the porter reads the information, and signals the train to leave at 4.26pm; the transformation process in this case is interpreting information and getting a cargo from A to B. The environment is, in some ways, the area where we need to draw our boundaries. The environment includes the climate of the firm, the influence of pressure groups and the whims of politicians. From the eclectic mix of stakeholders inherent in many operations, we need to make some judgement about the degree to which they affect the system for the impending decision or programme of actions. The boundary is therefore both dynamic and conceptual. We shift our boundaries to include or exclude components and entities. We do this when we focus on particular subsystems within the whole.

We can relate the 'special interest of the observer' to two factors: the person's *Weltanschauung* ('world view' – illustrated later) and the observer's motivation for describing the systems. Checkland (1993) lists three interests: curiosity, problem solving and design. It the latter two that are our primary concern. Decision-makers use soft systems analysis (SSA) to gain a clearer understanding of the nature of the system so that they can implement some change to it.

Activity 6.3

The local authority for the area in which you work has decided to stimulate the use of public transport, bicycles and motorcycles to reduce the level of road congestion. In the future, greater restrictions on city centre parking will be introduced; roads will have more space devoted to cycle and bus lanes.

For the above decision identify the various groups and individuals who will be affected and the possible consequences of the development. Try to define the parameters under the italicised headings within Daellenbach's definition above. A suggested answer can be found in Appendix 1 to this chapter.

6.3.3 Feedback and resonance

There are many industries and systems that are adapting in response to the environment. Systems that are not adapting, or which respond in the 'wrong' way, tend to go out of business. Businesses that follow the 'me too' approach along a redundant evolutionary path are also likely to suffer. But how were the dinosaurs to know that a meteor would strike the Earth and wipe out their species? And in this case it was probably best not to know anyway. However, such radical environmental turbulence is rare for business systems.

Dynamics is the study of system changes over time; it examines the nature of the feedback processes that shape the way the firm develops. This is somewhat different from the most common approach of evaluating system change, which is one of *comparative statics* (comparing one snapshot with another and noting the changes); this is the practice that occurs with *benchmarking*. In dynamics we try to determine the environmental forces and their rate of evolution.

Feedback systems are difficult to map. Figure 6.4 illustrates the feedback between three systems. These could be individual people in a meeting, or organisational responses to world environmental changes, for example the interaction of three people in a meeting discussing quality problems at work. Supervisor A accuses worker B of being lax. Manager C responds by warning B of the dangers to the firm of poor work. B responds by accusing A of not informing C of their concerns about a certain product. C responds by dismissing B from the meeting and castigates A for poor communication.

A firm decided to open a new facility in a new location; this provided fertile ground for rumour about the long-term viability of the existing facilities. This led to an increasing level of publicity regarding this issue. If existing customers disseminate this uncertainty to potential new customers or agents who begin to believe that there is a risk of closure, then rumours of closure might become a self-fulfilling prophecy. In reality the old facilities did close but as part of a new build in the same location.

Rapid technological change in the latter half of the twentieth century is having a levelling effect across all cultures and a profound effect on humanity. It is marked by innovations in production processes in agriculture, manufacturing and services and the introduction of information and communications technologies.

In parallel with the technology revolution has been the emergence of multinational and global corporations. Companies such as Shell, Microsoft, General Motors, Du Pont, Mitsubishi and Nestlé have power bases rivalling that of some governments.

If we add to this the changing environmental, religious and political concerns of the world, we find in many cases that the simple cause and effect model (the input–transformation–output model) of decision-making cannot cope with the complexities of many of today's decisions.

Systems theory provides an approach to decision-making that is holistic. Rather than treat problems as if they are associated with a subset of the system, such as a functional group, systems theory relates the problem to the bigger pic-

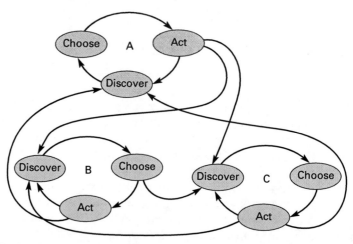

Figure 6.4 Feedback between three systems

Source: adapted from R. Stacey, 1996

ture, includes qualitative and quantitative observations and includes a dimension of time. Many problems are labelled as operational, financial or organisational. For example, quality problems are labelled as an operational issue, whereas the solution may be a combination of personnel, operational and financial strategies. Many problems are dealt with over short timespans, with no account of the history, or *dynamics* of the situation. Many problems once solved are forgotten – we forget about the problem and move on to the next, without learning, or feeding back into the system the nature of the problem, *cybernetics*.

Organisational cybernetics is a systems approach to understanding how systems interrelate, by attempting to map the feedback loops that work within the system. The theory attempts to describe how companies learn, using negative feedback loops to determine where they went wrong in the past. For example, the demand for a product depends not only on customer behaviour but also on how the firm manages price and quality. The firm affects the customer, who then affects the firm. Management style will affect success, but success will affect management style. Cybernetics does not attempt to identify the nature of the feedback loops, it assumes they are there, in a 'black box', working to keep the firm in the right direction.

6.3.4 Self-organisation and autopoietic systems

The term *autopoiesis* (self-acting and formative, or self-production and replication) has its foundations in the field of neurobiology but has been a theme of biological studies for many years. Varela (1984) defines an autopoietic organisation as:

> a network of productions of components which (i) participate recursively in the same network of productions of components, and (ii) realize the network of productions as a unity in the space in which the components exist.

In other words, a system which works together to produce the same outputs time after time. Krogh and Roos (1995) identify four properties of such a system:

1 *Autonomy* – the system is self-governing.

2 *Simultaneously open and closed* – the system is aware of external conditions, but not directly influenced by them.

3 *Self-referential* – the system learns from internal rather than external processes.

4 *Observing* – the system surveys the environment, but does not draw from it.

Within this framework, knowledge becomes self-generating. Words and phrases have specific meanings within the originating system (unlike jargon which is specific to a particular process, these terms may well be in common usage, but with different meanings). In essence, what individuals and outside entities bring into the firm is absorbed, but not acted upon. The system takes note and creates its own mechanism for the input; the input does nothing to affect the immediate nature of the system. Information (and knowledge) is generated within the organisation. In physical terms like silicon rubber, impenetrable when struck, but flowing when left to its own devices.

Conversely, *allopoietic* (all formative) systems react to inputs from the environment. Every part of an allopoietic system interacts with the environment, but to a central purpose – the benefit of the allopoietic system itself. Ideally the system works in synergy and is symbiotic within its environment, rather like a parasite.

We can draw parallels with the terms 'allopoietic' and 'autopoietic' within business. Decisions are often made more on grounds of internal dimensions: politics, personalities and power (autopoietic), than on rational and ethical responses to the environment (allopoietic), internal rather than external inputs (this is illustrated in Figure 6.5). For example, lately it has been fashionable for firms to restructure and downsize themselves, at least on paper. Sometimes this results in displaced staff. In an allopoietic firm these people would be either made redundant or, if they have a continuing useful purpose, found new jobs. In an autopoietic system, change is unlikely in the first place; if undertaken, these people would not be made redundant, but new positions created for them regardless of organisational benefits, negating one of the reasons for the restructuring in the first place.

It can be suggested that an internal referencing process that monitors and reacts to the 'health' of the system influences the continued existence of systems: systems are self-referential. We, as individuals, learn from experience; organisations (implicitly a collection of individuals) can be assumed to do likewise. Hence if we assume that an organisation is autopoietic in nature, the only way it can be studied is from an internal frame of reference. Although external observers may experience and record the outputs from such a system, they are not able to determine the mechanisms that produced them.

For organisations, similarity occurs in the use of language: manufacturing industry talks of capacity, bottlenecks, cost, reliability and value added; education talks in ratios, performance, duties and responsibilities; and services talk of queues, customer service, employee scheduling and cleanliness. Attempts to change (or introduce) new terms prompt legitimate inquiry into the relevance and meanings of the terms to enable new shared understandings (or misunderstandings) to occur. Bottery (1994) offers insights into this when comparing business and educational management, from the perspective of an education tutor. For example, when comparing commercial and non-profit organisations, he suggests that 'commercial organisations have a limited number of goals and constituencies to which they must answer; non-profit organisations have numerous and conflicting goals and constituencies' (Bottery 1994: 130), which is debatable.

Self-organised criticality is concerned with system change towards a critical state between order and disorder. Whereas deterministic chaos (Chapter 3) tends to

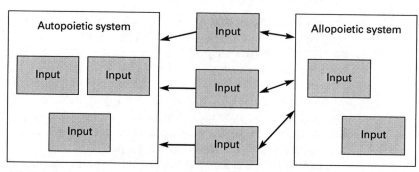

Figure 6.5 Autopoietic and allopoietic systems

start at the beginning of a chaotic process, self-organised criticality explores the mechanisms and principles governing the final critical state within a system that has the capability to organise behaviour. Bak *et al.* (1988: 356) define self-organised criticality as being where 'the system naturally evolves to the state [of self-organisation] without detailed specifications of the initial starting conditions (i.e. the critical state is an attractor of the system)'.

Self-organised systems assume that weak or low-dimensional chaotic forces govern systems behaviour. This is a common phenomenon in nature and one might expect social systems to exhibit similar behaviour. An analogy comes from the world of simulated biological systems. Ray (1992) describes the Tierra simulation. In this simulation, a computer organism is created. This creature lives and duplicates itself within the boundaries of part of the computer memory. The creature is programmed to undergo random mutations and is destroyed by a terminator after a certain period. As the simulation is run for some time the population ebbs and falls according to mutations which initially avoid the terminator, but are later counterbalanced by mutations that are parasitic and superparasitic, rather like a large organisation.

As decisions imply change, then an awareness of factors affecting the boundaries of the organisation are important, should we wish to break through them. As our organisations step towards a new market they may not simply be hampered by the external factors of that market, but also by the internal pressures that seek stability.

Systems theory provides an analytical and philosophical framework for describing the nature of a system from dynamic and cybernetic perspectives, acknowledging that objective and subjective, known and unknown parameters influence the way the system is evolving.

6.4   Research and diagnosis

How well we evaluate a problem or come to a good decision is related to the abilities of the decision-maker to diagnose the situation and agree parameters for good and bad. These abilities are influenced by numerous factors, some of which we return to in later chapters:

- the time available
- the culture
- the person
- the cost and benefit

6.4.1   Time

The time devoted to problem solving depends on the perceived importance and priority of the problem. Managers often deal with symptoms and strive to create short-term fixes. This is a valid strategy: why waste time investigating a problem if an educated guess resolves it? If the problem recurs or patently affects performance over a longer period then greater efforts to resolve it are initiated. However, often no time is available to progress beyond the 'fix it' stage, because another 'fix it' problem has arisen. More seriously, the 'fix it' stage often covers up underlying deficiencies that really do need resolving.

6.4.2 The culture

We address the issue of culture in Chapter 13. It may be the case that culture inhibits problem solving. For example, some managers may thrive on troubleshooting and solving short-term crises, hence not very much care about permanent solutions. They may be rewarded for such behaviour. It is in these managers' interest not to look too deeply into the initial cause of the problem. In extreme cases, managers may consciously or unconsciously create problems in order to manage them. Alternatively, the firm may have a climate of fear, discouraging staff from reporting problems, as a result problems maybe swept under the carpet.

6.4.3 The person

There are four authors of this book. When deciding to write it, each of us may have made the decision based on a different outlook on life. The first may have seen it as a way to increase his personal wealth (the materialist). The second (the educationalist) may see it as a way to pass on his knowledge to a wider audience. The third may see the book as an opportunity to develop skills in writing (the creative artist). Finally, the fourth may see it as a way to increase his power in the organisation (the politician). However, it is more likely that for all of them a combination of factors will be evident. To analyse a system we must be aware of our own perspective and prejudices, but also be aware that others are looking at the same system, but interpreting it in a different way. To make matters complicated, decisions often have multiple objectives and seek to achieve a variety of outcomes, some of which may be mutually exclusive. Most businesspeople would seek to maximise profit, whilst taking account of stakeholders' interests.

Bias is inherent in many of our conscious and unconscious actions. When faced with a decision-making situation we will draw upon our experiences to help guide us in our approach to the situation. Our world view or *Weltanschauung* associates our perceptions of the system with our position within it and our prior conditioning. Any observations are likely to be limited and possibly flawed, unless we are self-aware of our biases and preconditioning. Determining this world view will also play an important part in defining the performance evaluators used to measure the system performance. For the philosopher Wittgenstein, language is limited by thought, and unsayable things exist. What we understand from propositions comes from an analysis of the context, and this analysis itself is limited by our own perception of reality.

> A police officer approached someone late at night who was crawling round the base of a streetlight. 'What are you doing?', he asked. 'I dropped a coin over there,' said the person, pointing to the middle of the road. 'Why are you looking here for it then?', replied the police officer. *'Because this is where the light is'*, came the response.

Our *Weltanschauung* is based, in part, on our interpretation of the information we have; the more information, the greater the field of view, the greater the awareness of a situation. If the person looking for the coin can get a torch, then the chances of finding the coin will be greatly increased. Similarly, decisions are based on the information available. This means that the decision is also limited by the information available. De Bono's (1976: 113) second law states:

> Proof is often no more than lack of imagination in providing an alternative explanation.

If data are interpreted or presented in a form that provides a certain outcome, with no alternatives, the decision-maker will have some degree of confidence in that decision. Although the decision may be not be the best, it is the only explanation available. This links back to the discussion on bounded rationality in Chapter 1 and satisfies rather than optimises the decision. Our own imaginations will in part dictate the information to be collected and included in the decision model. As decision-makers, we are faced with the need to gather as much relevant information in as short a time as possible. However, we cannot keep getting information as the decision has to be made eventually.

6.4.4   The cost and benefit

The degree to which we investigate, diagnose and model a decision scenario depends on a judgement of the likely costs and benefits of the study and likely outcomes. In some commercial cases, financial data can be applied to the situation. In other cases such as health, social and environmental issues, it is often difficult to get meaningful measures of value. For example, if we decrease the numbers of cars in a city centre, how will the quality of life of the users of the city be affected?

6.5   Diagnostic process

Structured approaches are preferred when the components of the system are well known to the observer, and mathematical or analytical tools can readily describe the activities. This method presupposes that the analyst is familiar with the most common basic structures encountered in systems. However, with structured approaches there is a danger that the analyst is led down a particular path that in many ways predetermines the outcome. For example, a major accounting firm audited a number of hospitals in the NHS. The area in which it was looking related to the operation of sterile services departments (the supply of bandages and surgical instruments) and it produced a report for each hospital. Independently, a government body commissioned independent experts to undertake a related study. As part of the investigation, the experts examined the reports from the accounting firm. Each report was almost identical, irrespective of differences in local operating procedures, the environment and demographics. Because the original reports had followed a particular style, they were useful only as financial benchmarks and offered no information on best practice.

Process approaches make no assumptions about the possible structure of the problem situation. The approach relies on building a model from the basic building blocks of inputs and outputs. The approach is more time consuming and complicated, but offers greater scope for innovation and invention. We address the issues of model building in Chapter 7.

Activity 6.4	Consider the operation of a small urban ambulance department as a system. It is funded and operated by local government on behalf of its tax-paying residents. Try to identify a world view of the following observers (i.e. what would be their primary interests and the influences of those interests?). This actually contradicts what a world view is, but is an exercise in thought.

1 The local hospital

2 The local tax-payers

3 The head of the ambulance service

There is an old Chinese proverb that sums up the importance of obtaining a relevant world view. It goes something like this:

The frog in a well decided one day to climb towards the light. As he rose the light grew big. When he reached the light, he was amazed to see how big the world really was, having previously seen only the green slimy walls and the light at the top. He did not like this, and was scared, so he jumped back down again.

It may be, however, that we are happy with the green walls and the effort involved in looking over the edge has little personal or organisational benefits.

6.6   Soft systems analysis

Activity 6.4 suggests that, for any given problem within a system, a solution may not meet the expectations of all interested parties. The first step in understanding a problem situation is to get a feel for the context of the problem area. Checkland's (1981) methodology can be summarised as shown in Figure 6.6.

The stages represent two kinds of activity. Above the line, the decision-maker is concerned with reality, describing, comparing models, deciding on strategies and implementing these. Below the line the complexities of the real world are deconstructed and rebuilt using the *language* of systems analysis. This language comprises the philosophical foundations of the method and the techniques associated with modelling as illustrated later in the chapter.

We need to familiarise ourselves with the situation, the processes, structures, the resources involved, including the people and the cultural influences and the sources of data and information. We also need to discover the relationships between the parts of the system, how A affects B.

For example, a person walks to a bus stop to go to town (Figure 6.7).

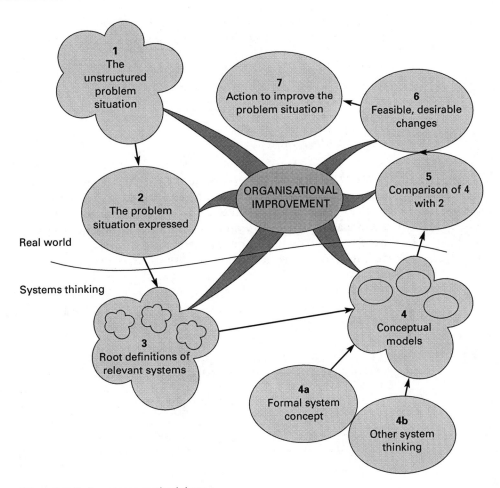

Figure 6.6 Soft systems methodology

We know that the movement of the person has been affected by the bus stop. When the bus appears the person will board and move off. *We* also know that the person controls the bus movements (if no one needs to be picked up the bus will not stop). How will this scene appear to someone from Venus (Figure 6.8)?

The controlling object might appear to be the bus, which is using the bus stop to capture and then eat the people.

Similarly, within a business, it is often difficult to determine the relationships between the various components.

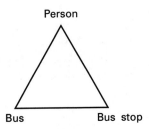

Figure 6.7 An Earth system

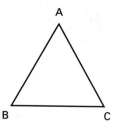

Figure 6.8 A Venus system

Many decisions have consequences that are potentially far-reaching. For example, if our firm is not making enough profit, we may decide to increase revenue, or reduce costs. If costs are to be reduced then we may need to reduce the numbers of staff or the amount of training. If revenue is to be increased, we may need to alter the price or adjust promotion. If price is increased then sales may fall; if costs are reduced then quality may be affected. If we continued in this fashion we would identify many relationships in the firm, but we may lose sight of the need for the initial decision. One way to keep track of and show the main points of the decision is to develop a problem map. For example, the profit problem looks like Figure 6.9.

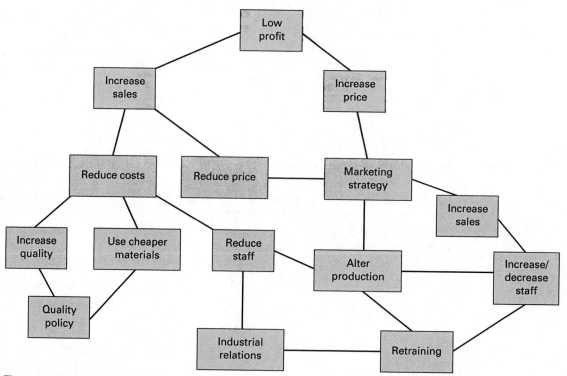

Figure 6.9 Profit problem map

6.6.1 **Rich pictures**

Another way to illustrate information, in a way that maintains an overview, is to draw a *rich picture diagram*, or rich picture for short. Buzan (1974) describes a useful technique for describing a situation called mind maps. Originally intended as a way to improve one's memory, the concept has proved useful in the analytical field. Checkland (1981), who has helped develop the concept of soft systems analysis, uses rich pictures as a first step in familiarisation with the situation, processes, structures, relationships, people and culture of the scenario.

Rich pictures might also be described as the 'big picture', a way, to use a cliché, of 'stepping out of the trees to see the wood'. Rich pictures are in essence cartoon-like summaries that can be read in any direction. This is an important difference from the other methods of describing a situation: verbal and written scenarios tend to be processed serially, whilst a picture can be processed in parallel. Remember that your perception of a situation, and your drawing of the picture, will be influenced by your *Weltanschauung*.

Daellenbach (1994: 52) identifies three major components of the situation represented in a rich picture:

1 *Elements of structure*. These are all aspects or components of the situation. They can be relatively stable, or change only very slowly in the timeframe implied in the situation. This would include all the physical aspects and components, such as physical structure, buildings, equipment and the products involved. It also includes logical, functional and intellectual structural aspects, such as organisational structure, rules, codes of conduct and services rendered.

2 *Elements of process*. These are the aspects of the situation that undergo change, or are in a state of flux, such as the flow of materials, flow of information and the decision-making that occurs.

3 *Relationship* between structure and process, and between processes. How do the processes interact? What affects these interactions?

Within the rich picture we would include both hard (quantitative) data and soft (qualitative) data. The hard data include financial and statistical information, structural information, products and processes. Hard data are sometimes subject to interpretation, so are not always a reliable indicator of reality – for example, we can massage accounts and statistics. The soft data include culture and climate factors such as relationships (power, friends), opinions, traditions and stories.

It is important the that rich picture is as accurate as possible. Linkages between entities should not be drawn unless they are observed to exist. Overuse of arrows may imply a structure or relationship that does not exist in our world view, one that we may fruitlessly decide to investigate further. Rich pictures do not imply solutions to problems; their purpose is to promote thought and debate, they are a heuristic device.

Rich pictures, in common with other forms of organisational analysis, contribute to greater understanding of a problem situation. They are particularly suitable for enabling understanding of the whole system and some of the intangible elements within it. When used in a group problem-solving scenario they can capture attention, as well as highlight areas possibly overlooked by other approaches. Key players and their relationships establish ownership of the issues.

Illustration 6.2 Problems in Ibiza

Susan and Ian waved goodbye to the raucous crowd of relatives and friends and climbed into the white Rolls-Royce, which was to take them to the airport at the start of their honeymoon. The plane left on time and, three hours later, it landed at Ibiza airport. They were whisked off to the hotel on the complementary service bus. The luggage was to follow later, in the luggage van. All was going well, until they checked in. The receptionist informed them that the hotel had had a problem with the bridal suite, which was situated on the top floor beneath a water tank in the roof. This tank had developed a leak two days earlier and had made the room uninhabitable for at least the next five days. All the other rooms were occupied. The holiday representative arrived about an hour later, was informed of this, and went away to try to find an alternative hotel. Two hours later, the representative returned and told the couple that a room had been found in a hotel half an hour away. Susan and Ian were relieved by this news. They reminded the representative of the need to send the luggage on and got into a taxi to the new hotel. The new hotel was pleasant enough, only smaller, without a bar and not near the sea. Both of these latter factors were important to the couple who enjoyed swimming and the night-life associated with the hotels nearer the beaches. They asked if the representative could try to find a more suitable hotel for the next day.

Luckily, they both had an overnight kit in their hand luggage, as the main luggage did not arrive that evening. They walked into the main resort area, which took about an hour, and caught a taxi back later in the evening. The next morning the representative did not visit the couple, who had waited at the hotel, expecting this. They went to the beach in the afternoon, although could not swim, because of the lack of swimming costumes. They tried to find the representative at the first hotel, but with no success. On the third day, the luggage and the representative turned up. The representative said that all the beach hotels were fully booked and that no other accommodation was available. By this time the honeymoon was half over.

The representative was responsible for the welfare and enjoyment of some 500 people spread over ten hotels, but primarily at three large beach hotels, and all within a 20 mile radius. A main part of her salary was from commission from the owners of local attractions, who paid a fee related to both numbers of visitors and bar takings.

The rest of the honeymoon passed without incident, but the couple did not enjoy the isolation of the hotel, and spent more than they intended on taxi fares. When they got back home they complained to the travel company and demanded a full refund of the cost of the holiday.

Activity 6.5 Draw a rich picture for Illustration 6.2 'Problems in Ibiza'. (It might look something like Figure 6.10.)

The rich picture attempts to describe things as they are perceived by individuals and groups (a shared consensus). We can try to describe things as they would be for the systems to exist and create a conceptual model. The conceptual model maps out the activities that need to be undertaken for the system to function. This does not imply that this should happen in the real world, as the objectives of the system may be flawed in the first place.

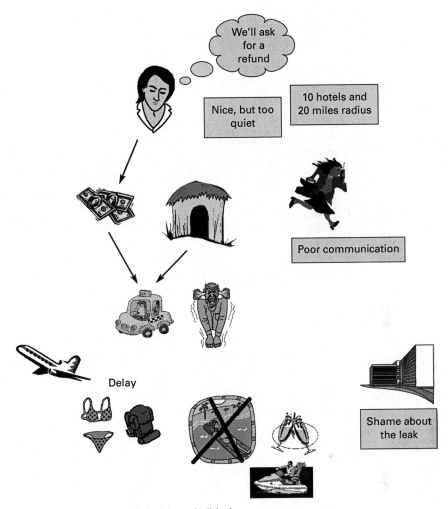

Figure 6.10 A Rich Picture of 'Problems in Ibiza'

6.6.2 Rich text

Rich pictures have a parallel in *rich text*. Take the following:

> I wander'd Lonely as a cloud that floats on high o'er vales and hills,
> When all at once I saw a crowd, a host, of golden daffodils;
> Beside the lake, beneath the trees, fluttering and dancing in the breeze.
> (William Wordsworth)

No doubt this verse conjures an image as you read it. Poetry may be 'over the top' when describing a system, and is fraught with potential misinterpretation. Metaphors, however, are commonly used to portray images about systems (or elements within them) that call upon generally felt experiences. This provides a link between something familiar and something less familiar. Common themes relate organisational issues to journeys, biological systems or even soccer. The importance of metaphor in developing understanding of a system is based on the suggestion that most thought is founded on a small number of taken-for-granted images, especially mechanical and biological ones. Morgan (1986) in his seminal text *Images of Organization* identifies the use of a range of metaphors.

Activity 6.6	**What does organisation mean to you?**
	1 Write a definition of an organisation.
	2 In relation to an organisation that you are familiar with, invent a metaphor that best describes what it is like and how it operates. For example, my old school was like a human being; its brain was the headmaster, the eyes the teachers, the blood the students. Or, my organisation is like a worn-out bicycle; it squeaks when it goes and the chain keeps coming off. Try if you can to get some colleagues to repeat the exercise.
	3 Now explain what you really mean by this metaphor.

Whatever your response to part 1 of Activity 6.6, it will probably have in it a reference to order, structure, planning and achievement of common goals. The response to part 2 is likely to be much different. Table 6.2 shows some examples from other students.

The questions to ask, once you have completed Activity 6.6 and compared your response to those of colleagues are:

- Why are there differences in the way organisations are perceived?
- Why is there is a tendency to use negative metaphors to describe the organisation?

All of these metaphors could relate to the same organisation but be reflecting a number of individuals' perceptions of it, or they may be a single individual's perception of a number of organisations. A person's perception of an organisation comes from his or her involvement with it, which will vary between people.

Once the generalities of the system have been established, we can then move on to investigating the parts of the system where the problem exists.

Table 6.2 The metaphorical organisation

Metaphor	Meaning
A chameleon	The organisation has the ability to rapidly change its appearance in response to threats and opportunities in its business environment
Keystone Kops	People race from one crisis to another without any overall plan
A circus	The original appearance is one of disorganisation, but is actually carefully organised and orchestrated
A dinosaur	The organisation is old, awkward, out of its time and place, doing things the same old way – unable to adapt, unaware of its environment, slow to respond – headed for extinction
A river	The organisation moves at a fairly slow pace, but is consistent and it gets things done, but tends to meander at times

6.7   Hard systems analysis

Hard systems analysis (HSA) enables us to look at parts of the system in greater depth. Rich pictures only create contexts for problems; they cannot provide direct solutions because they lack detail. At the end of the 'Problems in Ibiza' illustration, the only people aware of a problem are the young couple, the customer services department (when they receive the letter of complaint) and maybe the representative. Customer services is aware only of the symptoms, or results of the problem. In the illustration, the result is that the couple had a disappointing holiday. The causes are a lack of understanding of customer needs and requirements, which could imply problems with staff training or planning.

HSA is linked closely with the organisation's objectives and goals. These goals are expressed logically in the firm's mission statement and organisational objectives that attempt to define the boundaries within which the firm is operating.

HSA assumes that every system can be disaggregated into a number of subsystems; the components of those subsystems can be identified, and, as far as possible, quantified to provide an explanation of how they work. This process is called top-down decomposition of a problem area or area of concern.

We can identify the factors that need to be addressed when doing this top-down decomposition:

- Properties of the subsystem: purpose, definition, size, importance, inputs and outputs.
- Structure of the transformation process.
- Processes, series of logical steps, manual actions, algorithms, tasks.
- Communication of data, information and messages internally and externally.
- Controls, performance limits, management instructions that act as control functions.

For example, in the 'Problems in Ibiza' situation, we could look at the communication problem as broken down in Figure 6.11.

6.7.1   Hard systems methodology

The methodology adopted to solve a given problem can be modified to suit a given class of problem, or selected from a set of published methodologies with a specific aim in mind; this can be a cause of confusion. Not only do you have to think about a problem generally, you also have to think about a framework to solve it in general terms, i.e. a meta-methodology.

The following meta-methodology is based on a set of hard systems methods:

- Awareness and commitment
- Objectives, goals and constraints
- Alternatives
- Choice
- Model construction and validation
- Implementation

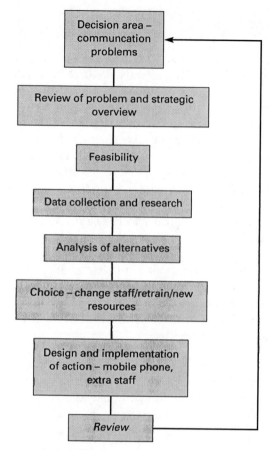

Figure 6.11 The systems analysis cycle

This methodology is neither exhaustive nor fully inclusive of all the methods in existence. It takes general concepts, themes and issues, and tries to identify the steps involved in a general hard systems approach. The steps are not linked in a chronological order. For example, model construction might come before alternatives.

Awareness and commitment

Awareness and commitment constitute perhaps the most important element, but not always the first stage. People may be aware of an inefficiency or ineffective operation, but be unaware of the underlying problem. A member of staff or consultant may bring the problem to attention, but unless the issue is causing pain (maybe more pain than other painful problems) to senior managers, a strategy for resolving the problem is unlikely to generate commitment.

Schein (1987) develops the process by which managers actively seek to alter the way things are done. He develops Lewin's model for social change, the stages being:

1 Unfreezing
2 Changing
3 Refreezing

The unfreezing change is where commitment is generated. There is a big step between seeking information about a decision and the actual changes that take place once the decision has been made. Schein (1987: 94) states: 'Potential clients must feel some pain or some disequilibria somewhere motivating them to seek help', and they must be able to seek help. He goes on to say that this usually involves both learning and unlearning elements. One can relate this to the *Weltanschauung* concept, where we realise our perception is no longer valid. This can be both anxiety provoking and confrontational.

Commitment may therefore come in various forms during the decision-making process. Initial commitment to look at a problem then requires further commitment to implement a solution. Initial commitment is vital and subject to the constraints described earlier. The person charged with exploring the issue must 'sell' the investigation and its possible consequences to other stakeholders in the system. The selling process often encompasses the stages described next.

Objectives, goals and constraints

Any decision needs to meet the needs of the organisation. These needs are often expressed in long-, medium- and short-term time horizons. The long-term is often expressed in the company's mission statement and indicates the main purpose for the organisation's existence. Underpinning the mission are the objectives for the firm over both long and medium terms. To meet the objectives a firm will set goals, 'mile posts' that they aim to reach on the road to success.

The work done for the Selby complex in Illustration 6.3 was initiated by the director of the coalfield, through an increasing level of industrial unrest, as well

---

Illustration 6.3

The Selby coal field in Yorkshire consists of five interrelating mines that deliver, via a series of underground conveyors, coal to a central disposal point at Gascoigne Wood colliery. Coal from the complex is supplied to coal-fired generating stations at a price that reflects the quality of the coal. The greater the ash-content of the coal, the lower the price. Ash in the coal is governed, in part, by the skill of the underground machine operators. Management needed a method by which it could allocate money back to each mine so that each mine could operate as an individual profit centre.

A model ROMASH (Run of Mine Ash) was developed that evaluated the amount of coal produced per colliery and the ash content of that coal. This can be simply done by measuring the thickness of the coal seam and recording the distance (length and depth) that the mining machines travelled. The initial model was inaccurate, as it did not take into account many other factors (principally intangible elements) including the skill (or lack of it) of the machine operators. Often, the machines went off-line and mined rock instead of coal, or geological anomalies went unrecorded. As disputes with colliery managers and mineworkers increased, revised models were created, data collection was improved and general awareness of the issues developed. Finally, commitments to issues beyond those that could be modelled and methods to control these were implemented.

The whole methodology was then adapted to a general system that could be applied to all collieries.

as an increasing financial penalty being levied by the major customer, the generating company. The objectives for changing the way in which coal production was accounted for were in line with the mission for the organisation, which was to provide products that customers were happy with at minimum cost. The study meets the medium-term needs of the complex, in that quality was crucial to customer satisfaction. The goal was to create a system that would provide information to enable some form of accountability to take place.

Alternatives

For many problem areas there will be a range of responses that individuals and organisations can make to address the issue. The range of possible and plausible alternatives is bounded by cultural constraints. Once the objectives have been established then the range of alternatives should be explored. For example, if a firm wishes to reduce the cost associated with inventory then it could implement a mathematical system of control, invest in information technology, implement a just-in-time system, or all three. Sometimes there will not be an obvious path for decision-makers to follow. In the Selby coalfield illustration, the accounting system that was developed was rather like increasing the numbers of police on the beat to reduce crime, rather than addressing the root cause of the crime itself. The crime (dirty coal) was the focus of continual attention, but difficult to eradicate.

Choice

We need to evaluate a number of alternatives in terms of meeting the organisation's objectives, with due regard to management's and stakeholders' expectations. The objective of 'reducing inventory costs' is a statement of intent, not something we can compare and contrast. We can turn it into a quantifiable goal by saying that inventory costs in proportion to turnover should be reduced by 20 per cent within two years. We can then assess our alternative strategies and establish performance measures.

We can classify the process of choice as the four Es:

- *Efficiency* (doing things right): Will the alternative provide the best use of resources?
- *Effectiveness* (doing the right thing): Will the alternative achieve the goal with minimum disruption?
- *Equity*: Will the alternative provide a positive financial contribution?
- *Efficacy*: Will the alternative achieve the goal, as well as satisfy the ethical responsibilities towards stakeholders?

Model construction and implementation

We discuss model construction and implementation in greater depth in Chapter 7. However, it is inevitable that some form of systems analysis is undertaken before a model can be expected to mimic the situation we are trying to simulate.

6.7.2 Graphical techniques

The essence of many methodologies is to draw pictures to aid understanding of the area of concern. The techniques illustrated are not meant to be exhaustive or exclusive. They are presented to illustrate different uses and levels of application. These graphical techniques are an essential part of an analyst's 'toolbox'. The imperative is fitness for purpose: if the tool is appropriate, use it.

Context chart

Context charts attempt to identify the main entities within a given system. For example, the problem map shown in Figure 6.9 may be broken down further using a specific model for evaluating the marketing issue (Figure 6.12).

Organisation charts

Organisation charts are traditionally used to identify the positions of people within the hierarchy of a firm. However, their use can be expanded to identify a range of relationships. This is of increasing importance within flat organisations and project-based structures.

Organisation charts offer little in the way of depicting how an organisation actually functions. As Mintzberg (Mintzberg and Van der Heyden 1999) states: 'The traditional organizational chart reveals a fixation on management, rather than showing the way in which a typical company accomplishes its work.' Organigraphs are an attempt to map out relationships within an organisation using hubs and webs that link products and processes.

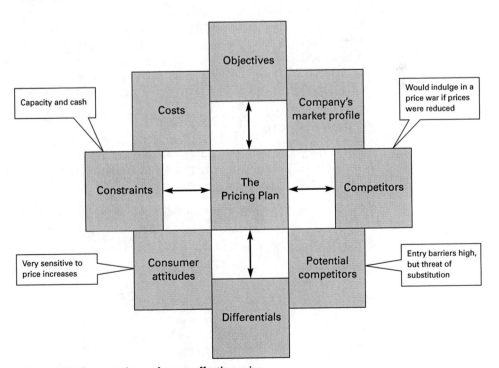

Figure 6.12 Context chart – factors affecting price

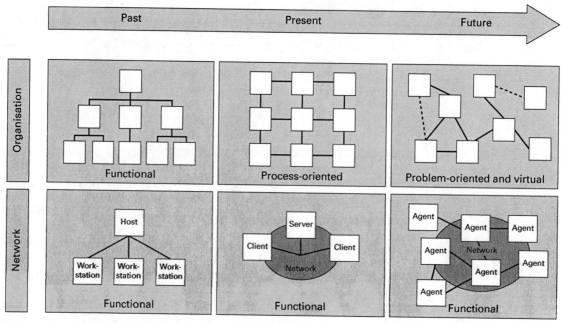

Figure 6.13 A dynamic view of a firm's evolving structure

Flowcharts

Flowcharts are the most commonly used method for describing a sequence of activities at both detailed and general levels. They are part of total quality management, computer programming, operational and project planning. Typically, sets of symbols are used that have a common meaning within the design activity concerned. Some of those used in computer systems programming are shown in Figure 6.14. These represent processes such as decisions, operations, storage and printing. Examples of flowcharts can be found throughout this book.

Data flow diagrams

Data flow diagrams are typically used to describe information flows within a system. Figure 6.15 illustrates the flow of information within a logistics process.

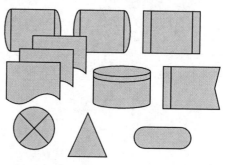

Figure 6.14 Computer flowchart symbols

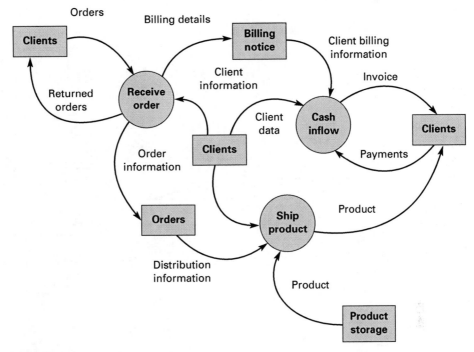

Figure 6.15 A data flow diagram for a logistics system

Precedence diagrams

Precedence diagrams are a special form of flowchart used in process and project design to help in evaluating time and resource constraints (see Chapter 10). An example is shown in Figure 6.16.

| Activity 6.7 | To practise using some of the techniques of HSA, choose one of the following and use as many of the techniques as you can: |

- Setting and assessing student work on a degree programme.

- Setting up an internet retail company.

- Deciding to build a new oil pipeline across your country.

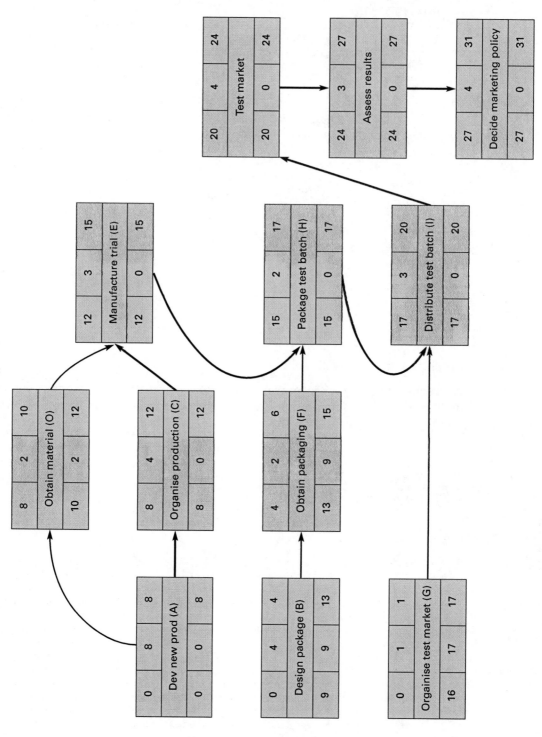

Figure 6.16 A critical path analysis precedence diagram

Illustration 6.4 Farming crisis

Management decisions are often concerned with maximising the use of resources and minimising costs. Often the decisions taken are local and do not affect the general population. In the case of farming, however, the culmination of local decisions is changing the environment in which we live. The pressures on farming are inextricably linked to national economic issues, in particular the need to feed a rapidly increasing world population. The farming industry faces a number of pressures:

■ *Price*. Produce is sold on the world market, hence prices are determined by low-cost producers. In the UK, the four major buyers can force farmers to meet these prices by sourcing from low-cost producers.

■ *Farmers*. The UK climate determines the range of crops and livestock that can economically be kept. This is restricted further by the major local resource of land. Land is finite and often suitable for only a narrow range of farming activities. Hence farmers cannot generally choose between wheat, cabbages, tomatoes, or sheep, cattle, ostrich and deer. In each case farmers look to achieve the highest yield per acre. For wheat farming, this encourages large fields and machinery and the use of chemicals to control pests and weeds. For cabbage farming, size is limited only by the additional irrigation required. Sheep would not be kept on high-grade pasture, and deer need high fences.

Experience has shown that farming for short-term profit and gains can impair the future productivity of the land. The short-term private view is in conflict with the longer-term public view. The longer-term view is one that external stakeholders might be expected to hold. However, there are times when governments take the shorter view in the light of real or imagined crises. For example, the authorisation of destruction of parkland or nature reserves to meet housing or food shortages.

Chemicals

In the UK, the use of chemicals to enhance product yield is subject to a variety of legislative controls. These controls are primarily aimed at preserving public and employee safety. For example, in many fruit enterprises, pest control is the most expensive and time-consuming growing practice. Where the concentration of fruit farms in an area warrants it, individual efforts are complemented by legislative measures including quarantine regulations to force removal of pest-laden, unattended orchards. Sometimes the most economical control procedure is biological in nature. There is increased research today to find and multiply parasites that kill fruit crop pests. Such biological methods are necessary as political pressures increase for banning DDT and other chemicals. Selection of varieties that are immune, resistant to attack or tolerant to specific pests, is a biological control procedure also widely used. Chemical control procedures, however, are relied on most heavily. Air-blast spray or mist-application machinery covering 70 acres (28 hectares) of trees or more in a day is now in common use.

Resource Management

It is often regarded as essential to the survival or the enrichment of an individual or a group to use resources in such a way as to realise immediate gains or profits. Such activities, however, may impair the future productivity of an area of land, exterminate a species, or destroy the usefulness of a site for any other purpose. In such a situation, the short-term private view conflicts with the long-term public view. Although many would argue that the public view should be more conservation oriented, emphasising proper safeguards to prevent deterioration of the environment, there are, nevertheless, times when governments take the short-term view in the face of real or imagined economic or political crises; they may, for example, authorise widespread destruction of resources as a temporary expedient to achieve a military goal or to strengthen the public treasury. However, crises will tend to become self-perpetuating if the destruction of resources weakens the country ecologically and economically. Thus, continued, unrestricted population growth in a country poorly equipped to manage its natural resources creates a continuing sense of crisis, because ever-expanding immediate needs are commonly met at the cost of future productivity and environmental stability.

For as long as human populations were small and the pressures upon the environment were limited, conflicts between long-term and short-term interests made little difference. Deteriorated lands could be abandoned and new lands found because there was sufficient time to permit natural repair of environmental damage. At present, however, with great and increasing numbers of people on a planet of limited capacity, conservationists are insisting that the difference between short- and long-term points of view be resolved in favour of actions that guarantee the survival of mankind.

Activity 6.8

1 Analyse the farming industry using soft and hard approaches. Identify as many elements of the system as you can.

2 Based upon this analysis, what measures should the government of your country consider to safeguard the interests of all stakeholders?

Illustration 6.5 The future of the coal industry

British mines produce some of the cheapest deep-mined coal in the world. It is not, however, the cheapest coal in the world. Coal prices on the spot market in Rotterdam are up to £10 per tonne cheaper than the cost of deep-mined British coal.

The chief users of coal in Britain are the electricity generating companies. If we consider first the national need for power, the country consumes about 300 million tonnes of coal equivalent power per year (the amount of power created from burning one tonne of coal). In 1971, forecasts for the consumption of coal put British Coal's (BC's) share of the energy market at about 200 million tonnes by the end of the century, with the remaining sources of energy coming from oil, nuclear, hydro-electric, experimental environmental power sources (wind, tide and wave power), and imported coal. On this basis, BC began an efficiency and expansion drive (The Plan for Coal) that led to the development of the Selby coalfield, and Asfordby Colliery, in the Vale of Belvoir, and estimated that about 150 collieries would meet this need in the year 2000.

In the mid-1970s, mineworkers went on strike and the government collapsed. In the late 1970s and early 1980s, power-generating companies began to complain that they were paying too much for coal, relative to world prices, and that, as these costs needed to be passed on, this was not good for the consumer. The government began a rationalisation process that again brought mineworkers out on strike for a year in 1983.

Other factors in the 1980s also began to influence the coal industry. Environmentally, coal is a damaging fuel. Emissions from coal-fired power stations include sulphur and nitrous oxides, which have been associated with acid rain, damaging forests in Scandinavia. EU regulations required these emissions to be reduced gradually over time. Some European generating stations, in Germany for example, began to fit flue gas desulphurisation units to the power stations that removed some of these pollutants.

The mining industry has always been one of the most dangerous to work in. The nature of the work leaves employees open to accidents at the site. In addition, many occupational health risks are encountered, such as black lung disease, pneumoconiosis, noise-induced hearing loss and skin complaints. The British industry is, however, regarded to be the safest in the world, with a strict regime of industrial surveillance and regulation.

In the mid-1980s, the British government decided to let market forces dictate the future for coal. It deregulated the generating industry, allowing any fuel to be used for electricity generation, and refused to subsidise pollution control measures for power stations. Up until this point, gas had been banned for use as a generating fuel, being seen as too valuable and convenient for domestic use to be used as an electricity-generating fuel. The newly privatised companies rapidly began constructing gas-fired generating stations, which offer low capital outlay, cheap fuel prices and low running costs.

The deep-mined coal industry began to decline rapidly and imports of coal increased. Some of the imported coal was cheap, because of use of child labour (South America), or government subsidies (Poland, Germany) in countries that felt the need to maintain coal-related industries. In nearly all cases the foreign deep-mined coal is obtained from sources less safe than British mines.

The results of the closure of British collieries have been whole communities put out of work and into poverty, through the direct or indirect consequences of the closures. Although there is no proven link between poverty, unemployment and crime, crime has also increased in these areas. The government has reacted by directing investment into these areas to encourage alternative industries to develop.

Activity 6.9   Can we learn from the experience of the coal industry? If so, then use soft and hard systems analysis to help assess the future for electricity generation from gas-fired power stations.

Summary

The way we approach some decisions in business, the way in which we construct the framework of the analysis, is crucial to the decision-making process. Our understanding of the problem domain will generate more confidence in the final decision. Our identification of the factors that will affect the decision area will enable a greater chance of the best decision being made. As this chapter has demonstrated, systems theory and thinking can, in some cases, play an important role in this process. Systems philosophy can be applied to all systems, be they large or small, global or domestic. If we can sensibly draw boundaries and define the rules that are relevant then we might, just might, get a better decision than picking the answer out of a hat.

If people are involved in a decision-making process, the system is going to be complex, although the problems to resolve might be trivial. Furthermore, all systems become entropic if energy is not sustained.

Systems can be discrete or continuous. The same logic turns a continuous system into a discrete system.

Systems theory provides an approach to decision-making that is holistic. Rather than treat problems as if they are associated with a subset of the system, such as a functional group, systems theory relates the problem to the bigger picture. Systems theory takes into account the dynamics and organisational cybernetics within the context of the whole system within which the decision is being made.

Hard systems analysis enables us to look at parts of the system in greater depth. Soft systems analysis enables us to get an understanding, from a number of perspectives, of the problem area. The essence of hard systems analysis is to assume that every system can be disaggregated into a number of subsystems. To move beyond soft systems analysis we need to address, in detail, the various systems operating within the rich picture.

Hard systems analysis uses a variety of graphical techniques to illustrate the structure and processes at work within a situation.

? Decision diary

For a decision you have made recently or might make in the future, describe the problem situation using soft and hard methods of analysis. Referring back to Chapter 5, what implications does your analysis have for the appropriate methods for research into this problem area? Referring back to Chapter 4, can you identify any potential irrational issues that might alter the analysis?

References

Bak, P., Tang, C. and Wiesenfeld, K. (1988) 'Self-Organized Criticality' in *Physical Review*, B, 38.

Bottery, M. (1994) *Lessons for Schools?* London: Cassell.

Boulding, K.E. (1956) 'General systems theory – the skeleton of science', *Management Science*, 2(3).

Buzan, T. (1974) *Use Your Head*. London: BBC Books,

Checkland, P. (1981) *Systems Thinking, Systems Practice*. London: Wiley.

Checkland, P.B. (1993) *Systems Thinking, Systems Practice*. Chichester: Wiley.

Clough, A.H. (1987, first published 1862) *Where Lies the Land?* Newmarket, England: Brimax Books.

Daellenbach, H.G. (1994), *Systems and Decision Making*. Chichester: Wiley.

De Bono, E. (1976) *Practical Thinking*. London: Pelican, p.113.

Jacob, F. (1974) *The Logic of Living Systems*. London: Allen Lane.

Krogh, G. and Roos, J. (1995) *Organisational Epistemology*. London: Macmillan.

Mintzberg, H. and Van der Heyden, L. (1999) 'Organigraphs: drawing how companies really work', *Harvard Business Review*, 77(5): 87.

Ray, T.S. (1992) *Evolution, Ecology and Optimization of Digital Organisms*. Sante Fe Institute Working Paper 92–08–042.

Schein, E. (1987) *Process Consultation*, Volume II. Reading, MA: Addison-Wesley, p. 94.

Stacey, R. (1996) *Strategic Management and Organisational Dynamics*, 2nd edition. Harlow: Pitman Publishing.

Varela, F.J. (1984) 'Two principles of self-organization', in Ulrich, H. and Probst, G.J.B. (eds) *Self-Organization and Management of Social System*. New York: Springer Verlag.

Further reading

Boland, R.D. and Greenberg, R.H. (1988) 'Metaphorical restructuring of organisational ambiguity', in Pandy, L.R., Boland, R.J. and Thomas, H. (eds) *Managing ambiguity and change*. New York: Wiley.

Folkes, S. and Stubenvoll, S. (1992) *Accelerated Systems Development*. Englewood Cliffs, NJ: Prentice Hall.

Hicks, M.J. (1991) *Problem Solving in Business and Management*. London: Chapman & Hall.

Jennings, D. and Wattam, S. (1994) *Decision Making: An Integrated Approach*. London: Pitman Publishing.

Morgan, G. (1986) *Images of Organization*. Newbury Park. CA: Sage.

Palmer, I. and Dunford, R. (1996) in *Organisation Development*, Oswick, C. and Grant, D. (eds). London: Pitman Publishing.

Pondy, L.R., Boland, R.J. and Thomas, H. (eds) (1988) *Managing Ambiguity and Change*. New York: Wiley.

Rivett, P. (1994) *The Craft of Decision Making*. Chichester: Wiley.

Veryard, R. (1992) *Information Modelling: Practical Guidance*. Englewood Cliffs, NJ: Prentice Hall.

Vonderembse, M.A. and White, G.P. (1996) *Operations Management*, 3rd edition. St Paul, MN: West Publishing.

Glossary

Allopoietic: an open system, every part of which interacts with the environment, but as a single entity retains a central purpose.

Analogue: something that is analogous or similar to something else, but in another form.

Autopoietic: a largely closed system that creates its own inputs, and elements within it do not interact creatively with its environment.

Benchmarking: the process of comparison between two systems. For example, firms may compare financial performance between years or compare operational performance with that of competitors.

Closed systems: systems characterised by being generally unaffected by the environment they operate within.

Cybernetics: the science of communication and control theory that is concerned particularly with the comparative study of automatic control systems (as the nervous system and brain) and mechanical–electrical communication systems. Cybernetics has been adopted by social scientists to describe how organisations function through control processes of measurement and linear reactions to negative feedback. It assumes stasis, consistency and harmony.

Dynamics: systems dynamics refers to the elements affecting the behaviour of a system given positive and negative feedback processes. These behaviours can be linear or non-linear and can involve internally generated behaviour and non-equilibrium states.

Entropy:	a process of degradation or running down, or a trend to disorder.
Iconic:	a physical entity whose form suggests its meaning or purpose.
Open system:	a system that draws from and interacts with other systems.
Symbolic:	a method of representing systems using combinations of symbols, axioms and rules of inference.
Weltanschauung:	associates our personal perceptions to the world (or system) being observed – our world view.

Appendix 1 Answers to selected activities

Answer to Activity 6.1

Your answer to the first part may have included the elements shown in Figure 6.17, upon which your answer to the second part would be based:

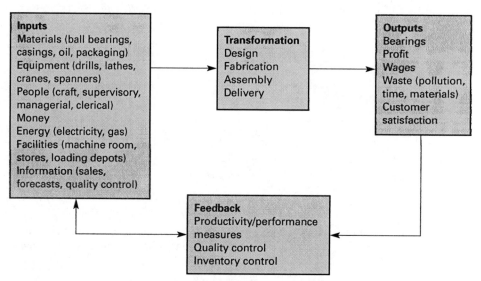

Figure 6.17 Input output model – Severn Bearings

Answers to the second part are likely to be varied, but the firm needs ways in which to improve both its quality and productivity. Possible solutions may include training, quality management initiatives, and production-related technologies.

Answer to activity 6.3

Group affected	Consequences
Components	Roads, vehicles, pedestrians, car parks, garages, time
Relationships	Relative geographical presence of entities and how they are currently linked: increased bikes – more bike repair centres; decreased car usage – reduced garage requirements; increased public transport – increased employment in public transport; reduced city centre parking – reduced fire risk because of faster response times %Road car < before; %Road alternative > before, Fewer cars = more buses, pedestrians, cycles Fewer city car parks = fewer cars, more anguish
Transformation process	The transformation process concerns the efficiency and effectiveness of getting resources between destinations within the city centre
Environment	Increased concern regarding safety and environmental issues. Need to be aware of special needs (doctors, disabled, delivery vehicles)
Activities and behaviour	Some groups will welcome the moves, such as cyclists, who may perceive a safer environment. Many would oppose such a move as a constraint on personal freedom. In the UK many people have not travelled by any means other than car for many years, hence may be resistant to the move. The council would have to be aware of this resistance and ensure that operators of the public transport adhered to high standards of quality
Inputs	The inputs include the various forms of vehicles involved, private cars, delivery vans, lorries, fire engines, police vehicle and ambulances. Inputs also include the goods and people contained within these vehicles, the energy they use, the time taken to complete the journey (including time taken in waiting for public transport) and national legislation
Outputs	Tangible outputs include fuel used. Intangible, objective outputs include costs incurred (either reduced or increased) and journey time changes. Intangible subjective outputs include stakeholder perceptions of the new system. For example, the police may find it better because of faster response times and a corresponding reduction in crime or increase in detection rates. Domestic travellers may find it depressing because of forced use of public transport or increased or inconvenient travelling time to enable them to park their cars
Observer interest	All the users of the transport system have similar aims, primarily to travel quickly and comfortably, at a price they can afford. The nature of these interests will manifest themselves in various forms. Many domestic users value the privacy and convenience of their own car. Commercial and public sector users are hindered by narrow roads, but equally suffer from increasing congestion.

Answer to Activity 6.4

1 The local hospital. As a customer of the ambulance service, you may have experienced some of the following:

- Poor communications, for example estimated patient arrival times.
- Poor availability, for example in routine patient transportation.
- Costs that are higher than you might expect.
- Unfriendly or uncooperative staff.

The factors recalled immediately are likely to be negative, as these tend to leave a greater impression on the mind.

2 The local taxpayers. As another potential or actual customer, you may have experienced some of the following:

- Poor timekeeping, delayed or cancelled transport.
- Poor communications, especially in respect to the first issue.
- Unfriendly or uncooperative staff.

3 As the head of the ambulance service you may have experienced:

- Conflicts regarding the amount of funding.
- Unfair criticism for circumstances beyond your control (congested roads).
- Poorly motivated staff.
- Changes in social and environmental factors that improve or impede performance.

7

Model building, simulation and forecasting

Learning outcomes

On completing this chapter you should be able to:

- Describe the model-building process.
- Create a simulation model for a problem situation.
- Develop and run a Monte Carlo simulation.
- Describe, apply and contrast various approaches to forecasting.

7.1 Introduction

Modelling is a popular pastime. Many of us have enjoyed games that mimic real life, for example model boats and houses. More recently we have immersed ourselves in fantasy worlds of myth and magic with computer games. This chapter is primarily concerned, however, with mathematical modelling, which underpins computer games and has for some time helped managers assess situations before they have happened. Here we will try to mimic situations using mathematical methods of description.

Simulation plays an important role in all of our lives. With it we try to mimic real experiences and situations, without the expense of developing the situation for real. Take, for example, the game of Monopoly. Using very simple rules, this game simulates the rise in fortunes of players in a mythical property letting market. The game would become unwieldy (for human play) if a complete set of rules, that mimic actuality, were included.

The simplest simulations can be described by using a mathematical representation, based on, for example, a physical or mathematical law. For example, Newton's laws of motion describe the ways in which bodies travel in relation to the forces placed upon them. His third law for instance states 'Action and reaction are always equal and opposite'. We can model this by using snooker balls on a table, or by the mathematical model that describes the conservation of momentum: $M_1 V_1 = M_2 V_2$ where M_1 and M_2 are the masses of the two objects, and V_1 and V_2 are the velocities of the snooker balls.

In business we use simulation to try to mimic the way that the firm, or elements within the firm, will respond to changes in operating characteristics. For example, a bank might simulate the effects of customer waiting times if it were to change the number of tellers working. Forecasting models are commonly used to predict the future and come in varying degrees of sophistication and complexity. Observations of the past coupled with awareness of present dynamics enables planners to make reasonable statements regarding future events.

This chapter takes us through the model-building process and the techniques of creating simulation and forecasting models.

7.2 Models

The illustration in the introduction referred to the game of Monopoly. In this game, the 'rules' of chance dictate the success or failure of the players. Whilst chance is an important part of life, we need to ensure that the probabilities are as near as possible based on reality. In Monopoly, the chance of hitting any spot on two rolls of the dice varies, the least likely are the second and twelfth spots (1/36), with the others varying (the seventh being the most likely at 1/6). In the game of Monopoly, we could begin to create a more realistic situation by removing the interactions with other players (the dice throwing) and replacing this income-generating device with information on revenues over time and costs associated with occupancy rates.

Activity 7.1   Write down some of the other factors that you might include to make the game of Monopoly more realistic.

We would start the detailed breakdown of the game by addressing the areas known as the *problem domain* and the *problem requirements*. In the Monopoly game the problem domain is the collection of properties in the various localities, with the associated revenues and purchase costs. Players picking up Chance cards incur additional costs, often related to property features. To make it more realistic we could introduce an estimate of fixed costs based on the number and type of properties owned. We could make an estimate of the amount of rent by building in information on average rents and figures on bad debts. The problem requirements are to make as much money as possible and to remove all competition.

Simulation models attempt to mimic the actions or processes of a physical system. Not all models attempt to do this; many, as you have already seen, or will see later in this text, just provide data relating to a specific issue. Table 7.1 lists some of the benefits to be gained from good models.

Models can be used to evaluate family finances. You may model your own cash flow which would include: gross income, tax rates, interest rates, loans, living expenses split into a dozen or so categories (the problem domain), to try

Table 7.1 The benefits of good models

Model trait	Benefit
Speed	Models are generally quicker to create and use than the real thing
Simplicity	Models cannot contain all the factors that affect the system (see Chapter 6); only the main factors should be included. This helps management or the problem owner to understand the main dynamics of a problem area. Whilst adding variables may make a model more accurate, this increase in accuracy must be balanced by the significance of the increase and the increase in costs to collect and analyse the data
Variety	Models, once created, are used to answer 'what if?' questions, and hence provide management with a greater awareness of the effects of a range of possible scenarios. In this vein, they must also be easy to manipulate. In the 1970s it took the mainframe computers of the time five days to produce a seven-day forecast!
Uniformity	Models will always produce a solution based on the same set of rules (which may be wrong, but at least they are consistent)
Adaptive	If changes in the system invalidate a model, then it should be fairly easy to adjust the component parts to adapt to the new situation
Cost	Models are cheaper to experiment with than reality
Convenient	Data preparation, input and updating should be easy

Activity 7.2   Write down some areas where models might be useful to yourself, or your firm.

to estimate what the monthly disposable income might be (problem require-ments). If the model were to predict expenses exactly, then it would need to incorporate information such as: the children breaking a window, the dog need-ing some veterinary treatment, the car needing a new water pump and the whimsical purchase of some new garden equipment. The main part of this model is based on data that are either certain or very predictable, such as the tax rate. The unknown factors are included by guessing a figure that might be spent per month on unforeseen items.

Models try to capture the essence of a real-life system; they can only be an approximation because the real world is complex. Figure 7.1 shows the relation-ship between reality and the model. Models mimic the real world we are trying to simulate. The purpose of the model is to quantify the situation, to provide infor-mation on the objectives. If the model is suitable, we can apply mathematical

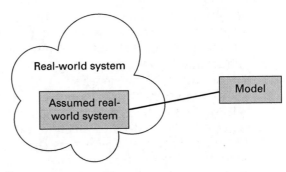

Figure 7.1 Models and reality

techniques, such as queuing theory or linear programming (see Chapter 9). If the system is too complex to describe mathematically, then we can use simulation to help imitate the system. Models can be constructed that use mathematical methods, simulation and heuristics in very complex situations.

To do this we can construct models of various forms. There are three types of model: iconic, symbolic and analogous.

- *Iconic models* are reproductions of physical objects, such as a model boat, usually to a different scale and with less detail. These are used to test a design, for example the seaworthiness of a new design of boat utilising a water tank.

- *Symbolic models* include a variety of flowcharting type techniques, as well as the mathematical models discussed later in the text. Flowcharts are one of the most useful and widely used of all the modelling techniques. They are a key feature of project management, operations management and quality management improvement processes. One of their greatest values is that they focus attention on the situation and force people to consider how the process is being conducted. This often leads to recognition of inefficiencies and suggestions for improvements.

- *Analogue models* are representations of the situation displayed in another form. For example, a railway company will have a display in its central control room that indicates the position of all of its trains. This will give the railway controller information on how best to manage train flow.

The model-creation process is circular, in that as it is being developed it is tested for accuracy, compared to real-world events, tested to see how it reacts to different inputs (sensitivity analysis) and adjusted, until management is confident that the solutions the model is providing are reliable enough to base a decision on. Software developments over the past 30 years have made such models commonplace for many activities.

Activity 7.3	What determines the contents of the assumed real-world system, and what should be included in the model? Hint: revisit Chapter 6.

William of Ockham, a fourteenth-century English philosopher, stated a useful heuristic:

Ockham's razor: Things should not be multiplied without good reason.

It is called Ockham's razor because he had a sharp and cutting mind. When modelling, we need to be very selective in what we include in the model. In Chapter 6 we saw that systems can be messy, with many possible influences and subsystems. We need to select only those parts that will have a significant effect on the outputs of the model.

The analyst needs to be aware of both 'hard' and soft' information and the relationships between them to be able to judge which of them needs to be incorporated in the model and which to leave out. This is often an iterative process. The model is built and tested, matched against reality and adjusted until acceptable results are obtained. Figure 7.2 illustrates how modelling fits into a management science methodology.

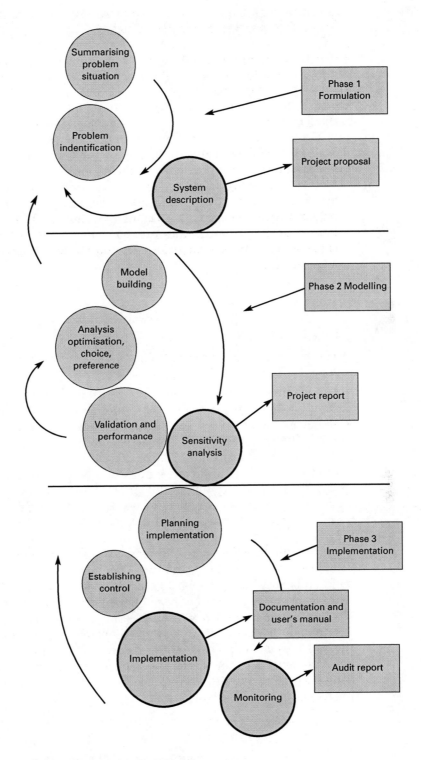

Figure 7.2 Management science methodology
Source: based on Daellenbach, 1994: 90

7.3 The modelling cycle

There are three influences on a problem domain: *entities*, *actors* and *processes*. Entities have *attributes*, which dictate their behaviour. Some entities are *permanent*, such as machines in a factory and the storage facility; some entities are transient or *temporary*, such as the job that a machine is performing. Actors are the *people* in the system covered by the problem domain. This would include the problem owner and the staff involved in the process. The processes are the *transformations* that are occurring in the system, such as the change in inventory level or the formation of the product from the resources.

Normally when we create a model we are concerned with the relevant *quantitative factors*, those that can be measured easily and are significant to the problem. *Qualitative factors* are intangible; they are subjective and cannot be measured directly, although they may be an important part of the decision. In an inventory example, the entities are the suppliers, the materials and the firm's storage facilities.

Activity 7.4	1 List all the qualitative and quantitative factors involved in a decision to purchase a car.
	2 Do the same for a house purchase.

In your answer to part 1 of Activity 7.4 you may have listed colour, style, comfort and aesthetics as the qualitative factors, and performance, cost and economy as the quantitative factors. For the house, design, smell, location and amenities might be listed as the qualitative factors, and cost, number and size of rooms, and state of repair as the quantitative factors.

Modelling is, then, an iterative process of successive enrichments. The initial model may well be very simple and far removed from reality; the model evolves, variables are included or excluded, towards a model that starts to match both the problem domain and the problem objectives. As the model becomes more complex, we compare the validity of the model with empirical observations. At some point, the predictive power of the model will cease to improve and additional complications become less significant. The number of pieces of information can build up rapidly. Rivett (1994: 132) describes a management consultancy group that created a model that addressed transporting coal in the north of England. The final model contained 500 variables and 625 constraints.

Although model building is cheap compared with testing with reality, it can still be an expensive process. At the start of the exercise we need to evaluate the potential benefits of the model and compare these with the costs of developing and operating it. We also need to take account of the risks of developing a useless model. Some of the costs include:

- *Data collection and analysis costs* – if the situation being modelled is complex, it is likely to require extensive data collection and analysis to verify the parameters.
- *Model construction and computation* – if the resultant model needs extensive computation, bespoke computer systems may be required.

- *Training and administration costs* – if the final system is going to require training of staff and changes in organisational methods.

Some of the benefits one might look for are:

- An improvement in *competitiveness*: – quality, productivity, flexibility, lead-time, cost.
- An improvement in *effectiveness* – making the right decision more consistently.
- An improvement in *efficiency* – maximising or minimising decision objectives.

There is also the effect of time. If the model takes a long time to construct, then the problem it was designed to address may not exist by the time the model is ready to give reliable results. Complex models are mostly used to mimic commonly occurring situations and situations that involve the firm in substantial costs, such as inventory control and resource scheduling systems.

On the mechanics of model building, Rivett (1994: 246) offers us six imperatives and nine principles that are worth repeating here:

The six imperatives:

1 Do *produce* an answer on time

2 Do *go* to the source of the data. Find out how they are collected, what is their value, and how accurate they are.

3 Do *listen* to people – what is the structure of the problem area, what is its technology?

4 Do *read* about the background of the organisation, its history and its management.

5 Do *understand* the people involved – not just the management, but all the stakeholders. What is their history, their motivations and their differing perceptions of the problem area?

6 Do *consider* whether there might be a simple lateral thinking exercise.

The nine principles:

1 It is not enough to think you understand what you read. Ask also what other people will understand.

2 Always question the data.

3 Think before you analyse.

4 Do not expect all distributions to be normal.

5 Objectives are not absolutes – they change even during a study.

6 Be ultra cautious in handling estimates of probabilities where there is no possibility of validation.

7 Examine the problem boundaries.

8 *On s'engage et puis on voit* (roughly, involvement enhances understanding).

9 'Go for the jugular'.

| Activity 7.5 | As a test of analytical thinking, write a sentence for each of the points mentioned by Rivett, explaining the importance of each. If you want to check your explanations get hold of the book! Rivett has written an interesting chapter on each point! |

7.3.1 An inventory issue

A common analogy to describe production flows is to liken the flow of material and products to the flow of water in a pipe. The minimum amount of water the better as it means less money tied up in materials. Hence, we need to have narrow pipes and fast flows to create the flow of water required. Inventory caters for inefficiencies in the system (this is explored further in Chapter 9). However, a just-in-time approach would involve the customer turning on the tap and the flow would come from the mains supply; like a shower, just the right amount of water delivered at the time it is needed. A planned approach would start with a full bath of water.

However, most firms will have pools of inventory the size of which will reflect the nature of the system and the uncertainties connected with it. For example, if we cannot predict demand, a stock of finished products is required to meet customer service levels (i.e. goods available when they want them). If suppliers have a lead time of two weeks, how reliable is this and are all of the materials usable?

We can create a simple model of how inventory levels change over time using four pieces of information:

1 rate of supply

2 reliability of supply

3 demand rate

4 demand consistency

It is typical that events, such as having materials delivered, will be associated with a degree of chance. For example, if you start work at 9 am you will set your alarm for 7 am, get in the car at 8 am and arrive at work at 8.45 am, usually. Occasionally things will go wrong, the alarm does not go off, the car will not start, or the roads are blocked, which then results in a late arrival. In model building we need to try to determine this variability and decide if it is important enough to build into the model.

Our inventory model at time t might then look like this:

$$\text{Inventory level}_t = \text{Inventory level}_{t-1} + \text{Delivery}_{t,t-1} - \text{Demand}_{t,t-1}$$

During the time interval t–1 until t, then, a delivery may or may not occur.

Whilst this model is accurate it does not help managers decide when to order more material, or how big that order size should be.

Activity 7.6	Consider the problem of inventory control. What additional refinements would you make to the model to make it more useful for decision-making?

The rolling stock figure (inventory level) should be a trigger for releasing an order. This is the reorder level and is dependent on demand during the lead time of the supplier. To this we could include the variability of demand, delivery and lead time to allow for things going differently from average. The order size, sometimes called the *economic order quantity*, is dependent on the balance between holding and ordering costs of the material. The earlier model is also weak as there are no stated rules. For example, you cannot have negative inventory, unless you allow order backlogs. We could state the new model in terms of a flowchart as shown in Figure 7.3. This is ready to be incorporated into a spreadsheet or other such computer program. The variable p prevents the model from placing duplicate orders. Further refinements would bring it closer to reality.

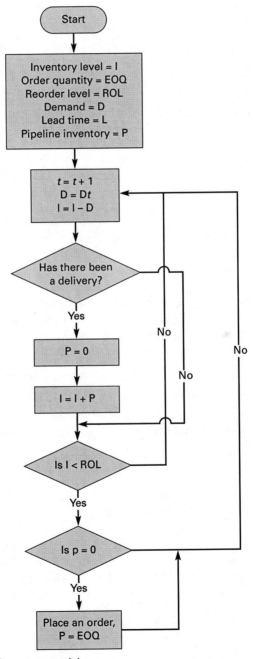

Figure 7.3 A refined inventory model

Consider the inventory model depicted in Figure 7.3. If we start with 100 units of inventory in January, assume 1 month lead time at a reorder level of 50, an order quantity of 50, variable demand (shown in the first row) and a period of 1 month; the model would give the results set out in Table 7.2.

Table 7.2 Inventory model

Time		Jan	Feb	Mar	Apr	May	Jun
Demand		30	60	40	70	50	40
P		0	50	50	50	50	50
Inv. carried forward	100	70	10*	20*	10*	10*	10*
Supply		0	0	50	50	50	50
Supply – demand		–30	–60	10	–20	0	10

	Jul	Aug	Sep	Oct	Nov	Dec
Demand	50	35	45	95	55	20
P	50	50	50	50	50	50
Inv. carried forward	10*	25*	30*	–15*	–20*	10*
Supply	50	50	50	50	50	50
Supply – demand	0	15	5	–45	**–5**	30

In Table 7.2 the asterisks indicate when an order is placed and the figures in bold indicate where the model is incorrect (given we cannot allow negative inventory). To counteract this we would have to adjust the reorder level or the order size, or reduce the lead time or the period between checking inventory levels.

Model effectiveness

Effectiveness depends on how well the real situation is represented, whether this is a wooden model of an aircraft in a wind tunnel, a CAD/CAM version of the same on a computer, or an architect's first draft of a new building. The advantages of models in the decision process are:

- conclusions and predictions have accuracy;
- risk is reduced by experimentation before implementation;
- they enhance understanding, stimulate creativity and evaluate alternative courses of action.

A flowchart is a simple system model with inputs and outputs. Figure 7.4 shows an example.

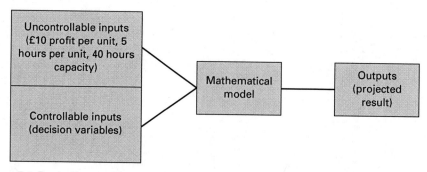

Figure 7.4 Production exercise

<table>
<tr><td>**Activity 7.7**</td><td>A production process is planning to use 100 hours per week available, profit margin at £9 per unit.</td></tr>
</table>

Activity 7.7 | A production process is planning to use 100 hours per week available, profit margin at £9 per unit.

1 Show that the profit will be £180, based on making and selling 20 items.

2 Produce a flowchart for the model, identifying the inputs (controllable and uncontrollable) and the output.

The number of available hours may either be uncontrollable, or controllable by management, hence it is a decision variable.

Deterministic and stochastic models

When there is complete control over the decision variables then these variables are deterministic. In a stochastic production model the number of hours to produce an item may not be exactly 5 but might vary between 3 and 6 hours. The product demand may be uncertain, or a host of other controllable, but variable, factors may influence the systems. With uncontrollable factors, it is more vital to predict the likelihood of the output being within a range of values. In this instance we have:

3 hours per item, so we can do: $100/3 = 33$ items at $£33 \times 9 = £297$ profit

6 hours per item, so we can do: $100/16 = 16$ items at £144 profit

Then, we should use a probability-based argument as discussed in Chapter 2.

7.4   Creating a simulation model

Simulation models, once created, are commonly evaluated on a computer. The quality of the output is directly related to the quality of the input data and the integrity of the model. 'Modelling is best planned on an incremental and parsimonious basis, with the expectation that the model will need to be enhanced as knowledge about the system develops' (Pidd, 1993: 13).

As indicated earlier, modelling can be an expensive process. We can often reduce the costs of this process and come to a workable model more quickly if we create prototypes. In the late 1960s and early 1970s, British Coal was at the forefront of using computers to assist decision-making. They used large mainframe computers and an empire existed that designed and programmed these machines to handle routine management decisions. The stock control system was one of the most advanced in the country. However, the development teams were often remote from the users, the objectives of the system not always clear and the problem boundaries not always clearly defined. It took large amounts of effort to alter the model to undertake more research and to reprogram the computer. With the development of cheap microcomputers, the need for meticulous model building began to decline. Systems changes become less onerous and Rivett's guidance begins to have less importance.

Illustration 7.1 A British Coal planning model

One system that bridged the gap between the old and the new technologies in computer modelling was COLLPLAN (*Colliery Plan*ning). COLLPLAN was commissioned by the head of planning for British Coal. The objective of the system was to provide collieries with a means by which they could plan the output from the colliery and estimate the resources needed to do this.

Models were created, on a mainframe computer system, based on critical path analysis and cost accounting techniques. A number of models were created to cater for the needs of different parts of British Coal. Each program became very complex and suffered from inaccuracies in its operation. It was recognised that the new microcomputers could be used to advantage here.

A new system was developed that was flexible in its approach. A set of general models was created that could then be linked to standard spreadsheet software. This new approach enabled users to adapt the model to their own particular requirements and model development and adjustment became much quicker and cheaper using this prototyping approach. The advent of microcomputers and developments in software has enabled modellers to rapidly create prototype models of a system.

These models do not, and indeed are not, intended to test all the possible outcomes of a decision scenario. In line with Rivett's first imperative, they should provide early indications of likely outcomes and are used as a tool to gain more knowledge and prompt more research into the system being simulated. Before we get to the stage of computer simulation we need to carefully develop a model that is going to be relevant, even at a prototype stage. These models should be evaluated manually before taking them to the computer modelling stage.

When we build a simulation model, we are concerned with how the entities are affected over time. In simulation modelling, entities are subject to *events*, or *processes*. When the *state* of the system changes then this is an event, such as a train arriving at a platform in a railway model.

Activity 7.8 Consider a busy road junction near to where you live. The local transport department is considering changing the traffic control system. It has a number of options: installing traffic lights, building a roundabout, or doing nothing. How would you go about building a model or models to help the transport department in this decision process? List all of the entities, activities and actors, and say whether they are temporary or permanent. For each one write a short description of its nature.

The model being developed in Activity 7.8 is somewhat different from that described in the earlier inventory model. In the supply of material, the firm actually has some degree of control over the parameters and can adjust the rate of supply and reorder levels. In the case of the traffic junction we cannot alter the supply, in this case the vehicle arrivals. We can measure the arrival rate of vehicles either by doing a manual survey at various times of the day, or by installing a traffic monitoring system to record the information. The entities include: the arriving vehicles (from all sides), the lights and pedestrians. The processes include: the lights changing, the vehicles moving off, and pedestrians walking across the road. The actors are the drivers and the pedestrians.

Activity 7.9 What might be the objective of the traffic department when the model is ready to mimic the various options? What factors would need to be considered?

The objective of the traffic department (Activity 7.9) could be to reduce accidents and keep traffic flowing smoothly. Factors other than those already identified would include the change in traffic movements over time. Demographic changes in car use and ownership, and local issues such as the development or removal of housing and industry, the effects of nearby businesses and schools and public events, would influence the system.

The event of a car (an entity) waiting at the junction is complicated by the fact that there are other junctions. The arrival rate of cars at each junction will vary throughout the day. The cars will wait at the junction for either the lights to change or a safe gap to appear, so that they can enter the island traffic.

7.4.1 Monte Carlo simulation

Monte Carlo simulation is a technique that mimics the way in which a system changes over time. It can be *event-based*, in which case the model alters the parameters every time an event occurs, or *time-based*, where increments in time prompt changes in the parameters when they are due.

Figure 7.5 illustrates a model of an event-based simulation for the road junction, where A_v = arrival time, IA_v is the interarrival time (the time between vehicles arriving).

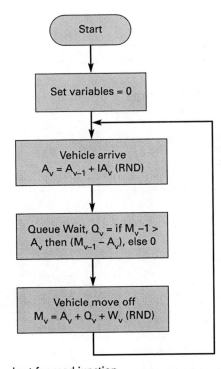

Figure 7.5 Simulation flowchart for road junction

Two important factors dictate how long the vehicle remains at the junction: the time waiting in the queue (Q_v) and how long each has to wait once it has reached the front of the queue (W_v). The term 'RND' is used to denote the use of random numbers to generate the times. Table 7.3 shows a summary of the data collected at a local busy junction; the complete set of data is shown in Appendix 3 of this chapter.

From the data, we can assign a distribution function (Figure 7.6). The actual results are and would be skewed differently during the day, with some periods showing longer or shorter interarrival times. Random numbers are assigned to the distribution function in proportion to the frequency of the event. Hence as 7–9 seconds occurs 14 per cent of the time, 14 numbers are allocated to it (more accuracy would be gained from using bigger numbers, but the data are not that accurate anyway, as it was only a sample of 86 cars on one day of the week).

The waiting time to move off is more normally distributed. Again, we can develop a distribution based on the observed values recorded in Table 7.4. This is shown in Figure 7.7.

Table 7.3 Interarrival times distribution (seconds)

Time	Frequency	%	Cumulative %	Rnd
≤3	10	12	12	1–12
4–6	15	17	29	13–29
7–9	12	14	43	30–43
10–12	25	29	72	44–72
13–15	13	15	87	73–87
16–18	8	9	97	88–97
≥19	3	3	100	98–100

Total 86

Table 7.4 Waiting times distribution

Time	Frequency	Cumulative %	Rnd
≤3	5	17	1–17
4–6	7	40	18–40
7–9	9	70	41–70
10–12	3	80	71–80
13–15	4	93	81–93
≥16	2	100	94–100

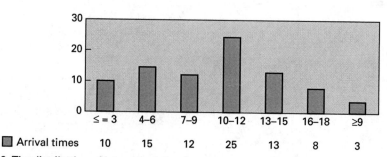

| | Arrival times | 10 | 15 | 12 | 25 | 13 | 8 | 3 |

Figure 7.6 The distribution of interarrival times

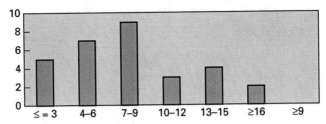

Figure 7.7 The distribution of waiting times

We can now simulate the flow of traffic at this junction using random number tables and our model. As the tables are in the form of a histogram, we need to take the midpoint for each distribution. So 7–9 becomes 8 seconds (in Table 7.4). Also, at the edges of the distributions we will assume that ≥ 16 is 17, ≤ 3 is 2, ≥ 19 is 20.

Activity 7.10

Using the random number table in Appendix 2, simulate the flow of traffic at the junction. To help you we have simulated the arrival and departure of the first five vehicles (Table 7.5). The random numbers in column 1 are used for interarrival time; the random numbers in column 5 have been used for the waiting time. How could the traffic department use this information to decide on the best policy to use?

Table 7.5 Simulation form

Column	1	2	3	4	5	6	7	8
No. car	Rnd	Inter-arrival time IA_t	Arrival time $(1+2_{(v-1)})$ A_t	Queue $(7_{(v-1)}-3)$ Q_t	Rnd	Wait for space W_t	Move off $(3+4+6)$ M_t	Time in system $(4+6)$
1	73	14	14	0	3	2	16	2
2	61	11	25	0	14	2	27	2
3	60	11	36	0	99	17	53	17
4	94	18	54	0	26	5	59	5
5	49	11	65	0	95	17	82	17

Appendix 1 shows a completed table. The information shows that there are occasional build-ups of traffic, but as mean arrival times are greater than mean waiting times there should never be a severe problem. A new model could be created that included traffic lights that, for example, were green (go) for two minutes and red (stop) for two minutes. This may then cut down on the overall waiting time.

Computers and simulation

The Excel spreadsheet has functions that generate random numbers. RAND provides a random decimal between 0 and 1, RANDBETWEEN provides a random number between two predefined limits. These enable simple simulations to be created rapidly. However, the distribution function still needs to be defined. RANDBETWEEN is ideal if the outcomes of an event are uniformly distributed over the given range (in Table 7.6 the range is 0–10). RAND can be used in con-

Table 7.6 Excel® random functions

RANDBETWEEN	RAND	Interarrival
7	0.759341	14
1	0.92206	17
7	0.344335	8
0	0.556881	11
7	0.915726	17
6	0.764861	14
7	0.035796	2
9	0.750822	14
3	0.075505	2
5	0.878614	17
8	0.687167	11
7	0.076721	2

junction with IF statements to guide the simulation on a course of action. For example, in Table 7.6 the interarrival times are determined by the formula:

=IF(H3<=0.12,2,IF(H3<=0.29,5,IF(H3<=0.43,8,IF(H3<=0.72,11,IF(H3<=0.87,14,IF(H3<=0.97,17,IF(H3<=0.99,20,0)))))))

7.5 Forecasting models

Forecasts are fundamental to all business activities. We need to be able to 'accentuate the positive and eliminate the negative'; this can be enhanced if we have some indication of the influences shaping the possible scenarios confronting the firm.

The 'big project' that diverts funds and management concentration has had, in many instances, disastrous consequences. An over-reliance on the success of one product or project can creep into a firm's strategy, so managers need to forecast whether their business could survive the complete failure or delayed start of a project. Reliance on single customers or suppliers can bring significant risks, even to the failure of the third party or through economic blackmail. Overoptimism is a recurring feature of business failures – for example the 'failure' of the Millennium Dome in the UK, where the Dome failed to meet forecast attendance figures. Accurate planning and forecasting are vital to the health of a business, and so it makes sense that business plans are reviewed for realism, accuracy and sensitivity to change. What are the threats and consequences if an important assumption is wrong by 5 per cent or 10 per cent in the forecast planning stage?

Inadequate, or missing, management information might suggest that managers have something to hide (possibly even from themselves) or that they do not have adequate skills to control the business. It is worth noting that some management teams who perform well during the good times find it difficult to survive the bad times.

7.5.1 Working forecasts

Most managerial activity is based on expectations about an uncertain future. Forecasts which are well reasoned and explicit are preferable to those implicit in the manager's mind and based on 'gut feel'. Working forecasts ought to be the synthesis of:

- an automatic forecast (usually quantitative), and
- subjective, the casual, irregular and routine source of information and managerial judgement.

It is obvious in many studies that practitioners rely heavily on judgemental forecasting methods. All forecasts should be subsequently compared with quantified business objectives. The final step is monitoring and control, i.e. compare performance achievement with planned activity levels. Naturally, this may lead to corrective action, modification to working forecasts and redevelopment of corporate goals.

Features of forecasting models

It is quite easy to justify the benefits of any forecasting model. These benefits should be compiled, because they increase understanding, identify key variables and permit variety in the values of options and parameters. Whilst simplicity is preferable, from any model a 'vision' of the future develops which, additionally, furnishes an estimate of the anticipated margin of error, which is an important element of the forecast.

Non-quantitative models form the contribution to the subjective part of the working forecast. The methods include: panel of experts, Delphi, market surveys or collaborative group work. Any subjective estimate may coincide with the quantitative estimates, but is subject to limitations, as it may under- or overestimate without full analysis or justification. However, we concentrate on a numerical perspective and philosophy, with an appraisal of the models' strengths and weaknesses.

7.5.2 Reasons to create a forecasting model

'The Meteorological Office [responsible for the British weather forecasts] give a 40 per cent chance of clear skies for the eclipse [of 11 August 1999], but they admit to a 30 per cent chance that they may be wrong' (*Daily Telegraph*, 5 August 1999). Such a statement is clearly odd, but our human need is for accuracy and comfort in the prediction, not an admission of the wide miss that could occur.

Forecasts are technically incorrect most of the time but their preparation must be done within the context of the available data, responding to the question, 'what do we think the future holds?' Giving an estimate for the margin of error is good practice. Attention on the forecast value alone is bad practice.

There is always the need to redevelop forecasts, which originate in the planning phase of any work. Operationally, the readjustment might occur if the actual situation diverges from the plan significantly, e.g. by 10 per cent or more, but that will vary from case to case. *Heuristic* decision rules may then take over, meaning that some principle or guideline is in force ('custom and practice'), but if you aim to control activities to within a defined margin of error then a tool-set is needed to adjust a pricing policy or minimise cost, or have in place enough personnel to achieve the desired outcome. A full-blown review of the financial situation ought to have supporting quantitative forecasts – out of courtesy alone. A marketing person could argue that product (or service) demand will generally shape the acquisition and supply of base materials, possibly a production plan for each office, depot or factory, with subsequent follow-up plans for the distribution from factory to market, consumer or user.

In short, the forecasting should cascade according to strategic requirements, the following factors being most important:

- growth of the demand;
- seasonal influences on change in response by consumer;
- uncertainties in consumer behaviour;
- price difference between competitors.

A suitable forecast will optimally predict a surplus or a shortage, and suspected deviations from planned quantities can be carefully minimised by regular forecasting.

Consumer demand has a random element reflecting the type of business. Demand for a washing machine is unpredictable, but demand for the motors that drive the washing machine are more certain as they are dependent on planned manufacture of the washing machines. A quantitative estimate of the historical variations will clarify the future variation. Can supply match demand exactly, or should we always ensure that supply and storage capacity are ahead of all anticipated demand? Is the cost of storage of inventory at the end of the month a problem? Is random variation more a cause of our planning problems than the seasonal variation?

7.5.3 Routine quantitative models

Commercial and business data are commonly portrayed by a series of chronological data values, where the horizontal axis represents time. Time includes all the factors that cause variation, and is a surrogate for all the independent variables that stimulate the response variable. This might include marketing effort, pricing policy and supply timings.

Typical stimulated response variables are customer demand, capacity provision, quality attributes such as the number of faults per week, or an index that evaluates change in something, such as the retail price index or the death rate.

Simple line graphs show the direct relationship between two variables. A weekly plot of shortages might show a situation out of control with an underlying trend of greater risk.

Time series models

Traditionally, three characteristics and effects in a time series model have interested forecasters:

- *Trend* (Figure 7.8), which is about growth and decline, especially in recent data values, although the entire history should be considered.

■ *Seasonal variation* (Figure 7.9), which is about repeated peaks and troughs in the data, visible from period to period and obviously significant. To apply a seasonal model, the seasons must be clearly defined and repetitive in nature, and have at least two replications. If you only had 18 months' data then you could assess the seasonal variation for the first 6 months only. A seasonal effect may increase or decrease as time goes on, or be merely constant.

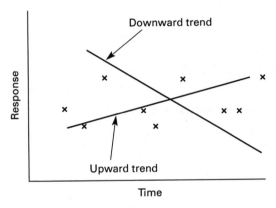

Figure 7.8 Trend with random variation

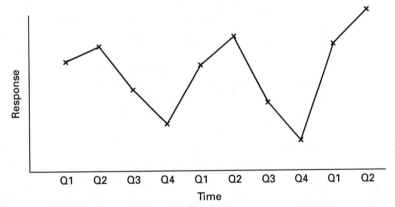

Figure 7.9 Seasonal variation increasing with time

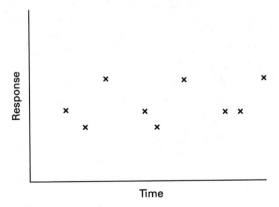

Figure 7.10 Random variation

- *Random effects* (Figure 7.10), the inability to prescriptively say that a value will occur because unseen influences are at work despite apparently equal circumstances to the previous period.

The 'cycle' that is apparent in some economies is too complex and sophisticated for our chosen models to estimate successfully.

Other textbooks, for example Morris (1996), Thomas (1997) and Anderson *et al.* (1998), provide the underpinning quantitative theory, we will merely give the formula being applied. Software, such as the Management Scientist (Anderson *et al.*, 1998) or Microsoft Excel® aids the calculation side and should be used where possible.

Three traditional, simple models can be fitted to a set of data to furnish what we might call 'preliminary' forecast estimates for the next time period, F_t:

- Moving average (*n* periods)

$$F_t = \frac{(A_{t-1} + A_{t-2} + A_{t-3} + \ldots + A_{t-n})}{n}$$

- Exponential smoothing

$$F_t = F_{t-1} + \alpha \, (A_{t-1} - F_{t-1})$$

- Linear trend projection

$$F_t = A + BX$$

The Multiplicative (or additive) seasonal model is covered in Illustration 7.2.

The forecast might utilise actual data values from the past (A_{t-1}, A_{t-2}, etc.), forecasts from the past (F_{t-1}) or estimated values (A, B, X), each being a meaningful contributor of information to the equation.

Additionally, such models can also incorporate a 'weight' that gives appropriate emphasis to data values, depending on whether the data are in the near or distant past.

Example 7.2   The following amounts (set out in Table 7.7) were spent by an author on his gas bills over a four-year period (Figure 7.11), values being payable per quarter. They are further charted in Figure 7.12.

Table 7.7 Gas data (£)

	Quarter			
	1	2	3	4
Year 1				65
Year 2	70	80	45	70
Year 3	80	85	60	85
Year 4	90	100	65	

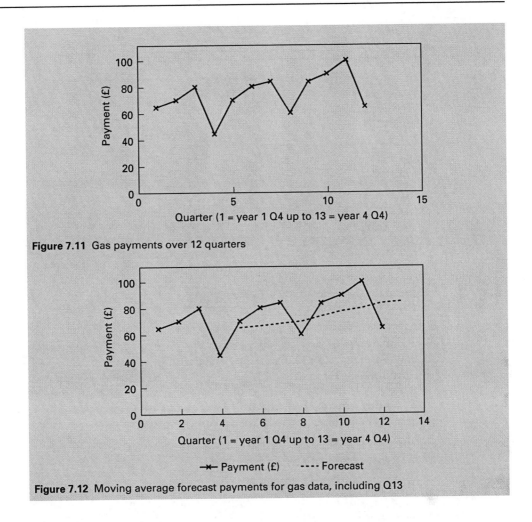

Figure 7.11 Gas payments over 12 quarters

Figure 7.12 Moving average forecast payments for gas data, including Q13

Moving average

Quarterly moving average figures are suitable, and will provide a forecast estimate for the next quarter, quarter 4 of year 4. A moving average could be the average of two values at a time, or three or four etc. For illustration purposes, we will take them four at a time (Table 7.8) and then position the moving average in (2) against the next actual value in (1) so as to estimate the forecast and its associated 'error' in (3), which is the numerical difference between (1) and (2).

As for judging the effectiveness of a model, it is normal to work out the 'squared errors', add them up and average them out. So, the sum of squared errors is 1,612.5 and the mean squared error is 201.6 (Table 7.8).

Several authors advocate the next value in (2) as the value for the forecast for Q4 of year 4. Others insist that a line be drawn from Q1 of year 4 forward to Q4 of year 4, having put the values of 65.00, 65.00, 66.25 etc. against their 'true' mid-point values, i.e. between Q1 and Q2 of year 2, between Q2 and Q3 of year 2 etc.

The Management Scientist (Anderson *et al.*, 1998) uses the former approach and we recommend that strategy too, as it avoids undue extrapolation across a long time period. The moving average values increase throughout, and the forecast of

Table 7.8 Moving average model calculations

	(1) Actual (£)	(2) Moving Average	(3) Error (1)–(2)
Year 1 Q4	65		
Year 2 Q1	70		
Q2	80		
Q3	45	260/4 = 65.0	
	Total = 260		
Q4	70	65.00	5.00
Year 3 Q1	80	66.25	13.75
Q2	85	68.75	16.25
Q3	60	70.00	−10.00
Q4	85	73.75	11.25
Year 4 Q1	90	77.50	12.50
Q2	100	80.00	20.00
Q3	65	83.75	−18.75
Forecast		85.00	

Total squared errors = 1,612.5
Mean squared error = 1,612.5/8 = 201.6

85.00 for Q4 of year 4 is 'about right'. The size of the errors may worry you, as they have a mean squared error of 201.6, which, when square rooted back into the appropriate units, is 14.2. This is then about 16.7 per cent compared to the forecast for the next quarter (14.2/85.00). The forecasts are shown in Figure 7.12.

Notice how each of the four data values contributes equally to the forecast, which may not be a satisfactory philosophy at all.

Exponential smoothing model

In this model, the idea of a weight (α, the exponential smoothing constant) appears in the formula and contributes to the philosophy that you may wish to give more emphasis to later data values:

$$F_t = F_{t-1} + \alpha(A_{t-1} - F_{t-1})$$

This formula uses information from the forecast in the previous period (F_{t-1}) with another value that is a comparison, or adjustment, according to the difference in the actual and the forecast from the previous period, $t-1$.

This idea is more likely to remove the influence of out-of-date data from the forecast. If α is set equal to 1 then $F_t = A_{t-1}$, and if α is set equal to 0 then $F_t = F_{t-1}$. Neither of these is a sound approach, so a value from 0 to 1 is used.

To illustrate the technique, let us try α equal to 0.4 and start the analysis with $F_1 = A_1 = 65$. The Management Scientist gives the results shown in Table 7.9 for the forecast and the errors.

The forecast for the next period is 79.36, which is below the moving average forecast value of 85.00, but notice how the mean squared error is much lower for the moving average model which implies that a generally tighter fit has been achieved by the moving average model. Hence, the preferred forecast is 85.0.

Table 7.9 Forecasting with the Exponential Smoothing Constant set at 0.4

		(1) Actual (£)	(2) Forecast	(3) Error (1)–(2)
Year 1	Q4	65		
Year 2	Q1	70	65.00	5.00
	Q2	80	67.00	13.00
	Q3	45	72.20	−27.20
	Q4	70	61.32	8.68
Year 3	Q1	80	64.79	15.21
	Q2	85	70.88	14.12
	Q3	60	76.53	−16.53
	Q4	85	69.92	15.08
Year 4	Q1	90	75.95	14.05
	Q2	100	81.57	18.43
	Q3	65	88.94	−23.94
Forecast	Q4		79.36	

Total squared errors = 3,050.7
Mean squared error = 277.34

Linear trend

The process of fitting a straight line model to a dataset is achieved mechanically or by computation. The formula we outlined above needs values for A and B, where A represents the intersection of the line with the vertical axis (where time is 0) and B represents the gradient of the line. Using software, the values shown in Table 7.10 are found.

$$\text{Linear trend projection} \quad F_t = A + BX$$
$$= 62.879 + 1.801\,t$$

where t is the time value for period t.

The forecast for period 13 is 86.29.

The mean squared error of 167.4 is even less than for the moving average model of 201.6, so this model then becomes even tighter on the closeness between the actual and the forecast. Hence, the forecast of 86.3 is more reliable than the others, but the weakness is that it probably ignores the seasonal differences in the spending on gas. This is clearly evident in Quarter 3, low spending.

Illustration 7.2 looks at an example of the seasonal model. It is also important to remember that the moving average model and the exponential smoothing models could take on other versions, because the choice of number of periods or the smoothing constant α could be varied. We have merely illustrated the forecasting procedure by picking on values and letting them generate the forecasts.

Critically, we should notice that these three models are appropriate only when the dataset is non-stationary, or when there is a simplicity about the data because seasonal or cyclical effects are absent.

7.5.4 Wider perspectives on forecasting

Economic efficiency is improved by relevant application of such techniques, especially at the microeconomic level and this will lead to improvements in the decision-making whether profit is the motive or not. Computers allow such fore-

Table 7.10 Forecasting with the Linear Trend model, including forecast errors

Year	Quarter	(1) Actual (£)	(2) Linear trend	(3) Error (1)–(2)
Year 1	Q4	65	64.68	0.32
Year 2	Q1	70	66.48	3.52
	Q2	80	68.28	11.72
	Q3	45	70.08	−25.08
	Q4	70	71.88	−1.88
Year 3	Q1	80	73.69	6.31
	Q2	85	75.49	9.51
	Q3	60	77.29	−17.29
	Q4	85	79.09	5.91
Year 4	Q1	90	80.89	9.11
	Q2	100	82.69	17.31
	Q3	65	84.49	−19.49
Forecast	Q4		86.29	

Total squared errors = 2,009.0
Mean squared error = 167.4

casts to be made almost instantly. The weakness of letting the software do the calculations is that we lose sight of the details of the technique. The forecast planner has to be aware of the theory of the model.

Assuming that the future will continue as the past, new models can be exported easily to reports (spot the danger?). The less certain we are about the future the more we move to non-quantitative models such as Delphi-type analysis. The regular and timely updating of the model as data become available will enhance the forecasting stature. Personal assessment has its place too. Irrational and unpredictable factors influence demand as well as supply. Angela (Illustration 7.2) has to react when the garage up the road raises its price by 2p a litre or runs out of diesel. So, she orders more and tries to avoid a stockout problem. The aim is to complement the decision-making with inputs of relevant magnitude and importance. Suppose there is a national raising of petrol prices, then the demand may drop, but only reliable data monitoring will help to quantify the impact. This random effect will be due to policy change rather than customer disloyalty.

Illustration 7.2 Forecasting for service levels

For four years, Angela has managed Ferguson's busy, independently run petrol station at Fort Trafford, during which time it has established an excellent reputation for quality and service. In order to maintain these high service levels, forecasting of diesel fuel requirements is critical. The business need is to supply to and meet demand and, from a company point of view, maintain optimum working levels, thereby reducing the amount of capital tied up in storage and also the loss of product in storage through evaporation.

In recent years, the trend in the UK has been towards diesel engine cars for economy and greater fuel efficiency. Official government data show that the number of cars, lorries and motorbikes on the roads will continue to increase for the foreseeable future. The introduction of cleaner, low-sulphur diesel fuels has also stimulated demand for diesel engine cars.

Angela has requested a forecast of the point in time when extra diesel storage will be needed to meet the continuing monthly growth in demand. To plan for the renewing or extension of the tanks (current capacity is 420,000 litres) is becoming inevitable and Angela worries about the effect of disturbance.

She recalls that on her MBA course an enthusiastic tutor once forced her to 'do a forecast analysis' of some sales data for an assignment.

Her day-to-day role concerns itself with many quantities, such as available types and levels of stock, or timing of arrivals. Each week, tankers deliver diesel on the five normal working days (but not bank holidays). On three days, a tanker brings a total of 32,000 litres of fuel (of which 15,000 litres is diesel, 15,000 litres is unleaded fuel and 2,000 litres is lead replacement petrol, LRP). On other days, the delivery is 20,000 litres of diesel and 12,000 litres of unleaded fuel.

In the shop at the petrol station, average daily sales are about £16,000 (of which £14,000 is fuel and the rest is other items such as confectionery, oil, snacks etc.).

An analysis of daily fuel sales shows diesel averaging 12,000 litres per day (about 56 per cent of total sales), with unleaded at 8,500 litres per day and LRP at 1,000 litres per day. The latter increased dramatically from January 2000 under new legislation.

Angela requests the last two years' diesel sales figures from head office reports (Table 7.11 and Figure 7.13). Quick inspection shows a general upwards trend, but with some unpredictable random variation.

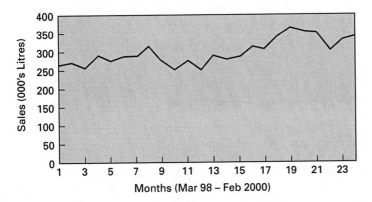

Figure 7.13 Two years' data of diesel sales to assess trend

Angela uses Excel® for all her graphs. To gauge the seasonal effect, she replots the 24 months' data into a 12-month window, with 2 years superimposed (Figure 7.14).

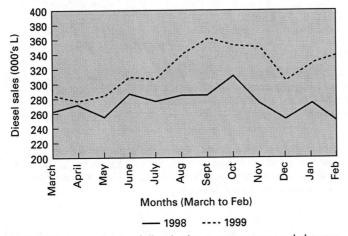

Figure 7.14 Two years' data of diesel sales to assess seasonal changes

Table 7.11 Last two years' diesel sales figures from Head Office reports

Month/Year	Month number	Actual sales (000 litres)
March 1998	1	264
	2	270
	3	255
	4	288
	5	276
	6	286
	7	285
	8	313
	9	273
	10	253
	11	274
	12	250
March 1999	13	285
	14	277
	15	286
	16	310
	17	306
	18	339
	19	364
	20	354
	21	351
	22	304
	23	330
February 2000	24	339

The obvious upwards trend does not disguise the selling pattern of diesel, which is consistently seasonal in nature over the 24-month period. A simple statistic, the range of the data for both 12-month periods (Table 7.12), reinforces the upward trend but also the wider variation in sales in year 2 (March 1999 to February 2000).

Table 7.12 Variation in diesel sales over a two-year period

Year	Range (litres)	From (litres)	To (litres)
1	60,000	253,000 (Dec.)	313,000 (Oct.)
2	87,000	277,000 (April)	364,000 (Sept.)

Angela is not too much concerned with the forecast for next month, but she does trust forecasting methods already, as she has surprised herself by accurately forecasting her gas and electric consumption at home using the Management Scientist software.

The question of the seasonal influence is clearer, as during both years sales peak during September and October, but in December sales drop somewhat, which is also apparent in May. With two pieces of data for all 12 months, it is possible to estimate the average seasonal effect (Table 7.14). The quantified seasonal effects can be assessed to determine whether there is a 'significant' month in which sales are especially high or low.

Angela also notes that diesel sales change month-on-month. For example, sales in October 98 are 10 per cent higher than September 1998 (313,000 vs 285,000 litres). This might be the effect of having more lorries moving goods for Christmas, or the worsening weather. Curiously, the same effect is not there in the second year's data, so we ponder whether it is a real effect.

Seasonal model

Usually, a multiplicative time series which incorporates the trend, seasonal effect and the random effect is sufficiently flexible to provide a forecast.

$$Y_t = T_t \times S_t \times I_t$$

where t is the time period in question, Y is the value that we need to forecast, T is the effect of the trend, S the effect of the season, and I the non-regular, random effect.

Forecasts are easy to produce using the Management Scientist for the number crunching. A further value, the mean squared error (MSE) is, subsequently, square-rooted to evaluate the margin of error.

Statistical analysis of the forecasting model

The Management Scientist results (Table 7.13) for the seasonal model are: actual sales, forecast sales and forecast error per month.

The MSE of 220,000 litres and the forecast for the next month (March 2000, month 25) of 343,330 litres are provided by fitting this model to this data.

As indicated earlier, the average monthly seasonal factors can be estimated by this calculating procedure (Table 7.14).

Table 7.14 shows that 'high season' is June, August and September, with October being 14.9 per cent above average. All the other months have 'below average' sales. July and November seem to be average, their indexes being close to 1.000. Sales are worst, seasonally, in February, being 11.2 per cent below average over the two years.

A complete statistical analysis of data would try fitting all four models, the linear trend and the seasonal model being absolutely fixed apart from the choice of the number of seasons. With the moving average and exponential smoothing models, a sensible choice and some fine-tuning need to occur so as to generate the best answers for each class of model. In Table 7.15, the results of fitting three moving average and one exponential smoothing model are given. Such results are easily derived using software.

Table 7.13 Comparison of actual and forecast diesel sales per month using the multiplicative time-series model

Month/year	Month	Actual	Forecast	Error
March 1998	1	264	251.40	12.60
	2	270	243.87	26.13
	3	255	251.36	3.64
	4	288	271.63	16.37
	5	276	268.13	7.87
	6	286	295.57	−9.57
	7	285	290.44	−5.44
	8	313	322.06	−9.06
	9	273	283.15	−10.15
	10	253	263.87	−10.87
	11	274	287.37	−13.37
Feb. 1999	12	250	262.45	−12.45
	13	285	297.37	−12.37
	14	277	287.80	−10.80
	15	286	295.97	−9.97
	16	310	319.13	−9.13
	17	306	314.34	−8.34
	18	339	345.78	−6.78
	19	364	339.10	24.90
	20	354	375.27	−21.27
	21	351	329.29	21.71
	22	304	306.30	−2.30
	23	330	332.97	−2.97
Feb. 2000	24	339	303.55	35.45

Table 7.14 Average monthly seasonal effect

Season	Seasonal index
March	0.993
April	0.949
May	0.963
June	1.026
July	0.998
Aug.	1.085
Sept.	1.051
Oct.	1.149
Nov.	0.997
Dec.	0.916
Jan.	0.985
Feb.	0.888

Using the MSE as the deciding criterion, the seasonal model is clearly the best model. Each of the historical data values is 'forecast' backwards into history so as to verify the suitability of the proposed model.

To estimate the margin of error on the forecast for the next period, it is routinely simple to calculate the square root of the MSE and then divide that by the forecast for the next period so as to estimate the percentage error for the model, as shown in Table 7.15.

Table 7.15 Results of fitting four models (ranked by size of the MSE, smallest first)

Model	MSE	Forecast for next period	√MSE	% error
Seasonal (12 seasons)	222	343.3	14.9	14.9/343.3 = 4.3
Exponential smoothing (0.7)	480	335.3	21.9	21.9/335.3 = 6.5
Linear trend	483	341.6	22.0	6.4
Moving average (2 periods)	514	334.5	22.7	6.8
Moving average (3 periods)	602	324.3	24.5	7.6
Moving average (12 periods)	1,531	320.4	39.1	12.2

This sort of presentation does confirm the consistency of the estimates for the next month's forecast, i.e. 343,300 litres. The company can expect about 4.3 per cent as a realistic prediction of the variation on the sales. Conversely, the moving average model with 12 periods is seen as a real no-hope model in all aspects. Inadvertently using it would generate a forecast of 320,400 litres, quite distinct from the best model.

Forecasting to when capacity might be exceeded

Angela knows that the time is coming when increased sales will require new tanks to store the diesel fuel. The tanks' capacity is 420,000 litres, but she needs to forecast when monthly sales will reach that level.

Figure 7.15 shows the forecast values for the period up to month 36, February 2001. In that time, October 2000 will furnish a predicted sales value which goes over the capacity. Angela realises she needs to be looking forward by about 8 months only before the shortages of diesel fuel get critical. These sales figures are, of course, subject to the 4.3 per cent margin of error predicted earlier, but Angela has to put in motion a plan to expand.

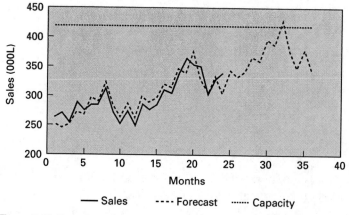

Figure 7.15 Forecast sales against the maximum capacity of the tanks (420,000 L)

She could also monitor traffic flows on the roads nearby or determine whether there are any environmental or civic changes coming forward, e.g. new road, shops, housing etc.

As identified earlier, the weaknesses of the exponential smoothing and moving average models are that they only predict one period ahead. The seasonal model is most useful in this respect because it can keep going 'into the future'.

A critical comparison of forecasting models

Target setting is a vital part of management. A clearly defined target, which is both realistic and achievable, can be monitored for signs of a variance. The target must be measurable and visible. There should be a better than 50 per cent probability of achieving the target. The target should concern achieving improvements rather than just increasing activity. Dates and times should be explicitly stated, and those responsible for achieving the target should be involved with setting it. A team leader should measure the progress of the team against the plan and the effect of the activities on the original problem. Measurement success criteria might include: the monitoring of progress against target; be clear and understood; be repeatable and consistent; and be responsive to action you intend to take.

Time series – assumptions and limitations

There are several assumptions to consider before we plunge into 'fitting' the model to a set of data:

- The forecasting model will continue into the future as it did with the historical data.
- Simple models provide forecasts.
- The rate of change ('trend') is constant only in the linear trend projection model.
- A model can be updated as new data arrives.
- Mean squared error is sufficient to discriminate between models.
- If casting bones work, use them!

There are some obvious limitations to these models

- The moving average and exponential smoothing models only forecast one period ahead.
- Missing data may have to be estimated.
- Time is the only independent factor considered.
- Forecast accuracy will improve if more variables could be added to the independent variables.

Some models are impossible to interpret, e.g. a 28-period moving average is technically possible, but is probably completely unrealistic.

Forecasting and strategic planning

It can also be argued that planning and scheduling are a multidisciplinary effort. The planning phase starts from the markets; simulated demand figures and the expected supply position convert into orders for products, and hence in the operational phase the actual operations for the period are determined.

In a simulation, the focus is likely to be on the growth or decline in the demand, the seasonal influences, the uncertainties in consumer behaviour and the price difference between self and competitors. The forecasts are adapted to give sufficient quantities for the demand level.

7.6 Models in practice

The widespread use of mathematical models is a recent addition to the managerial toolkit. The use of computers in modelling and simulation dates back to the late 1970s, when some labour intensive text-based software was available, which helped scientists simulate processes. The software has developed considerably since then, with powerful graphical packages being available that can run on personal computers. These packages utilise developments in chaos theory for data compression through similarity and Monte Carlo simulation concepts for mimicking events.

Apart from dedicated simulation software, a number of other systems can help in creating simulation models. The data for the exercises in this book has been evaluated using a spreadsheet package (Microsoft Excel®). Most companies now have such packages that deal primarily with management accounting issues. Their use is invaluable for developing 'what if?' scenarios. Apart from using computers to develop 'what if?' models, they are useful in being able to store large amounts of the data needed for decision-making. Throughout this text models are referred to when relevant. Table 7.16 lists some of these and the chapters in which they can be found.

Expert systems

An example of an expert system could be found in a car maintenance garage. There are many different models of cars, and not every mechanic could possibly be an expert on each type and model of car. Within the industry, the use of expert systems is becoming more common as skills become less common and more expensive to acquire. If the garage employs a mechanic who is an expert on Volvo gearboxes, we can capture that knowledge with a computer. Every time a problem occurs we can record the symptoms, the problem and the cure. When the expert is on holiday or leaves, a mechanic with basic skills, who is not an expert on Volvos or their gearboxes, can input the symptoms and the computer will advise on the best course of action based on this prior knowledge. If it is wrong, then the computer is updated with this new scenario and hence learns from the mistake.

Table 7.16 Mathematical models and their purposes

Model	Chapter	Purpose
Forecasting	7	Predictions of future events to aid in planning
Inventory control	9	To reduce inventory sizes to a minimum size, whilst providing a defined level of customer service
Cost/volume/profit – make-or-buy	8	Determines the breakeven point where the costs and profit to provide a product are the same as the costs to buy it
Financial appraisal	8	To judge the monetary worth of a course of action
Critical path analysis	10	Determines the shortest time to complete a project and the consequent non-critical activities
Expert systems	7	To provide intelligence
Decision trees	2	Evaluates the outcomes of alternative decision choices
Linear programming	9	Provides information on the best use of scarce resources
Transportation	9	Provides information on the best combination of alternative transport options

◆ Summary

Modelling and simulation help organisations understand complex situations by breaking the problem area down into well-defined parameters. The cause and effect relationships between the parameters can be measured, or estimated and quantified. The outputs from the model can then be used to aid in the decision-making process, and the development of the model helps in a general understanding of the forces at work within the organisation. There are a number of pitfalls in simulation development, not least the need to develop models quickly, before the need for a decision goes away. Computer modelling is a relatively new development and becoming accessible to small and medium-sized companies using cheaper high-powered personal computers. It is likely that more companies will routinely use simulation in the future to help gain a better understanding of their business and assist in the decision-making process.

? Decision diary

Find a local situation that involves inflows and outflows of people and queues. Try to create a simulation that models this movement. For example, you might choose the local post office, corner shop, or café.

If you are working, find out how the firm forecasts future demand. Also try to develop a model that forecasts your own finances over a six-month period. Base it on past bank statements. Then create a new forecast based on your predicted expenditure and compare the two. What lessons do you draw from this?

References

Anderson, D. R., Sweeney, D. J. and Williams T. A. (1998) *Quantitative Methods for Business,* 7th edition. Cincinnatti, Ohio: South-Western College Publishing.

Daellenbach H.G. (1994) *Systems and decision-making.* Chichester: Wiley.

Morris, C. (1996) *Quantitative Approaches in Business Studies,* 4th edition. London: Pitman Publishing.

Rivett, P. (1994) *The Craft of decision-making.* Chichester: Wiley.

Pidd, M. (1993), *Computer Simulation in Management Science.* Chichester: Wiley.

Thomas, R. (1997) *Quantitative Methods for Business Studies.* London: Prentice Hall.

Software

Anderson, D.R. Sweeney, D.J. and Williams, T.A. (1998) The Management Scientist (version 4.0 for Windows and Windows 95), a microcomputer software package (3.5″ disk). Cincinnatti, Ohio: South-Western College Publishing.

Glossary

Analogue models:	representations of the situation displayed in another form, so that the physical appearances are significantly different.
Delphi forecasting:	a panel of experts is asked individually and in private what they predict about the future. They provide an answer, which is then circulated to other members of the panel. Each member is asked to comment on each other's forecast and to revise his or her own in the light of the new wisdoms. In this way a consensus is hopefully gained, that is a synthesis of all the wise people.
Economic order quantity (EOQ):	the cheapest quantity of material to be ordered. A balance between inventory ordering and holding costs.
Heuristic:	a convenient term for the technique of investigation or decision that can be acquired solely by practice and experience.
Iconic models:	reproductions of physical objects, generally to a smaller scale. For example, a map can be on paper or on a computer screen.
Lead-time:	the time between placing an order and the order being delivered
Problem domain:	in many ways similar to the concept of a system as defined in Chapter 6. We need to define the components, relationships and activities within the problem area.
Problem requirements:	could involve providing more information and understanding about a system, or might involve maximisation of some variables and minimisation of others, such as profit and costs.
Symbolic models:	include flowcharts, symbols and mathematical models to simulate the real-life model. They are useful for testing, monitoring and dicussion purposes of the process being modelled.

Answer to Activity 7.10

Column No. car	1 Rnd	2 Inter-arrival time	3 Arrival time $(1+2_{(v-1)})$	4 Queue $(7_{(v-1)}-3)$	5 Rnd	6 Wait for space	7 Move off $(3+4+6)$	8 Time in system $(4+6)$
Arriving		IA_t	A_t	Q_t		W_t	M_t	
1	73	14	14	0	3	2	16	2
2	61	11	25	0	14	2	27	2
3	60	11	36	0	99	17	53	17
4	94	18	54	0	26	5	59	5
5	49	11	65	0	95	17	82	17
6	77	14	79	3	17	2	84	5
7	41	8	87	0	25	5	92	5
8	13	5	92	0	47	8	100	8
9	20	5	97	3	45	8	108	11
10	26	5	102	6	33	5	113	11
11	42	8	110	3	87	14	127	17
12	6	2	112	15	44	8	135	23
13	11	2	114	21	68	8	143	29
14	31	8	122	21	31	5	148	26
15	59	11	133	15	3	2	150	17
16	31	8	141	9	2	2	152	11
17	76	14	155	0	66	8	163	8
18	46	11	166	0	64	8	174	8
19	17	5	171	3	21	5	179	8
20	19	5	176	3	86	14	193	17

Appendix 2   Random number table

C1	C2	C3	C4	C5	C6	C7
73	77	84	60	87	26	3
61	94	82	62	42	86	14
60	52	66	92	41	15	99
94	34	65	9	18	82	26
49	73	97	16	99	54	95
77	98	89	59	67	41	17
41	55	54	71	70	87	25
13	52	42	17	56	7	47
20	76	75	8	35	86	45
26	13	15	77	10	41	33
42	98	11	88	16	57	87
6	44	71	9	46	27	44
11	99	76	65	54	59	68
31	9	58	32	25	77	31
59	25	31	35	55	30	3
31	84	98	40	81	77	2
76	36	56	25	8	71	66
46	24	67	18	88	76	64
17	1	85	24	0	30	21
19	4	19	85	66	29	86
74	82	13	12	89	88	24
9	42	35	76	61	2	58
41	20	97	94	31	32	57
82	36	27	83	78	37	52
34	68	12	74	68	17	12
49	45	49	37	83	81	53
49	33	83	87	41	25	47
96	35	70	60	12	53	56
13	5	13	51	41	95	28
89	60	67	15	5	40	9
46	87	43	27	5	49	100
88	26	67	27	69	28	89
54	17	7	36	70	7	52
65	22	91	47	87	84	54
88	20	63	8	93	77	47
8	66	51	7	100	47	16
35	49	74	22	37	62	23
53	9	71	69	3	59	54
24	74	49	84	93	16	36
97	11	35	19	80	45	99
92	26	91	89	26	31	96
35	39	55	67	49	8	11
18	67	40	1	25	36	94
78	2	74	2	48	63	60

Appendix 3 Data for road junction

Column Car arriving	1 Arrival time	Wait in queue	Wait for space	2 Move off	3 Time in system
1	0	0	3	3	3
2	2	1	8	11	9
3	5	6	5	16	11
4	8	8	14	30	22
5	11	19	6	36	25
6	13	23	8	44	31
7	16	28	8	52	36
8	19	33	13	65	46
9	21	44	5	70	49
10	24	46	7	77	53
11	28	49	3	80	52
12	33	47	3	83	50
13	36	47	10	93	57
14	38	55	16	109	71
15	43	66	9	118	75
16	45	73	7	125	80
17	49	76	3	128	79
18	54	74	9	137	83
19	59	78	14	151	92
20	62	89	7	158	96
21	67	91	3	161	94
22	73	88	6	167	94
23	89	78	12	179	90
24	97	82	8	187	90
25	109	78	10	197	88
26	123	74	5	202	79
27	132	70	17	219	87
28	135	84	5	224	89
29	141	83	13	237	96
30	155	82	5	242	87
Average		55.71	8.1		63.8
Standard deviation		29.1	4.0		29.51

Choice

Preface to Part Three

Given that we now have more information about the decision scenario (knowledge of uncertainty from Part One and knowledge of the decision environment from Part Two), we are often faced with a choice of actions. Part Three introduces some common methods by which alternatives are compared, evaluated and choices are taken.

In Chapter 8 we introduce methods by which decisions are judged in finance terms. Chapter 9 looks at management decision methods that are sometimes used to aid decision-making. This is followed in Chapter 10 by an examination of project management techniques that may be used to assist the decision-maker.

Financial decision-making

8.1 Introduction

Money has always been either directly or indirectly the pre-eminent factor influencing decisions in profit-making businesses. Every decision might be said to have a financial consequence, which reflects the effectiveness and efficiency of the business to achieve its strategic goals. A unique resource in terms of its simplicity of measurement, shared meanings and linear scaling, many quantitative models have been developed to assist the decision-maker to allocate and control money in the 'best' manner to achieve the objectives of the firm. Many of the chapters in this book have either a direct or indirect underpinning of financial decision-making. This chapter specifically addresses those models directly concerned with profitability and cost management.

Quite clearly, some knowledge of accounting principles and procedures is essential to the process of decision-making in a business at both national and international levels. But here we need to be cautious because a little knowledge is a dangerous thing. We need to approach 'management accounting' critically, and on this subject particularly, it is important to refer to other texts to develop a balanced perspective. Bear in mind, too, that what is accepted accounting practice in one country may not be so in another. Financial accounting in general is governed by strict procedures and protocols to provide a comparative and uniform basis for the evaluation of a firm's financial position, for tax purposes or for shareholders' use.

Whilst cost accounting systems have a manufacturing pedigree, the issues are relevant to services and are becoming increasingly important to non-profit organisations which need to account to an increasingly aware group of stakeholders.

An examination of the major texts in cost and management accounting indicates that the distinction between management and cost accounting is extremely vague, with some writers referring to the decision-making aspects in terms of 'cost accounting' and other writers using the term 'management accounting' or even 'financial accounting' (which is an unfortunate phrase as most accounting is done in financial terms). The terms are often used synonymously. What are we to make of this confusing state of affairs? First that we need to be wary of the terms used and to seek clarification of them in particular contexts. Second that accounting can be thought of as financial reporting systems, to external and internal bodies. And third, that we can roughly distinguish different kinds of accounting as follows:

- *Financial accounting* – the provision of information to parties outside an organisation such as shareholders, or those who have made loans to it.
- *Cost accounting* – tracing costs to products and jobs and with measuring departments, divisions and work centres in terms of pure economic performance in relation to the resource consumed in their operations.
- *Management accounting* – the provision of information to managers for decision-making, planning and control of resources.

Once decisions have been made, they may be implemented through a budget. We can distinguish three main types of budget.

- *Operating budgets* – the planned requirements for day-to-day activities within an organisation over a particular time, e.g. a month, a quarter or a year.
- *Capital budgets* – planned financial requirements for the long-term running of an organisation with regard to fixed assets and the forms of finance that the organisation needs.
- *Working capital budgets* – requirements for planned current assets and liabilities of the organisation with specific reference to the cash the organisation needs to finance its day-to-day operations.

Managers need financial information for three basic reasons, namely to enable them to:

- judge the monetary value of a product, process or project, so that they can
- maintain or improve the value, and
- hold staff accountable for the value.

Value might be defined as the difference between revenue or wealth and the cost of generating that revenue. The identification of relevant costs and revenues that reflect the value is often obscured by the complexities of the organisation. Sometimes, however, financial criteria are of secondary importance to qualitative criteria on deciding a course of action. For example, in decisions within the area of employee development, cost may be unimportant compared with issues of morale, employee relations and flexibility of workforce. However, cost cannot be ignored because it determines whether or not the firm can afford the particular programme of development. This has to be determined at some point so that a budget can be established to fund activities when they are planned to occur.

This also illustrates one of the major tasks facing managers – that of determining 'cost' or 'value'. The notions of certainty, uncertainty and scales of rationality further compound this issue. The nature of costs within a firm are such that the notion of accuracy is more apparent than real. 'True cost' is a misnomer, as many accounting data are based on estimation and approximation. The skill of a management accountant, and to some extent the manager interpreting the figures, lies in the ability to appreciate the scale or significance of the data and to analyse them in relation to the overall performance of the firm.

Conversely, the other major issue facing firms is revenue in the form of price and volume, whether this relates to internal pricing policy to create profit centres though *transfer pricing*, or through the determination of an external pricing policy for customers.

This chapter explores these factors and illustrates some of the more common approaches to financial decision-making.

8.2 The elements of cost

Johnson and Kaplan (1987: 131) describe the development of cost accounting systems. Manufacturing firms first developed cost accounting systems for two reasons:

1 to evaluate internal opportunities for gain from their resources;
2 to control the internal processes and activities that generated those higher returns.

The early forms of cost management systems were designed to enable managers get the most out of their business, i.e. to increase efficiency. A number of innovations in accounting have occurred since then. Notably, firms desire to evaluate accurately each product's contribution to the profits of the company. This information can then be used to plan profits in future years.

A number of complicated systems have been developed that aim to attribute a number of costs to a product. For example, when discussing the allocation of indirect costs in 1903, John Mann describes a system by which overheads are allocated to products based on weight and volume. This is a sensible approach given that the heavier a product the more energy will be required to move it; the bulkier a product the greater the floorspace it will occupy. The problem with the approach is that it did not take into account the process that actually produced the product. Many of the early systems were in fact pushed out not for reasons of unsuitability, but because of the high information and processing costs and possibly the need to comply with auditors who concentrated on inventory costing systems.

Inventory costing was the mainstay of management cost accounting from the 1920s. The occasional academic such as William Paton resurrected the ideas of attaching costs to a product as it flows along the process. However, he abandoned this idea in the 1970s by saying,

The basic difficulty with the idea that cost dollars, as occurred, attach like barnacles to the physical flow of materials and stream of operating activity, is that it is at odds with the actual process of valuation in a free competitive market. The customer does not buy a handful of classified and traced cost dollars; he buys a product, at prevailing market price. The market price may be either above or below any calculated cost figure.

(quoted in Kaplan, 1987: 139)

More recently, Goldratt (Goldratt and Cox, 1992) has proposed that inventory includes all of the assets a firm owns that are used in the creation of a product. In this respect inventory has less of a time implication. Traditionally inventory is transient, or should be, used over a short period. Using Goldratt's interpretation, then, buildings become inventory. Whilst this has some operational benefits, as one is drawn towards a continual return on investment approach to costs, it does divert attention to the need to turn round some inventory as quickly as possible.

Cost is, at a simple level, a product of price (in the form of the 'bought-in' cost or the cost of production) and volume. A more detailed definition would be:

The value of economic resources used in an operation to produce a good or a service.

As such, it is a measurable, rational and comparable factor that forms the basis of many decisions.

In the complex world of business, costs are normally split into three main categories: materials, labour and other expenses (Figure 8.1). Depending on the timeframe of analysis, they can be further categorised into *fixed* and *variable* cost. It is interesting to note that the shorter the timeframe the more fixed becomes the cost. Further division into *direct* and *indirect* (Table 8.1) costs allows analysis into the profitability of products and processes. For example, a hotel may have a cost structure as shown below, where the costs are not mutually exclusive, but the classification may provide for some analytical purpose:

Fixed cost:	Rent and rates
Variable cost:	Kitchen staff
Direct cost:	Linen
Indirect cost:	Electricity
Material:	Food ingredients
Labour:	Porters
Expenses:	Postage

In most cases, total aggregate cost is a combination of fixed and variable elements:

Total aggregate cost = Total fixed cost + Total variable cost

Profit is then simply expressed as:

Profit = Revenue − Total aggregate cost

When there is zero profit then:

Total aggregate cost = Revenue

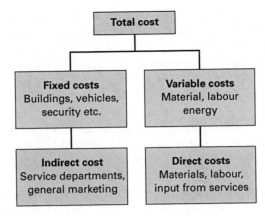

Figure 8.1 Cost structure

Table 8.1 Types of cost

Type	Description
Fixed costs	Assumed to remain unchanged over wide ranges of activities for any given time, regardless of whatever operational activity is taking place and regardless of the volume of production
Variable costs	Incurred in direct proportion to the level of activity that is taking place. If no activity is undertaken the variable cost is zero regardless of whether any fixed costs are being incurred
Indirect costs	Their existence depends on the general operation of the enterprise; they would remain even if a particular activity or action that is being costed had not taken place, e.g. the personnel department is an indirect cost
Direct costs	Arise solely because of the existence of an activity or the undertaking of an action (a product, service or department); they would not have occurred if the activity or action had not taken place

In other words, the organisation is breaking even and the point where revenue equals cost is called the *breakeven point*. Often this is portrayed in a breakeven chart (Figure 8.2).

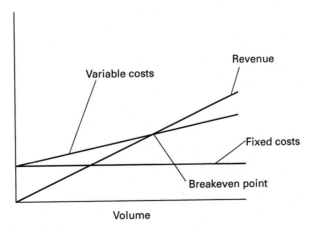

Figure 8.2 Breakeven chart

Within these categories of costs we also need to consider the way in which past costs are valued. Accountants consider the revenue lost as the result of a decision to be a cost, and cost savings as a result of a decision to be revenue.

Costs incurred prior to the present decision are considered to be *sunk*. For example, in the installation of a new management information system we would not consider the cost of the equipment if that equipment were already in place. *Disposal* costs are incurred when there is a mismatch between the book value of the item and the subsequent realised price. This occurs when the depreciation on the item has been incorrectly applied through incorrect estimates of the value of the item over time. (Strictly speaking, depreciation does not affect cash flow, it is primarily a financial accounting convention; however, if items are planned to be replaced then it helps to predict the effect on cash at that time.) Too much depreciation will result in a cash inflow, too little a cash outflow. However, neither should influence the decision to replace the machine, as they are not connected with the future profitability of the machine.

Opportunity cost represents the loss to the firm of revenue or savings in costs due to the chosen option. For example, if as a result of choosing project A, we cannot undertake project B, which would have independently generated £x, then the opportunity cost is £x. *Variable cost* is the increase in total cost when output is increased by one unit. *Marginal revenue* is the increase in total revenue when output is increased by one unit. *Contribution* (to fixed costs) is defined as the difference between revenue and variable costs.

Activity 8.1	Within the department of an organisation with which you are familiar, identify the main costs involved and classify them in as many ways you can. For example, a manager's salary may be directly associated with a product, indirectly associated with training costs, variable to another division and fixed from an organisational perspective (within a particular timeframe).

In a university department the costs incurred are largely labour related. Direct costs include tutors and administration staff, paper and some travel. Indirect costs include administration staff and managers, buildings and energy (as data are not normally collected on facility usage).

Cost units relate to items that proceed through the various parts of a service or manufacturing process. They are items that are so complete in themselves that they can be assumed to be an entity that has activities performed on it. These activities incur costs that are then attributed to the cost unit. Cost units can occur in both services and manufacturing environments. For example, units of service may be seats on a bus, or hours charged by an accountant. Units of production may be motorcycles, lipsticks, bank loans or loaves of bread, depending on the business.

Cost centres relate to individual parts of an organisation and may be identified as a department or sales region, or they may be oriented around a single item such as a machine, a vehicle or a person. The costs charged to cost centres are those that relate to its operation – for example, the depreciation of a vehicle or the expenses of a salesperson.

Profit centres are autonomous in that they receive the revenue from sales and are responsible for cost.

Activity 8.2	For an organisation with which you are familiar, try to identify the cost units and cost centres, or suitable areas if none are used.

Within a university, cost centres are often faculties and departments are budgetary control mechanisms, with the profit centre being the university central office.

8.2.1   Ascertainment of costs

There are two basic costing methods: *specific order costs* and *process costing.* In the former we attempt to determine the cost of producing a particular job, batch or order. The latter differs significantly in that the accumulations of costs associated with a process or department over a period of time are recorded. In both methods we are concerned with the nature of the costs associated with the inputs to the system, principally labour and materials. If every cost unit is different, then specific order costs may be chosen. In this case each activity must be identified and the costs associated with this activity must be associated with the product (often in the form of a job order). On the other hand, if every cost unit is the same then process costing can be used. Process costing determines the total operating costs of a process or cost centre and divides the total costs by the number of units that pass through it. For example, Kimberly Clark's facility near Grimsby manufactures Huggies™ nappies. A single machine operated by a handful of operatives produces thousands of nappies per day. This process is easily monitored in terms of costs, primarily materials, to get a cost per nappy.

These two cost methods are supported by a number of costing techniques, of which two are total absorption costing and marginal costing. *Total absorption costing* involves allocating all the fixed overheads to cost units. The cost units absorb the total costs of running the enterprise. Abnormal costs associated with a business that arise from time to time are not absorbed within the normal running costs and cost units are only charged with a fair share of the overhead costs of the business. The actual costs charged to a cost unit are:

Actual costs = Direct costs for labour and materials
+ A fair share of the business's indirect costs

The problem then involves determining what a fair share of the business's costs means. Although conventions have become established for some types of overhead incurred by business, there is still wide scope for subjective or qualitative judgement.

Marginal costing is a technique that enables us to determine the individual contribution of cost units to the profitability of the enterprise. To do this, the marginal cost of a cost unit is determined (basically it is the variable cost) and subtracted from the revenue that the organisation would receive from its sale. This difference between selling price and marginal cost is called *contribution* and can be determined by the expression:

Contribution = Selling price – Marginal cost

Total contribution is a function of the volume of units produced and sold:

$$\text{Total contribution} = \text{Volume (Selling price – Marginal costs)} \qquad (8.1)$$

Also, profit is a function of costs and revenues and can be related to contribution by:

$$\text{Profit} = \text{Total contribution} - \text{Total fixed costs} \qquad (8.2)$$

Equation 8.2 can be rearranged to provide the cost/volume/profit model as shown in equation 8.3:

$$\text{Volume} = \frac{\text{Fixed costs} + \text{Profit}}{\text{Contribution}} \qquad (8.3)$$

No indirect or overhead costs are included. We should only undertake marginal costing when it is reasonable to assume that any indirect costs will be the same regardless of whether one extra cost unit is produced. This tends only to be true over short time periods. Over periods of up to one month, many of the costs of a business remain fixed. Hence considering the contributions made between various products should result in alternatives that provide the greatest net gain for the business. However, this short-termism needs to be tempered by long-term visions and the needs for the firm to establish or develop new products and process that do not meet short-term financial criteria.

Analyses like the one described in the example can be displayed as a breakeven chart (Figure 8.3).

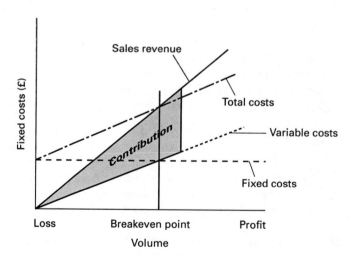

Figure 8.3 Breakeven chart showing contribution

Example 8.1

A manufacturing company has two products, A and B. Product A has a marginal cost of £10 per unit and product B a marginal cost of £20 per unit. The fixed costs for each product are £200,000. The market forecast for product A has identified an average selling price of £18 for the first 50,000 units and then £15 for the next 40,000 units. For product B the market forecast is a selling price of £34 for the first 30,000 units and any further units will be sold at £28. The organisation has planned for a profit of £250,000 for product A and £300,000 for product B.

Determine the number of products that have to be sold to achieve the profit requirements.

Solution

From equation 8.2 we have:

Profit + Fixed costs = Contribution

For product A this gives:

£200,000 (FC) + £250,000 (P) = Planned contribution = £450,000

The first 50,000 units gives a contribution of:

50,000 × (£18 − £10) = £400,000

This is £50,000 short of the planned contribution (£450,000 − £400,000). Therefore we must consider producing units that will sell for £15, providing £5.00 of contribution. Hence 50,000/5 = 10,000 units will need to be sold at this lower price; any more up to the planned 40,000 are an added bonus.

So the total number of units of A that need to be made and sold to achieve the plan is:

50,000 + 10,000 = 60,000

Activity 8.3

Using the information in Example 8.1:

1 Determine the number of units of B that need to be made and sold.

2 How many would have had to be made to meet the planned profit of £200,000 if the market forecast for product B had been:

   (a) 30,000 units at £40.00 further units at £32.00

   (b) 15,000 units at £40.00 further units at £35.00

   (c) 10,000 units at £45.00 further units at £40.00

8.2.2 Decision with limited resources

When considering marginal costs we need to take into account the economic justification for the comparison. An important factor of business processes is resources, some of which are scarce and limit the operations of the business. The limiting resources are normally labour, facility capacity (in the form of machines or other assets) or material restrictions. When these restrictions exist then it is necessary that the choice of alternatives is made not just with respect to highest contribution, but also with respect to the highest contribution per unit of limiting resource.

Example 8.2

A bakery produces two products: ginger biscuits and ginger cake. Both use ginger, although stocks are limited to 2,000 kg. The biscuits and cake are sold in bulk to a national grocery chain. Each batch of biscuits has a selling price of £45 and a marginal cost of £10. Batches of cake have a selling price of £35 and a marginal cost of £15. The biscuits require 5 kg of ginger and the cake 2 kg of ginger for each batch produced. Should we make biscuits or cake assuming no other restrictions?

Solution

The contribution from each product is:

Ginger biscuits:

				Scarce material requirement
Selling price	– Marginal cost	= Contribution		5 kg
£45	– £10	= £35		

Ginger cake:

£35	– £15	= £20		2 kg

This suggests that the biscuits are the more profitable, but on closer examination we can see that the biscuits provide a contribution of £7 per kg of ginger against the cake's contribution of £10 per kg of ginger. Therefore if we use all 2,000 kg of ginger to make the biscuits we would earn a contribution of $2,000 \times £7 = £14,000$, but the cake would earn a contribution of $2,000 \times £10 = £20,000$. Therefore the decision would be to make only cake. However, in reality many other resources will be restricting depending on the variety of the product mix; also the company may be forced into production of both products if the products are complementary. To resolve these complex decisions the linear programming technique, discussed in Chapter 9, is sometimes used.

Another aspect of marginal costing can be found in make-or-buy decisions, when resource restrictions limit production and it is possible to buy in a component from a supplier rather than produce it in-house, or where a company has to decide whether to produce a product or provide a service that can be obtained from an outside source. In both cases the procedure is similar to that relating to a single product. The supplier's price is compared with the total costs to the organisation for providing the product. The supplier's price and the firm's costs are related to the volume of production. Where the decision relates to a component part, then one consequence of this decision approach is that it identifies the opportunity cost, i.e. the income that would have been obtained if the product had been manufactured in place of the one that has been chosen or outsourced.

When we have a number of alternative products the steps towards a decision are shown in Figure 8.4.

Example 8.3

Example 8.3

A subassembly for a furnace (A) takes 25 hours to process on a heat-treating machine. It is sold for £200 and its marginal cost is £75. Another product B can also use the machine and takes 4 hours to treat. The marginal cost for B is £15 and it can be bought from an external supplier for £25. The company has to decide whether or not it should make or buy product B. The machine can only make A or B, time is constrained and there is no opportunity to purchase A.

Solution

To resolve this issue we must determine the contribution gained from a single item of A and the contribution lost when an item of B is not produced.

The contribution earned per machine hour when producing an item of A is £125 /25 = £5 per machine hour.

However, if an item of B had been made on the machine instead then 4 hours × £5 = £20 contribution could have been made because the production of product A has now been lost. This is the opportunity cost, which needs to be added to the cost of making B.

Therefore the full cost of making a unit of B is £15 + £20 = £35, which is more than the external supplier's price. Therefore the decision should be made to buy B and not to make it.

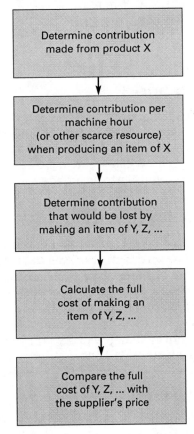

Figure 8.4 Determining opportunity cost

8.3 Materials costing

In manufacturing firms, materials often form the major cost. This cost is primarily the price paid for a specific quantity of material. Purchasing strategies can alter this through volume discounts and negotiation. Materials costs also include inventory costs, which are associated with storage and order costs and, if we run out, production loss costs.

The material from which a product is produced is an example of both a direct and a variable cost. However, in this process other material may be consumed (consumables), such as bandages, paper, welding rods, oil and water. These consumables may be a direct cost to the machine or activity, such as a bed on a ward, but only an indirect cost to the cost unit produced by the process, such as a patient (unless we have sophisticated monitoring systems that can record the number of bandages used on a patient).

Because of the significance of inventory costs and often the scope to reduce them, firms are drawn towards inventory reduction systems. From a macro perspective, for the production of company accounts or for product cost calculations, accountants use a number of conventions for valuing stock. A complication to this process is that materials are often bought and stored before being used. The price of the material when used may not match the price originally paid for it. Where firms can use just-in-time approaches of production control, this effect is reduced, but for many firms it is still a pertinent problem. To overcome this, certain general approaches are used to establish materials prices. A brief description of these is followed by examples of their use.

8.3.1 Specific prices

All stock valuation methods rely on knowledge of the price paid for inventory. When we are involved in special purchases, items obtained for non-standard or project-type work can be readily associated with a job and actual prices used to value the item. When the item is a regular purchase and prices fluctuate then we need more sophisticated methods.

8.3.2 First in, first out (FIFO)

FIFO is based on the assumption that the oldest materials (those that are received first) will be used first. Therefore the cost of a piece of material is the price paid at the time of the original purchase. For this to operate we need to be able to associate usage with delivery. As FIFO is based on actual cost it avoids problems of unrealised profits or losses. Stock is valued at current market prices, although at times of inflation or deflation undercosting or overcosting (respectively) can occur. If prices change rapidly and there is a high stock turnover, the system becomes difficult to monitor.

8.3.3 Average price

With this method, a moving average of the price of items being bought into the store is kept and this price is charged for all items used in production. In common with FIFO, it is based on actual costs incurred and does not give rise to unrealised profits and losses. However, it does not reflect current values as closely as FIFO, the degree of lag is dependent on the weights associated with the prices.

8.3.4 Last in, first out (LIFO)

LIFO is designed to reflect current prices in product costs by valuing issues at the price of the most recent purchase. Again it assumes that usage can be associated with delivery.

| Example 8.4 | A company bought the following numbers of 'thingies' on the given dates. |

Date	1 Feb	27 Feb	3 Mar	26 Mar	16 Apr	30 Apr	9 May
Number purchased	5	10	15	5	10	5	10
Price paid per item (£)	2.00	1.80	1.70	2.00	1.90	2.20	1.90

- LIFO – the cost is that of the last delivery, £1.90.

- FIFO – the cost is that of the oldest item in the store, £2.00 (unless we can identify that all of these have been used and we would then choose the next appropriate price £1.80 and so on).

- Average price – this could be either a simple average, £1.93, or more normally a weighted average (WA), £1.86 [from (5 × 2.00 + 10 × 1.80 + ... + 10 × 1.90)/(5 + 10 + ... + 10)].

- Specific prices are not relevant in this case as we have the inventory issue to contend with (in essence it will always be the latest price, in this case £1.90).

| Activity 8.4 | Evaluate the following stock prices |

Date	2 Feb	27 Feb	3 Mar	26 Mar	16 Apr	30 Apr	9 May
Number purchased	10	5	20	10	5	5	20
Price paid per item (£)	1.60	1.80	1.40	1.60	1.80	1.90	1.40

8.3.5 Material losses

In addition to cost valuation we are interested in the costs associated with material loss. These can be grouped into three categories: scrap, waste and spoilage.

Scrap is defined as a 'saleable residue discarded from a manufacturing process'. For example, sawdust from a sawmill, foundry trimmings, or even manure from a farm (if there is a market for them).

Waste is defined as having no value. For example, residue gases from a chemical process or dirt from a coal mine. The difference between scrap and waste is, then, an issue of recoverable value. As environmental regulations become more restrictive, it is likely in many cases that waste will find an increasingly high negative value connected with disposal and treatment.

Spoilage (or defective products) is defined as substandard units of product, which cannot be sold as perfect – although there may be a market for them in a factory reject store or the local Sunday market.

8.4   Human costs

Increasingly many of the human costs in a modern business are not directly connected with production (manufacturing or service delivery); they are part of overhead costs, for example marketing, personnel and finance departments. Unless the firm is organised along project lines then allocation of these costs to individual products is difficult.

Even the measurement of direct labour costs will contain some degree of inaccuracy. These inaccuracies reflect the fact that people are not consistent in their ability to perform uniformly over time and task, and that performance is an individual characteristic. So financial and operational measurements of performance are often derived from estimates, based on some form of research or empirical data. Performance data coupled with information on the task and wage rates enable estimates of human costs to be evaluated.

8.5   Machinery costs

Machinery costs have both fixed and variable considerations. Fixed costs relate to the costs of purchase and leasing; variable costs relate to the efficiency of the machine to convert the inputs to outputs. Decisions regarding these occur at both operating and strategic levels. At the strategic level we would be questioning whether a new machine or process might improve the value of the firm, by meeting organisational goals; at the operating level we would be seeking to improve efficiency in terms of productivity (output/input) by reducing waste, or by improving reliability though reducing unplanned breakdowns.

The costs associated with machines include energy, maintenance and breakdown. Decisions about energy costs are, for most firms, trivial in that they are largely unavoidable. For some businesses, cost reductions can be made through technology, for example the haulage business has gained from more aerodynamic vehicles and better engines. In firms where melting processes occur, such as the glass industry, heat exchangers make the best use of heat in exhaust gases. In manufacturing where large numbers of high-power machines are used, intelligent power distribution systems are used to reduce peak loading. These developments are often beyond the command of the firm. Hence, the aspects of machinery cost that can be influenced most are associated with the reliability and maintenance decisions. These are beyond the scope of this text, but references can be found later.

8.6 Activity-based costing

If, as managers, we can say with accuracy that a particular activity within a business is profitable, both financially and qualitatively, we can make a qualified judgement as to the efficacy of continuing with the activity. Activities can be costed at a micro level. For example, it is conceivable that a lecturer could itemise the costs associated with teaching. The university may ask the lecturer to manage the financial activities of a particular course. To do this, staff must be paid, rooms and equipment need to be hired and materials need to be obtained, all of which could be charged back to the university or student. In this case the tutor or course could be described as a *cost centre*. If the lecturer also generated income by recruiting and charging students, the course or lecturer unit would become a *profit centre*. If the tutor then started taking out loans and investing money, the tutor would become an *investment centre*. Activity-based costing (ABC) is central to the notion of establishing cost centres.

The objective of ABC is to measure and cost out all the resources used for activities that support the delivery of a product to a customer. This allocation of costs is achieved through the use of *activity cost drivers* and *resource drivers*, which are related to the volume of work undertaken. The process is illustrated in Figure 8.5.

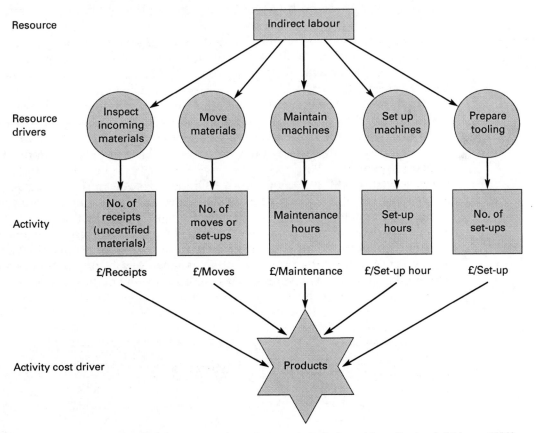

Figure 8.5 ABC: Expenses flow from resources through to products (adapted from Kaplan & Atkinson:1998)

Many ABC systems suffer from problems of initial accurate data collection and in assigning overheads in a representative manner. One such system was designed to improve accountability for the use of materials at a colliery. The system collected and collated information on materials ordered and delivered to the colliery. The materials were associated with particular activities. However, on investigation, many of the materials were used for other activities. The designed system relied on accurate reporting of materials usage by workers, and management needed to police and administer the system. This was a change in working procedures. The rigid nature implicit in the costing system was in conflict with the culture and uncertainties of the mining operations. In operation, the minutiae of data were not collected and the costing system was used only as an approximate indication of the true costs, but this in itself was of value. Owing to the system, managers were more keenly aware of the factors that influenced costs for the activities they were controlling and could help influence these in many ways. For example, one manager had a ton of wooden blocks delivered to a supervisor's office, to illustrate the point that the official had ordered sufficient quantity to last a year for the particular job they were ordered for.

A balance needs to be found between cost of operation of the financial system and the benefits gained from it. The benefit gained from measuring achievement and over/underspend and then using that information to improve the financial performance of the product or process.

This product-based costing (PBC) approach complements that of activity-based costing. If we can discover the cost of a product, which will be made up of the costs of the activities contributing to the product, and then relate this to the revenues, we can get an indication of the financial contribution of products to the goal of the organisation. However, PBC has to be developed from an understanding of activities' costs.

At each stage of the cost continuum in Figure 8.6, we dramatically increase the amount of data to be accumulated and allocated. Problems occur when we begin to examine the overhead costs and people associated with activities. A person may, for example, work on a variety of products or processes during the accounting period.

The concept of PBC makes numerous assumptions, not least that the data are a true reflection of reality. The programme illustrated in Table 8.2 might be one of a number of programmes offered. First thoughts might suggest that the direct costs are valid; however, often it is the case that staff working on one project might allocate time to another. This happens if there have been poor estimates of work requirements. The indirect costs are often assigned in arbitrary fashion, based upon historical data, which in itself may have been a whim of the cost clerk.

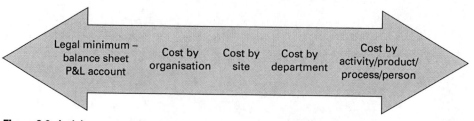

Figure 8.6 Activity cost continuum

Illustration 8.1 A PBC costing system

To illustrate the concept of PBC we can examine a training programme. Indirect costs are apportioned as a percentage of direct staff costs at the level shown in Table 8.2.

Table 8.2 A PBC costing system

Modules	Module contact hours	Direct staff costs	Operating expenses	Indirect costs	Total module costs	Number of students per module	Cost per student module
ELP1	10	1,763.63	1,250	1,975.27	4,998.90	30	166.63
ELP2	10	1,963.63	1,250	2,199.27	5,422.90	30	180.76
OM1	30	2,290.90	650	2,565.81	5,536.72	18	307.50
Man1	45	3,436.36	450	3,848.72	7,780.09	16	486.25
Mark1	30	2,290.90	600	2,565.81	5,486.72	18	304.81
Fin1	30	2,290.90	450	2,565.81	5,336.72	18	296.48
Eco1	30	2,290.90	450	2,565.81	5,336.72	18	296.48
Eco2	30	2,290.90	450	2,565.81	5,336.72	18	296.48
Acc1	30	2,290.90	550	2,565.81	5,436.72	18	302.04
Acc2	30	2,290.90	550	2,565.81	5,436.72		
Programme total	**765**	**71,600.00**	**19,950**	**77,952.00**	**16,9502.00**	**184**	**921.00**

8.6.1 Evaluation of ABC

A number of benefits and limitations with ABC are evident. ABC coupled with strict management control will push the organisation to constantly address its cost base. It will provide better understanding of cost drivers and the relative importance of the system costs. The system will reward the organisation with information on costs, but at the same time may limit the organisation's ability to respond flexibly to the environment. Product development may be hindered unless adequate measures are developed to ensure the high costs of development are fairly attributed, through techniques such as *life cycle costing*. There are many products offered by firms that overlap profit centres, are experimental, or are clearly not contributing to the financial goals. Any detailed cost analysis would most likely result in these initiatives being suspended, perhaps to the detriment of the firm.

It is of interest and value to senior management to implement a comprehensive cost system, but junior managers may not cooperate fully in the implementation and operation of such a system unless they can perceive a value in this.

8.7 Long-term decisions

The way in which a firm invests its money is crucial for the long-term viability of the business. The value of a firm comprises an appraisal of its current earnings and assets and its future growth potential. The growth potential is directly related to the ability of management to identify and select those projects and initiatives that have the greatest payback for the firm.

8.7.1 Project selection

Many firms use financial appraisal techniques to judge the return on a particular course of action. Financial accounting conventions designed to meet yearly reporting procedures are not appropriate, as the decision needs to consider the whole life of the project. At any one point in time a firm will be involved in routine cash management connected with its ongoing activities (which may include routine management of projects) as well as being faced with the choice of developing new products and procedures. The firm is likely to be faced with a number of projects that must be appraised and ranked so that those projects that fit best with the firm's objectives are undertaken. Given that in many firms the maximisation of shareholder wealth is a primary objective then those projects that offer the best return for money are often the most attractive.

In reality the choice is not always simple. Given that technology is changing rapidly and market requirements evolve and disappear, simple financial considerations are just one of the many screens that a particular project may face. Meredith and Mantel (1995: 42) suggest the following selection criteria are the most important:

1 *Realism.* The model should reflect the decision situation, this would include the pluralistic objectives of the firm and the managers. Common measurements systems should be established, because without them meaningful comparison of projects is difficult. For example, project A may enhance the firm's competitiveness in terms of improving speed of delivery, but project B may increase market share by implementing a new production facility. How can we judge between them? The model needs to take into account the firm's limited resources such as capital or personnel. The model should also take into account risk in terms of operational and market parameters.

2 *Capability.* The model should be sophisticated so that parameters can be altered to meet managers' 'what if?' scenarios. The model should be able to optimise, so that the comparisons that management deem to be important are evaluated and the best mix of projects is selected.

3 *Flexibility.* The model should provide valid results within a range of conditions that the firm may experience. It should be easily modified or be self-adjusting in respect to environmental, legislative, technological and organisational changes, for example changes in pollution regulations, tax laws, or the company's objectives.

4 *Ease of use.* The model should be reasonably convenient, be quickly executed, easy to use and understandable. It should not require special or additional interpretation, data that are difficult to acquire, excessive personnel or unavailable equipment. The model variables should match those that managers believe to be significant to the project. Finally, it should be easy to simulate the expected outcomes associated with investments in different project portfolios.

5 *Cost.* Modelling and data-gathering costs should be low relative to the cost of the project and must be less than the potential benefits of the project. All costs should be considered, including data management and implementation and running costs of the model.

The first part of this chapter looked at costs in some detail. For many long-term capital projects, accurate estimation of such costs is difficult and arguably fruitless. The costs of data collection or estimation may well mean that the project is doomed before the start or at least faces a poor chance of success.

Financial models for project selection

A large majority of firms use finance as a sole measure of acceptability for judging the acceptability of a new project. Some of these methods are discussed here. One common factor with all methods is a record of the predicted net cash flows. *Net cash flow* is the cash flowing into or out of the firm during a given period, it is the difference between revenues and costs. It is symbolised here by CF_i, where the subscript i indicates the period. When $i = 0$ then this is the initial period where, in many projects, the majority of the finance is committed.

Payback Period

The payback period is defined as the number of periods it takes for the project to repay the initial investment. Algebraically we can define it as:

$$\sum_{i=0}^{k} CF_i \geq CF_0$$

We determine which has the smallest value of k, the payback period. This is often expressed in years. For example, we can see from the following cash flows that the payback period is exactly at the end of the second year.

Year	0	1	2	3	4
Net cash flow (£) (CF)	−35,000	20,000	15,000	10,000	10,000
Sum (£) (ΣCF)	−35,000	−15,000	0	10,000	20,000

This method ignores cash flows beyond the payback period. However, it does provide a poor measure of risk: the faster the payback period the less risk to which the firm is exposed.

Average rate of return

The average rate of return is the ratio of average annual profits (either before or after taxes) to the initial investment in the project. Assume in the example just given that the average annual profit is £14,000, then:

$$\text{Average rate of return} = \frac{£14,000}{£35,000} = 0.4$$

The advantage of average rate of return and payback period is their simplicity. However, because they do not take into account the 'time value of money' both are inadequate for serious evaluation of an investment, unless it can be assumed that interest rates are near to zero and inflation is nil.

Discounted cash flow

This method, also referred to as the *present value* method (as well as hurdle rate, cut-off rate and similar terms), evaluates an investment according to a required rate of return. The method is derived from an appreciation of *future value*.

The value of a sum of money in a period in the future is given by:

$$FV = PV \left(1 + \frac{R}{100}\right)^N$$

where: FV = future value

PV = present value

R = interest rate as an annual percentage

N = the number of years of the investment

The term

$$\left(1 + \frac{R}{100}\right)^N$$

is known as the *compound factor*, as we are purely estimating the future value of the money invested in a compound interest fashion.

Example 8.5	If we invest £500 in a fund with an annual rate of interest of 5 per cent for a period of ten years then PV = £500, R = 5 per cent and N = 10 years, to give:

FV = £814

If we can guarantee that the rate of return will be 5 per cent over the next ten years then an investor will be indifferent to having £500 today or £814 in ten years' time.

The reciprocal of the compound factor is known as the *discount factor*, DF, calculated as

$$DF = \frac{1}{\left(1 + \frac{R}{100}\right)^N}$$

Given the information in Example 8.5, if we were guaranteed to receive £814 in ten years' time then that would equate to:

$$£814 \times \frac{1}{\left(1 + \frac{5}{100}\right)^{10}} = £814 \times 0.614 = £500$$

The discount factor, in this case 0.614, can be calculated from first principles using the previous formula, or more conveniently obtained from tables created for the purpose of evaluating present values, as shown in Appendix 2. Nowadays, though, calculators and spreadsheets often have sophisticated variations that allow a variety of types of present value calculations.

In an investment over a period of years, the *discounted cash flow* (DCF) method is used to determine how all of the relevant cash flows equate to present values to determine the *net present value* (NPV) of the investment. In other words, all payments and receipts over time are given a present value, when we sum all of these the NPV is obtained.

Given the information in Example 8.5 and an interest rate of 10 per cent per annum, we can create Table 8.3.

Table 8.3 indicates that the investment or project would add £9,910 [–35,000 + 18,180 + ... + 6,830] to the firm's assets.

Net present value can be expressed algebraically as:

$$NPV = A_0 + \sum_{t=1}^{n} \frac{F_t}{(1 + r)^t}$$

where: F_t = the net cash flow in period t,

r = the required rate of return

A_0 = initial cash investment

To include the rate of inflation during period t, we have:

$$NPV = A_0 + \sum_{t=1}^{n} \frac{F_t}{(1 + r + p_t)^t}$$

where p_t is the predicted rate of inflation or deflation.

Table 8.3 Net present value illustration

Year	0	1	2	3	4
Net cash flow	–35,000	20,000	15,000	10,000	10,000
Discount factor	1	0.909	0.826	0.751	0.683
Present value	–35,000	18,180	12,390	7,510	6,830
Net present value	9,910				

Internal rate of return

The internal rate of return (IRR) is the discount rate that equates to a present value of zero, that is the interest rate that simply allows the firm to break even on the project.

We require a value for r so that

$$\sum_{t=0}^{n} \frac{CF_i}{(1+r)^i} = 0$$

We can determine r by trial and error, graphical means or by iterative computer programs.

Using earlier data and a discount factor of 22 per cent, then 24 per cent, then 25 per cent we get by trial and error the figures shown in Table 8.4.

By trial and error we know the IRR is in between 24 per cent and 25 per cent. Figure 8.7 shows a graphical representation.

As you can see in Figure 8.7 the curve takes an inverse exponential shape, but a good approximation of the exact IRR figure can be gained from simply joining the dots and noting where the lines cross the NPV = 0 point. The actual IRR is 24.6 per cent (see Figure 8.7).

There are many more models based on the methods described. The variations generally attempt to introduce uncertainty into the process by closer analysis of cash flows over time or attempt to extend the analysis by considering other organisational projects and activities.

NPV overview

Meredith and Mantel (1995: 53) provide a useful overview of NPV methods for their relevance to managerial decision-making:

Table 8.4 Internal Rate of Return (IRR) illustration

Year	0	1	2	3	4
R = 22%					
Net cash flow	−35,000	20,000	15,000	10,000	10,000
Discount factor	1	0.8197	0.6719	0.5507	0.4514
Present value	−35,000	16,394	10,078.5	5,507	4514
Net present value					1,493.5
R = 24%					
Net cash flow	−35,000	20,000	15,000	10,000	10,000
Discount factor	1	0.8065	0.6504	0.5245	0.423
Present value	−35,000	16,130	9,756	5,245	4,230
Net present value					361
R = 25%					
Net cash flow	−35,000	20,000	15,000	10,000	10,000
Discount factor	1	0.8	0.64	0.512	0.4096
Present value	−35,000	16,000	9,600	5,120	4,096
Net present value					−184

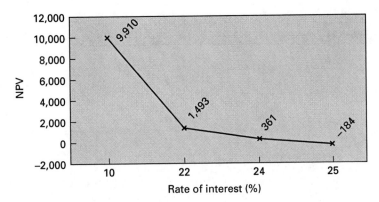

Figure 8.7 NPV vs % rate of interest

Advantages

- The undiscounted models are simple to use and understand.
- All use readily available accounting data to determine the cash flows.
- Model output is in terms familiar to business decision-makers.
- With a few exceptions, model output is on an 'absolute' profit/profitability scale and allows 'absolute' go/no-go decisions.
- Some profit models account for project risk.
- Some models include the impact of the project on the rest of the organisation.

Disadvantages

- These models ignore all non-monetary factors except risk.
- Models that do not include discounting ignore the timing of cash flows and the time value of money.
- Models that reduce cash flows to their present value are strongly biased towards the short run.
- Payback-type models ignore cash flows beyond the payback period.
- The IRR model can result in multiple solutions.
- All are sensitive to errors in the input data for the early years of the project.
- All discounting models are non-linear, and the effects of changes in the variables or parameters are generally not obvious to most decision-makers.
- Those models (with the exception of commercial success risk factor) that incorporate the risks of research mislead the decision-maker. It is not so much that the research and development process is risky as that the time and cost required to ensure project success is uncertain.
- Some models are oriented only towards evaluation of new products.
- All these models depend for input on a determination of cash flows, but it is not exactly how the concept of cash flow is properly defined for the purpose of evaluating projects.

Example 8.6

A firm that manufactures in the UK and sells to the UK and American markets has to choose between making product A or B. Table 8.5 indicates the cash flows involved.

Table 8.5 Cash Flow 1

Year	Cash outflows Production UK(£000)	Marketing UK(£000)	USA($000)	Cash inflows Sales UK(£000)	USA($000)
Product A					
0	1,200				
1	300	20	35	500	150
2	300	25	40	600	200
3	350	30	45	700	200
4	400	30	45	700	300
5	500	40	50	650	400
6	550	45	65	650	450
7	650	55	75	500	500
Product B					
0	1,500				
1	250	30	45	400	200
2	250	30	50	500	200
3	300	30	55	500	300
4	350	35	55	550	350
5	350	40	65	600	450
6	400	40	65	650	550
7	400	50	75	550	700

The viability of the projects will be judged using the NPV method with a discount factor of 10 per cent. However, to ensure comparability we must convert the cash flows to a common currency, in this case pounds sterling. An exchange rate of £1.00 to $1.50 is used to give Table 8.6. For example $150 becomes 150/1.5 = £100.

We can now determine the total cash outflows and inflows for both products and their present value, as shown in Tables 8.7 and 8.8, respectively.

Table 8.6 Cash flow 2

Year	Product A Marketing USA (£000)	Sales USA (£000)	Product B Marketing USA (£000)	Sales USA (£000)
0				
1	23.33	100	30	133.33
2	26.66	133.33	33.33	133.33
3	30	133.33	36.66	200
4	30	200	36.66	233.33
5	33.33	266.66	43.33	300
6	43.33	300	43.33	366.66
7	50	333.33	50	466.66

Table 8.7 Discounted cash outflows

Year	Production	Marketing	Total	P/V factor	PV @ 10%
Product A					
0	1,200		1,200	1	1,200
1	300	20 + 23.33	343.33	0.909	312.09
2	300	25 + 26.66	351.66	0.826	290.48
3	350	30 + 30	410	0.751	307.91
4	400	30 + 30	460	0.683	314.18
5	500	40 + 33.33	573.33	0.621	356.04
6	550	45 + 43.33	638.33	0.564	360.02
7	650	50	755	0.513	387.32
Total					**3,528.03**
Product B					
0	1,500		1,500	1	1,500
1	250	30 + 30	310	0.909	281.79
2	250	30 + 33.33	313.33	0.826	258.81
3	300	30 + 36.66	366.66	0.751	275.37
4	350	35 + 36.66	421.66	0.683	288.00
5	350	40 + 43.33	433.33	0.621	269.10
6	400	40 + 43.33	483.33	0.564	272.60
7	400	50 + 50	500	0.513	256.50
Total					**3,402.16**

Table 8.8 Discounted cash inflows

Year	UK sales	US sales	Total	P/V factor	PV @ 10%
Product A					
0				1	
1	500	100	600	0.909	545.40
2	600	133.33	733.33	0.826	605.73
3	700	133.33	833.33	0.751	625.83
4	700	200	900	0.683	614.70
5	650	266.66	916.66	0.621	569.25
6	650	300	950	0.564	535.80
7	500	333.33	833.33	0.513	427.50
Total					**3,924.21**
Product B					
0				1	
1	400	133.33	533.33	0.909	484.80
2	500	133.33	633.33	0.826	523.13
3	500	200	700	0.751	525.70
4	550	233.33	783.33	0.683	535.02
5	600	300	900	0.621	558.90
6	650	366.66	1,016.66	0.564	573.40
7	550	466.66	1,016.66	0.513	521.55
Total					**3,722.50**

Summarising these figures we get the NPV for each product (Table 8.9).

Table 8.9 Comparison NPV Product A and Product B.

	Product A	Product B
	£	£
P/V of cash inflow	3,924.21	3,722.50
P/V of cash outflow	3,528.02	3,402.16
Net present value	**396.19**	**320.33**

Both products give a positive return, but the decision would be for product A for greater value. This sort of decision becomes more difficult if exchange rates fluctuate.

Activity 8.5	For the data in Tables 8.5–8.8, would the decision alter if the exchange rate changes to £1.00 to (a) $1.3 or (b) $1.6?

8.7.2 Balanced scorecard

Johnson and Kaplan (1987) elucidated a shift in the relative importance of financial data when making strategic decisions. They recognised that many of these decisions defy simple financial analysis because they involve issues that are not quantifiable. To address this, a 'balanced scorecard' approach was developed to try to link financial and other strategic objectives. Four perspectives are addressed:

- *Financial perspective.* This is included to summarise those elements of the decision that lend themselves to financial analysis.
- *Customer perspective.* This reflects the importance of customer satisfaction within targeted markets as a measure of product quality.
- *Internal business perspective.* This section identifies those internal processes that enable the firm to gain competitive advantages. Kaplan (1998) splits these into three distinct areas: innovation, operations and post-sales service. Each of these could be subdivided into headings that illustrate speed, cost, quality, flexibility and dependability dimensions.
- *Learning and growth perspective.* The importance of organisational development through the evolution of a firm's people, systems and organisational procedures is recognised in this perspective. How firms are training employees, enhancing technology and structuring themselves to cater for changing conditions is articulated though measures of employee retention, satisfaction, skills and training and by measures that capture the effectiveness of communication channels.

An illustration of a scorecard is shown in Figure 8.8.

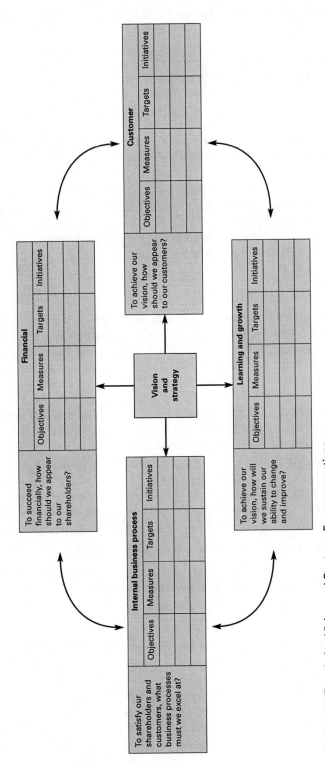

Figure 8.8 Translating Vision and Strategy: Four perspectives
Reprinted by permission of Harvard Business School Press. From *The Balances Scorecard: Translating Strategy into Action* by R.S. Kaplan and D.P. Norton. Boston, MA 1996, p. 9. Copyright © 1996 by the Harvard Business School Publishing Corporation; all rights reserved.

8.8 Short-term financial decisions

In the short term, managers are concerned with the creation of the cash flows that enable a continual supply of resources. Decisions revolve around adjusting variables within their control to create greater efficiencies. Short-term financial decisions are generally constrained by budgetary controls. The Chartered Institute of Management Accountants (CIMA, 1998) defines a budget as:

A quantitative statement, for a defined period of time, which may include planned revenues, expenses, assets, liabilities and cash flows.

A budget should reflect a realistic expectation of events and not be overly ambitious or cautiously pessimistic. As in real life it would be pointless for the average person to budget for a Rolls-Royce and disappointing to budget for a moped, if he or she can afford a car. The budgeting process involves planning, coordinating and communicating, and control activities.

8.8.1 Budgetary planning

Budgetary planning is based on predictions of sales revenue and resource costs. Normally the budget is planned over a one-year cycle in periods of one month (less, if appropriate). If, during that period, changes to product mix are intended then the relevant cost/income behaviour needs to be catered for. Planning compels consideration of the availability and cost of resources, inventory levels, labour recruitment and availability, plant and premises costs. Timings of cash movements need to be predicted: these are often a critical factor in the continuation of any business. The fact that profits are generated from planned activities does not mean that a corresponding cash inflow will occur when the activity is completed. Many firms have short-run liquidity problems despite efficient and effective operations, simply because of the time difference between paying for resources and receiving payment from customers. Planning helps to identify when during the year these types of problem might occur and the firm is then in a better position to take remedial action. The plan enables the firm to:

- obtain finance to cover a short-term cash flow shortage;
- avoid a short-term anticipated shortage of resources, such as material or labour, by seeking alternatives or substitutes;
- put to some other use anticipated surplus resources such as cash, facilities, materials or labour.

The simplest of all budgets is the cash flow forecast. In this method only relevant revenues and costs are considered. This prevents managers attempting to recover costs on the options being considered. All other considerations being equal, the most profitable option to choose is the one that, over the life of a project or circumstance, gives the greatest net financial gain to an organisation.

The phrase 'all things being equal' does mean that qualifications to the simple use of the techniques are necessary. Strategic or tactical considerations affecting particular actions or projects may have to be taken into account but they are not easily costed as cash flows. For instance, customer goodwill or public image may affect the organisation if certain actions are undertaken, but these, although important to the organisation with respect to its future viability, are difficult to equate to cash receipts or expenditures. Other considerations revolve around the problems of depreciation and the value of money over time.

8.8.2 Coordinating and communicating

Many departments within a firm would work in blissful ignorance of the activities of other departments if it were not for such activities as budgetary planning. Money, and certainly a limited supply of it, forms a common bond between departments, as each department vies for its share. In this process the strategic aims and objectives are transformed into real and meaningful goals for each department and hopefully an overall common understanding of the firm's processes. The classic, but dated, debate relates to serving the needs of production or the market. Clearly it is foolhardy to produce the most technically excellent product in the world if it cannot be sold, and likewise, it is stupid to produce a product for a mass market if the cost exceeds the price customers would pay.

The budget, then, forms a common link between the activities of departments and aids decision-making by indirectly relating local decisions to corporate profit performance and other objectives. Within the coordinating effect of the budget each department would be inclined to make decisions that improve the performance of the department, but not necessarily the firm as a whole. Budgets create a form of synergy.

8.8.3 Controlling

Mr Micawber, languishing in the debtors' prison, laments to David Copperfield, 'if a man had twenty pounds a year for his income, and spent nineteen shillings and sixpence, he would be happy, but ... if he spent twenty pounds one [penny] he would be miserable' (Dickens, 1850).

Mr Micawber, a well-liked and respected gentleman, could not control his finances, which resulted in his short stay in a debtors' prison. His creditors bore him no malice, except that it was human nature to expect to be paid.

Although we are unlikely to see a chief executive gracing the same meagre apartments as Mr Micawber, the principles and consequences of not meeting expenses with revenue are similar. Firms often have multi-million pound turnovers and the problems of control of expenditure are magnified by many modern day Micawbers in the system – managers and staff who have no real grasp of how money is being spent and what is being received. Historically we have moved on from the inadequacies of the regimes of the nineteenth century and have developed budgets to help control expenditure.

A budget is only as good as the use it is put to. If we consider business activities as projects then we develop a budget in the *setting phase*. Control only begins with the *operating phase* and parallel *feedback/forward phase*. The baseline budget is compared with current expenditure and revenue, and areas of divergence are highlighted. More proactively, the latest predictions can be fed into the budget to enable potential issues to be identified before they happen. The budget enables responsibility to be delegated away from senior executives and managers, without losing control. Junior managers have the freedom to act within the confines of the budget.

In project management there are two main variances from budget: the *schedule variance* and the *cost variance*. The schedule variance gives us an indication of the achievement of work related to time. If less work is done at a certain point in time then, in theory, the costs associated with the work performed will be less. The schedule variance is evaluated from the actual cost of work performed (ACWP) and the budgeted cost of work scheduled (BCWS). The cost variance compares actual costs (ACWP) and budgeted cost of work performed (BCWP) for the work performed to date. This is illustrated in Figure 8.9. A combination of these variances is called the *critical ratio*. The critical ratio is useful as it offsets good and bad ratios to give an arguably good measure of the health of a project. The critical ratio is expressed as:

$$\text{Critical ratio} = \left(\frac{\text{Actual progress}}{\text{Scheduled progress}} \right) \times \left(\frac{\text{Budgeted cost}}{\text{Actual cost}} \right)$$

Any result that returns a value of greater than unity indicates that the project or activity is on target; less than 1 indicates that something is wrong.

Modern technology helps managers to collect and analyse more data than ever before and the information available for making judgements is becoming more accessible. However, there are still costs associated with both the collection and use of this data. On the one hand we may have the capability to define accurately the costs associated with the most trivial of activities, on the other we need to question the application of these data to decision-making and management.

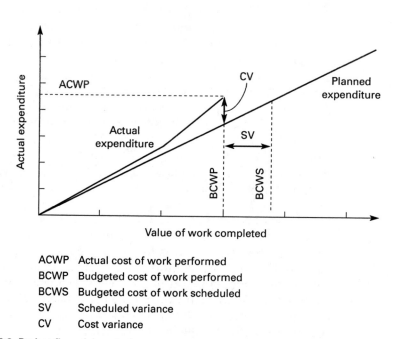

ACWP	Actual cost of work performed
BCWP	Budgeted cost of work performed
BCWS	Budgeted cost of work scheduled
SV	Scheduled variance
CV	Cost variance

Figure 8.9 Project financial control

| Example 8.7 | Table 8.10 shows the progress on a project. |

Table 8.10 Financial variances and critical ratio

Task number	Actual progress		Scheduled progress		Budgeted Cost		Actual cost		Critical ratio
1	20	/	30	×	600	/	400	=	1
2	25	/	35	×	650	/	650	=	0.71
3	30	/	30	×	425	/	575	=	0.74
4	30	/	20	×	700	/	700	=	1.5
5	35	/	40	×	650	/	500	=	1.13
6	35	/	40	×	380	/	260	=	1.28

Table 8.10 indicates that task 1, although behind schedule is also behind cost so, unless it is a 'critical' activity (see Chapter 10), is on target. Task 2 however is behind schedule but has met the anticipated cost, hence is likely to overrun the budgeted cost. Task 4 is well ahead of schedule at the same cost, and so on. A positive critical ratio is good, a negative one bad.

8.9 The dangers of control

Whilst there are obvious attractions and real benefits to be gained from knowing what your cash flows are, cash control and a focus on profit as the leading objective of a firm can bring with it unwelcome organisational effects. For instance, *resource dependency theory* suggests that competition for scarce resources may result in *ethnocentric* behaviour within an organisation (Brewer, 1986). A previously cooperative group may become dysfunctional as it pursues its own self-interest to the exclusion of others (Kramer, 1991). Bhallacharya (1985: 37) points to the dangers of preoccupation with financial measures of performance:

> A company can increase its short term profit very easily. Cut down vital capital expenditures, reduce essential services, slash depreciation, and the return on investment will look splendid – for a time. The question is, for how long? ... There is a point also to be made about non-financial factors, some of which indicate a great deal about future performance of a company. Such factors as the industrial relations record, absenteeism, productivity performance, the ability or otherwise to meet deadlines, product quality and design and the extent to which customers are satisfied, are obviously eloquent pointers to the company's prospects, both for the present and the future.

This point is reiterated by Drucker (1989: 59):

> To emphasise only profit, for instance, misdirects mangers to the point where they endanger the survival of the business. To obtain profit today they tend to undermine the future ... To manage a business is to balance a variety of needs and goals ... the very nature of business enterprise requires multiple objectives which are needed in every area where performance and results directly and vitally affect the survival and prosperity of the business.

Drucker goes on to suggest eight areas that should be used when judging a firm's performance: market standing, innovation, productivity, physical and financial resources, profitability, manager performance and development, worker performance and development, and public responsibility.

In 1900, Edouard Claparède argued that more thought is placed on the size of a child's shoes than on the size of their minds. In parallel, more managerial effort is spent determining and operating elaborate financial control systems than in ensuring that these resources are thereafter used carefully and wisely. Take, for example, the all too common end of year budgetary spending spree.

However, Hamel and Prahalad (1994: 159) make the point that if top management devotes more effort to accessing the strategic feasibility of projects in its resource allocation role than it does to the task of multiplying resource effectiveness, its value-added will be modest indeed.

So we need a balance: time spent in evaluation and time spent in control will both add value, so long as clear understanding of objectives is obtained and retained.

8.10 Spreadsheets

Spreadsheets are an essential tool for performing financial analysis. Systems such as Lotus123 and Microsoft Excel® have powerful facilities that include data analysis, model templates and graphical facilities that enable firms to perform a vast range of evaluations. Figure 8.10 illustrates one such template in the Excel® system.

However, spreadsheets (or, more correctly, spreadsheet programmers) are prone to error. Freeman (1996), in a survey of spreadsheet use, found that 90 per cent of spreadsheets with over 150 lines contained at least one significant for-

Machine A

Year	Outgoing Cash	Incoming Cash	Net Cash
0	12,500	0	−12,500
1	0	2,000	2,000
2	0	4,000	4,000
3	0	5,000	5,000
4	0	2,500	2,500
5	0	3,500	3,500

Lower Discount Rate	10%
Higher Discount Rate	15%
Present Value at Lower Discount Rate	12,761
Net Present Value at Lower Discount Rate	**261**
Present Value at Higher Discount Rate	11,221
Net Present Value at Higher Discount Rate	**−1,279**
Internal Rate of Return	10%
Profitability Index at 10%	1.02%

Machine B

Year	Outgoing Cash	Incoming Cash	Net Cash
0	15,000	0	−15,000
1	0	3,000	3,000
2	0	6,000	6,000
3	0	5,000	5,000
4	0	3,000	3,000
5	0	4,000	4,000

Lower Discount Rate	10%
Higher Discount Rate	15%
Present Value at Lower Discount Rate	15,975
Net Present Value at Lower Discount Rate	**975**
Present Value at Higher Discount Rate	14,137
Net Present Value at Higher Discount Rate	**−863**
Internal Rate of Return	13%
Profitability Index at 10%	1.07%

Figure 8.10 Spreadsheet solution (based on Barrow, 1998)

mula mistake. Similar studies (Davis and Ilkin, 1987; Panko, 1996) suggest that the users of such spreadsheets were normally very confident in the model's integrity, although in reality the models contained significant errors. Perhaps the most worrying thing about these revelations is the implicit trust and resultant complacency that the perceived infallibility of the models encourages.

Summary

In this chapter we have made a tentative step towards explaining some of the vocabulary and methods used in financial decision-making. Underpinning the concepts within the chapter is a variety of approaches and conventions that are particular to companies and countries. However, the foundations of financial decision-making, costs and revenues, are universal. Fundamentally, firms spend money – costs – and generate money – revenues. The timeframe over which this occurs is important as money loses value over time through notions of inflation and the cost of borrowing. How costs are allocated is important in order to reflect the true value of a product or process. Information on costs is collected and used to make these judgements; the trade-off between knowledge and benefits of knowledge is important. Finally, data collection is fraught with possible inaccuracies and open to a range of manipulative mechanisms that can give a false impression of a situation.

Decision diary

For a recent decision try to identify the associated financial variables. What factors limit the accuracy of these variables? How important to the decision were the financial issues?

Thinking back to Chapter 7 on forecasting, how are budgets set in your firm? Are they set based on a forecast taken from historical data, or from a prediction of likely expenditure, or a mixture of the two?

References

Barrow, C. (1998) *Accounting: Financial Management for the Small Business*. London: Kogan Page.

Bhallacharya, K. (1985) 'Accountancy's faulty sums', *Management Today*, February.

Brewer, M.B. (1986) 'The role of ethnocentricism in intergroup conflict', in Worchel, S and Autin, W.G. (eds) *Psychology of Intergroup Relations*. Chicago: Nelson Hall.

CIMA (1998) *CIMA Study Text*. London: BPP Publishing.

Davis, N. and Ilkin, C. (1987) 'Auditing spreadsheets', *Australian Accountant*, December.

Dickens, C. (1850) *The Personal History of David Copperfield*. London: Chapman & Hall.

Drucker, P.F. (1989) *The Practice of Management*. London: Heinemann Professional.

Freeman, D. (1996) 'How to make spreadsheets error-proof', *Journal of Accountancy*, 181(5).

Goldratt, E.M. and Cox, J. (1992) *The Goal*, 2nd edition. Croton-on-Hudson, NY: North River Press.

Hamel, G. and Prahalad, C.K. (1994) *Competing for the Future*. Boston, MA: Harvard Business School Press.

Johnson H.T. and Kaplan R.S. (1987) *Relevance Lost: The Rise and Fall of Management Accounting*. Boston, MA: Harvard Business School Press.

Kaplan, R.S. and Atkinson, A.A. (1998) *dvanced Management Accounting*, 3rd edition. London: Prentice Hall.

Kaplan, R.S. and Norton, D.P. (1996) *The Balanced Scorecard: Translating Strategy into Action*. Boston, MA: Harvard Business School Press.

Kramer, R.M. (1991) 'Intergroup relation and organisational dilemmas: the role of categorisation processes', *Research in Organisational Behaviour*, 13.

Meredith, J.R. and Mantel, S.J. (1995) *Project Management: A Managerial Approach*. Toronto: Wiley.

Panko, R. and Halverson, R. (1996) 'Spreadsheets on trial: a survey of research on spreadsheet risks', *Proceedings of the Hawaii International Conference on Systems Sciences*.

Further reading

Souder, W.E., (1983) 'Project evaluation and selection', in Cleland, D.J. and King, W.R. (eds) *Project Management Handbook*. New York: Van Nostrand Reinhold.

Glossary

Average price:	an accounting term used for stock valuation; the price of all items (of the same kind) is used to form a moving average price.
Breakeven Point:	the point at which total revenue equals total cost. Below this point costs are greater than revenue and the firm is making a loss, above this point revenue exceeds costs and the firm makes a profit.
Direct costs:	those costs that arise solely because of the existence of an activity or the undertaking of an action, and which would not have occurred if the activity or action had not taken place.
Ethnocentric:	the belief that one's own group is superior.
First in, first out (FIFO):	an accounting term for stock valuation; the price of the earliest item is used to cost the product or process.
Fixed costs:	costs that are assumed to remain unchanged over wide ranges of activities for any given time, regardless of whatever operational activity is taking place.

Indirect costs: any cost that is not direct, whose existence depends on the general operation of the enterprise and which would remain even if a particular activity or action that is being costed had not taken place.

Last in, first out (LIFO): an accounting term for stock valuation; the price of the latest item is used to cost the product or process.

Life cycle costing: considers initial costs of a project and estimated future cash flows, both costs and revenue. Both first costs and future cost streams should include factors such as inflation, cost escalation, taxes and depreciation of assets.

Marginal costing: is a technique that enables us to determine the individual contribution of cost units to the profitability of the enterprise. To do this, the marginal cost of a cost unit is determined and substracted from the revenue that the organisation would receive from its sale. This difference between selling price and marginal cost is called contribution.

Net Cash Flow: the cash entering or leaving the business. Normally calculated on a weekly or monthly basis and is the difference between revenue and cost.

Opportunity cost: the loss to the firm of revenue or savings in costs due to the chosen option.

Process costing: this method of cost allocation is used to help determine the costs of particular departments and processes. These costs can then be allocated to the products that pass through that particular stage.

Resource dependency theory: the notion that competition for scarce resource may transform a normally cooperative group into one that pursues its own self-interest.

Specifice order costs: the cost of a specific batch of products is evaluated. Used when the activities and resources used to create a product are easily identified and quantified.

Specific prices: the actual price of an item used to cost a process or product.

Time value of money: inflationary conditions mean that money generally loses value over time. One dollar today will buy more than one dollar tomorrow. This effect implies that the longer we can delay expenditure and the quicker we can create revenue the more profit we can generate. This effect underpins many of the financial appraisal models used in practice.

Total absorption costing: involves allocating all the fixed overheads to cost units.

Transfer pricing the price charged when one sector of an organisation provides goods or services to another sector of the organisation.

Variable costs: costs that are incurred in direct proportion to the level of activity that is taking place. If no activity is undertaken, the variable cost is zero regardless of whether any fixed costs are being incurred.

Answers to selected activites

Activity 8.3

1 Profit + Fixed costs = Contribution

For product B this gives;

£200,000 + £300,000 = Planned contribution = £500,000

The first 30,000 units gives a contribution of:

30,000 × (£34 − £20) = £420,000

This is £500,000 − £420,000 = £80,000 short of the planned contribution. Therefore we must consider producing units which will sell for £28, providing £8 of contribution. Hence:

$$\frac{80,000}{8} = 10,000 \text{ units}$$

will need to be sold at this lower price. So the total number of units of B that need to be made and sold is:

30,000 + 10,000 = 40,000

2 (a) For a market forecast of 30,000 at £40 and further units at £32 then the increased price leads to an increased contribution of:

30,000 × (£40 − £20) = £600,000

Therefore the number of units that are required to be produced and sold is:

$$\frac{500,000}{20} = 25,000$$

and there is no need to sell at the lower price.

(b) For a market forecast of 15,000 at £40 and further units at £35 then the contribution is:

15,000 × (£40 − £20) = £300,000

This is a shortfall of £200,000, hence 200,000/15 = 13,333 units at £35 need to be made and sold giving a total of:

15,000 + 13,333 = 28,333 units

(c) For a market forecast of 10,000 at £45 and further units at £40 then the contribution is:

10,000 × (£45 − £20) = £250,000

This is a shortfall of £250,000, hence 250,000/20 = 12,500 units at £40 need to be made and sold giving a total of:

10,000 + 12,500 = 22,500 units

Activity 8.4

Date	27 Feb	3 Mar	26 Mar	16 Apr	30 Apr	9 May
Number	5	20	10	5	5	20
Price	1.80	1.40	1.60	1.80	1.90	1.40

LIFO = 1.4

FIFO= 1.6

Average= 1.64 (Weighted average = 1.54)

Appendix 2	Discount table

Discount factor %					Year					
	1	2	3	4	5	6	7	8	9	10
1	0.9901	0.9803	0.9706	0.9610	0.9515	0.9420	0.9327	0.9235	0.9143	0.9053
2	0.9804	0.9612	0.9423	0.9238	0.9057	0.8880	0.8706	0.8535	0.8368	0.8203
3	0.9709	0.9426	0.9151	0.8885	0.8626	0.8375	0.8131	0.7894	0.7664	0.7441
4	0.9615	0.9246	0.8890	0.8548	0.8219	0.7903	0.7599	0.7307	0.7026	0.6756
5	0.9524	0.9070	0.8638	0.8227	0.7835	0.7462	0.7107	0.6768	0.6446	0.6139
6	0.9434	0.8900	0.8396	0.7921	0.7473	0.7050	0.6651	0.6274	0.5919	0.5584
7	0.9346	0.8734	0.8163	0.7629	0.7130	0.6663	0.6227	0.5820	0.5439	0.5083
8	0.9259	0.8573	0.7938	0.7350	0.6806	0.6302	0.5835	0.5403	0.5002	0.4632
9	0.9174	0.8417	0.7722	0.7084	0.6499	0.5963	0.5470	0.5019	0.4604	0.4224
10	0.9091	0.8264	0.7513	0.6830	0.6209	0.5645	0.5132	0.4665	0.4241	0.3855
11	0.9009	0.8116	0.7312	0.6587	0.5935	0.5346	0.4817	0.4339	0.3909	0.3522
12	0.8929	0.7972	0.7118	0.6355	0.5674	0.5066	0.4523	0.4039	0.3606	0.3220
13	0.8850	0.7831	0.6931	0.6133	0.5428	0.4803	0.4251	0.3762	0.3329	0.2946
14	0.8772	0.7695	0.6750	0.5921	0.5194	0.4556	0.3996	0.3506	0.3075	0.2697
15	0.8696	0.7561	0.6575	0.5718	0.4972	0.4323	0.3759	0.3269	0.2843	0.2472
16	0.8621	0.7432	0.6407	0.5523	0.4761	0.4104	0.3538	0.3050	0.2630	0.2267
17	0.8547	0.7305	0.6244	0.5337	0.4561	0.3898	0.3332	0.2848	0.2434	0.2080
18	0.8475	0.7182	0.6086	0.5158	0.4371	0.3704	0.3139	0.2660	0.2255	0.1911
19	0.8403	0.7062	0.5934	0.4987	0.4190	0.3521	0.2959	0.2487	0.2090	0.1756
20	0.8333	0.6944	0.5787	0.4823	0.4019	0.3349	0.2791	0.2326	0.1938	0.1615
21	0.8264	0.6830	0.5645	0.4665	0.3855	0.3186	0.2633	0.2176	0.1799	0.1486
22	0.8197	0.6719	0.5507	0.4514	0.3700	0.3033	0.2486	0.2038	0.1670	0.1369
23	0.8130	0.6610	0.5374	0.4369	0.3552	0.2888	0.2348	0.1909	0.1552	0.1262
24	0.8065	0.6504	0.5245	0.4230	0.3411	0.2751	0.2218	0.1789	0.1443	0.1164
25	0.8000	0.6400	0.5120	0.4096	0.3277	0.2621	0.2097	0.1678	0.1342	0.1074
26	0.7937	0.6299	0.4999	0.3968	0.3149	0.2499	0.1983	0.1574	0.1249	0.0992
27	0.7874	0.6200	0.4882	0.3844	0.3027	0.2383	0.1877	0.1478	0.1164	0.0916
28	0.7813	0.6104	0.4768	0.3725	0.2910	0.2274	0.1776	0.1388	0.1084	0.0847
29	0.7752	0.6009	0.4658	0.3611	0.2799	0.2170	0.1682	0.1304	0.1011	0.0784
30	0.7692	0.5917	0.4552	0.3501	0.2693	0.2072	0.1594	0.1226	0.0943	0.0725
35	0.7407	0.5487	0.4064	0.3011	0.2230	0.1652	0.1224	0.0906	0.0671	0.0497
40	0.7143	0.5102	0.3644	0.2603	0.1859	0.1328	0.0949	0.0678	0.0484	0.0346

9 Programmed decisions

9.1 Introduction

The foundations of modern quantitative methodology were laid during the Second World War, where the careful allocations of resources were critical to the performance of the warring factions. The basics of scientific management were developed earlier by Henry Fayol (1841–1925) and Fredrick Winslow Taylor (1856–1917). Both extolled the value of information and analysis to design, monitor and control work efficiently. These aspects of quantitative decision-making are still the subjects of substantial amounts of research, often resulting in complex algorithms containing hundreds of variables and solved iteratively on a computer. Quantitative decision-making is, in itself, a huge area of study. University library shelves are crammed full of texts devoted to quantitative methods for managers, operational research, and systems theory, and there are professional bodies of these disciplines in many countries. This chapter aims to introduce a conceptual understanding of one branch of management science, that of mathematical modelling to create programmed decisions.

Whilst some philosophers will argue that nothing in life, or business, is certain, it is often the case that we can assume that some things are so probable that they are certain. For these sorts of decision we can assume that once the decision has been taken then the consequences will be known. These 'simple', often routine, decisions are normally characterised by a known set of objectives, are not weighed down with conflict or human influences, and can lend themselves to programmed decision-making methods.

Take, for example, the case of an individual who buys tins of soup. The local supermarket will almost certainly have many tins of soup and you can leave it to the last minute to buy one because the times when the supermarket will not have any soup are rare. Further, the outcomes of 'soup' or 'no soup' are possibly not too important. We can make the decision only to buy soup as required, rather than keep a stock of it in the cupboard. Inventory decisions are important to many firms and they form a focus for the chapter.

Alternatively, a town authority may have a policy determining the replacement of its roadside light bulbs. Suppose there are two choices: change the bulbs when they fail, or change all the bulbs, irrespective of failure, on a regular basis. Two objectives can be identified: minimise the cost of maintenance, and ensure a safe level of lighting. The causes and effects of the decision parameters are easily quantified, and a model can be created to handle a variety of circumstances.

Other routine decisions that lend themselves to automation are those of scheduling, whether it is the scheduling of production through a manufacturing process, or the scheduling of staff within a service industry, or vehicles within a transportation system.

Management science offers us tools, techniques and methodologies that enable us to deal with managerial problems. Emotions, ethics and psychology are not part of this process, although may form part of the overall judgement. Management science deals with the collection, interpretation and presentation of data. However, because of the importance of qualitative aspects of decision-making, it is important to understand the limitations, assumptions and specific applicability of the methods in question. In some cases, management science can help us to quantify qualitative factors, by subjective scoring and assessment of risk.

This chapter examines some aspects of programmed decisions and builds on the issues of risk, systems analysis and modelling found in Chapters 2, 6, 7 and 10 (later).

9.2   Background

Turton (1991) has developed a simple grid to illustrate decision-making in relation to uncertainty (Figure 9.1). This model was an extension of much research into decision-making processes and uses the dimensions of cause and effect (clear or unclear) and objectives (shared/agreed or conflict) as a way in which to categorise decisions.

This chapter concentrates on decision-making that has clear cause and effects and shared and agreed objectives, or, as Turton implies, 'rational/ logical' decisions, where there is likely to be most chance of 'certainty'. Where we have unclear objectives but clear cause and effects we need to negotiate and compromise (as in some

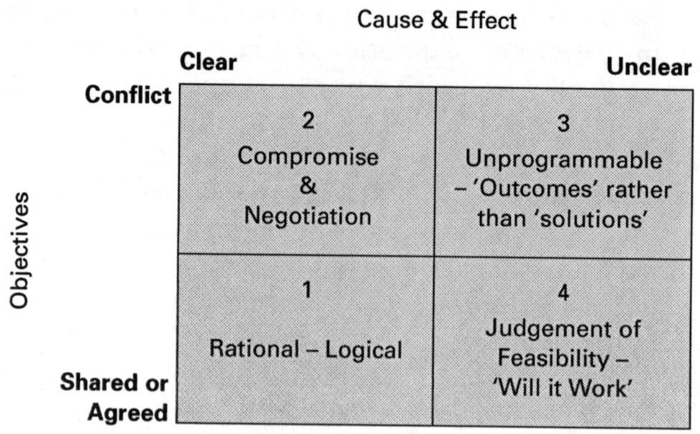

Cause & Effect

Figure 9.1 Model of decision making – types of uncertainty

Source: adapted from R. Turton (1991), Behaviour in a business context: Thomson Business Press

project management decisions). Where the cause and effects are unclear then politics, culture and other factors will affect the judgements made, as discussed later in Chapters 11, 12 and 13. In reality, the boundaries of Turton's model will be blurred. It is often the case that managers will attempt to use rational decision-making processes to aid in resolving issues that are political and, where there is a degree of conflict, to bolster or persuade. Rational decision-making can be used to back up a point of view 'if the model fits', but can be ignored if it does not. By 'fit' we mean match the decision-maker's prejudged decision or preference.

If we have certain or perfect information, how do we go about using it to make decisions? The benefit of decisions that can be solved by deterministic methods is that they can be solved more easily. You have already come across algorithms that have been used to determine the amount of stock to hold or to order, such as the economic order quantity in Chapter 7. These were developed from information that was assumed to be perfect; this is a simple example. In a sense, however, they also demonstrate that uncertainty is important. Imagine we need 100 units of product, but our supplier, on average, delivers only 90 per cent of what we order. The 90 per cent is an estimate of the likelihood of the order being filled in its entirety. The difference between modelling under certainty and modelling under uncertainty is the inclusion of the probabilities of certain events happening, generally termed *probabilistic* or *stochastic models* as opposed to *deterministic models*.

Activity 9.1	Consider the following 'everyday' decisions. Where would you place them on Turton's grid?

  1 Buying a house

  2 Accepting a job offer

  3 Paying a credit card bill

  4 Choosing a holiday location

  5 Going to work

How you rate each decision in Activity 9.1 will be personal, but the decisions may fall into quadrants 3, 4, 1, 2, 1, respectively.

9.3   Modelling under certainty

Many of the management science techniques discussed in this book are best performed on a computer. Indeed, the computer has made many of the techniques useful management tools, as opposed to academic exercises. Some mathematical techniques such as linear programming are possible (or justified in staff time) only beyond the trivial stage, if a computer is used. For example, within the chemical industry, equations with hundreds of variables are now routinely evaluated to enable firms to organise the most effective production and the cheapest sources of resources.

The computer also allows managers to experiment with 'what if?' scenarios to a much greater extent than in the past. This is an invaluable asset to managers wishing to compare the costs of various operational plans.

An interesting anecdote from the early days of operational research occurred during the Second World War. A team was evaluating the benefits of the use of the scarce resource of ammunition under various conflict situations. If we express the value of a bullet as its 'ability to inflict damage or injury', then the greatest effect comes from infantry rather than a gun crew on a bomber aircraft. This is because of the higher probability of a foot soldier hitting the target with a single bullet, compared with the aircraft. To illustrate, assume a foot soldier has a 20 per cent chance of causing damage and the gunner on the aircraft a 2 per cent chance. Mathematically, it is much more worthwhile to give all of the limited supply of bullets to the soldiers. So the decision to be made is: given the limited supply of bullets, should they all be given to the infantry, or should the bomber crews get bullets as well, leaving the infantry with fewer?

The final decision was made on psychological grounds. By not giving bullets to the bomber crews it was judged that aircrew morale would be affected; aircrews not able to defend themselves would be reluctant to take off. So, ammunition continued to be supplied to them.

Whilst management science offers useful tools to the manager to aid in the decision-making process, the solutions they offer must be evaluated in the context of the system in which they are being made. Quantitative methods, whether deterministic or probabilistic, contribute to the decision-making process. Figure 9.2 illustrates the role of quantitative methods in the decision-making process, competing with the more familiar qualitative methods categorised by management judgement and experience.

Deterministic models take no account of variability, compiled under the assumption that a given set of inputs will produce a given set of outputs. We can determine the effect of variability on the model by adjusting the level of inputs and analysing how sensitive the model is to these changes. This is described as *sensitivity analysis*.

The economic order quantity (EOQ) model introduced in Chapter 7 is not very sensitive to changes in the inputs. Figure 9.3 shows how the costs alter with a change in the number of units ordered. For this particular example, an EOQ of 62.5 might be rounded up to 70 or down to 50 with little effect on the total costs.

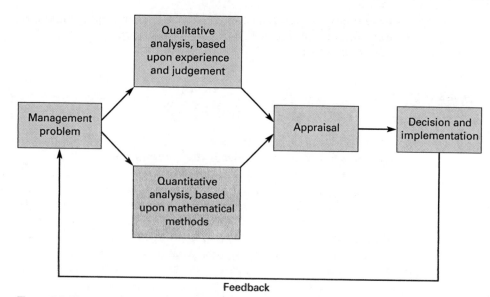

Figure 9.2 The role of quantitative methods

Many of the deterministic models used by managers to aid in the decision-making process are in this form. Some important models of this nature were introduced in Chapter 8 when we examined the management accounting approach to decision-making.

There are a number of techniques that centre around the problem of allocation of scarce resources, e.g. money, labour, machinery, time, and materials. Linear programming (LP) is the major methodology used to assist in these types of decision. The use of LP here allows for a result that is a specific number, an 'answer'. For example, if you wish to invest money in two units trusts in the ratio of 2:1 then you will invest 33.3 per cent in one unit trust and 66.7 per cent in the other. However, a large number of problems require an integer solution, for example in the allocation of labour. You normally cannot schedule half a person (the exception is when the person can work variable hours). This variation of LP is called *integer programming* and will only produce solutions in an integer form. Another example where simple LP does not provide an adequate solution is when there is more than one objective. For example, a company may

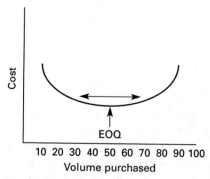

Figure 9.3 Sensitivity of the EOQ model

have the objectives of maximising market share, minimising costs and maintaining full employment. To resolve these problems a technique called *goal programming* is utilised.

9.4   An inventory model

The management of inventory has long been recognised as one of the most important issues facing managers on a routine basis. Historically, inventory management has revolved around mathematical modelling of the supply system to achieve two objectives:

- to meet customer service levels;
- to minimize inventory costs.

This section uses inventory control to illustrate the process of mathematical modelling. To do this, a brief outline of inventory issues is first provided, which is then followed by the model creation process.

9.4.1   Reasons for holding inventory

In Goldratt's (1993) novel *The Goal*, inventory is used as one of three factors that determine a firm's performance, the other two being operating expense and turnover. Within *The Goal*, a struggling factory gets to grips with its inventory conflicts and eventually becomes successful. Goldratt defines inventory as all of the firm's assets that it would use to create a product that might eventually be sold. For most firms, the major items of inventory that require management attention are those that are consumed on a regular basis.

Inventory takes three forms:

- *Material inventories* – those inventories of raw materials required for production.
- *Product inventories* – those inventories of finished products.
- *Work-in-progress* – those inventories of part-finished products.

The reasons for holding material inventories are:

- *Safety stocks* are used to smooth work flows within the production system, to take into account any shipping delays, or increased variations in production. Whilst they exist because of uncertainty and unreliability, it is obviously in the interest of the firm to minimise them wherever and however they can.
- *Economies of scale* are often associated with bulk purchases as well as providing lower order (transport) costs per item. This is likely to influence a firm's procurement and supply policy.

- *Safeguard and seasonal stocks* anticipate some disruption of supply. This can occur with some seasonally produced goods, or when we predict industrial or political instability. After the 1974 UK coal strike, power stations gradually increased stocks of coal to almost a year's worth so that when there was another strike in 1983, which lasted a year, the lack of domestic supply did not significantly affect electricity production in the UK.
- *Purchase savings* might take advantage of an unusually low price for a product. If soup is cheap at the local supermarket you might be tempted to buy dozens of cans.

Some reasons for holding product inventories are:

- To save on *transportation costs* so that full vehicles can be dispatched.
- To gain *production economies*, by having long production runs of particular products.
- To manage *seasonal demand* where large peaks in demand can often only be met through stocks from earlier production, such as chocolate Easter eggs, or Chinese moon cakes.
- To maintain *customer service* – finished inventory goods will be kept in stock to increase the speed of response to a customer demand.
- To provide *stable employment* by meeting demand fluctuations through inventory levels that enable a firm to smooth labour requirements, as opposed to hiring and firing staff or using subcontracting.

Work-in-progress (WIP) inventory includes those items of material that are within the production transformation system. At an accounting milestone, such as preparation of the end-of-year accounts, there will inevitably be some stock in this situation. During the course of the year, WIP will vary according to the types of product being produced and the efficiency of the system in converting the materials to finished goods.

The supply chain pipeline (Figure 9.4) helps to illustrate the links between suppliers and customers; the smoother the flow, the greater the effectiveness of the company. If the pipe is full of kinks and bends, the flow will become erratic, like the water in a water pipe. Inventory size is equivalent to the volume of water in the pipe, the capacity being the amount of water flowing per minute. If we

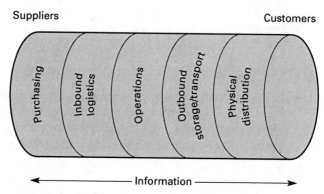

Figure 9.4 The supply chain pipeline

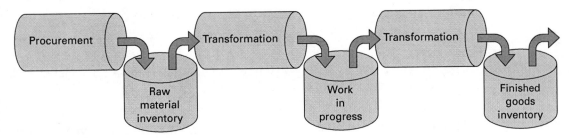

Figure 9.5 Broken pipe

Source: Teale, 1999: 196

reduce the diameter of the pipe we decrease the volume of water, but we then need to increase the speed of flow to achieve the same capacity.

A closer analogy is shown in Figure 9.5, where we have pools of inventory between the transformation processes. Whenever a pool of inventory occurs, we lose value. The pipeline is sometimes referred to as the *value chain*. It is important that value is added at each stage. Customers must perceive that value is added, either in the form of price or service (Teale, 1999).

The pipeline links the suppliers to the customers, with material travelling one way and information both ways. Customer dissatisfaction can occur if any one part of the chain fails. We can apply the pipeline approach to all activities within the supply chain and even extend the principles to supporting activities, such as the management of spare parts and capital purchases.

We need to minimise inventory for many reasons, not least the costs associated with it. Retailers, for example, would like to minimise not just for the savings in costs, but also to increase the value-adding area of the shop, the area where customers buy goods. In contrast, they also need to ensure that goods are continually available to customers. They could operate a just-in-time (JIT) system if they have a very responsive supplier. Multiple retailers have more scope to reduce inventory than unaffiliated, independent stores who are forced to keep small warehouses (lockups).

9.4.2   Inventory control

The important issues are:

- Inventory classification (what to control?)
- Reorder levels (when to order?)
- Economic order quantities (how much to order?)
- Application of modern technology (how to order?)

To develop a system to control inventory we need to have an understanding of the costs and benefits of such a system. These costs include the initial development as well as the continuing operational costs associated with data collection and analysis. The benefits are mainly connected with the costs saved by having a reduced stock.

Inventory costs

One criticism of material costing systems is that they tend to focus on purchase costs rather than on the total cost associated with purchasing, delivery and storage of the item and, as Goldratt eloquently identifies, the cost associated with lost turnover should we run out of inventory.

The costs associated with stock are:

- *Procurement (order) costs*, such as delivery costs, purchasing staff costs, management information system costs.
- *Holding costs*, such as storage costs, interest charges, depreciation and loss.
- *Production costs* due to lost production or inefficiency. Inefficiency costs refer to the fact that inventory can often disguise production inefficiencies.

The first two categories of costs work in opposite directions. As the quantity ordered increases, the effects are that the procurement cost per item decreases and the total cost of holding increases (Figure 9.6). An important decision in inventory control is to determine the right balance of holding and procurement costs. However, focusing on this trade-off should not shift management attention away from finding ways of cutting procurement costs. Production costs, in the form of stockouts, are potentially the greatest and reflect decisions on stock levels.

Inventory classification

In resolving inventory issues, we need to understand the costs associated with holding inventory. This needs then to be balanced with the costs of running out of inventory. But before we consider these costs the company must get an understanding of the scale of the inventory issues. There is no point in spending valuable management time examining and developing expensive inventory control procedures for items that do not require such measures. For example, a manufacturing firm would have a different inventory control system for office paper from the one it has for electronic parts for one of its products.

To classify inventory we can adopt a technique called ABC analysis where class A items are the most important and class C the least important to the firm. This analysis is based on Pareto's law, which separates the 'trivial many' from the 'vital few'.

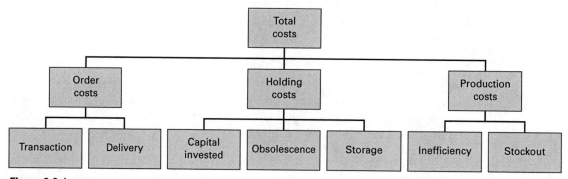

Figure 9.6 Inventory cost structure

- Category A items (20 per cent of items used) account for 80 per cent of inventory value.
- Category B items (30 per cent of items) account for 10 per cent of inventory value.
- Category C items (50 per cent of items) account for the remaining 10 per cent of value.

The data in Table 9.1 are an extract from a small electrical company's inventory records.

We need to implement a control system to minimise stock levels, but prevent shortages. Which items would we develop a sophisticated system for?

To categorise the items in ABC format (Table 9.2), we first calculate the annual cost (multiply the annual demand by the unit cost). These figures (annual £-volume) can then be ranked in descending order so as to calculate the cumulative percentage value (100 × cumulative value/total value). Table 9.2 indicates that items 1 to 4 are the main cost elements in category A; items 5 to 7 are the category B items and items 9 to 15 represent the 'trivial many' in category C. Any control system would focus on items 1 to 4. Items 9 to 15 would be controlled using simple container systems. The data are illustrated in Figure 9.7.

When we have classified our inventory we can turn our attention to developing the appropriate control system.

Economic order quantities

We now address the issue of how much inventory to order. To do this we have to create a mathematical model (commonly called the economic order quantity, EOQ). The EOQ can be represented graphically as shown in Figure 9.8.

To create our basic model we assume that demand is constant, that cost per unit is not dependent on the order quantity, the entire delivery is made at one

Table 9.1 Inventory costs

Description	Unit cost (£) (item or per 100 metres)	Average weekly usage	Standard deviation of use (over lead time)	Lead time (days)	Current inventory
Grommets	0.05	300	55	20	650
5mm T/C cable	23.55	1.25	0.52	21	200 m
Fibre optic line	2.50	75	5	18	715 m
Metal sheet	2.00	75	8	17	245
IC system	5.00	75	9	21	150
II system	4.50	75	7	21	163
Clip (croc)	0.17	75	15	21	2,745
Monitor	20.00	75	5	12	278
12 V battery	8.00	75	7	21	171
Sealant	5.00	15	1	15	145
Circlip	0.07	300	45	7	1,250
Boxes	0.48	75	9	10	220
Packing	3.50	7	0.87	10	68
Bags	5.60	3	0.23	10	4
Labels	1.10	2	0.08	10	7

Table 9.2 ABC analysis

Item number	Item name	Annual demand	Unit cost £	Annual £-volume	Cum. % (items)	Sum £	Cum. % £
1	Monitor	3,900	20	78,000	6.7	78,000	44.3
2	12 V battery	3,900	8	31,200	13.3	109,200	62.1
3	IC system	3,900	5	19,500	20.0	128,700	73.2
4	II system	3,900	5	17,550	26.7	146,250	83.1
5	Fibre optic line	3,900	3	9,750	33.3	156,000	88.7
6	Metal sheet	3,900	2	7,800	40.0	163,800	93.1
7	Sealant	780	5	3,900	46.7	167,700	95.3
8	Boxes	3,900	0	1,872	53.3	169,572	96.4
9	5mm T/C cable	65	24	1,531	60.0	171,103	97.3
10	Packing	364	4	1,274	66.7	172,377	98.0
11	Circlip	15,600	0	1,092	73.3	173,469	98.6
12	Bags	156	6	874	80.0	174,342	99.1
13	Grommets	15,600	0	780	86.7	175,122	99.6
14	Clip (croc)	3,900	0	663	93.3	175,785	99.9
15	Labels	104	1	114	100.0	175,900	100.0
	Total			**175,900**	**800**		

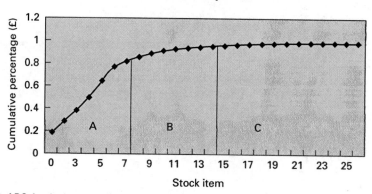

Figure 9.7 ABC Analysis

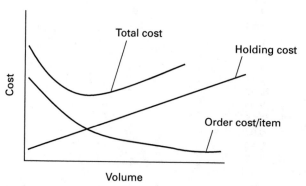

Figure 9.8 Inventory costs

time and that ordering and holding costs are known and independent. With some algebraic manipulation we get:

$$EOQ = \sqrt{\frac{2DC_0}{C_h}}$$

where D = annual demand rate

C_o = variable ordering cost

C_h = variable holding cost

The assumptions underpinning the simple EOQ model make its use in practice very limited. However, based on this simple model of economic order quantities a number of other models have been developed. Each model addresses the issue of EOQ and attempts to match it to practice, for example by taking into account price discounts on volume orders, and including time lags in production and delivery.

Example 9.1

Sue Eel buys oil for Salmon Garages. The demand for oil is constant at 20 barrels a month. Each barrel costs £50, the cost of processing an order and arranging a delivery is £60 and holding cost is £18 a year. What are the economic order quantity and total costs?

Solution

It is helpful to list the data in consistent units:

D = 20 × 12 = 240 units per annum

C_o = £60 an order

C_h = £18 per unit per annum

Using these values in the EOQ formula gives:

$$EOQ = \sqrt{\frac{2 \times 240 \times 60}{18}} = 40 \text{ units}$$

The cost of ordering is 60 × 240/40 = £360

The cost of holding stock = 18 × 40/2 = £360

These costs are the same, as one would expect, as the minimum point of Figure 9.8 is where the two lines cross, i.e. the costs are the same.

The costs of the barrels is 240 × 50 = £12,000

The total cost for the year is £12,720

Reorder level

Another important concept in inventory control is when to reorder. Reordering should take place before the item is used up and must take into account the amount of time it will take for the order to be processed and delivered, the *average demand* and *lead time* during that period. If these two factors are incorrectly estimated then a *stockout* occurs, or the firm will carry too much inventory. To counteract stockouts, *safety stocks* are held that are derived from an estimation of the variability of demand during the lead time.

To evaluate safety stocks we might assume that lead time and demand will vary according to a statistical distribution, in this case the normal distribution. We also use our judgement as to the *service level* we are going to provide the customer. Service level indicates the level of risk of actually running out of stock and can be found from normal distribution tables. Table 9.3 shows for any given system the service level Z (the number of standard deviations from the mean) which equates to the probability of running out of stock.

We can use the following formula to indicate the reorder point:

$$M = D \times L + Z\sigma_d$$

where: M = reorder level

D = demand during lead time

L = lead time

Z = service level (the number of standard deviations from the mean)

σ_d = standard deviation of demand over the lead time

Example 9.2	Given that the lead time for the delivery of oil in the Salmon garages example above is two weeks, what is the reorder level?

If the supplier cannot guarantee delivery within the two-week period, and if the use of oil varies to give a variation of demand during the lead time of three barrels, what reorder level would be required to provide a service level of at least 95 per cent?

Solution

Demand/week = 20/4 = 5 barrels

Reorder level is $D \times L = 5 \times 2 = 10$ barrels

Reorder level with safety stock. A 95 per cent service level or higher equates to a stockout of 5 per cent or lower or a service level (Z) of 1.64 using normal distribution tables. Hence:

Reorder level = $10 + 1.64 \times 3 = 14.92$, i.e. 15 barrels

Table 9.3 Service levels and probability of stockout

Service level (Z)	Probability of stockout (%)
0	50.0
1	15.9
2	2.3
3	0.1
4	0.0

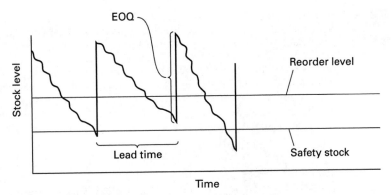

Figure 9.9 Inventory levels with instant replenishment

Figure 9.9 illustrates how these concepts relate to inventory levels over time with instant replenishment.

9.5   Linear programming model

Linear programming (LP) is commonly used to solve resource allocation problems provided that the problem can be defined in mathematical linear functions such as $ax + by + \ldots = c$. To use an LP model the problem must be formulated mathematically, solved and then translated into real terms. Also, the decision scenario must have a clear objective, within a set of constraints. LP is eminently suitable for problem solving under strong terms of certainty and with agreed objectives and strong cause–effect relationships in the system when:

- we need to maximise or minimise some parameter. For example, we may wish to minimise materials costs, increase revenue or maximise machine utilisation. This parameter is referred to as the *objective function*.

- The problem is limited in the number of solutions by a set of *constraints*. For example, the number of activities a sports centre can run is limited by the availability of staff, rooms and time. Hence, LP problems maximise or minimise a parameter subject to constraints on the system. The sports centre may wish to maximise room utilisation (the objective function), subject to staff availability, costs being less than a target value, and time of opening from 9 am to 9 pm. These constraints need to be mathematical in nature and not qualitative.

- There must be a number of alternative solutions (otherwise there is no decision to be made). For example, the leisure centre may be able to offer aerobics, jujitsu, and dance classes in one room and the relative mix of these can be altered. The LP would attempt to find the best mix to maximise, in this case, the room utilisation. If there were no alternatives to the mix then we would not need LP.

- The objective function and constraints must be described in terms of linear relationships. For example, X + Y = Z is a simple equation. Sometimes, the relationships are expressed in terms of linear inequalities such as A + B ≥ 0 to represent a minimum requirement in the model, or as C + D ≤ 10 to signify that a maximum number of resources (10) is available in this constraint.

Example 9.3

A garden furniture company, Rustica, wishes to determine the number of benches and picnic tables to produce to maximise the profit to the company. It has estimated that the profit on a bench is £9 and on a table is £6. Two processes are undertaken. The furniture is constructed then preserved by painting on a wood preservative. Each bench takes 4 hours to construct and 2 hours to paint. Each table takes 3 hours to construct and 1 hour to paint. Three employees are available to do the painting and they work 120 hours per week in total. Nine employees are involved in the carpentry work and they work 260 hours per week in total. Formulate the scenario as a Linear Programme.

Solution

The constraints are the hours available to do the painting and construction. Naturally, the only objective is to maximise the profit but it might be under discussion that the wastage has to be minimised too. This is dependent on the number of benches and tables produced. We will call the number of benches made X_1 and the number of tables made X_2. The LP model is:

Maximise profit = £9X_1 + £6X_2 (Objective function)
Subject to: $2X_1 + 1X_2 \leq 120$ (Painting constraint)
                $4X_1 + 3X_2 \leq 260$ (Construction constraint)
                $X_1, X_2 \geq 0$ (Non-negativity constraints)

We need the last constraint because it is impossible to produce less than zero tables or benches. As this is a two-dimensional problem we can solve it graphically. The procedure for doing this is as follows:

1 Set up a graph (Figure 9.10) so that X_1 is the horizontal axis and X_2 is the vertical axis (this will mean that the area above the horizontal axis and to the right of the vertical axis will satisfy the non-negativity constraints).

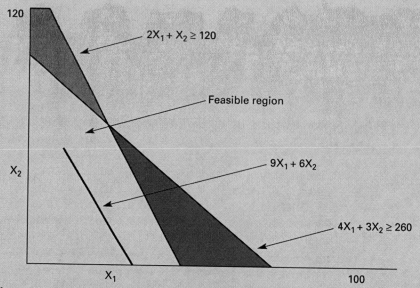

Figure 9.10 Rustica graphical formulation (not to scale)

continued

2 For each of the two constraints:

   (a) Set $X_1 = 0$, solve for X_2, and plot this point. For the painting constraint we get (0, 120) and (60, 0).

   (b) Set $X_2 = 0$, solve for X_1, and plot this point. For the construction constraint we get (0, 80) and (60, 0).

   (c) Connect these two points with a straight line.

- Determine the feasible side of the line. If the origin (0, 0) satisfies the inequality then the feasible region will be the side of the line that includes the origin. Shade this area to show where a feasible set of solutions will lie.

3 Find the optimal point:

- From the shading done for each constraint, the feasible region has been determined. Within this region a number of solutions are possible.

- Choose an arbitrary value for the objective function and solve the equation as before so as to plot this objective function on the graph.

- Move the objective function line up to a corner point to maximise the value of the objective function, or down to minimise it. That point will be the optimal solution and the coordinates will represent the optimum values of X_1 and X_2.

One way to do this is to draw a parallel line at a point furthest from the origin that still lies within the shaded area, i.e. set profit equal to 100 and then solve for X_1 and X_2. In the case of Rustica, $100 = 9X_1 + 6X_2$, therefore if $X_1 = 0$ then $X_2 = 16.6$, and if $X_2 = 0$ then $X_1 = 11.1$. We can then plot these two points, i.e. (0, 16.6) and (11.1, 0).

Referring back to Rustica, we can solve this graphically by generating straight lines that mark the feasible and unfeasible solutions for the constraints. For example, for the first constraint we can plot a line based on the values of X_1 and X_2.

If we set $X_1 = 0$ then $X_2 = 120$.

If we set $X_2 = 0$ then $X_1 = 60$.

Plotting the constraints on the graph we can see where the feasible solutions are. Any mix of products that lie within the shaded region of the graph is feasible. To discover the maximum profit we need to use the objective function. If we nominally set a profit of £400 then the line representing the objective function is:

$$400 = 9X_1 + 6X_2$$

If we set $X_1 = 0$ then $X_2 = 67$.

If we set $X_2 = 0$ then $X_1 = 44$.

We can plot the line on the graph as before. By altering the profit we can move the objective function so that it reaches its maximum value within the constraints. If plotted to scale then we would find that the solution would be $X_1 = 50$ units and, correspondingly, $X_2 = 20$ units.

The maximum profit in Rustica's case is $9 \times 50 + 6 \times 20 = £570$ obtained from producing 50 benches and 20 tables per week.

| Activity 9.3 | Solve the following linear programming problem graphically. |

Maximise $3X_1 + 3X_2$

subject to:

$2X_1 + 4X_2 \leq 12$

$6X_1 + 4X_2 \leq 24$

$X_1, X_2 \geq 0$

| Activity 9.4 | Dixon & Mason are suppliers of high quality wedding cakes. Two styles are produced: the three tier or the four tier. Both are produced in the same manner. The three-tier cake requires 2 hours of baking and 1 hour of preparation. The four-tier cake needs 3 hours of baking and 2 hours of preparation. During the next production period, 240 hours of baking time and 140 hours of preparation time may be used. Each four-tier cake will make £25 profit, but each three-tier cake only £15 profit. Formulate and solve this LP production mix problem to find the best mix of cakes that yields the highest profit. Use the corner point graphical method (as shown earlier). |

9.6 Linear programming assumptions and applications

Linear programming is restricted to those problems that:

- are linear. Many business costs change in a complex manner subject to a variety of dependent effects, and changes in one variable may affect changes in another;

- have a single objective. Many decisions involve trade-offs between competing objectives of cost, quality and speed;

- have a continuous objective variable. The LP provides fractional solutions, which often do not match reality.

In the longer term, the use of such models requires management to continually review the integrity of the model. For this reason, LP is a useful tool to aid in continual improvement programmes, as without regular reviews continued use of the model could be potentially damaging to the firm.

LP is most useful over the short term. Learning (or experience) curves can affect job times; machinery reliability can affect production rates. It is often the case that the variables do interact. The addition or deletion of a new product may in the longer term increase, or reduce, customer loyalty.

One of the major benefits of conducting an LP exercise is that it focuses attention on the problem area. The more attention the problem area is given, the more certain will be the data input to the model and the more reliable the results. The use of LP, as with all of the other models, is not to make a decision for a manager, but to improve confidence in the decision made and to provide management with evidence for change.

9.6.1 Software

In practice, many LP problems are routinely constructed and resolved by computer. To illustrate the use of software, the Rustica problem is solved using the Excel® Spreadsheet tool Solver.

On the spreadsheet a cell is identified as the target cell. This cell contains the objective function. So we would enter the formula for this and state whether this is to be maximised or minimised.

In Table 9.4 the formula is:

=9*D4+6*E4

We then define the cells that need to change. In this case there are just the two parameters: benches and tables, X_1 and X_2.

We set the constraints slightly differently from how we set them in the earlier method in so far as the independent variable is stated first and allocated a cell, as shown in Table 9.4. Within the Solver tool the constraints are defined as:

H4>=2*D4+E4

H5>=4*D4+3*E4

D, $E4, >= 0

When the problem has been defined we press Solve and the solution is shown in the target cell. As before, the firm makes £570 from producing 50 benches and 20 tables.

Table 9.4 LP using Solver

B	C	D	E	F	G	H
3		X1	X2		Constraints	
4	570	50	20		Painting	120
5					Construction	260
6					Negativity	0

 Activity 9.5   Try formulating Activity 9.4 on the Excel® Solver system.

◆   **Summary**

Programmed decisions are common, wherever routine, regular and non-contentious decisions need to be made. The need to create such an approach arises when the decision area becomes arduous and time consuming for individuals to undertake as part of their normal duties. The models created are often underpinned by substantial work by specialists in research and mathematics. As such they can be expensive to create. Once the model has been created it has to be maintained. One reason why firms do not perform as well as they might is because the data or models on which routine decisions are made are out of date or not representative of a changed situation.

One of the most useful of the management science approaches to decision-making is linear programing. Linear programming is the starting point for many methodologies that help indicate courses of action when we have certain information. We need to have a clear idea of the objectives of the model and of the constraints that the model is subject to. Deterministic models are commonly used to resolve allocation problems, such as the number of products to produce, or the routes of delivery vehicles. We need to be careful to ensure that the model is kept up to date if it is to be used on a regular basis.

Decision diary

Reflecting on your recent decision situations, which, if any, could have benefited from an LP approach? Try to formulate a model to resolve one.

References

Goldratt, E. (1993) *The Goal.* Aldershot: Gower.
Teale, M.W. (1999), 'Supply chain management', in Greasley, A. (ed.), *Operations Management in Business.* Cheltenham: Stanley Thornes.
Turton, R. (1991) *Behaviour in a Business Context.* London: Chapman & Hall.

Further reading

Anderson, D.R., Sweeney, D.J. and Williams, T. (1991) *An Introduction to Management Science.* St Paul, MN: West Publishing.
Taylor, F.W. *The Principles of Scientific Management.* New York: Harper & Row.
Turton, R. (1991), *Behaviour in a business context.* London: Thomson Business Press.
Vonderembse, M.A. and White, G.P. (1996) *Operations Management: Concepts, Methods and Strategies.* St Paul, MN: West Publishing.

Glossary

Normal distribution: the most widely used continuous probability distribution in statistics is the normal probability distribution. The curve is typically bell-shaped and represents the distribution of probabilities around a mean of μ, standard deviation of σ. Probabilities for the normal distribution can be computed using tables for the standard normal distribution that has a mean of zero and a standard deviation of one. Typically the curve is used to compute the chances of success or failure of a given system. For example, in inventory control that would be the chances of running out of stock; if two standard deviations stock above the mean are kept, that would equate to about two per cent.

Sensitivity analysis: a technique for determining how the outputs from a formula change with respect to changes in the input parameters.

Appendix 1   Answers to selected activities

Activity 9.3

First draw the graph with the axis (X) and X_2 (normally Y) representing the non-negativity constraints.

Second solve for each constraint, i.e. for constraint, 1 if $X_1 = 0$, $X_2 = 3$; if $X_2 = 0$, $X_1 = 6$. Two points (0, 3) (6, 0) are obtained. Plot these on the graph and join together to form the first boundary of constraint.

Solve for the next constraint. This will give (0, 6) and (4, 0). Draw the second line.

Draw the objective line. Select a suitable value for the function. e.g. 6:

$$6 = 3X_1 + 3X_2$$

Solving gives (0, 2) and (2, 0). Plot this line.

Next move the line parallel to the objective line until it reaches the boundaries of the constraints.

In this case there is one feasible solution: $X_1 = 6$ and $X_2 = 4$. The solution generates a value of 12.

Activity 9.4

Call three-tier cake X_1, four-tier cake X_2.

Objective function:

Maximise $15X_1 + 25X_2$, subject to:

$2 X_1 + 3X_2 \leq 240$ (Baking constraint) Points (0, 80), (120, 0)

$X_1 + 2X_2 \leq 140$ (Preparation constraint) Points (0, 70), (140, 0)

$X_1, X_2 \geq 0$ (Non-negativity constraint)

If we let profit = 300 then two points on the objective line are (0, 12) and (20, 0).

We get a solution of 56 three-tier and 42 four-tier cakes giving a profit of £1,890.

We can check the solution by putting the values back into our constraints and ensuring that these still hold true. In this case we find we have slack within the baking operation, i.e.

$2 \times 56 + 3 \times 42 = 238$, a slack of 2 in baking

and

$56 + 84 = 140$, no slack in preparation

This implies that the graphical solution, although good, is not perfect. The best mix is shown in the answer to Activity 9.5 (below), which shows the Solver version. This indicates 60 three-tier and 40 four-tier cakes to give a profit of £1,900.

CHAPTER 10

Time management: project decision-making

10.1 Introduction

From the desire to be successful there has grown a structured methodology, sometimes referred to as a project management 'body of knowledge', which enables project managers to assimilate new management thinking, including current systems work. This complements the more historical, traditional tools and techniques employed by project managers for the purpose of circulating information of a verbal, tabular or graphical nature. In this chapter, we develop a network of project activities from the starting point of a life cycle which is assessed to generate subsidiary information on the schedule of each activity as part of an integrated plan.

A successful project management team is thorough in its planning, data research and constraint identification. Working towards realistic targets for control, the team will be timely in posting warnings about failure and checking off the milestones of success. Using appropriate software tools to prepare diagrams and charts, project progress can be monitored against management objectives for time, cost and quality.

10.2 Project characteristics

In the 'Ask Bill Gates' column of *Management Today* (December 1999, p. 36), the question posed by a reader was: 'How does somebody impress you at interview?' Mr Gates (chairman of Microsoft) answered concisely: 'I want to know if a candidate has formed a complete model of how a company or project works'. His general advice to job applicants was 'to find out as much as possible about a company in advance'. In general, this advice applies to all types of projects at their research stage and, as the project unfolds through its lifecycle, there has to be careful monitoring of progress data so as to capture the uncertainty for management attention.

Many projects are special, exhibiting unique characteristics that manage to effect 'change' within the corporate, business or functional level of strategic decision-making of an organisation (Slack *et al.*, 1998: 76). For example, British Rail's Advanced Passenger Train (APT) of the 1970s was technically quite impressive as it developed the idea of a tilting train. The funding and hence the idea later fell away but there have been two direct developments of the APT. First, the Class 91 locomotive which powers most east coast mainline trains very successfully was a direct development of the APT. Second, the current imports from Fiat of Italy for the Virgin train operator can also be shown to descend from the APT. Britain did not have the political resolve to finish the project but was very good at initial conception and design.

Let us define a project as 'something that induces change that has a planned beginning and an agreed ending'. Introducing new methods, technologies, facilities or buildings might be typical changes. 'Normal work' usually focuses on effective, correct management of routine operations so as to achieve replicated, consistent output. Projects tend to be judged on three major dimensions: time, cost and quality. This compares with the classical five performance objectives in operations management of cost, speed, quality, flexibility and dependability discussed by Slack *et al.* (1998: 51–66). When there is a commercial, social or technical requirement to be 'better', then projects seek to transform the system to provide the improvement.

A thorough project management approach would investigate the enhancements for which the project was commissioned. The proposed enhancements could originate from a variety of other projects, and so project management is identified as a continuous philosophy for success and elimination of failure from normal, routine working practice.

Consider the following simple examples of projects with a social or cultural purpose: decorating a room, building a new theatre, organising a special celebration such as a wedding, teaching a child to ride a bicycle, or going on a holiday to an unknown country. Hence, everyday activities can be classed as 'projects' when they require some investment of money or time and can be evaluated for their quality.

Many construction projects are purely commercial, highly technical and complex, e.g. building Hong Kong's new airport to carry 70 million passengers a year, or the late 1990s dash towards internet commerce through website trading via the installation of a communications network with online shopping facilities. Other projects may be commercially pressing, such as gaining ISO 9000 approval, taking over another business, selling a new product in an overseas market, or perhaps developing online material for students on a distance learning education programme. The importance of 'time' management to these endeavours is obvious.

Projects are often famous for the quality of their success or failure. The building of the Egyptian pyramids was an awesome undertaking that has been preserved for thousands of years, but the ethical implications of hundreds of deaths in their construction are open for discussion. The landing of troops on the beaches in Normandy, France, in June 1944 was a logistical success of timeliness but, again, many were killed. The British Lending Library on Euston Road, London, opened many years late and massively over-budget but is world-class in terms of its facilities. Other projects might demonstrate superb timeliness or an element of surprise in achieving success owing to the quality of the opportunities offered.

The purpose of project planning is to evaluate and define the work so that it can be managed and completed successfully. An innovative project is, hence, 'investigative', testing assumptions and identifying obstacles. In comparison, an operation 'produces' the same item or furnishes the same service but is forced to improve on a more continual basis. For the most part, line managers work in the operational mode.

A project manager, traditionally, oversees five major objectives: the work to be done, by whom, at what cost, to what quality and within what timescale. Quality, cost and time can be 'soft' objectives, perhaps negotiable but depending on the latitude agreed between sponsor, project manager and end user. For example, project acceptance by a customer may have to occur although the quality and time are not exactly to plan but the costs have exceeded a fixed budget (Figure 10.1).

A project normally has quantitative estimates of its planned budget and the human and material resources needed to achieve the five major objectives. The project may be distinctive because of the degree of complexity around the technical, social or cultural purpose, the need for absolute completeness, the improved competitiveness or the enhanced customer benefits. Conversely, projects may be initiated exclusively for internal benefits such as preserving jobs,

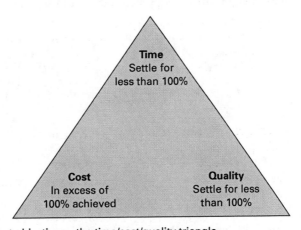

Figure 10.1 Project objectives – the time/cost/quality triangle

enhancing team spirit or providing continuity in a time of change. The risks involved are usually notable, being low, medium or high according to whose perspective you take (Chapter 2).

10.3 Systems concepts

The input–transformation–output model (Chapter 6) is equally valid when considering project management issues (Figure 10.2). Inputs are transformed over the project timescale into 'better' outputs. Such processes involve new techniques in the face of time, cost and quality constraints.

The influence the environment has on project activity will be one of the major features of a system. Describing the role of feedback in a system is important. Likewise, distinguishing between positive and negative feedback in the system and reacting to the implied consequences is essential in managing a timescale.

10.3.1 Information management

An evaluation of management competences by Williams (1996: 301–22)) showed that extracting information, analysing and presenting data are vital skills for hard-pressed project management personnel. This covers skimming through data, interpreting and summarising only that which is relevant but getting the desired information.

As information technology continues to impact on our lives, the managerial decision-making process will continue to adopt yet more computer-based techniques. However, total faith in resource scheduling packages, project management programs, spreadsheets, etc., is unwise. These programs do not just 'do the analysis' at the 'touch of a button', as some people often presume. However, we must have confidence in software to consistently maintain the integrity of data output because there is little doubt that it has improved enormously since the microcomputer was in its infancy in the 1980s.

Classical planning techniques can be applied to any project of any type. A basic diagramming approach facilitates information sharing and communication

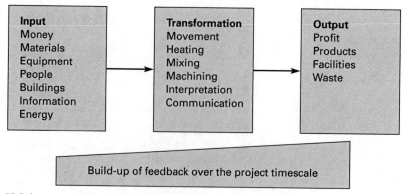

Figure 10.2 Input–transformation–output systems model

provided that the project data have a consistent format, preferably electronic for speed. These features are evidence of a well-managed approach to the project, above all when personnel join and leave through the life cycle.

It is easy to justify the systematic, iterative nature of plan development. Complementary risk assessment (Chapter 2) depends on timely anticipation of the scope of work and accuracy of the plan. Graphical presentation of time, cost and quality data helps all team members to get a common perception of pressures and issues (with all the incumbent psychological pain, Chapter 3) before addressing any recovery action. The importance of sharing data for the achievement of a project in the optimum time, and the tension imposed by short timescales, can make humans react to implied change in many dysfunctional ways.

10.3.2 Project life cycle

Owing to the unique nature of projects, there is no typical life cycle. For example, Kerzner (1992: 82–90) advises that even in mature industries, such as construction, a survey might find ten distinct life cycle definitions. Each phase could be viewed as a small project, with a repetition of similar management processes, but four major stages in the life of a project seem consistent. The germination of the idea, the growth in operational activities, maximum activity through the maturity stage and, finally, into the closedown period, with audit and handover to signify 'death' (Figure 10.3). Successfully identifying project roles, interfaces and systems of the life cycle is a vital aspect of project planning. This promotes discussion and debate about the types of organisational and technical skill to be recruited onto a project, whilst evaluating the 'effort' or cost to accomplish the work to the prescribed level of quality.

Activity 10.1	Your latest DIY project with some friends is to erect a shed in your garden, with a view to storing tools, bicycles and equipment.

1 Describe what occurs in the four stages of the project life cycle.

2 Describe the planning required in each stage of work, and identify the issues the further you get into the project plan.

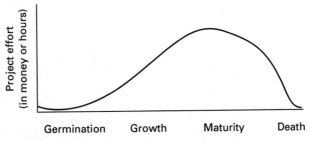

Figure 10.3 Life cycle and timescaled approach to the project effort
Source: adapted from Turner, 1999

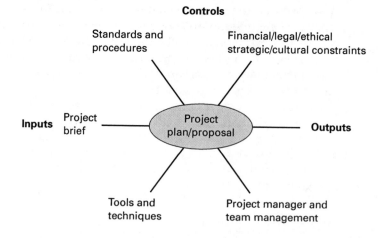

Figure 10.4 Mechanism and control of project inputs

For each stage of the life cycle, the project requires the scheduling and estimation of resource requirements, with appropriate development of teams and organisational plans. Procedures for accurate and timely control of a project must be established so as to minimise risk and ensure some measure of success over constraints, in line with project strategy and agreed standards. Turner (1999: 11) speculates that estimates of project costs in the germination phase can be wrong by up to 20 per cent, but in the maturity phase control is normally to within 5 per cent of the agreed figure. Summarily, project planning can be seen as a battlefield with many management viewpoints (Figure 10.2 has been extended into Figure 10.4). The criteria are defined by use of tools and techniques, but the constraints imposed by finance, culture, legalities etc. are to be overcome by human intervention. The project management team proactively possesses an overseeing responsibility for 'control' and 'mechanism'.

Once the project is growing towards maturity, with completed work and costs accumulating, problem solving occurs as managers will be fighting the fires lit by the seen, and unseen, constraints and outcomes. At project termination, a review and audit could provide a recyclable project plan with all the improvements and benefits drawn together into a quality-based document. Fresh customer focus and competitiveness might be explored in a strategic sense in the light of a changed appreciation of, for example, the marketing interface, the management of technology or the reduction in costs.

10.4 Project planning for time

Time is one of the three primary objectives (Figure 10.1) to be managed in any project. To generate a project timescale, the seminal idea pioneered in the 1950s of a *critical path analysis* of the project predicts the 'least time' to completion, rewarding the project manager with a plan of time schedules for each activity. Using electronic-based software (e.g. a Microsoft Excel® spreadsheet) or a dedicated project management package (e.g. Microsoft Project®), an integrated plan can be created for time and cost management, with allocation of resources.

Later in this chapter we will ponder the reasons for success and failure in a project, although there are some difficulties in definitively judging these depending on the perspective taken. Clearly, it will be necessary to judge the effort and management attention required for the project timescale.

10.4.1 Initiating a project plan

A project will tend to have one overarching purpose of a commercial, cultural, technical or social nature. Originating from the project proposal, the purpose will be agreed between the major players such as the sponsors, users, project teams and project managers. Project management is sometimes seen as a 'hard' subject, quite technical, and so less attention is possibly paid (incorrectly) to the 'softer' issues such as team-building and morale that are crucial to successful completion. 'Success' demands team-building, formation of a style and culture for the project to which these parties agree, at least contractually.

The germination stage of the project idea (see Figure 10.3) will, normally, produce a 'project initiation' document which might typically mushroom to detail the expected timescale from germination to death (Figure 10.5).

This is all very thorough – but how do we get to know the duration of this passage from germination to death?

10.4.2 Target times for project activities

It is normal to develop a plan by listing the activities. As an example, the following project (Table 10.1) is for the construction of a garage next to a house, with a target start date of Wednesday, 15 January 2003. Usually, work must occur in a five-day working week (Monday to Friday). Provisional estimates for the durations are

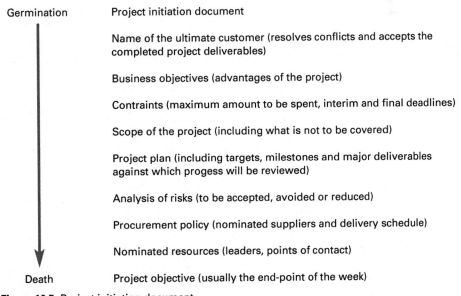

Germination — Project initiation document

Name of the ultimate customer (resolves conflicts and accepts the completed project deliverables)

Business objectives (advantages of the project)

Contraints (maximum amount to be spent, interim and final deadlines)

Scope of the project (including what is not to be covered)

Project plan (including targets, milestones and major deliverables against which progess will be reviewed)

Analysis of risks (to be accepted, avoided or reduced)

Procurement policy (nominated suppliers and delivery schedule)

Nominated resources (leaders, points of contact)

Death — Project objective (usually the end-point of the week)

Figure 10.5 Project initiation document

Table 10.1 Project data for building a garage

Activity number	Activity name	Duration (days)	Preceding activity numbers
1	Start of project	0	None
2	Level the site	3	1
3	Construct wall units	15	1
4	Construct doors	5	1
5	Obtain roof unit	5	1
6	Dig foundations	7	2
7	Install wall units	2	3,6
8	Paint walls	2	7
9	Install door	1	4,7
10	Paint door	1	9
11	Erect roof unit	1	5,7
12	Paint roof	2	11
13	End of project	0	8, 10, 12

given, in days, as well as the identities of the preceding activities. The inclusion of the anticipated logical links, or constraints, between activities thus models the complexity of the project. For simplicity, we assume that an activity can start when the preceding one has finished. Such a list might be standard for such a garage, or partially innovative in some way. For example, the wall units are pre-cast and might be constructed off-site, thus requiring only two days for installation. A more traditionally built garage might require walls to be built on-site.

We have nominated the durations as though they were absolutely accurate, but developmental activities often have quite wide margins of error attached to the duration estimates. For example, when MBA students are asked what their time estimate is for completing their next assignment, estimates typically range from 5 to 40 hours. In practice, the work done might range from 3 to 50 hours. The unknown and the uncertain are awkward to quantify, which may be an immediate, theoretical weak spot in the project plan.

10.5   Project network diagram

In 'draft' form, it is best to present all the activities in one network diagram showing links between tasks (Figure 10.6). In line with the style of modern project management computer software, the box (node) represents an activity and the line symbolises the constraint between two activities. Known as *activity-on-node analysis*, this basic presentation is quite effective.

(Note that many teaching textbooks on this work still use 'activity-on-arrow' analysis in which the lines represent the activity and the boxes signify the start and end of the activities. We avoid this style which is not compatible with modern software.)

10.5.1   Draft analysis of the project timescale

The objective is to estimate the total time required for the project. *Critical path analysis* starts the clock ticking from zero, merely adding the durations to the

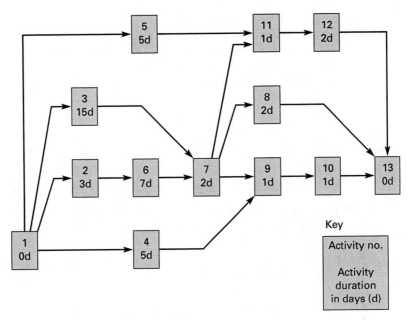

Figure 10.6 Garage project: draft network diagram

start time in order to get the finish time. To help familiarise you with the concept of the critical path, three of the paths of activities in the garage network are listed with their accumulated total durations in Table 10.2a.

| Activity 10.2 | Complete the remaining five paths through the garage network, with their timescales. |

Your answer to Activity 10.2 should have included the activity paths and durations shown in Table 10.2b.

Table 10.2a Garage project: durations of the paths of work

Activity path	Duration (days)	Total duration (days)
1-2-6-7-9-10-13	0+3+7+2+1+1+0	14
1-2-6-7-8-13	0+3+7+2+2+0	14
1-2-6-7-11-12-13	0+3+7+2+1+2+0	15

Table 10.2b Garage project: durations of other paths of work

Activity path	Duration (days)	Total duration (days)
1-3-7-9-10-13	0+15+2+1+1+0	19
1-3-7-8-13	0+15+2+2+0	19
1-3-7-11-12-13	0+15+2+1+2+0	20
1-4-9-10-13	0+5+1+1+0	7
1-5-11-12-13	0+5+1+2+0	8

You will surely agree that this manual counting method is quite tedious, but it does provide the critical path (longest timescale). This is 20 days in length, through activities 1-3-7-11-12-13. This path, paradoxically, is the shortest time in which the garage project is planned to complete. All other paths are predicted to complete in less than 20 days. For example, path 1-2-6-7-11-12-13 is planned for only 15 days and some of its activities will have some slack time (float) of 5 days within which the project manager might reschedule activities. For now, we note that the plan for the garage project of 20 days will start on Wednesday, 15 January 2003 and finish on Tuesday, 11 February 2003.

10.5.2   Critical path analysis – when to start and finish?

The benefits of this type of analysis for predicting the project timescale are covered thoroughly in the literature (Reiss, 1997: 44–62; Thomas, 1997: 431–91; Slack *et al.*, 1998: 617–19); Maylor, 1999: 76–90;). Calculating the critical path by hand is appropriate only if the network is less than 10 activities, but most real projects have at least 20 activities. Project planners would therefore analyse a project with computer assistance.

The project planner should know when an activity is planned to start and finish, as follows. Determine the earliest possible time that an activity can start; add on the duration to the start time; and the earliest possible time that the activity can finish is found. A cut-down version of a project with six activities (Table 10.3) to produce a textbook to a deadline is used to illustrate this.

The corresponding network diagram is shown in Figure 10.7.

Table 10.3 Precedence table for the book project

Activity code	Activity description	Duration (months)	Preceding activities
A	Initial consultation with publisher	3	–
B	Prepare proposal	2	A
C	Sign contract	1	B
D	Write material	18	B
E	First proof-read	4	C,D
F	Final proof-read and publish	6	E

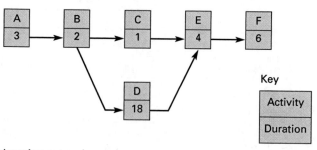

Figure 10.7 Book project network

Forward pass

The calculation of the earliest time that each activity can start and finish forms the 'forward pass'. Without even thinking about real calendar dates, let the clock start ticking so that activity A begins the project at time 0, its earliest start. By adding its duration to the start time, with a three-month duration, its earliest finish time is time-point 3. The general rule is that an activity's earliest finish (EF) equals its earliest start (ES) plus its duration (DU), i.e.

$$EF = ES + DU$$

Activity B can then begin as early as time-point 3. The duration of 2 months drives its earliest finish as time-point 5. For activity D, the earliest start time is also 5 but the duration of 18 means that the earliest finish is 5 + 18, which is 23 months (Figure 10.8).

Activity C takes only 1 month, with a planned earliest start time of 5 and earliest finish of 6. The difficult question is, when can activity E begin? It depends on activities C and D being finished. They provide finish times of 6 and 23, and hence the earliest that E can begin will be the later of the two, at time-point 23. E's earliest finish will then be at 27.

Finally, activity F can begin as early as 27, and with a 6 months' duration it is planned to finish at time-point 33 so that the planned publishing project timescale is 33 months (Figure 10.8). Note that the latest start (LS) and finish (LF) dates will be generated through the backward pass.

Backward pass

Assuming that the project timescale of 33 months is an acceptable timescale for the project manager, then we can also ask the question, how late can any activity possibly finish without disturbing the 33 months deadline? Likewise, how late can an activity possibly start? The 'backward pass' technique of planning uses a formula to determine the latest start time (LS) of an activity with duration DU from the latest finish time (LF):

$$LS = LF - DU$$

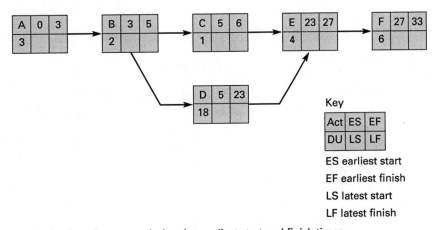

Figure 10.8 Book project network showing earliest start and finish times

Initially, we consider the final activity (or activities) in the network. The latest possible finish for activity F is time-point 33. Its latest start time (LS) must be 33 − 6 = 27, which you might notice gives the same time as the earliest time for this activity from the forward pass. This implies that activity F has no flexibility in its scheduling, but more of that in the analysis of slack time.

If F can start as late as 27 then E can finish as late as 27, so that E's latest start time is 27 − 4 = 23. This time-point is then passed back to both activities D and C to give their latest finish times of 23. Hence, the latest start time of C is worked back to be 22, but for D it is worked back to 23 − 18 = 5.

The most difficult answer to get is the next one. For activity B, do we have a latest finish time of 5 or 22? Hypothetically, if B were to finish as late as 22 then the project would slip by 17 months (addition of durations of 18, 4 and 6 months from D, E and F would take the end date of the project to 50). Hence, the appropriate latest finish for B has to be 5.

The rest is simple arithmetic. The latest start for B is 5 − 2 = 3 and this is passed through to A whose latest finish time is 3 and its latest possible start is 0.

All of the derived data (latest start and finish) from the backward pass is now available (Figure 10.9).

Using the results from the critical path analysis (Table 10.4), all interested parties in the project can meet to address amendments to durations or debate the risk points in the plan, e.g. where start and finish dates might need to be rescheduled.

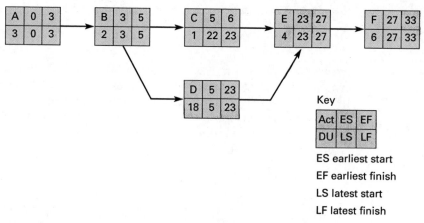

Key

Act	ES	EF
DU	LS	LF

ES earliest start
EF earliest finish
LS latest start
LF latest finish

Figure 10.9 Book project network showing all the derived start and finish times

Table 10.4 Tabulated critical path results for the book project

Activity	Activity name	Duration (months)	Preceding activity	Start times Earliest	Start times Latest	Finish times Earliest	Finish times Latest
A	Initial consultation with publisher	3	None	0	3	0	3
B	Prepare proposal	2	A	3	5	3	5
C	Sign contract	1	B	5	6	22	23
D	Write material	18	B	5	23	5	23
E	First proof-read	4	C, D	23	27	23	27
F	Final proof-read and publish	6	E	27	33	27	33

Activity 10.3

Return to the garage project (Table 10.1 and Figure 10.6). Examine activity 2, 'level the site' and activity 6, 'dig foundations'. Use the following timescale to help you plan the work. For example, time-point 3 means 'late on the Friday afternoon, 17 January'. In the forward and backward passes, this value of 3 will also carry through into the next working day, Monday, 20 January.

The first day of work is Wednesday, 15 January. The dark blocks show that no work takes place on Saturday or Sunday.

Day	W	Th	F	S	S	M	Tu	W	Th	F	S	S	M	Tu	W	Th	F	S	S	M	Tu	W	Th	F	S	S	M	Tu
Date	15	16	17	■	■	20	21	22	23	24	■	■	27	28	29	30	31	■	■	3	4	5	6	7	■	■	10	11
Timepoint	1	2	3			4	5	6	7	8			9	10	11	12	13			14	15	16	17	18			19	20

1 Start the clock ticking from time-point 0 (zero). What are the earliest times that activity 2 and activity 6 can start and finish?

2 'Explode' the information boxes of Figure 10.6 into the style of Figure 10.8 and begin to tabulate the results from part (1) for activities 2 and 6.

3 The project can commence on Wednesday, 15 January 2003 and work can take place on Monday to Friday each week. Convert the times found in part (2) into 'real' dates.

This project can begin as early as Wednesday, 15 January 2003 when time equals 0 (zero). The three days work of activity 2, 'level the site', anticipates that the earliest it will finish will be by Friday evening. Represented as an early finish time of 0 + 3 = 3, Friday, 17 January is the scheduled date to finish.

Subsequently, the earliest that activity 6, 'dig foundations', can begin is time-point 3, which corresponds to the start of the next working day, Monday, 20 January. The earliest finish of this activity is time-point 3 + 7 = 10. Time-point 10 corresponds to Tuesday, 28 January because the 7 days on which work could occur are Monday through to Friday (20–24 January), and also the Monday and Tuesday of the next week. Planned to finish as early as Tuesday evening, the date of 28 January can be displayed in the activity's information box.

The basic boxes in Figure 10.6 are now 'exploded' into the style of Figure 10.8 to include very relevant project data as real dates, as shown in Figure 10.10.

Both activities have planned earliest start and finish dates. The total duration of these two activities is 10 days, but as the project progresses the work might not go exactly to plan and hence it might impact on any dependent activities.

Presenting critical path analysis information

In the garage project, activity 7, 'install wall units', depends on two activities (3 and 6) being finished. 'Dig foundations' (activity 6) is due to be completed on Tuesday, 28 January. Consequently, activity 3, 'construct wall units' (15 days

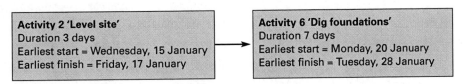

Figure 10.10 Information from the garage project, showing early start and finish dates

duration), is planned to start on Wednesday, 15 January, with completion by the end of Tuesday, 4 February. Hence, the earliest that activity 7 can begin is Wednesday, 5 February, the next working day, and it is more dependent on the completion of the construction work (activity 3).

Activity 10.4

1 Compile a complete critical path analysis of the garage project. Set the clock ticking at time 0 (zero) and display the forward pass and backward pass results in the style of Figures 10.8 and 10.9.

2 For each activity, using a 2003 calendar as given in Activity 10.3 with Wednesday, 15 January as the starting point, convert the results from part (1) into 'real' dates.

The complete analysis (Table 10.5) tabulates the project plan ready for attention to any changes to the plan. The critical path is through activities 1, 3, 7, 11, 12 and 13, a total length of 20 working days, as we found in Activity 10.2. Note that, in practice, an activity of zero duration or one day's duration starts and finishes on the same day.

The accompanying bar chart, drawn in Microsoft Project® (Figure 10.11), shows a timescaled analysis for easy communication to personnel, even those who are inexperienced at managing the project.

The complete network diagram, drawn using Microsoft Project® (Figure 10.12), shows all activities. Compare this with the more basic diagram of Figure 10.6, but note that the bar chart and the network diagram are crucial tools to stimulate discussion and agreement among project personnel concerning the prospects of success or failure in managing the project timescale.

Table 10.5 Critical path analysis results for the garage project

Activity	Duration (days)	Predecessors	Earliest start	Earliest finish	Latest start	Latest finish
Start of project	0	–	Wed 15/01/03	Wed 15/01/03	Wed 15/01/03	Wed 15/01/03
Level site	3	1	Wed 15/01/03	Fri 17/01/03	Wed 22/01/03	Fri 24/01/03
Construct wall units	15	1	Wed 15/01/03	Tue 04/02/03	Wed 15/01/03	Tue 04/02/03
Construct doors	5	1	Wed 15/01/03	Tue 21/01/03	Mon 01/02/03	Fri 07/02/03
Obtain roof unit	5	1	Wed 15/01/03	Tue 21/01/03	Fri 31/01/03	Thu 06/02/03
Dig foundations	7	2	Mon 20/01/03	Tue 28/01/03	Mon 25/01/03	Tue 04/02/03
Install wall units	2	3, 6	Wed 05/02/03	Thu 06/02/03	Wed 05/02/03	Thu 06/02/03
Paint walls	2	7	Fri 07/02/03	Mon 10/02/03	Mon 10/02/03	Tue 11/02/03
Install door	1	4, 7	Fri 07/02/03	Fri 07/02/03	Mon 10/02/03	Mon 10/02/03
Paint door	1	9	Mon 10/02/03	Mon 10/02/03	Tues 11/02/03	Tues 11/02/03
Erect roof unit	1	5, 7	Fri 07/02/03	Fri 07/02/03	Fri 07/02/03	Fri 07/02/03
Paint roof	2	11	Mon 10/02/03	Tue 11/02/03	Mon 10/02/03	Tue 11/02/03
End of project	0	8, 10, 12	Tue 11/02/03	Tue 11/02/03	Tue 11/02/03	Tue 11/02/03

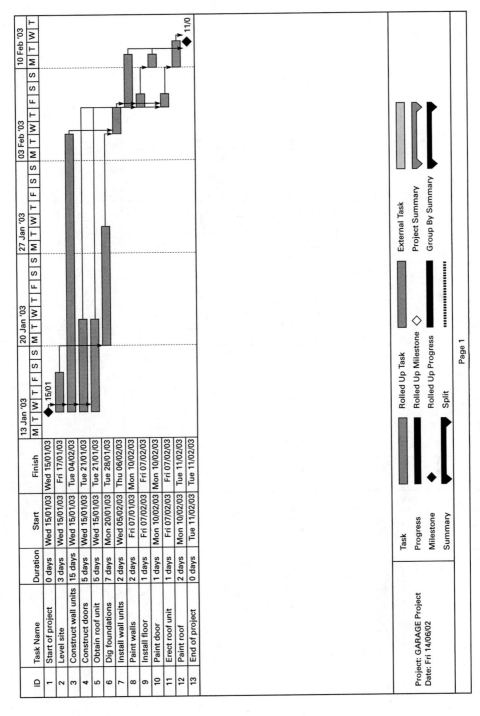

ID	Task Name	Duration	Start	Finish
1	Start of project	0 days	Wed 15/01/03	Wed 15/01/03
2	Level site	3 days	Wed 15/01/03	Fri 17/01/03
3	Construct wall units	15 days	Wed 15/01/03	Tue 04/02/03
4	Construct doors	5 days	Wed 15/01/03	Tue 21/01/03
5	Obtain roof unit	5 days	Wed 15/01/03	Tue 21/01/03
6	Dig foundations	7 days	Mon 20/01/03	Tue 28/01/03
7	Install wall units	2 days	Wed 05/02/03	Thu 06/02/03
8	Paint walls	2 days	Fri 07/01/03	Mon 10/02/03
9	Install floor	1 days	Fri 07/02/03	Fri 07/02/03
10	Paint door	1 days	Mon 10/02/03	Mon 10/02/03
11	Erect roof unit	1 days	Fri 07/02/03	Fri 07/02/03
12	Paint roof	2 days	Mon 10/02/03	Tue 11/02/03
13	End of project	0 days	Tue 11/02/03	Tue 11/02/03

Project: GARAGE Project
Date: Fri 14/06/02

Task		Rolled Up Task		External Task	
Progress		Rolled Up Milestone ◇		Project Summary	
Milestone ◆		Rolled Up Progress		Group By Summary	
Summary		Split	

Page 1

Figure 10.11 Bar chart of the garage project, showing early start and finish dates

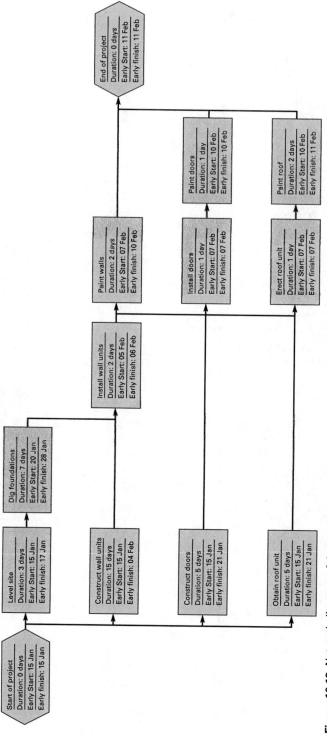

Figure 10.12 Network diagram of the garage project

Total float

It is especially important to recognise which activities are risky. The critical path referred to earlier is an itinerary of work with no free, spare time. The activities are rigidly scheduled such that the earliest start dates and the latest start dates are identical, likewise with the finish dates. The numerical difference in these two dates evaluates the amount of spare time available on each activity without impacting on the project's end date. Hence, in two ways:

Total float = Latest start date – Earliest start date

Total float = Latest finish date – Earliest finish date

For example, on activity 6, 'dig foundations', total float is the difference between Monday, 20 January and Monday, 27 January – exactly 5 working days. The management team uses these results and determines the tactics necessary to reach the project end date on time, given that some activities have no float available. These risks might prove to be critical unless they are managed capably and to the schedule required.

To conceptualise the float on an activity, the unused time between the planned early start time and planned latest finish time (Figure 10.13) for any activity measures the spare time. It is also possible that an activity eventually commences as late as its latest start date. If so, the total float will have been consumed from the earliest start date to the latest start date.

Clearly, where both start dates are equal there is no total float for that critical activity. A skilful planner will replan and reauthorise resources according to where there is the most appropriate need in the project.

Finally, looking back to Figure 10.12 (the complete network diagram), we decide to purchase an extra piece of kit for the garage, e.g. a workbench. Placing a telephone order on Wednesday, 15 January, we are informed that the arrival of the workbench is planned for 5 weeks' time (a lead time of 25 working days) from the start date, hence falling on Tuesday, 18 February. Two activity boxes can be added to the network to integrate this work into the plan. The boxes represent 'order' and 'receipt of kit' activities, with the 25-day lead time symbolised by the constraint. This development implies that the project end date would grow from 11 to 18 February.

Then, of course, we might need a power supply to the garage for the workbench – which generates another activity to be managed.

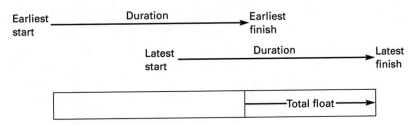

Figure 10.13 Total float for an activity

10.6   Project risk management

Projects fail for any number of reasons. The causes of these failures may be non-repeatable, unpredictable or plain uncertain. Sometimes, people are the cause, including innocent third parties.

10.6.1   Why do projects succeed and fail?

A project is successful when costs do not escalate, when the business purpose is fulfilled, the product or facility is accepted by the client or sponsor, and the quality level is acceptable to all parties. The five performance objectives of operations management as discussed by Slack *et al.* (1998: 51–66) of cost, speed, quality, flexibility and dependability are helpful in terms of focus but there are still some difficulties in judging the success and failure of a variety of projects. We need to manage more than the mechanics of the work. We have to think about and plan for the relationships and human interfaces within the project for administrative, strategic and operational errors (sometimes apportioned according to reasons of 'manpower', 'machines', 'materials' and 'methods').

The causes of failure are often ignored, somewhat perversely, so that they repeat themselves frequently (Chapter 2). Risks can be categorised in many ways, e.g. legal, perhaps involving civil law. Risks may be external (predictable or unpredictable) or internal (technical or non-technical). The objective remains to remove or reduce the risk by brainstorming, trend analysis, deflection by passing the risk to somebody else, or by contingency planning. This approach would be important when assessing the project timescale and evaluating the pressure points where slippage might occur.

The question of managing a project timescale successfully might boil down to whether using a 'fixed duration for an activity' is a secure way to manage the project timescale effectively. The consideration of how optimistic, or pessimistic, we might be about the fixed durations is important. Likewise, are we more likely to encounter a duration near to the fixed duration or will it be much longer? Design activities of a ground-breaking nature remain difficult to estimate and hence must be managed carefully to the agreed duration. It is appropriate to build in an estimate of the range of the duration, traditionally called a PERT (project evaluation and review technique) analysis but not taken any further here.

There is an old adage that project completion is a bit like driving a car. You have to start slowing down earlier to avoid a crash. Experience shows that project activities will always expand to fill the time of available resources.

10.6.2   Project planning exercise (risk assessment table)

The risk assessment of a project might be presented for discussion as a table of activities and resources, each of which is categorised as having high or low probability of occurrence, with high, medium or low impact on the time, cost or quality of the project. This is illustrated in Table 10.6 for the first 6 activities of the garage project in accordance with some of the ideas in Chapter 2.

Table 10.6 Risk assessment of the garage project

Activity/ resource	Risk	Probability	Impact on time/ cost/quality	Action proposed to avoid/minimise	Contingency plans
1	Weather impacts	High	High	Detailed planning needed Tight control	
2	Weather and equipment	High	High	Obtain advance approval for equipment	
3	Supplier fails to deliver	Low	Low	Confirm with all suppliers	
4	Technical difficulty	Low	High	Preliminary design Start earlier	
5	Company cancel	High	Low	Seek alternative roof	
6	Weather, equipment and manpower	Low	Low	Confirm all resources Extra trained staff needed	

10.6.3 Software tools to manage the timescale

Software tools play a massive role in supporting large projects. Sadly, the facilities offered by project management software and other types of business software stimulate the inherent dangers posed by reliance on electronic systems, but a manager must be free to exert control that is both human as well as technical. Many different types of project management software are available, with various features in the functionality of the software.

The inequality between a poor and a good project manager often lies in the planning, reflecting the quality of the decision-making about how tasks will be performed, who will perform them and when they will be accomplished. Planning things via desktop software does a little towards minimising overall project risk, especially if matters concerning people, resources and finance are not programmed directly into the timescale analysis.

10.6.4 Diagrams as communication tools

The bar chart (usually called a Gantt chart, after its originator) and the network diagram are interchangeable, containing exactly the same information pertinent to start and finish times for each task. It makes sense to produce and update these efficiently with project progress data as necessary.

The auxiliary total float time (sometimes denoted as slack, slippage or leeway) can be recycled to enhance overall project timing and can be shown on these diagrams. Critical path methodology is a popular way in which to present the information about project activity timings and it is important to know what such dedicated software can achieve or not achieve (not all software offers the same functions, facilities or speed of thought especially when dealing with large, complex projects of, say, two thousand activities). Project people have to model the reality of the complex project, their data coming from historical inputs and even historical personnel as best estimates.

10.7   A normative model?

What have we developed? A project network seems to be normative, a simulation model of the complexity of the project because it attempts to provide advice on what should happen and when. Recall, though, what was said in Chapter 1: a simple normative model tends to assume that decision-makers possess perfect knowledge, know all available options and can predict all possible outcomes.

The network is usually 'conscious' (breathing with progress data, perhaps half-spent, and 10 per cent late!), but choice of courses of action might be limited. Courses of action can be suggested, and relevant information may be available, but evaluating options is not the strength of the type of analysis we have described.

The network is 'ongoing' and helpful to the meeting of the time objective, and it desires the state of affairs in the project to improve by reinforcing timeliness and commitment – and action from a group of people who are supposedly committed to the success of the project.

Hence, because many authors who adopt or describe normative models acknowledge the models' limitations, we could treat network analysis as useful but badly defined, lacking finesse and subtlety or realism – a typical weakness in a mathematically based model. Its strength lies in getting teams together, reminding them of their duties and regularly forcing the parties to react to risks.

◆   Summary

Recognising the need to plan activities which form a project is important in managerial decision-making because managing time is one of the three main objectives in a project. The significant stages in the life of a project require appropriate managerial skills to bring success. From the agreed project specification should flow a methodology, integrating all parties. For these parties, a timescaled analysis is evidence of complementary planning to enhance the chance of a successful project outcome. A critical path analysis of any project will produce a timescaled plan with optimal start and finish times for each activity, with a bonus that the value of total float for each activity is calculated so that managerial focus on the most critical tasks will lead to better time management.

?   Decision diary

Observe new and old projects in the media which catch your attention. Investigate the focus on timescale and try to predict what the risks are to the company that is overseeing the project.

What are likely to be the repercussions to the project if the timescale is not achieved?

References

Kerzner, H. (1992) *Project Management – A Systems Approach to Planning, Scheduling and Controlling*, 4th edition. London: Van Nostrand Reinhold.

Maylor, H. (1999) *Project Management*, 2nd edition. London: Financial Times/Pitman Publishing.

Reiss, G. (1997) *Project Management Demystified*, 2nd edition. London: Spon.

Slack, N., Chambers, S., Harland, C., Harrison, A. and Johnston, R. (1998) *Operations Management*. London: Financial Times/Pitman Publishing.

Thomas, R. (1997) *Quantitative Methods for Business Studies*. London: Prentice Hall.

Turner, J.R. (1999) *The Handbook of Project-based Management*, 2nd edition. New York: McGraw-Hill.

Williams, C. (1996) 'Management competence and the management education needs of science graduates', *Management Learning*, 27 (3): 301–22.

Glossary

Activity-on-arrow analysis: an alternative approach to analysis of a project timescale, in which the lines represent the activities linked by circles (or boxes) which hold data on the start and finish times of the activities in the project. An antiquated and irrelevant style of presentation if the project is to be managed by software.

Activity-on-node analysis: the preferred mode of analysis of a project timescale, in which the box (node) represents an activity and the line symbolises the constraint between two activities. The basic presentation is in line with the style of modern project management computer software.

Backward pass: a set of logical calculations which obtain the latest possible finish time and latest possible start time for each activity in a project.

Critical path: the sequence of activities which have no spare time and which must start and finish on the scheduled dates otherwise they put the project end date in jeopardy.

Forward pass: a set of logical calculations which obtain the earliest possible start time and earliest possible finish time for each activity in a project.

PERT (project evaluation and review technique): a control method developed during the construction of the Polaris submarine project. The emphasis was on providing some understanding of the risk and how that risk could affect the timing of the project.

Total float: a calculation which shows how much free time there is in which to complete an activity. If the total float is zero the activity is critical.

PART FOUR

Implementation

Preface to Part Four

The final part of the text examines the factors that influence and affect the implementation of decisions. Great value can be obtained by spending time evaluating decision scenarios, collecting information, exploring potential outcomes and so forth. However, if this is done blindly, without considering the wider and more subjective aspects of implementation, decisions can go sadly wrong.

Decisions need to be accepted and respected. Unless people believe in the decision, a number of unwelcome and possibly dysfunctional organisational effects may occur. In Chapter 11 we discuss the nature and influence of group dynamics on decision-making. In Chapter 12 the notions of organisational power and politics are explored. In Chapter 13 cultural issues from both organisational and international perspectives are examined. In Chapter 14 we conclude with an introduction to the ethical aspects of decision-making.

In each of these areas there is potential for conflict to occur. This may be for a variety of reasons, for example a clash of personality within a group, fear of speaking out because of leadership style, or personal and organisational values being at variance with the context of the decision.

Group processes

On completing this chapter you should be able to:

■ Distinguish between task and process activities within groups.

■ Understand how process affects task completion and group effectiveness.

■ Examine the advantages and disadvantages of group decision-making and the different ways that groups can be used in organisations.

■ Understand the dynamics of multicultural groups.

■ Explore your own experience of group decision-making.

11.1 Introduction

Why have we chosen to address group decision-making in the section on implementation? Implementing decisions usually requires coordination of, and collaboration with, others. Rarely, if ever, do managers put a plan into operation by relying on their own skills and endeavours. Groups (be they quality circles, autonomous workgroups, planning groups and so on) are increasingly being seen as the medium in which operational problems are identified, diagnosed, addressed and solved. Equally rarely, however, is much attention paid to improving the effectiveness of these groups in a systematic and rigorous way. The common assumption seems to be that if you put a number of people together, then something will happen. As a result, success is left to chance rather than design. Alternatively, a pseudo-scientific approach is adopted, in which through some technique or device for 'forming the perfect team', managers fool themselves into thinking that they have tackled the complex issue of creating a productive group. Experience has shown, however, that there are no panaceas. There are, however, ways in which groups can become more effective. We suggest that, ultimately, this happens through informed experience. The experiencing will be left to you, but what we can do here is provide you with some concepts and practices that we believe to be relevant and valuable when considering decision-making. You may have heard the saying 'a camel is a horse designed by a committee'. The saying is generally used as a warning about the disadvantages of making decisions by group, certainly in terms of outcome. However, the saying could equally be interpreted positively. Why not think of it in terms of the creative potential of making decisions in this way? After all, the camel has its uses, and it is certainly unique. What the saying also seems to imply is that the processes involved in producing the outcome (the camel) must be flawed in some way. But what constitutes good, as opposed to bad, processes? Moreover, do good processes necessarily lead to positive outcomes?

11.2 Self and others

In discussing groups we paradoxically begin by talking about self. Groups could be described in terms of a meeting of selves. Some, but certainly not all, theories of group interaction acknowledge the role of the individual in groups. Social psychologist George Herbert Mead (see Clark *et al.*, 1994), proposed that, as self-conscious people, we came to define who we are through reflection upon our interactions with others. Obviously some people and groups of people are more important to us and have more influence on us. Mead referred to these influential people as 'significant others'. He distinguished this from what he called the 'generalised other', which refers to the way in which we personify and embody others' expectations of us. We learn to think, feel and act as a result of the pressures exerted on us by both significant others and the generalised other.

After mirrors, we now turn to windows. Communication is a continual process of giving feedback to, and receiving feedback from, others. This is, of course, done verbally and non-verbally. The following model is a helpful way of gaining personal insight into the relationship between the self as we view it and the self as viewed by others.

11.2.1 The johari window

The johari window is a model which conceptualises the possible ways in which individuals may communicate and give feedback to each other. It was developed by Luft (1970). Arguably, the process of giving and receiving feedback is one of the most important concepts in human interaction. Feedback can be verbal or non-verbal communication to a person or group and can provide valuable information as to how behaviour is affecting them or the state of their feelings and perceptions. Feedback is also a reaction by others, usually in terms of their feelings and perceptions, as to how the behaviour of others is affecting them.

The following model, a communications window, illustrates how individuals can give and receive information about themselves and others (see Figure 11.1). The four areas of the window are: the open area, the blind area, the hidden area and the unknown area.

The open area contains things that the individual knows about him/herself and which others in the group know. It refers, for example, to thoughts and feel-

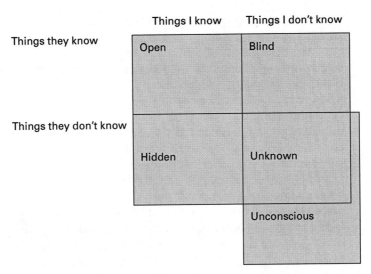

Figure 11.1 The Johari Window

ings that are openly exchanged as people share information with others. Behaviours fit into this category as they are public and available to everyone. The open area increases in size as the level of trust increases between the individual and others, and vice versa.

The blind area contains information that the individual does not know about him/herself, but which the group may know. We communicate all kinds of information of which we are not aware, but which is obvious to others. This information may include mannerisms, intonation of voice and other things about ourselves that, perhaps, we take so much for granted that we are not aware of them.

The hidden area contains things the individual knows about him/herself but of which the group is unaware. We keep this information hidden from others because, for example, others may reject us if we share our true thoughts, feelings and perceptions about the group or other individuals in the group.

The unknown area contains things that neither the individual or the group knows about the person. This may include early childhood memories, latent potential and unrecognised skills. Since knowing all about oneself is extremely unlikely, the unknown is shown in the window so that part of it will always remain unknown. The unknown area, therefore, forms part of our unconscious thoughts, feelings and motivations.

As a group progresses an individual reduces his or her blind area by receiving feedback from the group. We would need to develop a receptive attitude to encourage members to give us feedback. The more we do this the more the vertical line in Figure 11.1 will move to the right (see Figure 11.2).

Open	Blind
Hidden	Unknown

Figure 11.2 Ask for feedback

Another consequence of group behaviour can be the reduction of the hidden area. To do this we would have to give feedback to the group by sharing our feelings, perceptions and opinions. The johari window presents some interesting issues when considered in the light of decision-making. Normative and prescriptive decision-making models abound in the literature. Such models often assume that the capacity for increasing the information at one's disposal is increased as communication increases. This would seem likely. However, the issue of communication in itself is treated as non-problematical. People communicate naturally and the purpose of communication is to clarify. As we see from the johari window, the notion that communication is non-problematical is open to doubt. Communication serves not only to clarify but also to obscure. We may communicate, or choose not to communicate, in order to protect ourselves from perceived or real attacks from others. We may also choose to misinform others in trying to present our particular view of events. We may even be totally unaware of what we are communicating to others. Put another way, if our self was a product to be launched on the market, would we have the sole rights to distribution and marketing? Inevitably, others are free to interpret our image and our communications in ways that we would not necessarily wish them to.

Mead, mentioned earlier, argues that people are social in their nature, so that important processes of socialisation occur within groups. He points to our ability to empathise with another, or to take on the role of the other. We could describe this as 'putting ourselves in another's shoes'. This process not only enables us to have an appreciation of the other but also allows us to see ourselves through the eyes of the other. So we can see that groups afford us opportunities to receive direct feedback from others and also to engage in more speculative activity through the internal process of empathy. These external and internal processes are inextricably linked with who we are and how we come to see ourselves. So, although the focus of this chapter is on group processes, it is worth thinking about the extent to which our membership of various groups helps us to define who we are.

11.2.2 The looking-glass self

Cooley (1922) developed the notion of the looking-glass self to explain that our self-concept (the way in which we see ourselves) develops as a result of the way in which significant others see us. This notion is not unique to Cooley, but it does provide a useful metaphor when considering how the self is formed. We learn about the world and about ourselves by looking into the 'mirror' (significant others such as parents, guardians, teachers and so on) who reflect back what we should be and do. Thus we learn about appropriate behaviours, opinions, attitudes and values. Of course, we do have a say in the matter. The way in which we internalise, or make sense of, socially learned phenomena in our own unique way, is an important factor. We do not always reflect the image that may have been intended. Groups can be a powerful mirror for our own behaviour, as many of the studies mentioned in this chapter will show.

Later in the chapter we will return to examine other aspects of your list of groups that you compiled for Activity 11.1. If you had little difficulty in answer-

Activity 11.1

List all the groups to which you belong. Highlight in green the groups you enjoy belonging to. Similarly, highlight in red the groups you do not enjoy. From your green groups, try to decide which one you most enjoy. Now, from your red groups, choose the one you enjoy least of all. Write down the reasons for your selections. What is the size of the smallest group you belong to? What is the size of the largest group you belong to? How many members do you think there needs to be for a group to exist? At what point does a group become so large as to be considered an organisation rather than a group? Given your own experience of groups, what do you consider to be the optimum size?

ing these questions this may signify that to some extent you have already theorised about groups, although you may never have been forced to address this as a subject for analysis. There is no consensus on what constitutes the maximum size of a group, although some writers do offer an opinion on the optimum size.

11.3   Definition of a group

The following definition by Schein (1988: 145) is a useful starting point:

> [A group is] any number of people who (1) interact with one another; (2) are psychologically aware of one another; and (3) perceive themselves to be a group.

It might be a useful exercise to return to the list of groups you generated in Activity 11.1 and check that each of them fits within Schein's definition.

Writers often distinguish between group structure and group process. Group structure is used to describe 'the relatively stable pattern of relationships among the differentiated elements in a group' (Buchanan and Huczynski, 1997: 209). Group process deals with 'the sequence of interaction patterns between the members of a group' (Buchanan and Huczynski, 1997: 225). As the authors point out, there are clearly overlaps between the two. For instance, status and power are often dealt with as structural issues; communication and leadership as process issues. From this it would seem obvious that communication patterns within a group, for example, will more than likely be affected by the status of its members. In this chapter we do not distinguish between the two in the context of decision-making. We simply set out some concepts that have been learned from research and put into practice and should, in turn, help to improve your practice. Some of the ideas we explore have been generated through research into decision-making in groups in particular; others are more general theories that provide a useful wider context for decision-makers who want to understand the nature of groups. Either way, we believe they are relevant to the decision-making process.

11.4 Characteristics of a group

Dunford (1992) describes four characteristics of groups:

- roles
- norms
- conformity
- cohesiveness

11.4.1 Roles

We would generally expect there to be some differentiation among the group members in terms of what they do in the group. We might expect some members to be concerned with process functions and others to be concerned with task activities. Table 11.1 provides a useful inventory of group roles.

Table 11.1 Inventory of group roles

	Role	Function
A.	**Task**	
	Initiator	Most active in setting objectives and initiating action
	Expert	Has and provides specialist advice
	Evaluator	Assesses progress, analyses problems
	Implementer	Focuses on implementation details, timing and methods
	Procedural technician	Emphasises the importance of rules, procedures and precedent
	Representative	Spokesperson/liaison/negotiation for the group
B.	**Maintenance**	
	Exemplar	Exemplifies the group's ideals in personality, attitudes and behaviour
	Encourager	Praises, supports, empathises
	Confronter	Brings conflicts out into the open
	Harmoniser	Mediates, conciliates
	Tension reliever	Reduces formality, introduces humour
C.	**Disruptive**	
	Dominator	Seeks to dominate discussion and to impose own views/objectives
	Absentee	Withdrawn, uninvolved
	Aggressor	Attacks others; ridicules; hostile, sarcastic
	Smotherer	Compulsively nice; stifles attention to conflict
	Recognition-seeker	Boastful; highlights own achievements
	Confessor	Reveals personal fears, failings; uses group as a therapy session

Source: Dunphy, 1981

Many other typologies such as this exist. Belbin's (1993) typology is probably the most widely known (see Table 11.2).

Group or team?

Note that Belbin uses the word 'team' rather than group. The words have increasingly come to be used interchangeably. Is there a difference? Perhaps you would like to speculate about this and consider whether you belong to what others have labelled a team, for instance in a sporting activity or a work context? What makes a team different from a group?

Teams can be distinguished from groups in that each member of a team plays a *predetermined*, complementary role in achieving a common group purpose, as in sporting teams, for instance. The notion of predetermination is important. It implies intent and purpose, supplied and reinforced by tactical planning by one

Table 11.2 Useful people to have in teams

Type	Typical features	Positive qualities	Allowable weaknesses
Implementer	Conservative, dutiful and predictable	Organising ability, practical common sense, hardworking, self-discipline	Lack of flexibility and unresponsive to proven ideas
Coordinator	Calm, self-controlled and self-confident	A capacity for treating and welcoming all potential contributors on their merits and without prejudice. A strong sense of objectives	Laid back – may appear disinterested at times
Shaper	Highly strung, outgoing and dynamic	Drive and a readiness to challenge inertia, complacency, ineffectiveness or self-deception	Proneness to impatience, irritation and provocation
Plant	Individualistic, serious-minded and unorthodox	Creativity, imagination, strategist	Up in the clouds, inclined to disregard practical details or protocol
Resource investigator	Extroverted, enthusiastic, curious and communicative	A capacity for contacting people and exploring anything new. An ability to respond to challenge	Liable to lose interest once the initial fascination has passed
Monitor Evaluator	Sober, unemotional and prudent	Judgement, discretion and hard-headedness	Lacks inspiration or the ability to motivate others
Teamworker	Socially oriented, rather mild and sensitive	An ability to respond to people and to situations and to promote team spirit	Indecisiveness at moments of crisis
Completer/ finisher	Painstaking, orderly, anxious and conscientious	A capacity for follow-through. Perfectionism	A tendency to worry about nothing

Source: Belbin, 1993

or more of the team members themselves, or by some external agent. The term 'group' is a more generic term for an aggregate of individuals who interact with each other in some way, not necessarily to achieve a common stated aim, or to have any clear purposeful direction.

Whilst the distinction between teams and groups could be dismissed as a semantic issue, in reality the notions of genuine, common tactical purpose and intent are important distinguishing features. Work teams and 'teamwork' abound in the language of organisations and management; team leaders, for example, have come to replace supervisors. Many such teams are really groups of people who share a tenuous loyalty to each other, and a tenuous commitment to goals often imposed on them by powerful individuals either inside or outside of the group. They may have a behavioural commitment, but psychologically and emotionally they have not necessarily 'bought into' stated goals and are, therefore, lacking in genuine purpose and intent. What really distinguishes a team from a group is the notion of *genuine*, not just behavioural, commitment to each other and to their common aims; genuine compromise on behalf of the individual; and a joint sense of purpose or mission. Of course, genuineness is difficult, if not impossible to measure. Hence, ultimately, being a member of a team rather than a group is something that one *feels*. And if every member shares that feeling and expresses it in some way, either consciously or unconsciously, then the team is more likely to be a successful one.

Consequently, a team is by necessity a group, but a group need not be a team. Moreover, managers cannot readily create teams by labelling them as such. Creating teams requires skill, commitment, time, will, and, ultimately, luck.

Teams usually help to create or are created by a wider systemic order. For example, in a sporting context, teams form parts of leagues and competitions in which other teams compete. The increasing use of the word 'team' ultimately seeks to promote a metaphor of sporting competition, thus perpetuating the idea that organisations are arenas for regulated competition. If we adopt a political metaphor, the notion of teams falls down. Teams are inherently ordered and by their very existence promote functional order; just as no single player is bigger than the team, no single team is bigger than the league. Teams compete in a framework of sporting conduct and no individual must bring the game into disrepute. A team runs the risk of being suspended if it does not comply with the rules, regulations and normative expectations of the wider system. Consequently, teams within an organisational context ultimately serve the purposes of the dominant stakeholders in the wider social system, usually managers. Little wonder, then, that teams have become such a popular phenomenon in making organisational decisions.

The underlying assumption behind typologies such as Belbin's is that personality is, to a large extent, fixed and that there is a consistency in people's behaviour; that is, personality can be described in terms of *traits*. Such traits, for example, 'sober', 'emotional' and 'prudent' affect the ways in which people make decisions in a consistent manner. In effect, we *think* and *do* as a result of what we *are*. This contrasts with the view that roles and self are not necessarily synonymous. This view would stress, for instance, that a manager can exhibit very different behaviours in a work context and in an outside-of-work context. People take on roles as they would take on parts in a play, albeit less consciously.

The context of situations, and not just our personality and experiences, determines to a great extent the role that we play. Social contexts provide us with a predetermined set of unwritten rules that we culturally acquire (that is, learn) as we grow up. These unwritten rules are sometimes called norms.

11.4.2 Norms

According to Schein (1988: 76) a norm can be defined as:

> a set of assumptions or expectations held by members of a group or organization concerning what kind of behaviour is right or wrong, good or bad, appropriate or inappropriate, allowed or not allowed. Norms are usually not articulated spontaneously, but members can state them if asked to do so.

The following are examples of typical group norms which involve both doing and being: 'we should get to meetings on time'; 'everyone should participate in some way'; 'we control our emotions'; 'we're informal; we use first names'.

Activity 11.2	Following Schein's lead, identify what you consider to be two very different groups to which you belong. Reflect on how the group norms differ in each of the groups. Given the issues we have covered in this chapter, what do you think are the many and varied factors that determine group norms?

Norms often only become apparent when they are transgressed. This has huge implications for decision-making as norms can serve the purpose of relieving us of the need to make routine decisions on a continual basis. If no norms existed we would be placed in a position of having to cope with high levels of uncertainty, and having to continually negotiate and renegotiate perceptions, meanings, reactions and so on. Clearly this would cause us so much cognitive and emotional stress that our lives would become unbearable. Norms, therefore, serve a positive psychological and emotional purpose. However, they are also potentially dangerous in decision-making situations. Not all decisions are routine and programmed, as life is inherently uncertain. Managers cannot always predict people's behaviours, nor can they always accurately predict future events.

Inquiries into disasters often come to similar conclusions. A key contributory factor is often the lack of thought shown by the participants involved. In an analysis of the Tenerife air disaster in 1977, in which 583 people died, Weick (see Frost *et al.*, 1991: 118) argues that disasters occur as a result of the following combination of factors:

- Interruption of important routines.
- Regression to more habituated ways of responding.
- The breakdown of coordinated action.
- Misunderstandings in speech-exchange systems.

Clearly, norms play their part in such events as key decision-makers, in this case air crew and air traffic controllers, were said to have behaved in habituated ways.

11.4.3 Conformity

Another possible pitfall of making decisions by group can be that individuals may bow to peer pressure, thereby acting in ways that do not truly reflect their thoughts or feelings. Evidence from research has shown that individuals, when placed under pressure, will behave in ways that they feel are wrong. Famous examples are the often quoted studies of Asch and Milgram (see Buchanan and Huczynski, 1997).

Both studies point to the importance of recognising conformity as an important dimension when addressing group decision-making. Asch's work involved setting up experiments in which a group of people were asked to do a fairly simple task, that is to identify which of three straight lines they were shown was of the same length as one they had previously been shown. Of the seven members of the group, six were actually people who had been planted in the group by Asch. In other words, only one was a genuine unknowing participant; the other six had been told to lie about which one of the three lines they believed to be the correct one. Asch's research concluded that 75 per cent of respondents accepted the majority decision, even though they showed signs of being uncomfortable with the decision.

Milgram's work was not directly concerned with group decision-making but it does have implications for the issue of authority in groups. He set up an experiment in which a volunteer was required to administer electric shocks to individuals (out of sight in another room) who failed to answer questions correctly. In fact, the electric shocks were fake, although the participant did not know this at the time. Although the participant could not see the victim, he could hear the (pretended) cries of pain that the individual was told to emit when the electric shocks were being administered. Milgram found that two out of every three volunteers administered what they believed to be fatal levels of electricity because they were instructed to do so by an authority figure.

Activity 11.3	Reflect on the group norms you identified in Activity 11.2. Are the norms helpful in terms of how the groups operate? Are they applied oppressively in order to secure conformity at all costs? We suggest you use the exercise 'what to look for in groups' in Appendix 1 of this chapter as a way of structuring your analysis.

11.4.4 Cohesiveness

When we talk about cohesiveness we are actually focusing on the process rather than the task activities of groups. Through establishing roles, norms and mechanisms of control, a group establishes a sense of cohesiveness. A cohesive group is one that establishes clear roles, powerful norms and a high degree of control. This can be a positive phenomenon as energy is channelled in order to achieve a common purpose. As we have seen in this chapter, humans are social beings who develop a sense of self through interacting with others. As part of this process the individual may have to compromise his or her own ways of seeing and doing. The findings of Asch's and Milgram's studies suggest that this is not always positive. There is a degree of loss of individuality for the common good;

this may lead to groups' ignoring important information in order to maintain cohesion at all costs. Some authors have pointed to the fact that groups can be so cohesive that they become dysfunctional, and this leads to negative outcomes. The most notable of these authors is Irving Janis, whose work is considered later on.

11.4.5 Task and process

Whenever people come together in groups they use their skills and abilities in a number of different ways. These can be categorised in two ways:

- In terms of the job itself, they bring with them their expert, professional or technical skills, associated for instance with disciplines such as management, engineering, finance, law, or medicine.

- They also need to cooperate with the other people in getting the job done, using skills such as listening to others' ideas, sharing their own ideas, and establishing a common understanding.

In the first instance, they are dealing with the job – the task that needs to be performed; in the second instance they are concerned with the social skills of cooperation and interaction in achieving the task.

Illustration 11.1 Task-oriented and process-oriented groups

A task-oriented group

Eva was a member of a part-time, postgraduate research group. The group was very focused on the task of discussing individual research projects. Little or no attention was paid to the process of how they operated together as a group. Typically, topics were discussed in a very aggressive manner. If John put forward a point of view, Jim would immediately attack this. Ideas were rarely pursued in a constructive or supportive way. Individuals always had to be prepared to fight their corner. Eventually, Eva expressed her dissatisfaction to the other group members about this as she felt that the group was not giving each other enough support. Several members of the group were completely dismissive of her view. They were only concerned with talking about the contents of each other's research. In other words, they were extremely task oriented.

A process-oriented group

Peter worked in a small department in a business school. All of the group members taught in the same subject area. Individually they were all highly self-opinionated. There was a great diversity within the group. This was both a strength and a weakness – lots of interesting ideas were generated, but individuals were all so focused on their own agendas it was often difficult to gain support from enough of the others to actually make a decision about anything. It was not uncommon for a large part of their time at meetings to be spent discussing the relationships within the group and how they treated each other. Significantly, most of the focus was on negative aspects of process. People rarely expressed satisfaction about being a member of the group. They had great difficulty maintaining any focus on task and were viewed in a generally negative light by other staff within the wider organisation. In other words, the group was extremely process-oriented.

As can be seen from the examples in Illustration 11.1, giving attention to process issues is not inherently positive. Groups can focus so much on process issues that they become paralysed when confronted by a pressing task. One MBA student described his experience of working in an extremely process-oriented group in the following way: 'we keep taking the plant out of the pot just to check that the root system's okay. Well, we're in danger of killing the plant by showing such concern for it.' Likewise, showing too much concern for task may mean that we ignore the social mechanisms that serve to achieve it. This will, sooner or later, affect the ability of the group to achieve the task.

Activity 11.4

Go back to the list of groups you made in Activity 11.1 and alongside each indicate whether you think the general activity of the members is task oriented (T), process oriented (P) or task and process oriented (T/P). Can you discern any relationship between the groups you have highlighted in green as those you enjoy belonging to and their task or process orientation? If you do identify a relationship – for example if the groups you enjoy belonging to are predominantly task oriented – this may give you some insight into your own orientation.

It may also be worthwhile to think about the groups you have identified in terms of productivity. Reflect for a moment on which group you would identify as the most productive. Now reflect upon whether this is a task-oriented group or a process-oriented group.

Using the task and process classification it becomes apparent that productivity can be defined in different ways. A group that meets predominantly for the purpose of encouraging members to socialise may be termed a productive group in process terms although there may be no tangible outcomes in terms of task completion.

11.4.6 Fight and flight defences

The prospect of working in groups is not always positive. Many of us have negative experiences of group process and would, given a choice, work alone. However, the decision is often made for us by the way in which the organisational structure may be designed, or the way in which cultural values are operationalised. There is little doubt that we may learn a lot from working with others in group situations, but there is equally little doubt that the process can be an uncomfortable one at times. For example, we may be placed in situations in which we feel we have to disclose more information about ourselves than we would necessarily wish to; or we may find ourselves in confrontation with others. Such situations may lead us to question our own concept of the world, or to reject the ideas of others outright.

In order to protect ourselves in such situations, we may adopt defensive strategies. Such strategies are commonly classified in two ways: fight and flight. Although all defences are inherently evasive, fight defences refer to the individual moving towards the perceived source of conflict; flight defences refer to ways in which the individual moves away from the perceived conflict.

Fight defences

As the well-known English football manager and philosopher Brian Clough used to say, 'the best form of defence is attack'. According to Thoresen (see Pfeiffer and Jones, 1972: 117), behaviours associated with fight defences involve an individual competing with the facilitator (or person in charge of the group), expressing cynicism and challenging the group's psychological contract, or interrogating others. All are defensive strategies designed to draw attention away from one's own true feelings in the light of a perceived threat.

Flight defences

Flight defences are employed when an individual 'rides away from the sound of the guns rather than towards them', so to speak. They are ways of avoiding openness and genuine involvement in group process. Thoresen (see Pfeiffer and Jones, 1972: 117) draws our attention to the following flight defences: intellectualisation (in which an individual rationalises away his or her true feelings in order to avoid them); generalisation (the making of general impersonal statements in order to disown one's own feelings and thoughts); projection (attributing unacceptable and uncomfortable traits of self to others); rationalisation (trying to justify dysfunctional behaviours by substituting plausible, yet false, reasons in order to avoid possible real causes); withdrawal (either physical, emotional or intellectual).

11.5 Advantages and disadvantages of group decision-making

There are some generally accepted advantages and disadvantages of using groups to make decisions in organisations. An advantage, for example, may be legitimacy. The individual who makes decisions alone may be perceived to be autocratic. Decisions made by groups are likely to enjoy a wider consensus of legitimacy. This may lead to more psychological commitment for the implementation of the decision from members of the organisation. Ideologically, group decisions may be seen to be more legitimate through appearing to be more democratic. A disadvantage may be time sensitivity. There may be situations where there is insufficient time to allow for group decision-making – it generally being considered that a group takes longer to make a decision than an individual, as Schein points out in Illustration 11.2.

There is a difficulty in categorically stating what is an advantage and what is a disadvantage of decision-making in groups. As you will see from the theories that follow, many of the processes are double-edged swords. For example, the fact that individuals take greater risks in groups may be a virtue or a vice depending on the circumstances.

Illustration 11.2 Group decision-making

Schein (1969) identifies different ways of arriving at a group decision in relation to time:

Increasing speed of decision

1. Decision by lack of response

2. Decision by authority rule

3. Decision by minority

4. Decision by majority

5. Decision by consensus

6. Decision by unanimous consent

Decreasing speed of decision

Source: Schein, 1969

11.5.1 Risky shift

Dunford (1992:117) succinctly summarises the phenomenon of risky shift in the following way:

> The phenomenon of 'risky shift' is based on the discovery that groups will often select a riskier alternative than individuals (Stoner, 1968). Clark (1971) presents and assesses four possible explanations for risky shift:
>
> 1. The familiarisation hypothesis: as the risk is discussed within the group it becomes more familiar, less shocking.
>
> 2. The leadership hypothesis: those most prepared to take risks are likely to be those who emerge as leaders with associated influence over group decisions.
>
> 3. The diffusion of responsibility hypothesis: a group decision is less likely to be the responsibility of any one individual; blame for a poor decision will thus be spread, hence a risky decision represents only a partially shared risk to an individual.
>
> 4. The risk-as-value hypothesis: moderate risk has a more positive social value than caution, hence individuals will prefer, all things being equal, to be seen as risk-takers.

11.5.2   Cultural amplifier hypothesis

Schein (1988) argues that the circumstances represented by the risky shift phenomenon are more accurately explained in terms of what he calls the cultural amplifier hypothesis. This states that the group will focus upon and magnify the dominant cultural value(s) concerning the issue or problem with which they are dealing. In other words, as individuals from similar cultural backgrounds come together in groups it is likely that shared cultural beliefs, values and attitudes are reinforced and have a significant bearing on decision processes and outcomes.

11.5.3   Cultural diversity

As more and more corporations become global, cultural diversity is becoming an issue of increasing concern within organisations. Adler (1991) suggests that the diversity offered in multicultural groups can lead to higher productivity than homogeneous groups. Interestingly, Adler points to different national cultural orientations towards task and process. For example, he suggests that Germany and the USA tend to be task-oriented cultures, whereas Middle Eastern and southern European cultures are more process (or relationship) oriented. This can be a useful mix within a multicultural group, but the diversity needs to be managed, otherwise dominant members may tend to promote their own preferred task/process orientation within the group.

Illustration 11.3 Chelsea allsorts: not an Englishman in sight at the Bridge

A little bit of history was made at the weekend when Chelsea football club fielded a team consisting entirely of foreign players – the first time in the life of the Premier League or its predecessors that this has happened. The Blues' supporters have known for some time that, with the preponderance of overseas players in the squad, it was a question of when rather than whether, it would happen. The problem is working out what, if anything, fielding a team consisting of a Dutchman, a Spaniard, two Frenchmen, a Brazilian, a Uruguayan, a Nigerian, two Italians and a Norwegian might 'mean'.

It is not very many years since Chelsea was one of the most xenophobic of football clubs, with supporters booing foreign players when they came on the field – even on occasion their own players. All that belongs to history. Chelsea is now, at least on paper, the most cosmopolitan of clubs; manager Gianluca Vialli inspires deep loyalty among fans. Only the location of the club at Stamford Bridge anchors it in history. That is sufficient to ensure that victory with an all-foreign team (like Sunday's 2–1 win over Southampton) somehow reinforces the Chelsea-ishness of it all.

It is curious how Britain, so reluctant to share a single currency with the rest of Europe, has welcomed continental and non-European players to its bosom. Fifteen years ago it would have been as difficult to imagine that Chelsea would field an all-foreign team as it would for Paris St Germain to have listed an all-England squad. At this rate Chelsea will soon be accepting euros at the club shop. Of course none of this implies that Chelsea's manager is being anything other than totally meritocratic when he chooses the team each week. It is virtually certain that the team's indefatigable captain, Dennis Wise, will soon be back in the first team. But as no more than a prudent insurance policy he might find it sage to change his name by deed poll to Dennis Raisonnable.

Source: The Guardian, 28 December 1999

In what terms do you think the group is described as homogeneous in the *Guardian* article in Illustration 11.3?

It is neither the common skills nor the common purpose of the players in Illustration 11.3 that defines their homogeneity; it is their 'foreignness', that is, the fact that none of them is English. Ironically, its structural diversity is what gives it its commonality, its key defining feature. How often are workgroups defined in terms of their 'not' being something, rather than being something? For instance, how might one department define itself in terms of not being like other departments? Or how might a group of people define themselves in terms of having a 'common enemy' such as an autocratic boss?

Adler (1991) offers the following recommendations to ensure satisfactory performance by culturally diverse groups:

1 Select group members of a similar level of ability to enhance accurate communication, but with a diversity of attitudes to enhance creativity.

2 Give attention to cultural differences but avoid stereotyping; attempt to understand the way people in other cultures think, feel and act; look for the benefits that can flow from diversity.

3 Help the group to agree to a superordinate goal, one that transcends their individual differences. Such a goal can help give a sense of direction to the group's activities and often will reinforce the importance of cooperation between group members.

4 Avoid cultural dominance. If one culture provides the members in the more powerful positions, the contributions of non-dominant group members will be reduced. In particular, power should be distributed according to each member's ability to contribute to the task, not some preconceived idea of relative cultural importance.

5 Mutual respect by group members should be encouraged. This can be enhanced by selecting members of equal ability, making sure that the skills and accomplishments of individual group members are known within the group, and minimising early judgements based on cultural stereotypes. Give early and positive feedback to help the group see itself as a team and to reinforce the idea that good output can be produced despite, or even because of, the more complex task of reaching agreement that culturally diverse groups are likely to involve.

11.5.4 A 'garbage can' model of groups

The term 'garbage can' was coined by Cohen *et al.* (1972) to describe the idea that situations in which choices have to be made are primarily used by individuals as an opportunity to air their own problems and predetermined solutions. In other words, personal agendas are prioritised above the need to solve the problem at hand and, in so doing, issues that are not directly relevant are likely to be brought to the situation. This contrasts with rational approaches to decision-making which, for example, implicitly assume that people work towards achieving organisational goals in a logical manner. However, a lot of organisational behaviour is not particularly rational. Managers are often members of the groups they manage and, as such, if there is a problem or issue to be addressed they are part of it, not a neutral arbiter who can solve it as a rational, external agent. The behaviour of managers in organisations is not always directed in a rational purposive manner towards achieving organisational goals. Rather they seek through the exercise of power to pursue their own goals and objectives; they become embroiled in political manoeuvring, battling against other managers for a share of scarce resources. Groups often become the arena in which many of these battles are waged, albeit often subtly. Many management textbooks do not give any indication of this.

Whilst we are neither advocating nor condoning overtly political activity within and between groups in organisations, we should not ignore what is 'reality' for many managers. It is rare to find an organisation where social and political activity does not play a significant part in the range of activities which are enacted by the people in the organisation. So, it would be remiss in any consideration of decision-making in groups not to acknowledge that much of the activity is not directly concerned with the rational pursuit of organisational objectives.

Karen Legge (1984: 30) puts this very succinctly in describing the garbage can model:

> Briefly, Cohen *et al.* argue that in many choice situations ... although it is assumed that the main concern is with 'making decisions' in fact other activities seem equally important, such as fulfilling earlier commitments, justifying past actions, scapegoating or cementing loyalties, recruiting and socializing and game playing. As a result, a 'choice situation', rather than being regarded as an opportunity for rational problem-solving, may be more realistically conceptualized as: "... a meeting place for issues and feelings looking for decision situations in which they may be aired, solutions looking for issues to which there may be an answer, and participants looking for problems or pleasure" (Cohen *et al.*, 1976, page 25).

Again we see authors pointing to apparently irrational behaviour, certainly not directed towards organisational goals. The idea that a choice situation can be a meeting place for issues waiting to be aired has significant consequences for decision-making in groups. If this is the case, then group decision-making situations, for example meetings, may be the social contexts in which these issues are likely to surface. The implication is that individuals are unlikely to agree on the problems let alone solutions, as they bring their own open or hidden agendas to the table.

11.5.5 The Abilene paradox

One Sunday afternoon an American family 'decide' to go for a drive across the desert to visit the town of Abilene. The journey is not a pleasant one. It is a hot day, the desert is extremely dusty, the car hot and stuffy. They have a very poor meal at Abilene and return home. Back home the family members start to moan about the trip to Abilene, each in turn blaming the other members of the family for wanting to go in the first place. It transpires that none of the individual family members wanted to visit Abilene. Yet the family decided to go. Why? It is suggested that they went to Abilene because they were unable to articulate and manage the underlying consensus that existed within the group.

Harvey (1974), who developed the paradox, suggests an essential symptom and six sub-symptoms which would be present where it occurs. The essential symptom is stated as the inability to manage agreement. The six sub-symptoms are:

1 Organisation members agree privately, as individuals, as to the nature of the problem.

2 Organisation members agree privately, as individuals, as to the steps that would be required to cope with the situation or problem.

3 Organisation members fail to accurately communicate their desires and/or beliefs to one another.

4 With such invalid and inaccurate information, organisation members make collective decisions that lead them to take actions contrary to what they want to do.

5 As a result of taking actions that are counterproductive, organisation members experience frustration, anger, irritation and dissatisfaction with their organisation.

6 Finally, if organisation members do not deal with the generic issue – the inability to manage agreement – the cycle repeats itself with greater intensity.

Studies on group dysfunction generally focus on overt conflicts within a group, but the Abilene paradox reminds us that there can be problems with group effectiveness that are not directly about conflict. We say not 'directly' because it might be argued that at the root of the individual members failing to articulate their lack of desire to visit Abilene was a fear of being at odds with the other family members.

11.5.6 Groupthink

Janis (1982) coined the term 'groupthink' to describe what he regarded as the main negative aspects of making decisions in groups. Janis studied major political policy decisions in the USA and came to the conclusion that the apparently positive phenomenon of group cohesion can also lead to negative consequences as group members prioritise maintenance functions in the group over task functions. He identifies the following symptoms of groupthink:

1 The illusion of invulnerability: group members share a sense of being above criticism. This leads to overoptimism when it comes to taking risks.

2 Belief in the inherent morality of the group: group members feel they are acting morally and believe themselves to be beyond reproach.

3 Illusion of unanimity: there is a belief that decisions are based on unanimous agreement. Silence is seen as consent.

4 Collective rationalisation: group members make up reasons for their decision in order to make themselves look rational and correct.

5 Stereotyping of other groups: competitors are seen as incompetent or evil. This leads to the group underestimating competition.

Illustration 11.4 Directors 'too scared' to confront each other

Problems at the top remain unresolved because board members tend to shy away from confrontation

High-octane exits rarely happen at Japanese board meetings. Everyone is too polite – with the result that important issues remain unaddressed, for fear of confrontation.

This emerges from a study of leadership qualities in Japan and eight European countries. In Japan, 77% of senior managers questioned said problems damaging to the business were never raised because it would be too difficult to do so.

A similar reticence was exhibited by British directors: more than half of those in the sample would rather smile through gritted teeth than risk speaking their minds, says Professor Andrew Kakabadse, whose findings are described in his report, *Leadership in Times of Change*.

'People who are holding down top jobs don't bring up crucial issues because they're emotionally unable to do so – so they let the problems continue and the company deteriorate,' says Kakabadse, a professor of international management development at Cranfield School of Management, near Bedford. The result, he says, is a board that behaves like a dysfunctional family.

He cites the case of the marketing director whose efforts to improve his own performance are hampered by the defensiveness and political motivation of relationships at board level. 'He would like to bring those problems to the surface, but finds it impossible, because emotionally it's harder than putting up with it. If you're in a mid-management role and need to know about marketing, you're sent on a course; but if you're the director of marketing it is assumed you don't need any kind of course because you've been exposed to all the marketing issues your company is facing – so you get no outside help. Top people need personal development, but they are frightened to receive feedback in case their weaknesses are exposed – so it is more difficult to get them trained. It may be necessary to ask for an outside influence to come in, under the pretext of something else, like manager development. That would give the marketing director the opportunity to say he thinks the board needs further exposure to developing as directors. But it does require someone at the top to recognise the problem and do something about it.'

Because this is such a sensitive area, great delicacy is required to remove the sticking plaster and start the healing process. 'If top managers are not ready to discuss things, they need some discreet counselling process to give them emotional robustness,' says Kakabadse.

On those rare occasions when difficult issues are tackled, the Japanese make a better job of it than most of their European counterparts, says Kakabadse. 'Only the Swedish displayed a higher level of capability towards discussing and dealing with problems. The Irish, followed closely by the British, were the most likely to be immature and aggressive,' says Kakabadse.

Cultural differences are often used as an excuse to resist unwanted changes. 'If an American company introduced a reform that its Tokyo subsidiary did not want and it used the excuse that it would go against Japanese culture, nobody would dare to say, "you have to do things the way we do them in the United States",' he says.

Kakabadse also claims that the tough top executive is a myth: 'the macho image is for the rest of the world to see. If they started behaving like John Wayne with each other, they wouldn't get things done'.

Source: Margaret Coles, *Sunday Times*, 23 July 1995

6 Self-censorship: group members do not openly express any doubts about the decision, thus preventing any critical appraisal.

7 Direct pressure on dissenters: any individual who expresses concerns or doubts is pressured by the other members, and their loyalty to the group is called into question.

8 Mindguards: some of the members take on the function of shielding the group from what might be seen as criticism. Hence, any negative feedback is suppressed.

In order to avoid groupthink, Janis recommends the following guidelines:

1 Require each member to take on the role of 'critical evaluator', airing any doubts or objections.

2 Tell the leader not to state his or her position on an issue before the group decision.

3 Have several groups working simultaneously on the decision.

4 Bring in facilitators to appraise process issues.

5 Give one of the members the role of 'devil's advocate', and consistently question courses of action.

6 Don't underestimate competition from other groups.

7 When the group has reached consensus, encourage reflection and re-evaluate any possible alternatives.

11.6 Intergroup processes

We have, up to this point, concentrated on the processes that happen within groups (intragroup processes); we now turn our attention to what sometimes happens between groups (intergroup processes). Dunford (1992) points to ways that group members can be used, or manipulated, by outsiders to behave in particular ways so that the group, in turn, exerts pressure on other groups to fall into line. He describes the situation in a prisoner-of-war camp where the captors deliberately segregated the prisoners by race and undermined the pre-existing hierarchical relationships between the soldiers by ignoring rank. Often the most inexperienced men were put in charge of groups. This challenge to the normal order of things destabilised the prisoners. Rewards were given to those who complied with the captors' demands. 'Good' groups were rewarded; 'bad' groups were punished. Whereas it might have been very difficult for the captors to get the prisoners to conform en masse, by tackling the problem at group level they were able to bring about change. These factors made a significant contribution to making the prisoners much more manageable in order to achieve the captors' desired outcomes – to subdue the prisoners and use them for propaganda purposes.

11.6.1 Problems of intergroup competition

Schein (1988) identifies some common intragroup problems that emerge as a result of intergroup competition (Illustration 11.5).

Illustration 11.5 Problems of intergroup competition 1

A. What happens *within* each competing group?

Each group becomes more closely knit and elicits greater loyalty from its members; members close ranks and bury some of their internal differences.

The group climate changes from informal, casual playful work and becomes task oriented; concern for members' psychological needs declines while concern for task accomplishment increases.

Leadership patterns tend to change from more democratic toward more autocratic; the group becomes more willing to tolerate autocratic leadership.

Each group becomes more highly structured and organized.

Each group demands more loyalty and conformity from its members in order to be able to present a 'solid front'.

B. What happens *between* competing groups?

Each group begins to see the other as the enemy, rather than merely as a neutral object.

Each group begins to experience distortions of perception – it tends to perceive only the best parts of itself, denying its weaknesses, and tends to perceive only the worst parts of the other group, denying its strengths; each group is likely to develop a negative stereotype of the other ('they don't play fair like we do').

Hostility towards the other group increases while interaction and communication with the other group decreases; thus it becomes easier to maintain the negative stereotype and more difficult to correct perceptual distortions.

If the groups are forced into interaction – for example, if they are forced to listen to representatives plead their own and the other's cause in reference to some task – each group is more likely to listen more closely to their own representative and not listen to the representative of the other group, except to find fault with his or her presentation; in other words, group members tend to listen only for that which supports their own position and stereotype.

Source: Schein, 1988: 173

Schein (1988) goes on to describe the consequences of groups perceiving themselves as winners or losers as a result of organisational competition.

Schein (1988: 179–80) recommends the following steps in order to avoid intergroup conflict:

1 Emphasise organisational effectiveness and each group's role in achieving it.

2 Stimulate high interaction and frequent communication between groups.

3 Rotate members frequently between groups, or encourage mutual understanding of other groups' problems.

4 Avoid win–lose situations by avoiding competition for scarce resources; pool resources; share rewards equally.

> ### Illustration 11.6 Problems of intergroup competition 2
>
> #### C. What happens to the *winner*?
>
> Winner retains its cohesion and may become even more cohesive.
>
> Winner tends to release tension, lose its fighting spirit, become complacent, casual, and playful (the condition of being 'fat and happy').
>
> Winner tends toward high intragroup co-operation and concern for members' needs, and low concern for work and task accomplishment.
>
> Winner tends to be complacent and to feel that the positive outcome has confirmed its favorable stereotype of itself and the negative stereotype of the 'enemy' group; there is little motivation for re-evaluating perceptions and stereotypes or re-examining group operations in order to learn how to improve them, hence the winner does not learn much about itself.
>
> #### D. What happens to the *loser*?
>
> If the outcome is not entirely clear-cut and permits a degree of interpretation (say, if judges have rendered it or if the game was close), there is a strong tendency for the loser to *deny or distort the reality of the losing*; instead the loser will find psychological escapes like 'the judges were biased', 'the judges didn't really understand our solution', 'the rules of the game were not really explained to us', 'if luck had not been against us at the one key point, we would have won,' and so on. In effect, the loser's first response is to say 'we didn't really lose!'
>
> If the loss is psychologically accepted, the group tends to seek someone or something to blame; strong forces toward scape-goating are set up; if no outsider can be blamed, the group turns on itself, splinters, surfaces previously unresolved conflicts, fights within itself, all in the effort to find a cause for the loss.
>
> 1. Loser is more tense, ready to work harder, and desperate (the condition of being 'lean and hungry').
>
> 2. Loser tends toward low intragroup co-operation, low concern for members' needs and a high concern for recouping by working harder in order to win the next round of the competition.
>
> 3. Loser tends to learn a lot about itself as a group because its positive stereotype of itself and its negative stereotype of the other group are disconfirmed by the loss, forcing a re-evaluation of perceptions; as a consequence, the loser is likely to reorganize and become more cohesive and effective once the loss has been accepted realistically.
>
> *Source*: Schein, 1988: 174–5

He suggests that managers find the fourth point most difficult to accept because of the inherent assumption that competition is a healthy state to be in. Whilst he acknowledges that this may hold true in the short term, he argues that in the long term it is to the detriment of the organisation and will lead to the negative consequences mentioned above.

Summary

You may have realised by now that there are a great many complementary and overlapping theories of groups. You have at your disposal several theoretical frameworks to help you analyse group decision-making activity. In the course of this chapter we have asked you to perform several quite detailed analyses of groups to which you belong. The theories presented have practical applications. However, if you believe that you now have the knowledge to fully understand groups, then you are mistaken. The saying 'the more you learn, the less you know' applies to groups as much as to anything else. The more theories you come across, the more alternative interpretations of events emerge. None of them is 'right', but if they provide you with insight into your own actions and the actions of others, then they have served a useful purpose.

Decision diary

1 With regard to the johari window theory, do you find, for example, that you are more open in one group than another? If so, what do you consider to be the factors that contribute to this?

2 You may note that a factor can be both positive and negative – for example, a cohesive group is likely to work more effectively than a less cohesive group, yet the more cohesive a group becomes, the more likely it is to display the symptoms of groupthink. Can these contradictions be managed?

3 Performing such detailed analysis of the groups you belong to may have highlighted aspects of membership of those groups which you have not considered before. Has this had any impact on your perceived level of satisfaction in each of the groups considered?

In addition to these three questions you might like to read the list of things to look for in groups (see Appendix 1). Choose a group to which you belong and observe them over a period of time, say a week. Use as many of the questions as you can to analyse what happens in the group, keeping notes whenever you can. In doing so, remember, as we have seen in this chapter, in all human interactions there are two major ingredients – task (sometimes called content) and process. The first deals with the subject matter or the task upon which the group is working. In most interactions, the focus of attention of all persons is on the content. The second ingredient, process, is concerned with what is happening between and to group members while the group is working. Group process, or dynamics, deals with such ideas as morale, feeling, tone, atmosphere, influence, participation, styles of influence, leadership struggles, conflict, competition, cooperation, etc. In most interactions, little attention is paid to process, even when it is the major cause of ineffective group action. Sensitivity to group process enables group problems to be analysed earlier, and dealt with more effectively. Since these processes are present in all groups, awareness of them will enhance a person's worth to a group and enable him or her to be a more effective group participant.

References

Adler, N.J. (1991) *International Dimensions of Organizational Behaviour*. Boston: PWS-Kent.

Belbin, M. (1993) *Team Roles at Work*. Oxford: Butterworth Heinemann.

Buchanan, D. and Huczynski, A. (1997) *Organizational Behaviour: An Introductory Text*, 3rd edition. Hemel Hempstead: Prentice Hall.

Clark, H., Chandler, J. and Barry, J. (eds) (1994) *Organisation and Identities*. London: Chapman & Hall.

Cohen, M.D., March, J.G. and Olsen, J.P. (1972) 'A garbage can model of organizational choice', *Administrative Science Quarterly*, 17 (March): 1–25.

Cooley, C.H. (1922) *Human Nature and the Social Order*. New York: Scribners.

Dunford, R. (1992) *Organisational Behaviour: An Organisational Analysis Perspective*. Reading, MA: Addison-Wesley.

Frost, P.J., Moore, L.F., Louis, M.R., Lundberg, C.C. and Martin, J. (eds) (1991) *Reframing Organizational Culture*. London: Sage.

Luft, J. (1970) *Group Processes: An Introduction to Group Dynamics*, 2nd edition. National Press.

Janis, I.L. (1982) *Groupthink: Psychological Studies of Policy Decisions and Fiascos*, 2nd edition. Boston, MA: Houghton Mifflin.

Legge, K. (1984) *Evaluating Planned Organizational Change*. London: Academic Press.

Mullins, L.J. (1999) *Management and Organisational Behaviour*, 5th edition. London: Financial Times/Pitman Publishing.

Pfeiffer, J.W. and Jones, J.E. (eds) (1972) *Annual Handbook for Group Facilitators*. San Diego, CA: University Associates.

Schein, E.H. (1969) *Process Consultation: Its Role in Organisation Development*. Reading, MA: Addison-Wesley.

Schein, E.H. (1988) *Organizational Psychology*, 3rd edition. Englewood Cliffs, NJ: Prentice Hall.

Weick, K.E. 'The Vulnerable System: An Analysis of the Tenerife Air Disaster' in Frost, P.J., Moore, L.F., Lovis, M.R., Lundberg, C.C. and Martin, J (eds) (1991) *Reframing Organisational Behaviour*. Newbury Park, CA: Sage.

Further reading

For a general exposition of the development of group theory we recommend the relevant chapters in Buchanan, D. and Huczynski, A. (1997) *Organizational Behaviour: An Introductory Text*, 3rd edition. Hemel Hempstead: Prentice Hall.

For Mead's thoughts on the self, refer to the reading in Chapter 2 of Clark, H., Chandler, J. and Barry, J. (eds.) (1994) *Organisation and Identities*. London: Chapman & Hall.

We also recommend that you watch the film *12 Angry Men*, directed by Sidney Lumet, screenplay by Reginald Rose. You will recognise many of the behaviours described in this chapter.

Glossary

Groupthink: a term describing the dysfunctional group process that may result in negative outcomes in group decision-making.

Intragroup processes: actions and behaviours that are manifested within a group.

Intergroup processes: actions and behaviours that are manifested between groups.

Process-oriented group: a group that mainly concentrates on the interactions that are happening within the group rather than on the task or the outcome.

Task-oriented group: a group that mainly focuses on achieving the task at hand.

Appendix 1 | # What to look for in groups

Participation

One indication of involvement is verbal participation. Look for differences in the amount of participation among members.

1 Who are the high participators?

2 Who are the low participators?

3 Do you see any shift in participation, e.g. highs become quiet; lows suddenly become talkative. Do you see any possible reason for this in the group's interaction?

4 How are the silent people treated? How is their silence interpreted? Consent? Disagreement? Disinterest? Fear?

5 Who talks to whom? Do you see any reasons for this in the group's interactions?

6 Who keeps the ball rolling? Do you see any reason for this in the group's interactions?

Influence

Influence and participation are not the same. Some people may speak very little, yet they capture the attention of the whole group. Others may talk a lot but are generally not listened to by other members.

7 Which members are high in influence, that is, when they talk others seem to listen?

8 Which members are low in influence – others do not listen to or follow them? Is there any shifting in influence? Who shifts?

9 Do you see any rivalry in the group? Is there a struggle for leadership? What effect does it have on other group members?

Styles of influence

Influence can take many forms. It can be positive or negative; it can enlist the support or cooperation of others or alienate them. How a person attempts to influence another may be the crucial factor in determining how open or closed the other will be towards being influenced. Items 10 to 13 are suggestive of four styles that frequently emerge in groups.

10 *Autocratic.* Does anyone attempt to impose his or her will or values on other group members or try to push others to support his or her decisions? Who evaluates or passes judgement on other group members? Do any members block action when it is not moving in the direction they desire? Who pushes to 'get the group organised'?

11 *Peacemaker.* Who eagerly supports other group members' decisions? Does anyone consistently try to avoid conflict or unpleasant feelings from being expressed by pouring oil on the troubled waters? Is any member typically deferential towards other group members – gives them power? Do any members appear to avoid giving negative feedback, i.e. who will only say what they think when they have positive feedback to give?

12 *Laissez-faire.* Are any group members getting attention by their apparent lack of involvement in the group? Does any group member go along with group decisions without seeking to commit him/herself one way or the other? Who seems to be withdrawn and uninvolved; who does not initiate activity, participates mechanically and only in response to another member's question?

13 *Democratic.* Does anyone try to include everyone in a group decision or discussion? Who expresses their feelings and opinions openly and directly without evaluating or judging others? Who appears to be open to feedback and criticisms from others? When feelings run high and tension mounts, which members attempt to deal with the conflict in a problem-solving way?

Decision-making procedures

Many kinds of decision are made in groups without considering the effects of these decisions on other members. Some people try to impose their own decisions on the group, whilst others want all members to participate or share in the decisions that are made.

14 Does anyone make a decision and carry it out without checking with other group members (self-authorised)? For example, he or she decides on the topic to be discussed and immediately begins to talk about it. What effect does this have on other group members?

15 Does the group drift from topic to topic? Who topic-jumps? Do you see any reason for this in the group's interactions?

16 Who supports other members' suggestions or decisions? Does this support result in the two members deciding the topic or activity for that group (handclasp)? How does this affect other group members?

17 Is there any evidence of a majority pushing a decision through over other members' objections? Do they call for a vote (majority support)?

18 Is there any attempt to get all members participating in a decision (consensus)? What effect does this seem to have on the group?

19 Does anyone make any contributions which do not receive any kind of response or recognition (plop)? What effect does this have on the member?

Task functions

These functions illustrate behaviours that are concerned with getting the job done, or accomplishing the task that the group has before them.

20 Does anyone ask for or make suggestions as to the best way to proceed or to tackle a problem?

21 Does anyone attempt to summarise what has been covered or what has been going on in the group?

22 Is there any giving or asking for facts, ideas, opinions, feelings, feedback or searching for alternatives?

23 Who keeps the group on target? What prevents topic jumping or going off on tangents?

Maintenance functions

These functions are important to the morale of the group. They maintain good and harmonious working relationships along the members and create a group atmosphere which enables each member to contribute fully. They ensure smooth and effective teamwork within the group.

24 Who helps others get into the discussion (gate-openers)?

25 Who cuts off others or interrupts them (gate-closers)?

26 How well are members getting their ideas across? Are some members preoccupied and not listening? Are there any attempts by group members to help others clarify their ideas?

27 How are ideas rejected? How do members react when their ideas are not accepted? Do members attempt to support others when they reject their ideas?

Group atmosphere

Something about the way a group works creates an atmosphere which, in turn, is revealed in a general impression. In addition, people may differ in the kind of atmosphere they like in a group. Insight can be gained into the atmosphere characteristic of a group by finding words which describe the general impressions held by group members.

28 Who seems to prefer a friendly congenial atmosphere? Is there any attempt to suppress conflict or unpleasant feelings?

29 Who seems to prefer an atmosphere of conflict and disagreement? Do any members provoke or annoy others?

30 Do people seem involved and interested? Is the atmosphere one of work? Play? Satisfaction? Taking flight? Sluggishness?

Membership

A major concern for group members is the degree of acceptance or inclusion in the group. Different patterns of interaction may develop in the group which give clues to the degree and kind of membership.

31 Is there any subgrouping? Sometimes two or three members may consistently agree and support each other or consistently disagree and oppose one another.

32 Do some people seem to be 'outside' the group? Do some members seem to be 'in'? How are those outside treated?

33 Do some members move in and out of the group, e.g. lean forward or backward in their chairs or move their chairs in and out. Under what conditions do they come in or move out?

Feelings

During any group discussion, feelings are frequently generated by the interactions between members. These feelings, however, are seldom talked about. Observers may have to make guesses based on tone of voice, facial expressions, gesture and many other forms of non-verbal cues.

34 What signs of feelings do you observe in group members: anger, irritation, frustration, warmth, affection, excitement, boredom, defensiveness, competitiveness, etc.?

35 Do you see any attempts by group members to block the expression of feelings, particularly negative feelings? How is this done? Does anyone do this consistently?

Norms

Standards or ground rules may develop in a group that control the behaviour of its members. Norms usually express the beliefs or desires of the majority of the group members as to what behaviours should or should not take place in the group. These norms may be clear to all members (explicit), known or sensed by only a few (implicit), or operating completely below the level of awareness of any group members. Some norms facilitate group progress and some hinder it.

36 Are certain areas avoided in the group (e.g. sex, religion, talk about present feelings in group, discussing the leader's behaviour, etc.)? Who seems to reinforce this avoidance? How do they do it?

37 Are group members overly nice or polite to each other? Are only positive feelings expressed? Do members agree with each other too readily? What happens when members disagree?

38 Do you see norms operating about participation or the kinds of questions that are allowed (e.g. 'If I talk, you must talk'; 'If I tell my problems you have to tell your problems')? Do members feel free to probe each other about their feelings? Do questions tend to be restricted to intellectual topics or events outside of the group?

Source: adapted from: Pfeiffer and Jones, 1972: 21

12 Power and politics

Learning outcomes

On completing this chapter you should be able to:

- Distinguish between the related concepts of power and authority.
- Identify key sources of power in organisations.
- Identify and differentiate political behaviours.
- Appreciate and evaluate how an understanding of power and politics affects the way in which managers make decisions.

12.1 Introduction

When asked to describe sources and effects of power in their organisations, managers often identify ways in which they are affected by power rather than ways in which they exert power. Perhaps it is easier to identify the ways in which others influence us, or maybe we choose to underestimate or de-emphasise the ways in which we affect the behaviour of others. Having power is often seen as a reflection of a successful organisational career. Most, if not all, organisations are hierarchical and power is often determined and discussed in relation to our position in the organisational structure. However, we may hold power over others for a host of other reasons. We explore these reasons in this chapter. In addition, we explore the concept of organisational politics and identify a number of political 'games' that are commonly played in organisations. We believe that an understanding of such games leads to a more realistic appreciation of the decision-making process, particularly with regard to implementation.

12.2   Sources of power

In order to examine the concept of power more closely, and to distinguish it from authority, we will address the influential theory of French and Raven (see Cartwright and Zander, 1968). The authors identify the following five sources of power:

1 *Reward power.* The ability of A to reward B with something that will motivate or satisfy B in such a way as to comply with A's demands or wishes. Examples of reward power may be the use of pay, promotion, increased responsibility or personal praise.

2 *Coercive power.* Coercive power is based on fear. B perceives that A has the ability to punish him or her if B does not comply with A's demands or wishes. Examples may include the fear of dismissal, formal warnings, reprimands, or even physical or psychological violence (for instance, bullying in the workplace).

3 *Legitimate power.* This is based on authority. B perceives that A has the right to influence B because of A's position or role within the organisation. This is based on position power, that is, one's organisational role, rather than personal relationships. An example of this is the notion of managerial prerogative, or a manager's often unquestioned right to manage.

4 *Referent power.* Referent power is based on B identifying with A in some way. This is often referred to as charismatic power. A may have power over B not necessarily through reward, fear or authority but through personal respect and esteem.

5 *Expert power.* This is based on holding expertise or knowledge that someone else does not hold but which may be useful to that person. For example, a medical consultant working in a hospital may have power over a manager through his or her medical expertise. Conversely, the manager may have power over the clinician by having greater knowledge of the financial implications of decisions, thereby determining the resources that may be available to the clinician.

French and Raven's categorisation is useful because it allows us to start operationalising the concept of power. One broad way of differentiating sources of power is in terms of their being a property of the organisation.

Organisational sources of power can be more easily removed from the individual or group in that they are more reliant on the structuring of the organisation. These structural sources include the individual or group's position in the organisational hierarchy, access to critical resources, and access to symbols of power such as company cars.

Personal power is more dependent upon personal characteristics and therefore cannot be so easily removed. Individuals can have power as a result of who they are rather than what they are. For example, someone who has been in the organisation for a long time may have power as a result of his or her experience rather than their position in the official hierarchy.

To some extent, however, classifying sources of power as a property of the individual and/or the organisation is somewhat spurious. In reality, sources of power overlap and cannot be so easily distinguished. For example, think about

Illustration 12.1 Y2K? Why no bug?

As the year 2000 loomed, a new phenomenon appeared – the millennium bug. This strange creature that no one had ever seen sent a chill through industries, commerce and governments across the globe. Was this the harbinger of Armageddon after all? Would vital services be decimated? Would the entire global economic system end up as a meal for the bug's voracious appetite? Something had to be done about what came to be called the Y2K problem. In Great Britain, British Aerospace spent in the region of £100 million on 'bug repellant'; British Telecom was believed to have spent £300 million. The British government spent an estimated £430 million on updating systems in the public sector. In total, governments and organisations worldwide were said to have spent £360 billion in meeting the menace. The only European government that was believed to have done little to tackle the problem was the Italian government. January 2000 came and went, and the bug did not surface. Minor glitches were reported in the trading systems of 12 Japanese brokerages, but no global catastrophe. Some started to voice doubts as to whether they needed to have spent so much money preparing to meet the menace. One business leader was quoted as saying, 'a lot of people made a lot of money out of this. A lot of consultants, software vendors, and a lot of people writing books'. Others said it was money well spent; it had been 'a genuine and very serious problem', affirmed a spokesperson from a large business organisation. So, was this as a result of the financial resources and human endeavour that had been channelled into keeping the nasty little creature at bay? Or could it be that there never was such a creature? There were no significant problems in Italy.

Activity 12.1 What issues does this raise in terms of French and Raven's sources of power? For example, how do you think that expert power has been demonstrated, and by whom?

the extent to which we attribute expertise to particular *roles* in organisations or society in general. For instance, you may assume that managers have achieved their position of authority as a result of some kind of expert knowledge and experience. You may attribute this to the role itself by holding the assumption that we work in meritocratic organisations in which we get what we deserve. Alternatively, you may attribute this to the *person* by primarily assuming that managers achieve positions of power in organisations by means of their personality, personal motives or serendipity. Nonetheless, French and Raven's typology does encourage us to examine the subject in greater depth. Like beauty, the recognition and appreciation of power is ultimately in the eye of the beholder.

Gareth Morgan (1986: 159) identifies 14 sources of organisational power:

1 *Formal authority.* The right to manage, or managerial prerogative, is an example of power based on formal authority. Within organisations, the right to manage is legitimated in a number of ways, for example through the idea of hierarchy. The power to make decisions therefore becomes a structural, legitimate right given to individuals as they rise in the hierarchy.

2 *Control of scarce resources.* All resources, be they financial, material, human or technological, are invariably limited to some extent. The degree to which we have access to such resources may determine our power to make or influence decisions.

3 *Use of organisational structures, rules and regulations.* As Morgan points out, organisational structures, rules and regulations are often portrayed as rational instruments aimed at the efficient achievement of goals, but from a political perspective can be understood as instruments in the struggle for political control. In terms of managerial prerogative, the right to make decisions is a fundamental management privilege. Through the act of decision-making, managers continually reinforce their prerogative to manage. In fact, when managers do not make decisions, they may be criticised by subordinates, peers and superiors. It could be said, then, that the right to make decisions becomes a *duty* to make decisions.

4 *Control of decision processes.* Morgan distinguishes three interrelated elements: decision *premises*, decision *processes*, and decision *issues and objectives*. The first involves the control of agendas rather than direct involvement in the decision or the decision-making process in question. If you have the power to present the decision alternatives for discussion then you have a great deal of influence on potential outcomes. Strategic decisions that are passed down for implementation serve to control the agenda of decision-makers at a lower level. The power of senior managers can be asserted through the use of language used to present the problem or decision options in a certain way thereby reinforcing a particular set of values and beliefs about preferred outcomes. The second element involves more direct and overt control about how the decision is made and concerns such questions as who should be involved, timescales, order of agenda items etc. The final element concerns the influencing and shaping of issues through more direct contribution to discussions and active involvement.

5 *Control of knowledge and information.* This relates to item 2 in that information can be viewed as a resource and can also be related to French and Raven's notion of expert power. Individuals defined as experts are more likely to influence decisions that concern their area of expertise in that the expert will have an air of authority that is less likely to be challenged by others.

6 *Control of boundaries.* The individual's position will determine the extent to which he or she is privy to information from other areas of the organisation. Such people can act as 'gatekeepers' between individuals or departments and can be selective in the way they wish to present a problem or issue. This is not necessarily dependent upon hierarchical power. For example, secretaries, personal assistants and 'front-line' staff (at the 'interface' with customers) are often important organisational gatekeepers. Middle managers are often powerful controllers of boundaries, selectively sifting information on account of their pivotal role in the organisation.

7 *Ability to cope with uncertainty.* As Morgan suggests, organisation implies interdependence, and individual actions may well impact upon other parts of the organisation in unpredictable ways. The way in which these uncertainties are dealt with may be an important source of power in terms of ability to react quickly and effectively.

8 *Control of technology.* This is an increasingly high profile source of power because of the rate of new technological change and globalisation. Technology can be used to serve the interests of particular individuals or groups.

9 *Interpersonal alliances, networks, and control of 'informal organisation'.* This is the 'it's not what you know but whom you know that matters' factor. People form alliances and networks within the organisation as a result of personal and political needs.

10 *Control of counterorganisations.* Counterorganisations are organisations that have been legitimately established to form a counterbalance to the existing dominant, legitimate source of power. The most obvious example is that of trade unions. Other examples include consumer organisations and environmental lobbies which can become extremely powerful in their own right and can act as a significant influence on organisational decision-makers.

11 *Symbolism and the management of meaning.* Morgan focuses on three aspects of symbolic management: the use of imagery, the use of theatre and the use of gamesmanship. The use of images, language, symbols, ceremonies and rituals is an important mechanism for shaping organisational members' views and therefore for shaping power relations. This can be related to the idea of managing organisational culture in order to control people's behaviour rather than directly and overtly controlling them. For example, the notion of empowerment suggests that decision-making is devolved to people in organisations who have not traditionally held decision-making responsibility. Another way of viewing this is that they are being subtly manipulated and controlled (because they are doing more for the same amount of money).

12 *Gender and the management of gender relations.* Organisations have been viewed by some writers as patriarchal in that they are built upon gendered assumptions about what constitutes effectiveness. Organisations are often spoken about in terms of rationality, as are managers, but this is often gendered as a male attribute. As Morgan points out, adjectives stereotypically used to describe males include logical, rational, aggressive etc. Females are more often spoken about in terms of being intuitive, emotional, submissive and empathic. The stereotypically male adjectives pervade the language of organisations and organisational decision-making. Language is political in that it encourages and reinforces particular world views.

13 *Structural factors that define the stage of action.* As we said in the introduction to this chapter, managers often talk about the constraints that are placed upon them rather than the power they themselves have. As Morgan points out, managers can be powerful in terms of one or more of the sources identified yet constrained by other structural factors. This constraint can be real or imagined, depending on your point of view. The perception that our behaviour is somehow constrained by other forces acts as a mechanism that disempowers us.

14 *The power one already has.* When people believe that they have power and this is reinforced by the way others react to them, then this can be an empowering aspect of power. In other words, power breeds power. There have been high profile examples of individuals who have been regarded as powerful and influential and have, therefore, had little difficulty in attracting funds, although near bankrupt.

Activity 12.2 Try to think of a recent occurrence in an organisation with which you are familiar that illustrates one or more of the sources of power identified by Morgan. Describe what happened and explain why you think it relates to the chosen source(s) of power.

12.3 Dimensions of power

In essence, our interpretation of sources of power depends on our underlying assumptions about the nature of power. Lukes (1974) explores the nature of power in some depth and distinguishes between three dimensions of power.

The first refers to observable behaviours and conflicts and can thus be used to describe Dahl's (Lukes, 1986) definition of power as the ability of A to get B to do something that B would not otherwise have done. Although useful as a starting point for analysis, this definition presents an oversimplification of power relationships in organisations. It does not adequately reflect, for instance, that power is as much a structural phenomenon as an interpersonal one.

The second dimension Lukes uses to describe what Bachrach and Baratz (see Lee and Lawrence, 1985: 146) identify as 'nondecision-making'. Power involves not only the ability to act, but also the ability to not act. Hence, power can be used unobtrusively to control agendas and to limit the scope of decision-making. In other words, power can be used to decide whether or not to make decisions, or to misrepresent a decision context. So, for example, a manager can set the context for a decision that is made at a meeting by deciding to present only selected facts in order to prevent certain issues from being discussed.

The third dimension of power describes the way in which power can be expressed through taken-for-granted assumptions. Our thoughts, perceptions and actions, argues Lukes, are shaped by this process of socialisation that discourages us from identifying alternative forms of expressing ourselves or identifying our true needs. With regard to decision-making, this third dimension leads to an interesting philosophical question: do we ever make decisions or do we simply behave as we have been programmed to behave through social conditioning?

12.4 Hierarchy and decision-making

Organisations do not make decisions; people do. Decisions are, however, often made by individuals in the name of the organisation. Managers may blame structural failings for their actions, but ultimately it is management that helps to create and sustain those structures in the first place. Most, if not all, organisations are structured hierarchically and therefore create a framework of asymmetrical power relationships. This has its advantages as hierarchies tend to create stable and clearly defined channels of communication, as well as systems of responsibility and accountability. Individuals have a psychological need to be controlled to some extent. We recognise the principle of hierarchy from an early age, for example through the early socialisation processes of schooling, so not only are we willing to be subjugated to higher authority in some way, we actually come to expect it. We also expect to relate with others in a hierarchical way, for example managers are expected to manage (control) and if they are not seen to be managing according to widely recognised criteria their competence may be called into question. The disadvantages of hierarchy tend to centre on its psychological consequences for individual and group decision-making behaviour. Hierarchy concentrates the power of decision-making at the higher levels of the organisation and consequently not everyone in the organisation will be as committed to organisational goals, which may reflect the interest of the few. As organisations have become more conscious of the needs of the customer and with the increasing use of new technology, decision-making has been devolved to the lower levels where the interaction with the majority of customers generally takes place.

Relating to Lukes' (1974) notion of the third dimension of power it is interesting to note two points:

- The structuring of organisations is accepted as a managerial prerogative, that is, managers have the right to adopt structures that they deem suitable and this is rarely questioned. In fact, it could be argued that it is accepted as natural. This gives managers a great deal of decision-making power in that there may be discussion about the *forms* of structure to be adopted but the *nature* of the right to structure remains unquestioned. In essence, structures may change, but underlying power structures (for instance, the manager's right to make decisions) remain unaltered.

- Alternatives to traditional ways of structuring organisations in order to perpetuate asymmetrical power relationships are rarely explored. There are a few high profile examples of alternative structure (for instance Semco and Oticon). In the main, however, we tend to accept the fact that organisations are far from democratic. As humans we are socialised into accepting this reality from an early age as we are born into family structures that are based on hierarchical principles, and are schooled into accepting the right of others to hold legitimate decision-making power over us. We may, therefore, find it easier to avoid having to make decisions.

12.5   A framework of power: unitarist, pluralist and radical perspectives on conflict

Fox (1966) first identified what has generally become known as the traditional view of organisational conflict: the unitarist view. With its emphasis on harmony and integration, the unitarist, or 'happy families', view looks upon managers as organisational peacekeepers. Conflict is regarded as an unnecessary evil to be minimised and certainly not tolerated, and therefore illegitimate. Any conflict that does emerge is, therefore, a failure to manage organisational processes. Problems may be explained in terms of communication problems or bad decision-making. Emphasis may be placed on processual detail (for example, managers not making the 'right' decisions, or not implementing decisions 'correctly') rather than on political issues (the incompatible needs of different stakeholders). In contrast to the unitarist perspective, Fox (1966) identified the pluralist perspective. Pluralism, with its acknowledgement of the needs of different stakeholders, recognises the inevitability of organisational conflict in the management decision-making process.

Both perspectives acknowledge the pivotal role of managers in organisational decision-making. They may differ on the purpose of management decision-making, but management's right to make decisions is never questioned.

However, a more radical perspective on conflict points to the exploitative nature of management in organisations. Organisational conflict is regarded as a structural phenomenon resulting from competing social forces which clash on a daily basis. Managers manage on behalf of the owners of the means of production (shareholders and owners of capital) and, therefore, all decisions are set against a backcloth of exploitation in which managers control and take advantage of those who provide the labour (workers). This perspective imbues management decision-making with a much more macropolitical quality. Managers' decisions become the mechanism by which the structure of capitalism is maintained. The *types* of decision managers make, and the *style* in which they make them, may be products of the assumptions they hold regarding the nature of organisations, and how they conceptualise conflict in relation to the unitarist, pluralist, radical typology.

12.6 An enactment view: implications of 'owning decisions'

The phenomenon of organisational structure is often presented as an objective one. Indeed, much of the theory we have looked at so far bears testimony to the fact that, traditionally, authors have tended to be too concerned with presenting forms of structure and attempting to establish design principles. Emphasis has therefore been placed on the need to design organisations so that they perform to their optimal capability or, at the very least, in an efficient manner. The traditional approaches therefore largely assume a rational–technical perspective on human behaviour. This focus on the forms of organisational structuring has tended to divert attention from important issues concerning the nature of structuring.

More recent approaches have begun to distinguish between subjective interpretation and objective acceptance of organisational phenomena. In other words, the extent to which power is the product of human consciousness rather than something that exists outside of individual consciousness. Writers from a social construction perspective believe that reality is largely the product of human interaction and as such is maintained and perpetuated through everyday interactions, in other words humans are seen as actors who create, maintain and perpetuate power structures, rather than puppets who are merely affected by structural phenomena that are outside of their control. According to Morgan (1986: 132):

Organizational structure, rules, policies, goals, missions, job descriptions, and standardized operating procedures ... act primarily as points of reference for the way people think about and make sense of the contexts in which they work. Though typically viewed as among the more objective characteristics of an organization, an enactment view emphasizes that they are cultural artefacts that help shape the ongoing reality within an organization.

Morgan refers to the enactment view, that is that seemingly objective power 'structures' (for example, hierarchy or managers' right to manage) exist only because humans create and perpetuate them. Power structures then take on a life of their own in our blind acceptance of them and, in turn, affect our actions. This process can be described as a dialectical one in that decision-makers create, enact and perpetuate the organisation's power structures through their actions and interactions and the structures take on a life of their own and influence individuals by determining their behaviour and actions. In essence, power structures such as hierarchy can be said to acquire agency in becoming drivers of people's motives and actions.

Individuals internalise the meaning of power structures very differently because of their experiences, personality, motives and a host of other conscious and unconscious factors. For example, in a less hierarchical organisational structure an individual may be required to take on greater decision-making power. But what one person may define as an opportunity to develop personally (more responsibility) another may regard as a threat (more opportunity to make a mistake and be found out).

There have been calls for managers to do away with traditional, hierarchical, managerial representations of their organisations that bear little or no resemblance to what actually goes on (Mintzberg and Van der Heyden, 1999). It could cynically be argued that managers will be resistant to such changes as they are likely to be the ones who have the most to lose. A key part of the managerial function is to make the 'real' structure work, that is to manage the networking and 'customising' or 'humanising' of official systems and procedures that goes

---

Illustration 12.2 Measuring up

Whilst walking through the reception in a large manufacturing organisation, a senior manager noticed that a colleague was standing by the organisation chart holding a ruler. He realised that his colleague, a middle manager, appeared to be measuring the chart on the wall. When he asked him what he was doing, his colleague replied that he thought that his name appeared to be lower down the chart than another colleague's whose name he believed should appear further down as he was not as senior. However, he was reassured by the fact that it had actually been an optical illusion and the position of the other person's name was not in fact as high up the chart as his own. He went away happy.

In order to put the manager's actions in a wider context it is worth mentioning that, at the time, the organisation in question had six separate staff restaurants, each for different grades of staff, of which the 'managers' mess' was the most exclusive. Perhaps it is not so surprising that the individual was so preoccupied with status. His behaviour may not appear so irrational when explored in the light of organisational politics.

on in order to achieve results. If there were charts that clarified what we really did, that would be one more reason for not needing managers. It would hardly come as a surprise to anyone that official charts indicate an oversimplification of human interaction, which is far more complex and ambiguous. Organisational charts do not necessarily represent the diversity of power sources in the organisation, relying as they do on identifying formal sources of authority.

Some of the ways in which power is acquired, manifested and used are described in section 12.7.1 when we discuss political games. One of the aims of official organisational structure is to provide clarity and certainty in reporting relationships, but sometimes this may lead to what could be described as strange and irrational behaviour.

12.7 Organisational politics

Dunford (1992) suggests that the subject of power has traditionally been treated as secondary in the study of organisational behaviour, largely due to the fact that it has been viewed in pejorative terms in the context of the prevailing perspective of organisations as machine-like structures in which people behave objectively and rationally and pursue efficient economic goals.

Mintzberg (1983) distinguishes between legitimate and illegitimate uses of power in differentiating politics as an illegitimate subset of power. Politics can be seen as the use of power that is not formally sanctioned by the organisation: 'politics refers to individual or group behavior that is informal, ostensibly parochial, typically divisive, and above all, in the technical sense, illegitimate – sanctioned neither by the formal authority, accepted ideology, nor certified expertise (though it may exploit any of these)' (Mintzberg, 1983: 172). Others (Pettigrew, 1973; Pfeffer, 1981) discuss politics in less value-laden terms, regarding it as an inevitable consequence of people acting to enhance or protect their own interests.

The divergence in views reflects the different perspectives of politics that are found in many academic texts. The potentially positive outcomes of political behaviour and conflict are eloquently expressed by the character Harry Lime, played by Orson Welles, in the film *The Third Man* (1949), directed by Carol Reed and based on the novel by Graham Greene:

> In Italy for thirty years under the Borgias they had warfare, terror, murder, bloodshed – but they produced Michelangelo, Leonardo Da Vinci, and the Renaissance. In Switzerland they had brotherly love, 500 years of democracy and peace, and what did that produce? The cuckoo clock.

Views regarding the use of political behaviour are usually polarised as either legitimate or illegitimate. This issue of legitimacy and illegitimacy is important in relating power, authority and politics to organisational decision-making.

Jennings and Wattam (1994: 83) suggest, 'an understanding of political processes and behaviours is crucial to both decision-making theory and practice'. However, they go on to argue that a political way of looking at organisations is a metaphor, which if overused can lead to a paranoid view of organisational life. There are strengths and limitations in regarding politics as an organisational metaphor. In a positive vein, it can allow us to make sense of seemingly irrational behaviours and actions. We can acknowledge the diversity of goals that exist in the organisation, and seek to evaluate our own underlying goals and speculate about those of others. This may, in turn, lead to a more realistic and informed appraisal of the workings of the organisation. The limitation of regarding it purely as a metaphor is that when it comes to action, those that 'live' the politics rather than intellectualise them by placing them in a wider theoretical context, may come to set the rules of what Mintzberg (1983) defines as political 'games'. Politics tends to breed politics. Managers have the choice of (a) pretending that political behaviour does not exist, (b) recognising the existence of political behaviour, regarding it as illegitimate and trying to eliminate or prevent it in some way, (c) regarding it as an everyday phenomenon but choosing not to 'join in the games', (d) regarding it as an inevitability and 'joining in the games'. Whichever option is adopted, managers may find that they cannot avoid engaging in political activity, as others may determine their involvement for them.

Mintzberg (1983) describes organisations in terms of internal and external coalitions. Internal coalitions derive their power from four sources, or what he calls systems: the system of authority, the system of ideology; the system of expertise; and the system of politics. He regards the first three as legitimate systems because they exist to achieve overarching organisational goals. The political system exists when insiders do not accept legitimate authority; do not identify with the dominant ideology; or do not accept or use their expertise for the overall welfare of the organisation. He argues that political power arises in order to 'displace' legitimate power which is a product of senior management, or wherever there are 'gaps' in the first three systems of influence.

12.7.1 Political 'games'

Politics manifests itself in a number of 'games', each with their own set of rules, and each with a specific purpose. Mintzberg (1983:188) lists those shown in Table 12.1.

The insurgency games are played in order to resist authority, expertise or the dominant ideology. They are also played to effect some kind of organisational change. Mintzberg (1983: 188) defines a decision in terms of a 'commitment to action'. Between the commitment from senior management and the implementation by subordinates lie the problems. Decisions are not always executed according to how managers intended them to be. Those that implement them can exercise a certain amount of discretion. If the decision suits them, they can implement it with enthusiasm and try to ensure its success. Alternatively, when they believe that the decision will not be to their benefit, they can stall in some way. According to Mintzberg, operatives lower down in the hierarchy are more likely to play insurgency games because they feel the full weight of organisational controls and have most to gain from resisting authority.

The counterinsurgency games are games played by those in authority in order to deal with insurgency. Usually, rules and regulations are tightened in the face of a challenge to authority. This does not always work, as the insurgency is often symptomatic of a deeper dissatisfaction. Managers therefore adopt political means to tackle the problem, for example, by bargaining with the malcontents.

Table 12.1 Political games

Purpose of game	Game
Games to resist authority	The insurgency games
Games to counter the resistance to authority	The counterinsurgency games
Games to build power bases	The sponsorship game (with superiors)
	The alliance-building game (with peers)
	The empire-building game (with subordinates)
	The budgeting game (with resources)
	The expertise games (with knowledge and skills)
	The lording game (with authority)
Games to defeat rivals	The line versus staff game
	The rival camps game
Games to effect organizational change:	The strategic candidates game
	The whistle-blowing game
	The Young Turks game

Source: Mintzberg, 1983: 188

The sponsorship game entails a less powerful member of the organisation aligning him/herself with a more powerful person.

The alliance-building game involves individuals or groups creating support networks, often implicitly, among their peers. Thus managers, for instance, form interest groups that are often temporary and issue-based, in the sense that they support each other on specific issues that they believe to be in their common interest. However, they may part company, so to speak, when the issue is no longer in the spotlight.

The empire-building game entails setting out to acquire other people's resources, be they financial, material or human. Managers may become involved in 'turf wars' over positions in the organisation, and over the people who fill those positions. Salary and status are often dependent on the size of a manager's department, the size of his or her budget and so on. The possibility of 'stepping on someone else's toes' makes this a game with high risk attached.

The budgeting game is similar to the empire-building game but differs in so much as the participant does not wish to acquire territory in an aggressive manner, but to expand his or her own organically. The aim is to get more resources. Common tactics, according to Mintzberg, are: ask for too much because you know you will not get it all; bring out rational arguments to support your claim; suppress arguments that could call your claim into question; if necessary, bend the truth a little about your real needs; when the budget has been allocated, make sure you use it up even if it means wasting it – if you do not, the surplus will be cut from next year's request; if you can, hide some away as slack 'for a rainy day'.

Mintzberg (1983: 198) describes an extreme example of the game. The story involves a division of a large organisation which put in a request to head office for capital funding for a large chimney to be constructed. This is queried as the centre cannot see why on earth they would want a chimney. A representative flies out to the division only to find out that an entire plant has been built without the approval of the centre. The justification is that the request for a new plant would most probably have been refused on economic grounds as a large capital project, so it was equipped through plant expense orders which were not likely to be queried. The only thing that eventually brought the matter to the attention of the centre was the chimney, which exceeded the $50,000 expense order limit.

The expertise games can take two forms: they can be used to attack others or to defend the game players from attack by others. Professionals play an attacking game by calling upon their monopoly of skills and/or knowledge as a lever to get what they want. This can obviously be likened to expert power, mentioned earlier. A more defensive use of expert power involves experts keeping their knowledge to themselves in order to maintain their power base and to resist any attempts to dilute it in any way. In protecting their position, they may seek to mystify their role and function in some way. Goffman (1959: 76): 'As countless folk tales and initiation rites show, often the real secret behind the mystery is that there really is no mystery; the real problem is to prevent the audience from learning this too.'

The lording games are played by those who choose to 'lord' their power over others in some way. It involves the illegitimate use of legitimate sources of power. Interestingly, research into this kind of behaviour has tended to focus on employees lower down in the hierarchy. Roy's (1960) often cited study 'Banana time' gives vivid examples of workers 'lording it' over fellow workers and trying to establish informal 'pecking orders'. The suggestion is that when people have little official power and status, they look to establish these in informal ways.

The line versus staff game is described by Mintzberg as a zero-sum game in which one person or group wins at the expense of, and as a result of, its opponent's loss. The aim is to defeat your opponent. The line versus staff game is a classic played out in many organisations. The fact that staff functions do not form part of the line management structure often adds an element of ambiguity to the power relationship that exists between line managers and staff members such as personnel managers. Stereotypically, line managers' allegiances lie with the organisation, whereas staff members are often also affiliated to professional bodies.

The rival camps game is another zero-sum game which comes about when only two parties, be they individuals, groups or departments, are left to confront each other as a result of previous political games having taken place. The field is now clear as other rivals have been eliminated, suppressed or enveloped. Typically, a rival camps game might centre around a significant change in the organisation, with each camp being for or against the change.

The strategic candidates game is another that is played to effect some kind of organisational change. An individual or group looks to instigate some kind of strategic change by promoting its own 'strategic candidate'. It does so through legitimate means. The candidate need not be a person; it could be an idea or a project of some description.

Whistle-blowing has entered everyday language to a greater extent than any of the other games, with the possible exception of empire building. It involves an internal member seeking recourse to powerful external influencers when some moral has been transgressed, or some unethical behaviour exhibited. When an individual feels powerless within the organisation, an option may be to try to use external sources of power to counter the internal source. Organisational members sometimes use the press as a medium to expose issues or problems that they do not agree with and which they feel contravene ethical rules.

The Young Turks game is the final game mentioned by Mintzberg, and the one that he suggests is played for the highest stakes. A group of individuals align to depose the existing power-holder in order to change the organisation's strategic direction. This could be termed revolution or mutiny in that what is sought is a fundamental change in the systems of authority and ideology.

Illustration 12.3 Industrial sabotage

Railwaymen have described how they block lines with trucks to delay shunting operations for a few hours. Materials are hidden in factories, conveyor belts jammed with sticks, cogs stopped with wire and ropes, lorries 'accidentally' backed into ditches. Electricians labour to put in weak fuses, textile workers 'knife' through carpets and farmworkers cooperate to choke agricultural machinery with tree branches.

Our data include examples of acts which only temporarily disconcert the management, and of those which have shut an entire factory. Sometimes the behaviour involves only one person, but often the active or passive cooperation of hundreds is observable. It may occur just once or twice in the history of the industry or be an almost daily experience in the workers' life. To do justice to such a range of activity we use a broad definition of industrial sabotage – that rule-breaking which takes the form of conscious action or inaction directed toward the mutilation or destruction of the work environment (this includes the machinery of production and the commodity itself).

Source: Taylor and Walton, 1994: 321

Activity 12.3   How might you define the actions described in Illustration 12.3 in terms of Mintzberg's games?

Although the authors use the term 'industrial sabotage' to describe such incidents as those in Illustration 12.3, they could equally be described as examples of empowered, albeit illegitimate, decision-making, or vivid examples of organisational political games (such as insurgency). The illustration shows that either through active or passive resistance, all organisational members have the power to make or influence decisions. A manager's power to make management decisions is sanctioned by the organisational hierarchy and therefore regarded as a legitimate right, but in reality, as we have seen, there are many diverse sources of power in organisations. Some organisations are more conscious of 'harnessing' this power in a positive way. Pascale (1978: 153) points to this very poetically:

Overt strength is not unequivocally a desired attribute ... Reefs do not attempt to resist the sea like defiant walls of man-made steel and concrete. Instead, the reef extends wedges out in a seaward direction. The waves deflect off these wedges, one against the other. Consequently their power, rather than directed at the reef, is turned against itself. The reef does not insist on standing higher than the sea. In times of typhoon, the waves wash over the reef. And it survives.

It is sometimes the case that management decisions that are implemented to tackle problems, end up creating other problems. Indeed, we could suggest that if there were no organisational problems, we would not need managers, so it may be in the interest of managers to selectively perpetuate them rather than solve them. This could be a conscious or unconscious driver for managers' political actions in organisations. The actions described in the industrial sabotage example could be seen as symptomatic of underlying malaise as well as being problems in their own right. As decision-makers, it would be prudent for managers to question why people act in this way and investigate the possible causes of negative actions. For example, such behaviour may be caused by structural factors. Employees may feel alienated by what they regard as meaningless tasks and little responsibility. So, can these tasks be managed differently to take into account the negative effects on the people performing them? Alternatively, they could be caused by a mixture of structural and interpersonal factors. For example, are groups of people being encouraged to compete? If so, how is this being managed so that it does not deteriorate into conflict? There could be a host of underlying reasons, but if the decision-maker defines the negative actions purely in terms of being a problem rather than also being a symptom, the likelihood of addressing the real underlying issues diminishes. Productive long-term solutions may suffer as a result.

12.7.2 Personal interaction as politics

Some authors (Laing, 1967; Mangham, 1978) assume that political behaviour is to be found wherever people interact. Human interaction is in itself a political pursuit as we seek to influence the perceptions and behaviours of others as we go about our daily routines. Indeed, the way we make sense of our experiences and extrapolate our beliefs and values onto others is a political act. The growing trend towards mission statements and language about shared values in organisations, which express ideal states of power relations in organisations, can be viewed in terms of powerful stakeholders attempting to sell or tell their vision of the organisations to less powerful members of the organisation. As organisational members, we can easily forget that the messages that appear in slogans and rhetoric exalting us to view the organisation in a certain light or to behave in prescribed ways, are the product of individuals or groups of people with a vested interest. The words take on an agency of their own as we attribute them to 'the organisation' or to some faceless, machine-like bureaucracy of 'communication'.

At an interpersonal level, power is brokered on a daily basis. When viewed as a commodity, power, not money, becomes the lifeblood of the organisation. Arguably, without unequal power relationships it would be difficult to take decisive action in an organisation. It is, therefore, not the status *per se* of an individual that gives him or her the right to take decisive action, but the status differential between that individual and others. In our own experience of working with large groups of managers over a long period of time, it is obvious that managers find it difficult to take decisive action when there is a lack of status differential. For example, in classroom settings managers see themselves primarily as students among peers. The right to manage is therefore passed on to tutors, but when tutors attempt to 'take a back seat' and actively refuse to take on leadership roles, many individuals find it difficult to make decisions with or on behalf of their peers.

Bear in mind, however, that power and influence are not necessarily the same. For example, you might find that the person who speaks the most is allowed to because of their authoritative position, yet verbal support may not necessarily follow.

Organisations are arenas for the negotiation and renegotiation of power. Individuals and groups acquire and lose power on a continual basis. An individual who may be powerful in a particular context may lose his or her influence in another context. To this extent, power is context-specific and our personal interpretation and internalisation of power may be different according to the situation. It thus makes it difficult to discuss issues of power outside of specific contexts.

12.8 Recognising power: organisational symbolism

Organisational power may be likened to sources of energy such as electricity or natural gas. It may be difficult to perceive although it affects us all in some way or other. Being difficult to perceive, we have to provide indicators of its existence. Power is not a tangible phenomenon, it is a concept. As such, we cannot feel it or taste it, yet who would deny its existence? And what is the point of having power if it is not recognisable to those we seek to wield it over? As with any other concept, we are surrounded with *indicators* of its existence. Such indicators in themselves may be tangible (for example, a doctor's white coat, a manager's suit) or intangible (almost imperceptible behaviours such as the giving of eye contact, or tone of voice). Tangible indicators may be the 'trappings' that come with the job. Mangham (1988) argues that when an individual takes on a particular role, he or she is also required to exhibit corresponding behaviours. To use a dramaturgical metaphor, that is, to view organisations in terms of theatre, in order to make the part more genuine the individual requires appropriate props. The props in themselves become agents of power in that they influence the way people interact. For example, the police officer's uniform serves as an inanimate yet powerful agent that reinforces the legitimacy of the individual wearing it. The police officer's uniform is a universal example that most people could relate to. In organisational settings, however, inanimate objects take on a significance that is often irrelevant to those who are not members of the organisation. Organisational symbols therefore create an internal world of power relationships that mirror society at large but may simultaneously exclude or override its usual rules of behaviour.

In Illustration 12.4 the symbolic meaning of the fountain, as a signifier of the vice-president's power, was initially lost on the visiting manager, yet it seemed to be taken entirely for granted by the members of the organisation. Stories such as this serve to perpetuate the myths surrounding powerful figures.

Illustration 12.4 In residence

A senior manager in a 'world class' manufacturing company based in the UK visited one of its partner institutions based in the USA. The manager was struck by the opulence of the manufacturing site that was built in the shape of a quadrangle with mature, landscaped gardens at the centre. The focal point of the gardens was a particularly attractive fountain that, at the time, was not operating. When he inquired as to why this was the case, the manager was told that the vice-president was not on the premises. Intrigued by this, he inquired further. Apparently, the controls that determined whether the fountain worked or not, were situated in the vice-president's office. Much as the Royal standard flies over Buckingham Palace when the monarch is in residence, there seemed to be a definite correlation between the vice-president's presence on site and the operation of the fountain.

◆ Summary

We have chosen to place this chapter in the implementation section of the book, but it would equally have been at home in any of the other sections. Power and politics pervade every area of organisational life. Through an exploration of the nature of power, and by identifying political games, the decision-maker can come to a fuller appreciation of the inherent difficulties of implementing decisions. Moreover, the decision-maker can begin to analyse the extent to which his or her own decision-making process is influenced by the structural power relationships that exist within the organisation. Power can be viewed as a structural phenomenon or as an interpersonal one. In reality, it is both of these and more. Its presence is difficult to gauge, but we have tried to show that there are ways in which indicators of power can help us to make sense of decision-making situations. Power can be expressed symbolically through manifest ways, or more subtly through, for example, language. It may be the case that recognising these ways allows us to empower ourselves a little. Alternatively, it may just increase our frustration.

? Decision diary

Next time you are in a meeting, try to note the subtle ways in which power is 'traded'. For example, look for the following behaviours: Who gets the most/least 'air time'? Who gets the most/least eye contact? Who gets interrupted the most/least? Who gets the most/least verbal support after speaking?

Make a note of these behaviours in your diary. You may make some links here with Chapter 11 (group processes).

References

Cartwright, D. and Zander, A.F. (eds) (1968) *Group Dynamics Research and Theory*, 3rd edition. New York: Harper & Row.

Dunford, R. (1992) *Organisational Behaviour: An Organisational Analysis Perspective*. Reading, MA: Addison Wesley.

French, J.R.P. and Raven, B. 'The Bases of Social Power' in Cartwright, D. and Zander, A. (eds) (1968) *Group Dynamics: Research and Theory*. London: Tavistock.

Fox, A. (1966) *Industrial Sociology and Industrial Relations*, Royal Commission on Trades Unions and Employers' Associations, Research Paper 3. London: HMSO.

Goffman, E. (1959) *The Presentation of Self in Everyday life*. Harmondsworth: Penguin.

Jennings, D. and Wattam, S. (1998) *Decision-making: An Integrated Approach*, 2nd edition. London: Financial Times/Pitman Publishing.

Laing, R.D. (1967) *The Politics of Experience and the Bird of Paradise*. Harmondsworth: Penguin.

Lee, R. and Lawrence, P. (1985) *Organizational Behaviour Politics at Work*. London: Hutchinson.

Lukes, S. (1974) *Power. A Radical View*. London: Macmillan.

Lukes, S. (ed.) (1986) *Power*. Oxford: Blackwell.

Mangham, I.L. (1978) *Interactions and Interventions in Organisations*. Chichester: Wiley.

Mangham, I.L. (1988) *Effecting Organisational Change*. Oxford: Basil Blackwell.

Mintzberg, H. (1983) *Power In and Around Organizations*. Englewood Cliffs, NJ: Prentice Hall.

Mintzberg, H. and Van der Heyden, L. (1999) 'Organigraphs: drawing how companies really work', *Harvard Business Review*, 77(5):87.

Morgan, G. (1986) *Images of Organization*. London: Sage.

Pascale, R.T. (1978) 'Zen and the art of management', *Harvard Business Review*, March/April: 153.

Pettigrew, A. (1973) *The Politics of Organisational Decision-making*. London: Tavistock.

Pfeffer, J. (1981) *Power in Organizations*. Boston, MA: Pitman.

Roy, D. (1960) 'Banana time: job satisfaction and informal interaction', *Human Organization*, 18: 156–68.

Taylor, L. and Walton, P. (1994) 'Industrial sabotage', in Clark, M., Chandler, J. and Barry, J. (eds) *Organisation and Identities*. London: Chapman & Hall.

Further reading

Crick, B. (ed.) (1970) *Machiavelli. The Discourses*. Harmondsworth: Penguin.
Machiavelli, N. (1981) *The Prince*. Harmondsworth: Penguin.

If you replace the words 'city', 'state', 'principality', 'empire' and so on with the word 'organisation', and the words 'prince', 'king', 'emperor' etc. with 'manager' or 'director', and use your imagination, you may find that some things have not changed much in five hundred years. You may even recognise some of the political games mentioned by Mintzberg.

13 The cultural context

On completing this chapter you should be able to:

- Appreciate the ways in which organisational culture affects the decision-making behaviour of individuals.

- Explore the two-way relationship between organisational culture and management decision-making.

- Recognise and distinguish different perspectives on culture and evaluate how they might affect decision-makers' actions.

13.1 Introduction

In the early 1980s there was a proliferation of literature (Deal and Kennedy, 1982; Peters and Waterman, 1982) offering managers such advice as 'walk the talk' or 'stick to the knitting'. Managers were implored to become leaders and heroes rather than managers, to manage the culture in order to win the 'hearts and minds' of employees. This kind of approach has been disparagingly labelled 'guru theory', or 'Heathrow organisation theory' (a term coined by Gibson Burrell, referring to the London airport where such books may still be found in abundance in bookshops). Criticisms of guru theory tend to focus on the fact that the authors apply an atheoretical and retrospective methodology by, for instance, choosing already successful organisations as examples to be followed by others. Critics argue that the early chosen examples are no longer successful and this rather negates the argument that we should attempt to mimic the managerial approaches adopted in these organisations. The guru theorists tend to overemphasise the power that managers have to determine organisational success, and thereby de-emphasise such environmental determinants as the economy, for example.

Although there is much academic criticism of such an approach, a visit to an airport bookshop might suggest that guru theory is alive and well. Indeed, the lists of best-selling books in professional management journals tend to confirm that there is a strong market for such literature.

In this chapter we locate this populist view of organisational culture in a more complex, analytical framework. Whilst we readily accept the view that organisations do not make decisions, rather people do, we nonetheless also accept that organisational culture affects the decision-making behaviour of people within organisations. There is no doubting that the culture of an organisation can have significant implications for the way in which organisational members interpret their roles and relationships with others. We evaluate the dialectical relationship between organisational culture and decision-making, that is, the way in which culture affects the behaviour of decision-makers, and, in turn, the way in which the actions of decision-makers affect culture.

As Rosen (quoted in Frost *et al.*, 1991: 273–4) states:

Although culture emerges from action, it continuously acts back upon it as well, recreating and transforming action through the provision of meaning. To function in a setting, and to gain meaning from behavior, culture systems are more or less internalized.

13.2 A theoretical framework: integration, differentiation and fragmentation

Why do students of organizational culture dislike ambiguities? Why do we tend to notice (and value) that which is clear, stable, and 'orderly' (that which we can readily understand, measure, and control) and ignore that which is unclear, unstable, and 'disorderly' (that which is more fragmented, intractable, and difficult to control)? These preferences betray our professional identity. They reveal our professional culture's dominant values, interests, and beliefs.

– Debra E. Meyerson (quoted in Frost *et al.*, 1991: 255)

Why indeed? And it is not just students of organisational culture who seek clarity, stability and order, as we noted earlier in Chapter 1 when we looked at the case of the paradoxical platypus, or above in this chapter when we considered the popular appeal of gurus. Albert Camus, the French novelist and theorist, suggests that we are nostalgic for clarity. We therefore welcome and embrace theories that provide such clarity. On the other hand, Camus also reminds us that a postmodernist view of knowledge would indicate the impossibility of ever establishing absolute knowledge. It is, therefore, fair to say that there are probably deep-seated philosophical reasons why we remain open to what might be termed 'grand theory' – a theory which gives universal answers to problems. Whilst a lot of emphasis is generally placed on culture as a unifying force that is to be understood and harnessed for managerial utility, this represents but one view of the subject. Frost *et al.* (1991) draw upon the work of Meyerson and Martin (1987) by exploring the vast array of theories of corporate culture in terms of three distinct perspectives that appear in the literature: the integration perspective, differentiation perspective and the fragmentation/ambiguity perspective.

Integration perspective

This perspective presents and promotes the idea that culture is unified and unifying. Organisational culture is talked about in terms of integrating and bringing together all members of the organisation. Writers adopting this perspective therefore focus on discussing the importance of shared values and common goals and beliefs. The early work of Deal and Kennedy (1982) and Peters and Waterman (1982) would come under this category.

Differentiation perspective

Rather than focusing on unity, the differentiation perspective addresses issues of diversity. Emphasis is placed on the existence of subcultures as opposed to an overriding, cohesive culture. The presence of subcultures is recognised as an inevitable result of the differentiated nature of organisations and society. Individuals and groups will have their own particular needs, wants, beliefs and values, whether they are organisational or personal. This will lead to the creation of subcultures. The potential for conflict is therefore acknowledged.

Fragmentation/ambiguity perspective

This offers a completely distinct view of culture. The notion of clearly intelligible patterns of behaviour and shared meanings is challenged. Meanings are seen as much more fluid and transient than the theories from the other two perspectives would have us believe. Organisations are arenas in which social actors are continually negotiating and renegotiating meaning, so the extent to which culture can be clearly identified and managed is much more problematical.

The three cultural perspectives: towards synthesis?

We suggested at the outset of this book that we may be predisposed to view the world in particular ways; that we have our preferred paradigms. Just as we suggested then that integrating other perspectives with our own was problematical, so Frost *et al.* (1991) suggest that trying to integrate the three cultural perspectives outlined above is not only difficult but also to be avoided. They suggest that whilst acknowledging our own preferred, or 'home', perspective, we need to understand the other two. Attempts to integrate the three perspectives into some unifying theory would be a mistake and would undermine the value of the individual perspectives. They remind us:

> Martin and Meyerson insist that it is essential to remember that any single perspective can tell only part of a cultural story. In any context, at any time, the other two perspectives explain aspects of the culture that are ignored or misrepresented by the home perspective. When two of the three perspectives are suppressed, one of the suppressed viewpoints is usually fairly easily accessible ('Of course, I should have seen that'); the other perspective is usually deeply repressed because its acknowledgement would be threatening to current arrangements and understandings. In cultural research, as in psychoanalysis, the more a perspective is repressed, the greater the potential growth in understanding if the relevance of that perspective can be understood.
>
> (Frost *et al.*, 1991: 160)

We would argue that there is much value for us in our general exploration of different perspectives on decision-making in what Martin and Meyerson have to say about the use of the cultural perspectives in organisational analysis. If up to this point in the book you have been 'skipping' those perspectives you are less comfortable with, perhaps we should challenge you to revisit them now to see what you might discover. Of course, it occurs to us that if you are uncomfortable with more qualitative aspects of decision-making you may very well not be reading this!

Activity 13.1	Draw a picture of the culture of an organisation with which you are familiar. Try to do this instinctively. However, if this proves a strange or daunting task at first, a measure of perseverance should lead to some sort of drawing. What does your drawing depict? What do you think this represents? Do you think you have represented an integrated, differentiated or fragmented view of culture? How do you think others in the organisation (peers, senior managers, customers and so on) would depict the culture? If this reveals differences, can you account for them?

Our experience of getting many MBA students to undertake Activity 13.1 leads us to speculate that you may very well have produced a drawing which shows management's view of a neatly defined organisation (integration) but then goes on to show the ways in which wider organisation members are aware of the elements of differentiation or fragmentation. For example, a well signposted tarmac track leading up a sun-topped mountain offering up clear vistas across the distant horizon become multiple dirt tracks leading who knows where. And the peak, if there is one, is shrouded in mist with no sign of any horizon.

As Dunford (1992: 171) suggests

> The integration perspective is popular with managers because it is neat – it provides a view of culture as something coherent – it is not messy – it is seen, therefore, both as able to be encapsulated in a few clear terms and as manageable. However, although this perspective may be a comforting one for managers to hold, it is not necessarily the most useful if they wish to understand the complexity of organisations from a cultural framework.

A parallel can be drawn here between the popularity of integrative literature concerning organisational culture and the popularity of normative literature advising managers how to make decisions. Prescriptive approaches tend to simplify the complexity of the subject by ignoring the inherent contradictions that often face organisational decision-makers. Managers' concern with the practical can often encourage them to satisfice in the short term rather than develop more lasting solutions. Empirical research into management often suggests that a great deal of managers' time is spent 'fire-fighting' (dealing with problems in an ad hoc way and without time for reflection as they arrive in quick succession). Unsurprisingly, rather than develop the diagnostic capability to deal with their own unique circumstances, managers may choose to simplify the problems they face by turning their attention to approaches that offer an easy solution or by ignoring that there is a problem at all.

13.3   Culture as tangible and intangible

One of the most popular exponents of the importance of organisational culture as a way of analysing organisations is Edgar Schein. His work is typical of writers who draw attention to the distinction between tangible and intangible elements of culture. He talks about perceptions, thoughts and feelings, and alludes to behaviour through adaptation and learning. The image of an iceberg is sometimes used to illustrate these visible and invisible dimensions of culture. Only a fraction of an organisation's culture is immediately visible to the observer. The observer must infer what is happening under the surface by looking at what appears above water level. He or she can assume that an invisible mass has some bearing on what is observed, but can only speculate about the relationship. However, the longer one experiences the observable phenomenon, the more informed the speculation will be. Visible aspects include: artefacts, stories, gossip, humour, myth and physical surroundings. Aspects that are not immediately intelligible include: the history of the organisation and the values, beliefs and attitudes that underpin action.

Activity 13.2   Edgar Schein (quoted in Frost *et al.*, 1991: 247) defines culture as:

A pattern of shared basic assumptions,

invented, discovered, or developed by a given group

as it learns to cope with its problems of external adaptation and internal integration,

that have worked well enough to be considered valid, and, therefore,

is to be taught to new members of the group as the correct way to perceive, think, and feel in relation to those problems.

Where would you locate this definition in the integration/differentiation/fragmentation framework?

Do you remember the example of the character in the illustration in Chapter 12 who measured his position on the organisation chart with a ruler? Did this actually happen? According to another source this was actually a myth, a story that was prevalent in the organisation at the time. Shortly afterwards, the organisation chart was renamed an 'organogram' and a disclaimer was placed at the bottom saying that in no way did the chart represent people's relative status and that it was simply for clarity of communication channels. Perhaps the story gained credence as the organisation was changing to a flatter structure and the incident was used to signify the absurdity of the old structure. Perhaps the incident, if indeed there was an incident, was a driver of the change. Either way it serves as an example of the power of storytelling and its role in the development of organisational culture.

The notion of a cultural metaphor has major implications for decision-making. It draws our attention to the fact that decisions may be strongly motivated and influenced by the organisational setting in which individuals operate. The more tangible this setting becomes to organisational members, the more likely it is that decision-making will be framed or constrained. So, for example, when we talk about a strong culture, perhaps what we really mean is that the organisation is ideologically driven to the extent that individuals' actions are influenced and inhibited by a pressure to conform to what Schein calls 'a pattern of shared basic assumptions'.

In light of these pressures to conform, people develop 'good enough' solutions to deal with the problems of organisational life. Culture can be seen to bring clarity and a (common) sense of purpose where otherwise uncertainty might prevail. There is no such thing as a perfect culture in absolute terms and, whilst on some occasions the clarity derived from culture can facilitate 'appropriate' decision-making behaviour, in other situations it might be seen to be counterproductive, where more benefit would have been derived from embracing uncertainty. In so far as culture is commonly thought of as encapsulating shared values and beliefs, it is closely related to ideology.

13.4   Culture as ideological control

The former prime minister Margaret Thatcher is often used as an example of an autocratic decision-maker who appears not to have suffered fools gladly. Towards the end of her final term in office, the Cabinet – the key decision-making government forum – comprised yes-men. This is a view that was perpetuated in the media at the time and reinforced through satire, although, interestingly, it is denied by Margaret Thatcher herself in her autobiography *The Downing Street Years*.

It could be said that the Cabinet, Thatcher included, was merely enacting policies derived from the underlying ideology of the Conservative Party at the time, that is 'Thatcherism'. In the light of this ideological underpinning, the Cabinet may have become the mouthpiece of an established ideology that was driving the actions of key decision-makers. However, it should not be forgotten that the ideology itself was a product of human thought and activity. It became associated with, and enacted by Margaret Thatcher and her followers, and was based on the monetarist economic principles of thinkers such as Milton Friedman. Ultimately, the relationship between action and underlying ideology is a dialectical one, as mentioned earlier. In essence, culture is created by individuals. The danger lies in the fact that those individuals and their successors become trapped by the expectations imposed by that culture as it becomes reified as normality. More than a decade after her departure from office, the Conservative Party is still perceived to be in a state of disarray due to the loss of clarity following the collapse of the ideological underpinnings.

| Activity 13.3 | Can you think of a decision-making situation you have been in where you felt constrained by organisational factors? If so, how do you know that you were expected to act in a certain way? Put another way, how did you 'learn' about the culture of the organisation concerned? |

According to Morgan (1997)

> management has always been to some extent an ideological practice, promoting appropriate attitudes, values, and norms as means of motivating and controlling employees. What is new in many recent developments is the not-so-subtle way in which ideological manipulation and control is being advocated as an essential managerial strategy ... used to create an Orwellian world of corporate newspeak, where the culture controls rather than expresses human character.

In this quotation Morgan offers a more sinister view of the use of ideology in organisations. Culture is presented as a mechanism by which control is exerted.

Illustrations 13.1 and 13.2 provide contrasting examples of the way in which control can be exerted ideologically, and manifested in subtle and not-so-subtle ways.

Illustration 13.1 Happy Christmas!

This is a copy of an actual memorandum sent within a department of a large national company. Apart from changing names, the memorandum is reproduced almost verbatim.

Memorandum

To: **See below**

Subject: **STAFF DINNER – RAYMOND EXPECTS**

All,

Rather like 'England Expects' we have a 'Raymond Expects'.

We are all members of SPECIAL PROJECTS DEPARTMENT and throughout the year I expect loyalty from you, to me and to the department, and once a year I expect an open demonstration of that loyalty – the Christmas night out.

We are all members of SPECIAL PROJECTS and again loyalty and demonstration of that loyalty would be nice – the SPECIAL PROJECTS Staff Dinner.

There are things you don't enjoy, that cost you money that you don't have, but are expected of you when you take on the side of 'management'. Some of you are willingly taking the money for training on MBAs, degrees etc. Others simply enjoy the status and high salary.

Have a real think about it and we will discuss it before I submit the merit rise list.

Talk to your staff along the same lines and let's have a real turn out.

Perhaps the important issue in Illustration 13.1 is not that a manager is using what at face value is a happy, social occasion to reinforce his position of power but rather more it is the blatant manner in which it is being attempted (we can only speculate on what a fun time was had by all!). We might suggest that it may be commonplace to so 'hijack' such events, but that the perpetrators of such acts are generally more subtle about the manner in which they do so, although Gareth Morgan might disagree. Illustration 13.2 offers an example of a more subtle process of cultural control.

Illustration 13.2 A people culture?

Ricardo Semler is the chief executive of a family-owned organisation, located in Brazil, which manufactures valves, pumps and heavy-duty industrial equipment. Semler prides himself on doing away with traditional bureaucratic ways of running a business. There are no privileges for directors and managers, and employees set their own salary levels. Profits have risen and there is a long list of applicants for jobs. He managed the organisation along traditional lines for five years after taking it over but, disenchanted with the traditional command and control approach to managing, he slowly began to introduce more radical methods.

Semler believed that the key factor for successful management was trust, and consequently abolished all security checks and clock-in procedures at Semco. The reason behind this move was the belief that most people are trustworthy and should not be penalised on account of a small minority. He argues that shared commitment is necessary in managing change effectively and has therefore attempted to bring democracy into the workplace. Openness is encouraged in sharing information and salary levels are transparent. In an interview with Bruce Lloyd of South Bank University, London, Semler says:

> At Semco we try to do away with formalities which discourage team development. We encourage movement between projects and areas which helps team creation and recreation. We work on six monthly operational budgets – there is a tendency to have to rethink things every couple of months. Everyone knows what is going on. We do balance sheet training programmes – even for the cleaning ladies – and that helps trust. There is no classified information whatsoever. Salaries are known and we are not scared of the wrong information getting to competitors. The only real source of power within an organisation is information and the real test of an organisation's approach is whether this is really shared and open. By the democratisation of information you can take out layers of management and it really encourages teamwork ... Companies talk about democracy but the democracy we operate in our lives and political structures is rarely found in the work environment. Companies are still autocratically run and many have become museums of history. Not much has really changed in the last 300 years except techniques.

In Illustration 13.2, Semler offers a rare example of a radical way of structuring organisations in order to create a more democratic culture. It also serves as a reminder that the way in which an organisation is structured determines how people think about themselves, their work roles and their relationships with others. It has become more widely accepted that managers should manage through indirect means, that is, through managing culture. If we accept that a key function of management is to control, then Morgan's view is not as radical or critical as it might first appear.

Although Semco is often used as an example of a new type of organisation free of traditional ideological stereotypes of command and control hierarchies, a brief analysis of the language used by Ricardo Semler indicates that attitudes to hierarchy are more entrenched. Deeper aspects of culture are more difficult to alter.

Activity 13.4	Semler makes the following statement: 'We do balance sheet training programmes – even for the cleaning ladies – and that helps trust.'
	What do you think this statement suggests about the way that Ricardo Semler thinks about hierarchy? If hierarchy is not an issue then why pick up on cleaning ladies as an example?

Presumably, cleaning ladies are still regarded as the lowest stratum in the Semco hierarchy, otherwise why choose to single them out to illustrate the point? Note the use of the word 'even'. The language used is perhaps an indicator that all is not what it seems. Again this points to the possibility that we are still trapped in traditional values and ways of thinking, although the physical structures may be changing. However, it could also be said that only through action will we begin to change ingrained values and beliefs.

Semco may be seen as an example of the way in which emphasis is being placed on subtly managing through culture, strict recruitment, selection and peer pressure. Less emphasis is being placed on overt control, but control exists nonetheless. In fact some would argue that as people are empowered to take on greater responsibility they become more controlled as they buy into organisational values and goals to a greater extent than if they were coerced against their will. In essence, they believe that they have power that they do not really have.

13.5 Cross-cultural implications for decision-making

A senior manager in a multinational, American-owned manufacturing organisation recently visited a relatively new overseas plant in eastern Europe. One of the problems he was confronted with was that the local employees had been adversely affected by the company's insistence on displaying the organisation's value statements in large writing on the factory walls. On closer examination, it was discovered that the main reason for this adverse reaction was not that the employees necessarily disagreed with the statements, but that they associated the form of display itself with Soviet slogans and, therefore, ideological hegemony. Under the former Communist regime, it was common for Soviet propaganda to be publicly displayed in a similar way. The new propaganda, as they regarded it, evoked feelings of political, social and cultural subservience. The employees' reactions to the notices on the wall are examples of what Geertz (Frost *et al.*, 1991: 273) refers to as 'envehicled meanings'. The notices on the factory wall are the

> vehicles through which communication occurs. Symbols are here the 'objects, acts, relationships, or linguistic formations that stand *ambiguously* for a multiplicity of meanings, evoke emotions, and impel men to action.'
> (Cohen, 1974: 23, quoted in Frost *et al.*, 1991: 273)

With the continuing growth in the globalisation of many organisations, this example demonstrates that what may be innocuous in one culture may cause great alarm in another. It serves to highlight that the interface between organisational culture and the wider cultural context may lead to problems of misinterpretation and may require us to actively explore ambiguity. Truth and reality are, at best, shared and socially negotiated phenomena at a place and point in time. When the dimensions of place and time change, the meanings become ambiguous.

Geert Hofstede (1981) researched 116,000 employees in one multinational company operating in over 40 countries. The focus of his research was to try to understand 'value' differences between national cultures. From his findings, and subsequent reflection, he identified five dimensions by which national cultures can be compared.

1 Power distance

Power distance describes the extent to which a culture will accept differences between levels of status and power in its population. To what degree are people likely to accept and respect hierarchy and status differentials in their organisations? For instance, according to Hofstede's findings, Great Britain is low power distance and Singapore is high power distance. In other words, social status and power differentials are less likely to be tolerated in Great Britain than in Singapore. In the example of the American multinational, mentioned above, what is interesting is that the symbolic meaning of the 'slogans' was interpreted in vastly different ways. The organisation wished to create a lower power distance differential. In other words, it was trying to create more of a team culture by displaying and sharing common values. This was interpreted, through the previous structure of experience of the employees, as domination. The symbol, for them, was a reminder of a high power distance differential. In other words, it evoked memories of large, impersonal bureaucracies that had a major influence on their lives.

2 Uncertainty avoidance

Uncertainty avoidance draws our attention to the possibility that some cultures are inherently more tolerant of uncertainties than others. For example, countries such as Greece and Portugal are classed as high uncertainty avoidance countries. This suggests that the Greeks and the Portuguese are more likely to fear situations in which there is a perceived high level of uncertainty. Conversely, the UK is classed as a low uncertainty avoidance country, which suggests that the British are more likely to embrace uncertainty in a more positive way.

3 Individualism vs collectivism

Is independence valued more highly than social cohesion? This is the basic question addressed in this dimension of culture. Hofstede suggests that some countries' cultures value one above the other. One of Hofstede's interesting findings was that, in general, the wealthier economies tended to value individualism more highly. The poorer countries tended to place more emphasis on collectivism and community.

4 Masculinity vs femininity

This refers to the extent to which gendered roles are clearly differentiated. In high masculinity societies, gender roles in society are clearly different. Men's roles are defined in distinct ways from female roles. Each gender's roles are associated with a particular set of characteristics. For example, female roles tend to emphasise caring and sharing, whilst male roles emphasise competition and aggression.

5 Long-term vs short-term orientation

According to Hofstede, cultures can be differentiated according to their orientation towards short-termism and long-termism. Short-termist societies place emphasis on quick results. There are some parallels here with the notion of task and process in group activity which we addressed in Chapter 11. Short-termism is more akin to task orientation, with its consequent emphasis on results. Long-termism reflects a more process-oriented approach, placing emphasis on social factors.

13.6 A critique of culture as a metaphor

Our discussion so far has been based on the assumption that culture exists as a recognisable phenomenon and is, thus, routinely and non-problematically experienced by people in organisations. Even the ambiguity perspective, identified by Meyerson and Martin (1987), is an attempt to locate ambiguity in a recognisable wider theoretical framework, albeit a heuristic device. The question we could ask ourselves is 'can a culture really exist?' We could further explore this by asking whether culture is merely a metaphor for trying to conceptualise, synthesise or explain what we otherwise struggle to articulate.

The notion of organisational culture is inherently unifying and stresses commonality. It is, therefore, built on a deeper notion of shared meaning that is to be found, for instance, in most religions. Perhaps the idea that there is no ultimate meaning to life is too unbearable, and consequently leads us to seek meta-meanings in order subconsciously to affirm the purpose of our existence through meaningful activity. The more that such activity can be shared with others, the more value we can attach to it, hence the more meaningful it becomes. Decision-making activity in organisations that can be readily aligned with the espoused (usually by senior managers) common purpose is more likely to be encouraged and approved than activity that may be seen to undermine common goals. Furthermore, and reflecting on Rosen's quotation earlier in this chapter, individuals may well be predisposed to believing those who implore them to think, feel and act for the common good. If enough people believe in a certain point of view then, perhaps, that point of view can become 'truth', at least for a short period of time. The challenge for decision-makers is that truth is not necessarily so fixed and absolute. What constitutes truth at the point we make a decision may well change by the time the consequences of that decision become apparent. Indeed, truth may well be shaped by the decision itself.

Illustration 13.3 serves to show how tenuous the belief system might be within an organisation and how fairly 'heavy-handed' tactics are often required to 'bolster' the 'belief'. We might reflect that 'truth' is often achieved at a heavy cost.

Illustration 13.3 Does behaviour express thoughts and feelings?

An MBA student on a decision-making unit was asked to describe how the appraisal scheme operated at his organisation and how the scheme impacted on his actions. The company is a large local and national employer and the student was a middle manager in the organisation. He described how the managers had to demonstrate identified essential/desirable behaviours in their communications with their subordinate staff. These behaviours had been determined by senior management as being necessary to help to promote and achieve the company mission. He was appraised by his immediate line manager in terms of how well he had demonstrated these essential behaviours.

The student disclosed to the MBA group that he did not actually believe in the mission and its associated list of essential behaviours. However, in order to maintain his job security and to earn his annual performance-related pay, he nonetheless attempted to demonstrate the required behaviours in all his dealings with his subordinates. He was fairly certain that his performance was convincing and his staff had no idea that his enthusiasm for the company mission was anything other than genuine. In Goffman's terms, he kept his cynicism well off-stage (Goffman, 1959).

During the discussion the student, A, indicated that his immediate manager, B, was also assessed in the same manner within the scheme, i.e. his manager's manager, C, appraised B in terms of how well he had demonstrated the essential behaviours in his dealings with the MBA student and his peers. In fact, this procedure operated right to the top of the organisation's hierarchy.

A was asked if he thought that his manager, B, believed in the mission and the essential behaviours. He replied unreservedly in the affirmative. He was then asked how he knew this to be so. He replied that in all his dealings with him, B was always promoting the mission and its achievement, unreservedly.

'Oh', said the tutor. 'Just like you do with your subordinates?'

The speed with which the proverbial penny dropped for A was unforgettable, as indeed, was his reply:

'**** hell! No one believes it!'

 ## Summary

A great many views exist on the meaning and significance of organisational culture. Some authors are unambiguous about its meaning and clear about ways in which it can be applied in practice to understand the behaviour of people. Some even argue that knowing about culture can allow you to manage change more effectively. Others regard it as a more problematical phenomenon which offers no easily applicable solutions to understanding or managing in organisations. The spectrum of theoretical views is well embraced in Meyerson and Martin's integration/differentiation/fragmentation framework. Whatever your 'home perspective' on culture, there are implications for decision-making. Ultimately, as we have said elsewhere, decision-makers have to act. They share the stage with other actors who may or may not share their values or beliefs. The extent to which these values and beliefs are shared is determined by shared structures of experience, habituated behaviours, traditions and so on that we sometimes call 'culture'. It is, therefore, imperative that we take into consideration the cultural context in which we make decisions.

Decision diary

Refer back to Activity 13.1. Approach a colleague within the organisation you chose to depict in the activity. Ask your colleague to undertake the activity, without referring to your own drawing. Once completed, contrast and compare your representations of the organisation. In Activity 13.1 you were asked to speculate on how others might depict the culture. To what extent were your speculations appropriate in the light of your colleague's depiction?

References

Deal, T.E. and Kennedy, A.A. (1982) *Corporate Culture: The Rites and Rituals of Corporate Life*. Harmondsworth: Penguin.

Dunford, R. (1992) *Organisational Behaviour: An Organisational Analysis Perspective*. Reading, MA: Addison-Wesley.

Frost, P.J., Moore, L.F., Louis, M.R., Lundberg, C.C. and Martin, J. (eds)(1991) *Reframing Organizational Culture*. London: Sage.

Goffman, E. (1959) *The Presentation of Self in Everyday Life*. Harmondsworth: Penguin.

Hofstede, G. (1981) *Culture's Consequences: International Differences in Work-Related Values*. Newbury Park, CA: Sage.

Meyerson, D.E. 'Acknowledging and Uncovering Ambiguities in Cultures' in Frost *et al.* (eds) (1991) *Reframing Organizational Culture*. London: Sage.

Meyerson, D.E. and Martin, J. (1987) 'Cultural Change: An integration of three different views', *Journal of Management Studies*, 24, pp. 623–47.

Morgan, G. (1997) *Images of Organization*, 2nd edition. London: Sage.

Peters, T.J. and Waterman, D.H. (1982) *In Search of Excellence*. London: Harper & Row.

Rosen, M. 'Scholars, Travelers, Thieves: On Concept, Method, and Cunning in Organizational Ethnography' in Frost *et al.* (eds) (1991) *Reframing Organizational Culture*. London: Sage.

Schein, E.H. 'What is Culture?' in Frost *et al.* (eds) (1991) *Reframing Organizational Culture*. London: Sage.

Further reading

You might like to browse through back copies of the journal *Theory, Culture and Society* published by Sage Publications for some stimulating theoretical and practical discussions addressing the topic.

Glossary

Integration perspective: theoretical perspective that assumes culture is unifying and integrative. Conflict is, therefore, regarded as dysfunctional and avoidable.

Fragmentation perspective: theoretical perspective that accepts the existence of alternative forms of culture due to the different orientations, needs and desires of individuals and groups. Therefore, acknowledges the existence of, and potential for, conflict.

Ambiguity perspective: theoretical perspective that challenges the notion of culture as easily intelligible and manageable. Views meanings as transient and fluid. Regards culture as a social construct and, ultimately, as a subjectively defined phenomenon.

14 Ethics

LEARNING OUTCOMES

On completing this chapter you should be able to:

- Evaluate the importance of considering ethical issues as a decision-maker.
- Distinguish different models of ethics in decision-making.
- Develop an understanding of your own preferred ethical models as a decision-maker.

14.1 Introduction

I would not say that social importance is just as important as economic performance, but it is an important factor. We are not something separate – just a body of people founded by some shareholders, operating on their behalf. We are part of the structure of the town we work in and the lives of the people we employ and of the country we live in and I think it is ridiculous to pretend otherwise.

Sir Anthony Pilkington, Chairman, the Pilkington Group (quoted in Bloom, 1994)

Managers and academics are seeing the consideration of ethical issues in making business decisions as increasingly important. This interest is to some extent fuelled by the high public and media interest not only in business activities and events as major and tragic as the Bhopal incident but also in the relatively minor deceptions of small building firms popularised in *Watchdog*-type television programmes. Environmental issues, for example, are being given greater consideration than was previously the case as people are becoming more aware of the scarcity and finiteness of physical resources, a more cynical view is that 'green' issues are being treated as a necessary component of any successful marketing strategy. However, organisations are increasingly being pressured, be it through public opinion or government legislation, to take on board the concept of sustainability of resources. At an operational level this may entail, for example, financial penalties on the disposal of waste or financial incentives on the productive use of by-products.

Environmental issues are, however, only one particular facet of ethics. Most, if not all, decision-makers are at some stage confronted with a dilemma that highlights the often contradictory forces placed on the decision-maker to act in ways that do not conform to his or her personal beliefs and values. What does one do in such circumstances? There can be no one correct answer to such a question and numerous case studies have shown that individuals manage such dilemmas in different ways.

This chapter reviews the nature of ethical judgements and provides a framework that we can work within, to guide us through this complex area of decision-making. We provide no answers to ethical dilemmas, but attempt to clarify different theoretical ethical models that exist. It is hoped that this will to some extent help you to contextualise the ethical issues that may confront you as a decision-maker. This may even help you to identify with greater clarity the issues facing you and perhaps help you to make more informed decisions.

14.2 Ethical theories and moral choice

For many people, 'ethical' means 'my feelings tell me it's right'. Feelings are a very individualist and subjective thing, but shaped by and conforming to cultural issues. For some, feelings will include deeply held religious or spiritual beliefs; for others loyalty towards the well-being of the family unit may be the primary factor. For the organisation there is sometimes a conflict of interests, between the good of the company, the people within it as individuals, and the environment.

What is right and good has long been a source of debate. Socrates, 2,500 years ago, believed that we could educate people to act in ethical ways. Kohlberg (1981) also believed in this and provides a 'philosophy of moral development', which, although flawed in the original concept, provides a developmental path of reasoning that can be linked to educational achievement.

Forty years ago managerial loyalty was dedicated to the maximisation of profit. Its duty to society was only to provide wealth in terms of jobs for the employees and profits for the shareholders, within the boundaries of the laws of the land and accepted business practice. Friedman (1970) offers a realistic and often used get-out approach to decision-making. Decisions are justified by the quantified benefits to the firm: 'there is one and only one social responsibility of business – to use its resources and engage in activities designed to increase its profits so long as it stays within the rules of the game, which is to say engages in open and free competition without deception and fraud.' This statement has direct roots to Adam Smith's view of the business community. In the *Wealth of Nations* (published in 1776), Smith saw a natural balance, between individual initiative and desire for profit, being checked by others' desire to do the same. A moment's reflection suggests that moral integrity has to be the norm for business conduct. If lying, cheating and acting without respect for others were normal business behaviour, there would be few customers. Suppliers would ask for money before providing a service and employers would not trust employees. Business would soon grind to a halt. What this approach does not take into account is the qualitative aspects of the decision. For example, it is too easy to dismiss the free trip to the sea for the underprivileged children on cost grounds, and overlook the potential for generating goodwill in the community in which the company operates. It is difficult for managers to justify this approach in an environment that forces them continually to address the bottom line. Some companies can reconcile this issue by having policies, as illustrated later by Owen when referring to the General Electric Company, which actively promote community innovations. Budgets are set up to cater for these issues. The issues are managed so that the firm does get a return in the form of publicity.

However, although business operates in the short term with moral integrity with close groups and organisations, the boundaries have expanded. Companies talk in terms of stakeholders – all the groups that may have a vested interest in the way in which the firm carries out its business – other than the single share-holder body. These stakeholders include employees, suppliers, customers, the local community, and pressure groups such as environmentalists. Few of these groups have the firm's profit maximisation as their central interest. Indeed, shareholders themselves cannot be viewed as a single body and hence may not have a simple profit-centred view of the firm. Shareholders may include share-clubs, employees, investors attracted to 'ethical' or alternative business ventures.

Activity 14.1	Write down your own definition of ethics.

We are assuming that you found it difficult to come up with a definition in Activity 14.1. Indeed, it could be argued that trying to define the subject is not as beneficial a task as attempting to explore it. We attempt to do the latter in this chapter. You are probably about to encounter a 'new language' as we start to examine ethics in more detail.

The modern study of ethics is an amalgam of hundreds of years of ethical thought, from Stoicism through to universal laws. These dimensions help frame the ethical mix shown in Figure 14.1; the relative importance of each of the elements will constitute each person's ethical mix.

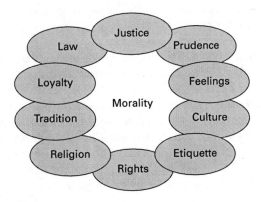

Figure 14.1 Ethical dimensions

The *Oxford English Dictionary* defines ethics as the 'science of morals in human conduct'. It defines morals as 'concerned with the goodness, or badness, of human character, or behaviour, or with the distinction between right and wrong'. The definitions are largely interchangeable. As individuals, we are all likely to have different perspectives on right and wrong but, for many, these perspectives are shaped by the society we live in, i.e. the religious beliefs, the laws, the culture and traditions. Personal morals are shaped by experience; collective experience shapes the ethics of a society. Business ethics are then drawn from the laws and values of individuals and society. Ethics and culture are inextricably intertwined, both being related to the basic attitudes, values and assumptions of individuals and societies. These definitions do not much help us to understand what ethics actually is, or how it relates to a business. One way to describe the difference between morals and ethics is to describe morals as those standards of behaviour an individual adopts, and ethics as relating to the underlying debate and study around moral philosophy. Integrity may be when the two converge.

14.2.1 Historical development of ethical thought

We can categorise ethical writing into two streams: popularist, where ethical issues are drawn to people's attention through novels and journalistic activities, and philosophical, where great thinkers attempt to develop ways to determine right from wrong.

Many writers of popular fiction have used ethics and moral values as a source of tension in their writings. For example, Jonathan Swift's description of the Yahoo's in *Gulliver's Travels* (published 1726) epitomises the worst of human behaviour in the eighteenth century, and authors such as Emile Zola in France and George Orwell in England describe perceived immoral behaviour of authorities. Awareness of ethical issues was brought to popular attention in Victorian times by writers such as Charles Dickens. His books, littered with reprehensible behaviour by many of the characters, served not only a romantic purpose, but were also a damning criticism of elements of society at the time. In the preface to *Nicholas Nickleby*, Dickens says in respect to schools:

> The author's object in calling public attention to the system would be very imperfectly fulfilled if he did not state now, in his own person, emphatically and earnestly, that Mr. Squeers and his school are faint and feeble pictures of an existing reality, purposely subdued and kept down lest they should be deemed impossible.

Much of the anti-social behaviour described by these authors has been prohibited by law, and in modern times replaced by a service culture. It has taken a set of disasters – the Exxon Valdez oil disaster, Union Carbide at Bhopal, India, the Zeebrugge ferry disaster (mentioned in Chapter 4) – to make firms and governing bodies consider the wider social implications of what they are doing.

If you pause to think, most books have an element of moral dilemma in them. These moral dilemmas are the driving force behind most soap operas on television. We are all intrigued as to how others react to these situations and we like to compare their responses with our own.

Activity 14.2   Dickens was 'whistle-blowing' on society, drawing attention to the apparent blindness of society in general to unacceptable behaviour. Dickens had little to lose in this respect, as he was not financially connected with the enterprises he castigates. How would you as an individual react if you disagreed on moral or ethical grounds with the activities of your employer? For example, if you worked for a food company and you suspected that the company was legally using a compound that induces a mild addiction to its products?

Activity 14.3   Try to recall some works of fiction you have read, or dramas you have watched, where ethical issues take a leading role in the development of the story. List these and briefly describe the ethical issue in question.

14.3   Stakeholder analysis

One of the earliest statements on business ethics, and a precursor to stakeholder analysis, was made by Owen D. Young in 1929 when he was head of the General Electric Company and quoted by Kerr (1996: 1013):

> It makes a great difference in my attitude toward my job as an executive officer of the General Electric Company whether I am a trustee of the institution, or an attorney for the investor. If I am trustee, who are the beneficiaries of the trust? To whom do I owe my obligations? My conception of it is this: That there are three groups of people that have an interest in that situation. One is that group of fifty-odd thousand people who have put their capital into the company, namely its shareholders. Another is a group of well toward one hundred thousand people who are putting their labour and their lives into the business of the company. The third group is of customers and the general public. Customers have a right to demand that a concern so large shall not only do its business honestly and properly, but, further, that it shall meet its public obligations and perform its public duties ... in a word, vast as it is, that it should be a good citizen.

The statement by Young has since been expanded and includes other major groups such as suppliers and even competing firms. Ethical issues often are of profound importance to pressure groups, such as environmentalists. A decision by Shell to dump an oil platform at sea generated a lot of negative publicity. Greenpeace, a pressure group, produced figures that related to the environmental impact and as a result some customers boycotted the company. The company then reversed its decision. It has since been an issue of debate as to who was correct in the estimation of environmental impact.

Activity 14.4   See if you can identify the internal and external individuals, groups and other organisations that you consider to be important stakeholders in your own organisation.

Go back to the list of stakeholders you provided in Activity 14.4. Think of a recent decision and try to rank those stakeholders in order of the importance you placed on each of them, either consciously or subconsciously, at the time of making your decision.

The most powerful stakeholders in terms of decision-making are managers. In *Readings in Strategic Management*, Michael Porter (1989) refers to a series of high profile mergers and acquisitions and concludes that 'only the lawyers, investment bankers and original sellers have prospered in most of these acquisitions, not the shareholders'. Managers are key stakeholders in organisations and therefore play a significant role in decision-making. In a survey published in 1980, it was found that 80 per cent of acquisitions resulted in falling profits, and therefore a reduction rather than an increase in dividend returns to shareholders. Research into the proliferation of acquisitions and mergers in the UK in the 1980s seemed to confirm this correlation. Research has also suggested that one important stakeholder group usually does benefit from merger activity: the senior managers from the acquiring organisation. It is worth distinguishing between profitability and growth. Organisations may indeed become less profitable as a result of merger activity but the likelihood is that the managers in the dominant organisation will be left with larger budgets and increased power and status. These are important motives for management action.

14.4 Behaviour and responsibility

Albert Carr (1968) suggests that 'the ethics of business are not those of society, but rather those of the poker game'. He puts forward the argument that business ethics are of necessity different from those of society in general. Businesses cannot afford to be ethically sensitive. The world of business is amoral because of its competitiveness: only the ruthless and purposeful will survive. Likening business to a poker game, certain behaviours are unacceptable, such as keeping an ace up your sleeve, but other behaviours are part of the game, such as distrust, ignoring friendships, deceptions and concealment.

14.4.1 Tit for tat

Robert Axelrod (1984) provides an interesting insight into cooperative practices between people (businesses?). Starting from a basic egoistic assumption – that we are all selfish – which is the best strategy for promoting cooperation? His research, based on the 'prisoners' dilemma, showed that tit-for-tat was the most consistently successful strategy.

The prisoners' dilemma situation is easily turned into a game by having two players with counters, C (cooperate) and D (defect). The rules are simple:

1 Try to get the highest score you can.
2 Do not reveal your intentions until your counter is displayed.
3 Score as follows: both cooperate = 3 points each.

4 Both defect = 1 point each.

5 1 defect 1 cooperate = defect 5, cooperate 0.

When examined closely tit-for-tat reveals four winning principles:

1 Be nice – never be the first to be nasty; be optimistic about human nature.

2 Be provocable – always respond to nastiness with nastiness.

3 Be forgiving – always accept peace offerings from the nasty with forgiveness.

4 Be clear – always allow the other side to know exactly what you will do.

These strategies work even when neither side is basically altruistic. Given the prisoners' dilemma situation, those who learn to cooperate consistently make the highest scores.

The factors affecting behaviour appear to be:

1 Predictability – knowing what others will do increases cooperation.

2 Certainty of future intention – where this is not present, the future holds no threat to defection.

3 Frequency of interaction – the more frequent, the more cooperative.

4 Identifiability of partner – the more identifiable, the more cooperative.

Axelrod points to some measures to improve cooperativeness:

1 Enlarge the shadow of the future – make future considerations at least as important as immediate gains.

2 Change the pay-offs – make it more profitable to cooperate and less to defect.

3 Teach people to care – through socialisation, habit formation and social ethos.

4 Teach reciprocity – show people how nice strategies benefit everyone.

5 Improve recognition abilities – what is being done and who is doing it.

The way in which managers behave ethically can be related in some respects to their leadership style. Christie and Gers (1970), for example, have identified styles based on the sixteenth-century writings of Niccolò Machiavelli. People are judged to have a high or low MACH, in respect to tactics, people and morality.

Activity 14.6	Imagine you are in a room with two other people. Someone comes in and puts £3,000 on a table to be distributed in any way the group decides. The game is over when two of you agree on the split. The fairest way would be to spilt the money evenly £1,000 each. Before you suggest this, one of the others suggests a split between you and them £1,500 each. Before you respond the other person suggests a £1,600/£1,400 split between you and them. How do you respond?

Your response to Activity 14.6 will to some extent reflect your tendency towards Machiavellianism. Niccolò Machiavelli, who might be viewed as an early political scientist, offered advice to rulers in his book *Il principe* (1513; *The Prince*), as to what they must do to achieve their aims and secure their power. Its relevance to ethics lies in the significance that it ignores usual ethical rules. 'It is necessary for a prince, who wishes to maintain himself, to learn how not to be good, and to use this knowledge and not use it, according to the necessities of the case.' It may be a satirical critique of the rulers of the time, but has now become synonymous with political cynicism, corruption and deviousness. Its value lies in the wider appreciation of the differences between the esoteric ethical theories of the philosophers and the realities of political (or business) life.

14.4.2 Ethics: a framework for analysis

We can categorise approaches to ethics into two broad themes: subjective and objective. Within the objective approach we either try to evaluate the outcomes of a decision with a cognitive approach, or we try to apply a uniform, rule-based system to help guide us in the 'right' way.

Subjective

Emotivism

How it feels to me. Individual conscience can be used to define right or wrong. This does not in any way counsel us on how our conscience should be informed and in that sense does not offer a theory of ethics. The obvious criticism is that we can do anything and if we think it is right, it is right. We cannot criticise the fanatic who commits a felony if he explains 'my conscience told me to do it'.

Wang Shou-jen, a Chinese philosopher, provides an eastern parallel with *intuitive knowledge* (of right and wrong). A story illustrates the meaning.

> A student of Wang Shou-jen caught a thief in his house and proceeded to give him a lecture on intuitive knowledge. The thief laughed and demanded to be shown where this intuitive knowledge was. The weather was hot and the student invited the thief to remove his coat, then his shirt. He continued, 'It's still too hot, why not take off your trousers?' The thief hesitated and replied, 'That does not seem quite right.' Thereupon the captor shouted: 'There is your intuitive knowledge!'

Egoism

What is in my best interest? Egoism says that an act is right when it best promotes the individual's long-term self-interest. In most instances this will result in responsible behaviour. For example, the egoist will avoid intemperance or injuring others, because they will be wary of the harms they may suffer if the anti-social behaviour rebounds on them. This breaks down if the egoist is in a powerful position where he or she can avoid recriminations, in fact the theory actually promotes violence in this situation as the right thing to do.

Relativism

What is right in the reference culture? Ethical relativism, like egoism, is one of the founding theories. It holds that an act is right when the social group to which one belongs approves it and wrong if it does not. There exists a dialectical relationship between organisational culture and the actions of people within the organisation, in which organisational members create and perpetuate the culture through their actions and interactions, and the culture then takes on a life of its own and acts in turn to influence behaviour and actions. Cultures, be they national or organisational, vary in terms of accepted and expected behaviours. Ethical relativism is a term used to describe the notion that an ethical behaviour may be grounded in terms of culture and therefore what is regarded as acceptable ethical behaviour in one organisation may be frowned upon in a different organisation.

A criticism of this theory is that a relativist will approve of actions performed by other societies if those actions are approved by that society (if they honour the belief, otherwise they would be deemed hypocritical). For example, if a relativist society believes that capital punishment is wrong for its own society and comes in contact with a society that approves it, then it must then concede that it is right for that society. Another variant is related to cultural differences. If we accept the ethics of other societies when trading abroad, we are sanctioning what may be unacceptable practices back home. The problem is simple: if you believe an action to be fundamentally wrong, can it ever be right in another context? Bribery, child prostitution, atheism cultural clashes, force us to examine priorities.

Activity 14.7	Interview a friend who works in a different organisation. Try to identify subtle differences in ethical behaviours that you put down to organisational culture.

Objective

Teleology/consequentialism

The cognitive or teleological approaches attempt to evaluate the circumstances to help determine the most appropriate actions. The *Oxford English Dictionary* defines teleology as 'the explanation of phenomena by the purpose they serve, rather than postulated causes'. Teleological theories are *consequentialist* because they take the consequence of the decision into account. The goal-centred approach does not set rules, but has as its major thrust the likely outcomes of a decision.

Utilitarianism

If the consequence can be measured by the value of the decision, we can describe that as its utility, hence the branch of teleology known as *utilitarianism*. Solomon (from the Christian Bible) displayed an example of utilitarianism (giving the most value to the most people) when he decreed that the baby should be divided in two (hoping, of course, that the real mother would not allow this, and hence arriving at a wise judgement). In teleology we try to maximise the value of the decision in the light of the benefits to those who will be affected by it. One of the criticisms of decisions for the greater good is that individual rights of minorities are sometimes overlooked. In the Solomon example, the rights of the child were not taken into account. Solomon may in fact have been demonstrating a variety of machiavellian wisdom, by arguing that the ends justify the means.

Utilitarianism takes many forms developed by a variety of philosophers, generally an action is right if:

■ Utilitarianism (Mill 1806–73) – that action produces the greatest amount of happiness for the greatest number of persons.

- Negative utilitarianism (Popper, 1902–94) – that action produces the least amount of suffering for the least amount of people.
- Preference utilitarianism – it satisfies the greatest number of people's needs and wants.
- Interest utilitarianism (see Parfitt, 1984) – it complies with our own interests (as these have been shaped over time to comply with societal norms and are intuitively right).

Deontology

Deontological (ruled-based) theories are also known as *nonconsequentialist* theories. Deontology revolves around a set of rules that a society has determined demonstrate acceptable behaviour. Society in this respect is a person or group in authority, for example god, parliament, board of governors. The rules are often strict and offer no room for compromise. For example, 'don't lie', 'don't cause pain'. This can cause conflict. For example, a hard-working employee, who is also useless at some aspects of the job and is sensitive to criticism, wonders why she is turned down for promotion. Does the employer explain the situation accurately, knowing that this will depress the employee, or does she lie to minimise the pain? The latter option is, of course, a consequentialist option.

Religious tradition is for many people a major source of ethical guidance. In business there are clearly going to be inadequacies for managerial ethical decision-making. Among the criticisms are the variety of religious teachings and the need for all of them to be interpreted.

Some of the most often quoted rules are those of Immanuel Kant (1724–1804). Kant's famous guide to ethics, the *categorical imperative*, the main focus of which is 'act only on that maxim through which you can at the same time will that it should become a universal law'. This tends to have the following implications:

- People are always treated as ends, never solely as means.
- Goodwill is the only good thing: intention.
- Always and only act as you would have everyone act.

This leads on to human rights as the counter to tyrannical abuse of power. Kant's respect of persons breaks down and sometimes has to acknowledge consequences. For example, thirteen people would drown if they all claim the right to life in a twelve-person life raft. If one has to be thrown out, then all would have to be.

Virtue theory

An alternative view of moral behaviour lies in the seminal work of Alasdair MacIntyre. In *After Virtue*, MacIntrye argues that modern moral thinking is problematical, since we have failed to sustain the tradition of the virtues.

Social contracts

Social contract theory is the view that morality is founded solely on uniform social agreements that serve the best interests of those who make the agreement. Social contract theory has evolved from natural law theory, specifically the theories of Grotius and Pufendorf. Plato (c. 427–347 BC) hints social contractarian themes within Book 2 of *The Republic*. One character, Glaucon, recognises that it is good for us individually to be unjust, although it is bad for us individually to suffer. We also recognise that if we do act unjustly, we will suffer injuries from other people. To avoid suffering injury, then, we should make contracts with each other by which we give up injustice and practise justice.

The definitive statement of social contract theory is found in Hobbes' *Leviathan*. Hobbes (1588–1679) argues that the original state of nature is a condition of constant war, which rational and self-motivated people would want to end. These people, then, will establish fundamental moral laws to preserve peace. The foundation of Hobbes' theory is the view that humans are psychologically motivated by only selfish interests. Hobbes argued that, for purely selfish reasons, the agent is better off living in a world with moral rules than in one without. Without moral rules, we are subject to the whims of other people's selfish interests. Our property, our families, and even our lives are at continual risk. Selfishness alone will therefore motivate each agent to adopt a basic set of rules which will allow for a civilised community.

There are several traditional criticisms of Hobbes' theory. First, critics questioned whether humans are as self-interested as Hobbes contends: many people have transcendent interests which focus on social, religious or political communities. Second, it is not clear that people who are fundamentally equal in the state of nature would be rationally motivated to attack each other, given only a 50/50 chance of survival. Third, the moral rules arrived at make demands of an agent which go beyond what is necessary for an agent's self-preservation, which is that agent's sole motive for making the contract. Fourth, the moral rules arrived at are only rules of prudence for people motivated by egoistic concerns. Thus, it is difficult to call this a 'moral' theory. Finally, it is not clear why we should consistently follow a moral rule (such as a prohibition against stealing) if we can occasionally violate that rule without being caught. Further, since we are motivated only by self-interest, we would have strong reasons to occasionally violate rules when that served our interests. Social contract theory, then, will obligate us to follow moral rules only to the point where it is necessary to keep society together. And this makes it a fairly weak normative theory.

Other social contract theories

After Hobbes, social contract theory developed in different directions. John Locke argued that the state of nature is a pre-political, yet moral, society where humans are bound by divinely given natural law. A social contract is made between citizens who institute a government to prevent people from occasionally violating natural law and showing partiality. Jean-Jacques Rousseau (1712–78) argued that the state of nature is not a state of war, but a state of individual freedom where creativity flourishes. Since a fully mature person is a social person, a social contract is established to regulate social interaction. This contract between citizens establishes an absolute democracy which is ruled by the general will, or what is best for all people.

Interest in social contract theory declined in the nineteenth century with the rise of utilitarianism, the theory that actions are right when they produce more benefit than disbenefit for society. Contemporary versions of social contract theory attempt to show that our basic rights and liberties are founded on mutually beneficial agreements which are made between members of society. John Rawls argues in *A Theory of Justice* (1971) that, in an original position, a group of rational and impartial people will establish a mutually beneficial principle of justice as the foundation for regulating all rights, duties, power and wealth.

A recent model for social contracts comes from Green (1994), who has proposed an alternative method for businesses to manage their ethical responsibilities. Neutral, omni-partial rule-making (known as NORM) attempts to define a methodology for establishing the moral rules of the firm. It has its roots in early philosophical thinking, particularly that of Kant. The guiding principle for NORM is: an action is right if it might be reasonably be thought of as being accepted by all members of society as a moral rule, that is, an abiding form of conduct known by everyone and open to everyone in similar circumstances.

NORM combines elements of deontological and teleological approaches. One advantage of this approach is that everyone is included. All the minority parties involved will accept the rules created under this system. This avoids one of the problems created by utilitarianism, the danger of whistle-blowing. To illustrate this, Green (1994) uses a case, the 'Desert island promise' (see Illustration 14.1).

Illustration 14.1 The desert island promise

A charter pilot and his elderly passenger are flying across a distant tropical sea when the plane's engine malfunctions and it crashes into the water near a desert island. Managing to make it ashore, the pilot and his passenger are stranded for weeks.

During their stay, the passenger reveals to the pilot that, as a hobby back home, he cultivates orchids in his garden. The plants, which he admits are not rare, or otherwise valuable, may survive a few more months on their own, but will eventually need care.

Several weeks go by and the passenger falls ill and is near death. He tells the pilot that he is extremely worried about who will take care of his orchids in the future, if he dies. He also reveals to the pilot that buried in a secret location in his garden is a sack of coins worth several thousand pounds.

'If I die and you survive,' he asks the pilot, 'will you make me a solemn promise? Please, locate the money and use it to endow perpetual care for my orchids. It is deeply, deeply important to me that these flowers do not perish.'

Looking into the pained eyes of the passenger, the pilot solemnly agrees. With a look of relief and gratitude on his face, the passenger dies. The pilot remains on the island for several more weeks and is eventually rescued. Returning to civilisation he visits the orchid-grower's home and locates the buried money. Debating in his mind whether he should donate the sum of money to a local charity, or merely use it to buy himself a new car, he leaves the garden – but not before ripping up the orchids and throwing them onto the compost heap.

Activity 14.8   For the desert island promise, can you justify on ethical grounds the behaviour of the pilot?

A utilitarian approach to ethical decision-making is displayed throughout Illustration 14.1. The decision-maker, the pilot, is always acting to maximise human happiness. Deontologically it is wrong to lie, or break promises, hence a deontological solution is difficult without the pilot suffering a guilty conscience when he pulls up the flowers.

NORM attempts to mitigate this type of conflict by pre-empting it – a difficult process when one is dealing with such an abstract situation, but the principles are valid. NORM uses a methodological approach that proposes moral rules and then examines their validity under a number of circumstances. The rules are updated and modified until an acceptable rule is obtained.

A proposed moral rule for the desert island problem might read as follows:

- 'It is right to break a promise to someone who is dying, if breaking the promise will do greater good later on.'

One of the problems with this rule is that it invalidates wills: deathbed wishes could no longer be treated as sacrosanct. Hence this rule would be rejected by some in society. An alternative may be proposed:

- 'Someone who has made a deathbed promise may not break that promise no matter what circumstances prevail later.'

This, on the face of it, appears a reasonable rule with no obvious serious drawbacks; most people could abide by it. However, there may be occasions when complying with the rule will harm society. For example, if the orchids were later to be found to be carrying some deadly disease, we might propose an exception to the rule:

- 'Someone who has made a promise to a dying person may break that promise if, by keeping it, it is likely to cause serious harm to society.'

NORM uses a commonsense approach to setting rules for conduct that may be encountered in the business. Green (1994), for example proposes a rule for business abroad:

- 'A businessperson, who is threatened with physical violence unless he or she becomes a party to fraud and embezzlement, may participate in these activities to the extent needed to ward off the threat.'

The above deontology-teleology theoretical model is a useful way in which to conceptualise the discussion on ethics.

14.5 Ethical development

The American psychologist Lawrence Kohlberg (1981) hypothesised that people's development of moral standards passes through stages that can be grouped into six moral levels. At the early level, that of preconventional moral reasoning, the child uses external and physical events such as pleasure, pain or punishment as the source for decisions about moral rightness or wrongness; the child's standards are based strictly on what will avoid punishment or bring pleasure. At the second stage, standards are based on personal outcomes, either the action is worth or not worth the person's efforts. At a third, that of conventional moral reasoning, the child or adolescent views moral standards as a way of maintaining the approval of authority figures, chiefly parents, and acts in accordance with their precepts. Moral standards at this level are held to rest on a positive evaluation of authority rather than on a simple fear of punishment. At the fourth stage, authority is deemed to include legal contracts. At the fifth stage the boundaries of approval extend to general society. At the final level, that of post-conventional moral reasoning, the adult bases his moral standards on principles that he himself has evaluated and that he accepts as inherently valid, regardless of society's opinion. The person is aware of the arbitrary, subjective nature of social standards and rules, which he regards as relative rather than absolute in authority.

Thus the bases for justifying moral standards pass from self-centred actions through a greater awareness of external actions, which tends to lead to an avoidance of adult disapproval and rejection to avoidance of internal guilt and self-recrimination. The person's moral reasoning also moves towards increasingly greater social scope (i.e. including more people and institutions) and greater abstraction (i.e. from reasoning about physical events such as pain or pleasure to reasoning about values, rights and implicit contracts). This transition from one stage to the next is characterised by gradual shifts in the most frequent type of reasoning; thus, at any given point in life, a person may function at more than one stage at the same time. Different people pass through the stages at varying rates. Finally, different people are likely to reach different levels of moral thinking in their lives, raising the possibility that some people may never reach the later, more abstract, stages.

The evidence for these theoretical stages comes from children's answers to moral dilemmas verbally presented to them by researchers, rather than their actual behaviour in time of conflict. Scientists have argued that many children display a more profound moral understanding than is evident in their responses on such tests. Others have argued that because even very young children are capable of showing empathy with the pain of others, the inhibition of aggressive behaviour arises from this moral affect rather than from the mere anticipation of punishment. Some scientists have found that children differ in their individual capacity for empathy, and, therefore, some children are more sensitive to moral prohibitions than others. There is evidence suggesting that temperamentally inhibited children whose parents impose consistent socialisation demands on them experience moral affect more intensely than do other children.

Carol Gilligan (1993) has proposed that, as well as Kohlberg's three stages of development (selfish, belief in conventional morality, postconventional), there are differences between males and females. These differences reflect elements of social conditioning and hence the ethical behaviour. Founded primarily on interview research, Gilligan has found that men and women use fundamentally different approaches. Since men have dominated the discussion of moral theory, the women's approach is often not taken seriously and is considered to be less developed and sophisticated.

However you rank the statements in Activity 14.9, the exercise serves to illustrate the problems of judging ethical behaviour. How can we attempt to systematise everyday behaviour into patterns which do not ultimately help with everyday practice and which reflect a series of conflicting ethical traditions? How can we:

- salute the perfection of an Olympic gold medal winner;
- apply utilitarian principles in the principle of triage to the wounded in war;
- be religious in idealising charity, compassion and equal moral worth;
- follow Kant and Mill in affirming personal autonomy?

Activity 14.9   At the time of his trial in 1961, Adolf Eichmann (the Nazi chief executioner), made a number of statements. Try to rank these in terms of Kohlberg's level of moral reasoning:

1 'In actual fact, I was merely a little cog in the machinery that carried out the directives of the German Reich.'

2 'I must say truthfully that if we had killed all the 10 million Jews that Himmler's statisticians originally listed, I would say "Good, we have destroyed an enemy". Where would we have been if everyone had thought things out in those days? You can do that in the "new" German army. But with us an order was an order.'

3 'If I had sabotaged the order of the one-time Fuhrer of the German Reich, Adolf Hitler, I would have been not only a scoundrel, but a despicable pig like those who broke their military oath to join the ranks of the anti-Hitler criminals in the conspiracy of 20 July 1944.'

4 'I never met him [Hitler] personally, but his success alone proves to me that I should subordinate myself to this man. He was somehow so supremely capable that the people recognised him. And with that justification I recognised him joyfully, and I still defend him.'

Business ethics is an increasingly discussed subject. You should find plenty of newspaper articles that deal with ethical issues either in business or wider society. We recommend that you scan as many newspapers as possible and cut out articles that you think highlight ethical issues. Two examples, both from a local paper, are provided in Illustration 14.2.

Table 14.1 summarises the arguments that you might put forward in your answer to Activity 14.10.

Activity 14.10 demonstrates the problems of defining the benefits of a decision: what is good for one sector of the community is bad for another. Where do we draw the boundaries? Should we view the decision on a world basis and consider those workers in South America and the pollution effects in Sweden? Ethical issues often have many sides to their argument.

One of the problems with utilitarianism is that it ignores the rights of the individual or minority group. For example, if an employee has to lie for his company regarding a certain situation, it may be for the best utilitarian reasons, but for the individual is morally wrong, as it is generally thought to be wrong to lie and deceive.

> **Illustration 14.2 Local ethical issues**
>
> **Party pooper**
>
> Nightclub dance floors across East Yorkshire could be deserted on New Year's Eve, because of archaic licensing laws. Club bosses in Hull have been told that they are unlikely to be allowed to serve drinks beyond 12.30 am on the big night due to the event falling on a Sunday. [A manager comments] 'These evenings are without doubt very special occasions and to deny the people of Hull the opportunity to celebrate them into the early hours will also leave many revellers disappointed.'
>
> **Marina plan is not plain sailing**
>
> Residents are divided into two clear camps on the issue of Bridlington's proposed £60m marina.
>
> Supporters insist it will bring more jobs and prosperity, and give the resort a bright new future.
>
> Objectors, however, are equally convinced it will rob the beaches of sand, play havoc with tidal flow and accelerate erosion.
>
> Source: *Hull Daily Mail*, 28 October 2000

Activity 14.10 In Chapter 6, Illustration 6.5 addresses the future of the coal mining industry. Reread this case and argue the decision to retain, or close down, the industry, from an ethical point of view. Categorise the arguments in terms of utilitarianism as indicated by the classification in section 14.4.2.

Table 14.1 Utiliarianism's answers to the future of the coal mining industry

Viewpoint	Argument
Utilitarianism	Keep mines open because, if mines are required then these are the best to keep open because of local and national community issues. The environment will suffer, so pollution prevention measures should be fitted to power stations
Negative utilitarianism	Keep mines open because less suffering will ensue not only in local communities, but also for workers abroad, as fewer people will be employed in hazardous conditions
Preference utilitarianism	Shut coal-fired power stations and hence close collieries because the British public will benefit from less pollution and cheaper energy costs
Interest utilitarianism	Subsidies are wrong and the coal industry is subsidised, hence remove subsidies. Free market is the ideal economic model, so deregulate the energy-generating market. Hence, unless the coal industry can compete it will close down

14.6 Green issues

For many companies the chief factor in their management of the environment is the need to stay within the law. Some companies insist that their suppliers have BS 7750 registration (an environmental quality certificate) in order to minimise their liability. Sadgrove (1996) has identified a matrix that positions companies according to their environmental performance (Figure 14.2). After a number of years of environmental hype, where ignorance was replaced by impulsive reactions by companies and governments as they became aware of the issues, firms are becoming more proactive in establishing environmental codes of practice. Sadgrove (1996) predicts a situation where original laws, which were ineffective, will be replaced by stronger legislation and more frequent court actions. This will force companies to adopt more proactive environmental policies.

Logistics issues are often the source of ethical and environmental analysis. They are visible and their effects can be immediately obvious to those they affect. Traffic, for example, causes air pollution, noise pollution, vibration and visual intrusion.

Many firms recognise the strength of feeling often associated with the development of new sites for their businesses, particularly with regard to the impact of increased levels of traffic. Just-in-time delivery, for example, comes in for criticism because of the potentially increased number of journeys to a manufacturer from a supplier. Minimisation of transportation costs has led to the centralisation of warehouses and also to 24-hour deliveries, which have positive environmental benefits. Cooper *et al.* (1991) have found that night-time delivery actually saves around 6 per cent in fuel costs because of increased efficiency.

However, for many environmentalists the main hope rests in legislation. Transport policies need to recognise the benefits of integrated policies that make use of environmentally friendly modes of transport such as rail, combined with efficient nodes (terminal, ports, stations), where materials are split up for road delivery to the final destination.

The use of decision trees (Chapter 2) is a useful way to try to quantify, or at least list, the potential outcomes of a decision. It becomes difficult to put sensible estimates of the probabilities of the outcomes occurring. For example, if an

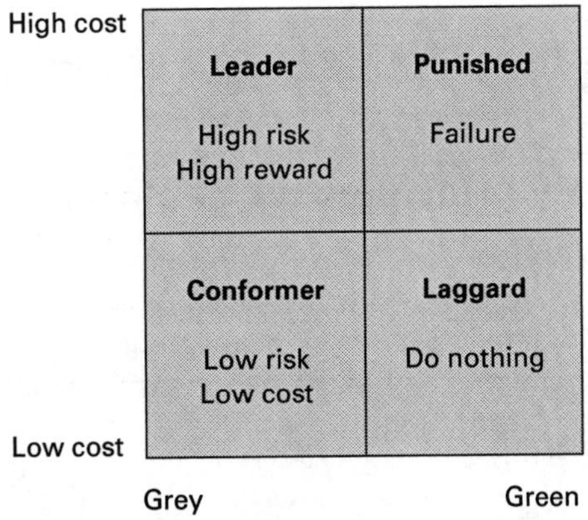

Figure 14.2 The Green Grid

Source: adapted from Sadgrove, K. *The Financial Times Handbook of Management*, with permission of Pearson Education.

outcome is the silting of the lake due to soil erosion, the firm may minimise this by preventative measures if it really becomes a problem. The benefit of using this, or similar methods, is that it helps identify cause and effect, and if we can identify these we are in a better position to do something about them. Of course, we need to identify the issue in the first place. If the colliery owners in the past thought that spoil tips would be a source of pollution and death in the future then they might have been more active in other forms of dirt disposal.

Illustration 14.3 Construction of the Aswan High Dam in Egypt

Many of the great technical achievements have not just brought about the increased value to society used to justify them. Sometimes unexpected undesirable consequences have occurred, which have outweighed the benefits of the initial project. The construction of the Aswan High Dam in Egypt is a possible example.

The dam, intended to enable irrigation and increase output for Egypt, initially increased agricultural production in the Nile Delta. With it came an unprecedented increase in schistosomiasis – a highly debilitating disease spread by water snails that thrive in the irrigation canals. It is claimed that 60% of Egypt's farm-workers (*fellahin*) are affected. Fertile silt, which prior to the building of the dam annually renewed the fertility of the lands it inundated, is now trapped behind the dam. In its place a massive increase in the use of fertilizers is needed to maintain output. That, together with poor drainage causes salinization, annually leaving large tracts of land unsuitable for agriculture. The loss of the silt previously carried past the delta into the Mediterranean has caused the sea to encroach upon the land, leading to further loss of land. The loss of the nutrients, previously fed into the Mediterranean, destroyed the sardine fisheries, which provided an essential part of the nation's diet. Finally, uncontrollable growth of water hyacinth in Lake Nasser causes excessive loss of water through evaporation. So the erection of the dam had a number of unexpected consequences, some of them disastrous. None were predicted and taken into account when the dam was erected. The decision to build the dam was largely a political power play between the USA and the old USSR, both hoping to incorporate Egypt within their sphere of influence.

Source: Daellenbach, 1994: 112

Activity 14.11   Use Illustration 14.3 to construct a decision tree.

14.6.1 Twenty principles for debate

The following classification of ethical ways of doing things, based on Hellriegel *et al.* (1995: 617), is formed from a survey of individuals from business, philosophical, religious and political arenas. To a great extent, the principles identified fit into the deontological-teleological classification. For example, number 5 is based on deontological reasoning if 'gut feeling' can be regarded as synonymous with 'established principles internalised by the individual through the socialisation process'. They demonstrate, to some extent, the 'as is' element of ethics as apposed to the 'should be' situation.

1 *Hedonist principle – if it feels good do it.* What feels pleasurable is not necessarily good for you or for anyone else; and by concentrating on your pleasure, you lose sight of the medium- and long-term consequences. It is the ethics of drug addiction.

2 *Psychological egoism – maximise one's personal gain and pleasure.* How would you feel if everyone attempted to maximise their personal gain and pleasure, which you would have to allow? People's maximisations would inevitably conflict at some stage, and there would be no means of resolving them.

3 *Might-equals-right principle – you are strong enough to take advantage without respect to ordinary social conventions and widespread practices or customs.* What kind of society would we live in if this were the dominant principle? Would you be willing to live with this situation if you were not the most powerful? It is the ethics of the tyrant.

4 *Conventionalist principle – obey the formal rules of your organisation and the laws of the land.* Can the law or any set of rules cover every ethical situation or dilemma? Are there not bad laws and bad rules? Should we have obeyed the laws in Nazi Germany, or rules in an organisation which break fundamental beliefs (such as a commitment against discrimination)?

5 *Intuition principle – go with your 'gut feeling' or what you understand to be right in a given situation.* How far is this sufficient? Does one not need to come to a decision at some time? How open and reflective can one be, given the myriad ways one's existence and perception of the world is determined?

6 *Organisation ethics principle – ask whether actions are consistent with organisation goals and do what is good for the organisation.* The interests of one's own organisation may not coincide with the wider good; the regulatory framework constraining the practices of ones' company may, for instance, not be strong enough to prevent considerable ecological damage.

7 *Means–end principle (the programmatic ethic) – ask whether some overall good justifies any moral transgression.* This has led to the Gulags in Soviet Russia and to ethnic cleansing in Bosnia. By allowing the adoption of any means, you may well destroy the possibility of an ethical end. It is the ethics of those denying an adherence to ethics in the means.

8 *Maximin principle – minimise the pain suffered by those worst affected by means of actions designed for the greater good.* If we attempt to build a society on this principle, will we ever provide enough incentive to the higher achievers? Is there a fixed constant that society can achieve? Will this amount be depressed by fixating on the poorer members of society; will it not be increased – and to their benefit – by concentrating on those who can contribute most to society?

9 *The principle of utilitarianism – act so as to help to produce the greatest happiness for the greatest number.* How does one measure happiness? Will one person's happiness (and capacity for it) be the same as another's? Should one cause severe hardship to one group if overall it causes the greatest happiness – such as imposing slavery? If we accept it, can any act be described as evil – will that not depend on how we measure the happiness/unhappiness it produces? It is the ethics of the arena.

10 *Professional ethics principle – do only that which can be explained or justified before a group of your peers.* This has to assume altruism by the profession towards clients and society, which cannot be guaranteed. Even if such a panel included interested lay members, there is no guarantee that they will fully understand professional discourse, nor any guarantee that the standards of one profession hold for another.

11 *The compliance ethic – obey the wishes of the most powerful.* This is the behaviour that all tyrants and autocrats want to see in other people – an open invitation to do what they want with no one standing against them. It is the ethics of the coward.

12 *Disclosure principle – ask how it would feel if the thinking and details of the decision were disclosed to a wide audience.* This ethic may simply encourage one to focus on public image, rather than attending to matters of conscience. Additionally, it may prevent one from taking account of concerns which are not the concern of the focal audience.

13 *Distributive justice principle – an individual's treatment should not be based on arbitrarily defined characteristics; apply rules designed to be fair to all.* What does 'fair' mean? Ought one to give everyone an equal share? Do you give more to one than another because of particular needs? Does everyone have a right to a basic minimum? Should we give more to individuals if their contribution to society is seen as more valuable than someone else's? Or should we base fairness on the attainment of some level of skill and knowledge?

14 *Categorical imperative principle – act in a way you believe is right and just for any other person in a similar situation.* Are there ever two situations so alike that one can say that one should adopt precisely the same decision and behaviour again? And if there is not, how useful is the principle in practice? Does it remain at such a general level that it has little practical use?

15 *Golden rule principle – do as you would be done by; look at the problem from the position of another person affected by the decision and try to determine what response the other person would expect as most virtuous.* But will others want what you want: is this not self-centred and probably culturally biased, and thus might it not impose unwanted attentions upon others?

16 *The principle of pluralism – act to preserve the rights of different groups with varied and possibly opposing values and aims.* Does this mean that we preserve the rights of groups to impose their values upon other groups? Do we sanction the right of any groups to impose their will upon individuals within that particular group? Should we tolerate the acts of a group if we totally disagree with their acts, even if everyone within the group agrees to the values and aims, and no one interferes with other groups?

17 *Autonomy – respect the right of others to decide for themselves what they think is right, wrong, forbidden or required, provided that they grant others this respect.* Can everyone have their own way all of the time? Can an organisation allow everyone to decide for themselves – could it function? What happens when decisions by different individuals collide?

18 *Altruism and empathy – attend to another's special need.* Will attention upon particular individuals prevent a necessary regard to wider concerns within society and the world at large?

19 *The ethic of professional reputation – act to futher the aims and interests of one's professional community.* Similar to the professional ethic, there is no guarantee that the profession will act in an altruistic way towards clients and society. It may be that the profession may abuse its position by acting to further its own aims and interests which may then make situations worse.

20 *The communal principle – act as member of a world community of beings valued in their own right.* Can one always treat people as an end in themselves? Does not the fact that we live our lives in and through organisations, mean that for much of the time we necessarily have to treat others, and expect to be treated, as a means to ends?

Activity 14.12   For some dilemmas that you are familiar with, how does each of the 20 principles affect the decision being made? For example, shall we punish a person for smoking cannabis for pleasure? If the person finds that cannabis alleviates a medical condition, should we punish him or her? How is it best to spend a limited healthcare budget within a hospital ward?

14.7   Case studies

The following five case studies have been gathered from a variety of sources. You are asked to perform an analysis of each of the situations. You should refer to relevant ethical theoretical frameworks. We have begun the analysis of Case 1 to demonstrate how you might apply ethical theories to the cases. We are grateful to David Simon for permission to use these cases.

14.7.1   Case 1: A taxing situation

An Inland Revenue inspector purchased a used car at an auction. Shortly after purchase the car became faulty. He returned to the car auction and challenged the seller to rectify the fault. The seller immediately denied responsibility, claiming that he was a private individual and not a car dealer. At the time the law afforded considerably less protection to purchasers who bought goods from a private seller than those who bought from a dealer.

When it became apparent to the tax inspector that he was not going to receive a satisfactory outcome to his complaint he went to his local trading standards officer (TSO) to ask for help in resolving the matter. Although the tax inspector could give details of the seller's name, knew that he operated out of a lock-up garage and frequented the city car auction, he could not provide a 'good' address for the dealer. The inspector confided in the TSO that he had accessed the appropriate Inland Revenue files to find an address for the dealer but had been shocked to discover that according to their records, he did not exist. This meant that not only was the dealer avoiding his legal liabilities as one who sold motor vehicles in the course of a trade or business, but he was also managing not to pay any income tax.

The TSO investigated the matter. He was able through his inquiries to trace the dealer to the lock-up garage but could never find him on the premises. He was unable to find a 'home' address for the dealer until one day he mentioned the case to a colleague. This particular colleague had worked for many years in financial services in the city and this, allied to his work in the trading standards department, meant he had an extensive network of what might loosely be termed 'informants'. He told the TSO that he would see if he could get an address for the dealer. Two days later he called the TSO aside in the office and gave him not only a good address for the dealer but also details of the bank where he held an account. He made it clear to the TSO that he should not ask him how he came by this information. The TSO inferred from this that less than legal means had been resorted to.

The TSO knew that he would need a court order to get access to the dealer's bank account and that it was unlikely in view of the offences being investigated that such authority would be granted. So he decided to go to the bank and see what reaction he got from the manager when confronted with the request to confirm details of the dealer's account and address. Although this was technically a little mischievous on the part of the TSO, it was not actually illegal for him to make such a request. The bank manager was totally bemused by the request. He went through to his office to check the details. The expression on his face confirmed that the dealer did indeed hold an account at the bank – but he refused to confirm this verbally to the TSO.

The dealer proved to be totally evasive to the TSO. Despite now having a good address the TSO was unable to establish contact with the dealer. Careful monitoring of private car advertisements in the local newspapers and extensive visits to the car auction were mainly fruitless, apart from about three advertisements. The TSO submitted a report to the procurator fiscal (the local prosecutor) recommending that the dealer be prosecuted for failing to disclose his occupation as a car dealer in those advertisements and for offences relating to the false trade descriptions applied to the car purchased by the tax inspector. The procurator fiscal concluded that there was insufficient evidence to support a prosecution and dropped the case.

The TSO visited the tax inspector at the Inland Revenue offices. He advised him of the decision and returned documents to the inspector. The inspector asked the TSO if he had found an address for the dealer as he could at least ensure that he could be made to pay income tax in future. The TSO confirmed that he had indeed found a good address. But unfortunately since he had discovered the information while acting under his authority as a TSO, he could not divulge the information, which was in the file he had with him, much though he would have liked to.

The tax inspector was clearly disappointed to hear this. He pointed out the irony that as law-abiding citizens he and the TSO were paying their taxes whilst this 'criminal' was avoiding all liability. The TSO said he was well aware of the irony but he was constrained by the legislation. On saying this the TSO placed the file on the tax inspector's desk and walked towards the window. As he looked out of the window, he remarked to the inspector, who was still at his desk, out of direct sight of the TSO, that it afforded a wonderful vista of the city. After a minute or so the TSO turned round to face the inspector. He picked the file up from the desk and bade him farewell.

To this day, the TSO does not know whether the tax inspector actually opened the file to get the details about the dealer's address. But occasionally he thinks about the incident and hopes that the dealer has at least joined the tax paying ranks of society.

Case 1: a suggested analysis

In terms of a stakeholder analysis, the most readily apparent stakeholders are the car dealer, the tax inspector and the TSO.

From an objective dimension, the car dealer is passing himself off as a private individual and therefore from a deontological perspective he is failing to fulfil his duty as prescribed by the various pieces of consumer legislation involved. Similarly, his failure to declare his earnings for tax purposes can be seen as a deontological matter. From a teleological perspective it might be argued that such are the car dealer's personal financial circumstances that he has to maximise his earnings as best he can.

From a subjective dimension, it could be that it simply feels right to him to act in this way and this is compounded by the possibility that he has seen others act in a similar way (subjective relativism).

The tax inspector, from a subjective dimension, operates in a different referent culture which places high importance on being law abiding (relativism). He also felt badly done by (emotivism), and clearly, buying a faulty vehicle was not in his best interest (egoism). In terms of the objective dimension we might expect to see most relevance in the deontological theories as this would be consistent with the subjective analysis. However, from a teleological stance, it seems that the inspector was prepared to use the records of the tax service for his own ends to find an address for the dealer. Similarly, he encouraged the TSO to breach his legal obligations by asking him to divulge the details of the dealer to him. We can see here that subjective ethical frameworks may sometimes contradict objective analyses.

Continue the analysis of this case by looking at subjective and objective dimensions in relation to the TSO.

In addition to these main stakeholders, there are other, less obvious but perhaps no less important stakeholders, including other 'honest' car dealers, law-abiding taxpayers, prospective car buyers, the procurator fiscal, the TSO's professional body and code of practice, the tax inspector's employers.

At first glance the relevance of these secondary stakeholders may seem inconsequential; however, we might come to see the apparently contradictory action of the tax inspector as justifiable when seen in the context of his concern that if others pay taxes then why should this dealer evade his responsibilities? Do you personally believe that this is a situation in which the ends justify the means?

In developing your analysis of the cases that follow you should try to think about the role of important stakeholders not directly referred to by the writer.

14.7.2   Case 2: Whistle-blowing

The editorial in *Accountancy Age* of 21 October 1993 read:

> Last week saw the launch of Public Concern At Work, a charity which sets out to help those who voice their concern about malpractice at the workplace – the whistleblowers.

Accountants are by no means exempt from such dilemmas; indeed they might often be the people best placed to discover evidence of wrongdoing. Despite the profession's high ideals, practical help has been limited. Former Guardian Royal Exchange accountant Robertson, for example, who brought concerns about some of GRE's transactions to the Inland Revenue and was sacked for his pains, found little help from within his own profession.

Since then (the mid-1980s), advice, including free legal advice, has been available to the accountancy bodies. Rules of confidentiality have been introduced to encourage members to seek counselling on ethical problems before it is too late.

But whistle-blowing is still a hazardous route, all too likely to leave the individual with integrity intact, but no job. If we are really serious about professional standards, we should be ready to protect the small number who stick out their necks to defend them, whatever the cost.

14.7.3 Case 3: Protection from theft

In an inner city area in Hull, various lock-up shops (i.e. shops not attached to residential premises occupied by the shop owners) had often been broken into during the night, and goods and money stolen. The owners of the shops alleged that the police had been able to do very little to prevent these thefts, and had been remarkably unsuccessful in tracing the perpetrators of the crimes.

Two well-built men called on the shopkeepers offering, for sums ranging between £250 and £500, to trace the people responsible for the thefts and to 'warn them off'. They alleged that they either knew, or could find out, who the likely perpetrators were, and thus would have more success than the police.

Several shopkeepers who took up the offer did find relief from the continual breaking in and theft. The police force warned that shopkeepers should be wary of such offers and should not take them up as they could potentially involve themselves in acts of violent retribution against the alleged offenders. The police stated that they were not aware of any connection between the men offering to trace and warn off the thieves and the thieves themselves, but that neither the shopkeepers nor any other citizen should take the law into their own hands.

14.7.4 Case 4: Factory closure

A large national company had a factory in a northern town where there was a high level of unemployment. The company alleged that this factory had been running at a loss for several years. In order to try to ensure the survival of the factory, the local managers (backed by the national management of the company) imposed a 20 per cent pay cut on the workers, and also retrospectively removed the bonus scheme which had been in operation. Thus the workforce was deprived of bonuses which they thought they had already earned.

This action precipitated a strike. The local management tried to recruit other local workers to fill the jobs, and at the same time issued notices to the striking workers reminding them that they were in breach of their contracts of employment, and that unless they reported for work on the Monday morning after the weekend they would be sacked.

The workers did not return to work, and at 6.00 am on the following Tuesday morning the local managers delivered redundancy notices to the homes of the striking workers. Two months later the factory closed down.

The striking workers took their case to a tribunal where they were awarded £1,000 each for unfair dismissal and arrears of bonuses already earned. The reason for the award was stated to be that the company was required by law to allow workers 24 hours to consider their position and report for work, and the redundancy notices had been issued only 22 hours after the workers had failed to report for work.

The workers believed that the strike had been deliberately precipitated by the management to make them breach their contracts so that they could be sacked without being entitled to redundancy pay.

14.7.5 Case 5: Shipyards and union solidarity

A shipyard on the River Tyne had almost run out of orders and was facing closure. The yard had almost completed the building of three frigates for the Royal Navy. Once the ships were built they would undergo substantial sea trials before being fitted out. There was substantial suspicion that the government might choose not to return the frigates for fitting out after the sea trials, but choose to take the frigates to another shipyard where the fitting out might be done more cheaply.

The trade union branch at the yard contacted the union branches in all the other British shipyards, asking them to agree not to undertake the work, should the frigates not be returned to the Tyneside yard for fitting out. With the exception of one yard in the south of England, located in an area where there had been no previous history of high unemployment levels, the union branches agreed. The branch secretary at the southern yard responded that his members too had families to support and needed the work, and that the union branch could not agree to reject the work if its management was successful in attracting the contract.

14.7.6 Case reflections

Having completed your analyses of the cases, reflect on whether you can identify any consistency in the way you have interpreted the cases. In other words, are you predisposed towards some ethical frameworks and not others? For example, do you find yourself relating more to deontological theories than to teleological theories or vice versa? On the other hand, if there is no apparent consistency, which may indicate that you tend to deal with the theories in a contradictory way, what implications do you believe this may have for your decision-making?

◆ Summary

The importance of ethical decision-making should not be underestimated either from a personal perspective or from the perspective of the firm. Ethical dilemmas can cause conflict and uncertainty, resulting in negative behaviour such as whistle-blowing. In decision-making we can follow a set of rules laid down by society, or weigh up each decision with regard to the greatest benefit. How the organisation reacts to ethical decisions may become an important issue concerning customer perceptions of the firm. As with other decisions, we need to be aware of the stakeholders in the decision. Of particular importance are those decisions associated with the environment. They can produce intense emotions and generate widespread negative publicity for the firm.

❓ Decision diary

For the decisions that you are involved with either at present or in the past, reflect on the rights and wrongs of them. Try to classify them using the models discussed in the chapter.

References

Axelrod, R. (1984) *The Evolution of Co-operation*. New Yorks: Basic Books.

Bloom, H., Calori, R. and de Woot, P. (1994) *Euromanagement*. London: Kogan Page.

Carr, A.Z. (1968) 'Is business bluffing ethical?', *Harvard Business Review*, 46(1): 143–53.

Christie, R. and Gers, F.L. (eds) *Studies in machiavellianism*. New York: Academic Press.

Cooper, J., Browne, M. and Peters, M. (1991) *European Logistics*. Oxford: Blackwell, Chapter 13.

Daellenbach, H.G. (1994) *Systems and Decision Making*. Chichester: Wiley.

Friedman, M. (1970) *The Social Responsibility of Business is to Increase Its Profits*. New York: New York Times Company.

Gilligan, C. (1993) *In a Different Voice: Psychological Theory and Women's Development*. Boston: Harvard University Press.

Green, R. (1994) *The Ethical Manager*. Macmillan: New York.

Hellriegel, D., Slocum, J. and Woodman, R. (1995) *Organizational Behaviour*, 7th edition. St Paul, MN: West Publishing Co.

Kerr, T. (1996) 'The Role of Ethics in Contemporary Management' in Crainer, S. (ed) *The Financial Times Handbook of Management*. London: Pitman, p. 1013.

Kohlberg, L. (1981) *Essays on Moral Development*. Toronto: Harper & Row.

MacIntyre, A. (1990) *After Virtue: A Study in Moral Theory*. London: Duckworth.

Porter, M. (1989) 'From Competitive Advantage to Corporate Strategy', in Asch, D. and Bowman, C. (eds) *Readings in Strategic Management*. London: Macmillan.

Rawls, J. (1971) *A Theory of Justice*. Cambridge, MA: Harvard University Press.

Sadgrove, K. (1996) 'Managing the Environment' in Crainer, S. (ed) *The Financial Times Handbook of Management*. London: Pitman, p. 1045.

Glossary

Deontology:	the 'science of duty'; is concerned with doing one's duty in terms of established ethical principles.
Interest utilitarianism:	deals with the greatest number of people getting what is in their best interest.
Negative utilitarianism:	deals with the least suffering for the fewest people.
Preference utilitarianism:	deals with the greatest number of people getting what they want.
Teleology:	'consequential' in ethical terms; decisions are made through evaluating the likely consequences of any action taken.
Utilitarianism:	a variant of consequentialism; the greatest pleasure for the greatest number of people.

Index